TRIAL ADVOCACY:

INFERENCES, ARGUMENTS AND TECHNIQUES

By

Albert J. Moore
Professor of Law
University of California, Los Angeles

Paul Bergman
Professor of Law
University of California, Los Angeles

David A. Binder
Professor of Law
University of California, Los Angeles

AMERICAN CASEBOOK SERIES®

WEST PUBLISHING CO.
ST. PAUL, MINN., 1996

COPYRIGHT © 1996 By WEST PUBLISHING CO.
610 Opperman Drive
P.O. Box 64526
St. Paul, MN 55164–0526
1–800–328–9352

ISBN 0–314–06530–X

 *TEXT IS PRINTED ON 10% POST
CONSUMER RECYCLED PAPER*

Printed with Printwise
Environmentally Advanced Water Washable Ink

To Sherrill, Andrea and Melinda

*

Preface

This book's premise is that effective trial advocacy is more than the use of good rhetorical skills. Asking properly-phrased questions and demonstrating oratorical polish are important skills, but alone such skills cannot transform witnesses' stories into substantively persuasive cases. For example, it is one thing to present a clear story about what happened on the night of a murder through such basic techniques as setting the scene and chronologically going through the events leading up to the murder. However, it is another to present the story in a way that incorporates and emphasizes one's arguments about how the events establish the killer's state of mind.

This book presents a systematic approach to persuasive trial advocacy. Readers will learn how to prepare for trial by marshalling evidence into persuasive bundles of evidence and inferences called "arguments," and then how to communicate those arguments effectively at all stages of trial, from opening statement to final summation. Awareness of how to prepare and present persuasive arguments is crucial because most evidence presented at trial is circumstantial. The probative value of circumstantial evidence rests on inferences drawn from generalizations, and one needs an understanding of how to identify evidence strengthening or weakening generalizatons if one is to present the most persuasive case possible.

Part One of the book is in essence a "blow up" of those one or two paragraphs of most existing trial advocacy texts that recommend that advocates prepare for trial by "organizing evidence into a persuasive presentation that will satisfy the elements of claims and defenses." Unfortunately, like the general bromide that one should "buy low and sell high," such recommendations do not help would-be trial advocates identify what facts they need to prove in any specific case, or the evidence tending to prove or disprove those facts, or how to organize such evidence into persuasive arguments. Yet whenever parties seek to persuade factfinders to accept their versions of events rather than their adversaries' versions, these topics are crucial to effective trial advocacy.

Thus, Part One presents an approach to developing persuasive arguments that readers can employ no matter what the substantive backdrop of a dispute (e.g., torts or contracts, civil or criminal cases), no matter whether a case is large or small, and no matter what the precise nature of factual conflicts. This Part shows readers how to construct three fundamental types of arguments to persuade a factfinder of the accuracy of one's version of events. It describes how to marshall evidence prior to trial according to these three types of arguments, including preparing responses to an adversary's likely counter-arguments. Part One also recognizes that factfinders may be persuaded by "silent" arguments (those addressed to a factfinder's emotions and prejudices), and describes how to identify and counter and sometimes even take advantage of such arguments.

Part Two marries content to presentation by exploring and illustrating effective trial techniques and strategies. This Part emphasizes how to translate one's pretrial arguments into the questions that are asked and the assertions that are put forward to a judge or jury at each phase of trial. Thus, Part Two shows how arguments prepared prior to trial shape questions asked during jury voir dire, evidence that one elicits during direct and cross examination, and the content of opening statement and final summation.

Students spend much of their time in law school analyzing substantive laws, and in many instances substantive laws are the product of social groups' desire for justice. But it's not too much of an exaggeration to say that the law cannot achieve social justice unless lawyers are able to establish the facts that animate the laws. Thus, in order to represent a client competently and help ensure that social policies created by legislatures and appellate courts are carried out by accurate factfinding, trial lawyers must understand the content of persuasive trial arguments and have the ability to communicate that content to judges and juries. This book is devoted to these twin goals.

> ALBERT J. MOORE
> PAUL BERGMAN
> DAVID A. BINDER

Los Angeles, California
August, 1995

Acknowledgements

We sincerely appreciate the contributions of our research assistants, especially Jaleen Nelson and Douglas McCormick, and also including Ray Caldito, Christy Pyland, Lisa Rosenthal and Jennifer Scullion. More than merely gathering materials from dusty library shelves and floors (the latter after one of our larger earthquakes), they genuinely collaborated and provided us with invaluable feedback both on our ideas and how we expressed them.

For critiquing drafts of various chapters and enhancing our understanding of arguments, we want to thank our colleagues Gary Blasi, Ann Carlson, Steve Derian, Cassandra Franklin, Jerry Lopez, Chris Littleton, David Sklansky, John Wiley and Pam Woods. Some of you have helped us in the past, and to you we can only say that you should have known better. Together, you all certainly changed the thrust of the book from the compilation of lowfat day-of-trial recipes that we initially set out to write.

Our thanks also to the UCLA Academic Senate and the UCLA Law School Dean's Fund for their generous financial support.

We also acknowledge the helpful comments of the participants in the Clinical Theory Workshop organized by Prof. Stephen Ellmann at New York Law School in February, 1994. Thanks also to Ruthann Robson from CUNY Queens for the insights we gained from her 1995 presentation at the UCLA Law School.

Our thanks to Mozart, whose music made the hours in front of the computer much more pleasant. But had he written "Flight of the Bumblebee" and "In the Hall of the Mountain King," the book undoubtedly would have been finished a year earlier.

Finally, a quick response to our esteemed and good friend Kenney Hegland, who kicked sand in our faces for languishing on the beach while he produced two books. When our eyes cleared, we noticed that his books were second editions. So, now we'll go back to the beach and figure we're "tide."

*

Summary of Contents

*

Table of Contents

PART ONE—SECTION B. CONSTRUCTING ARGUMENTS IN PREPARATION FOR TRIAL —PREPARING RESPONSES TO AN ADVERSARY'S CASE

*

TRIAL ADVOCACY:

INFERENCES, ARGUMENTS AND TECHNIQUES

*

Chapter 1

THE ROLE OF ARGUMENTS
AT TRIAL

———

You thought that the evidence favored your client, and you used all the right trial techniques. During direct examination you asked open questions which allowed your witnesses to enhance their credibility by testifying in their own words. During cross examination you used leading questions to control the scope of adverse witnesses' answers. And your evidence professor would have applauded the propriety of your questions.

Moreover, your personal style was impeccable. Your demeanor projected sincere belief in the justice of your cause. Your physical gestures were dramatic, your voice was authoritative, and your legal position was forcefully stated.

Nevertheless, the factfinder decided the case against your client. You are left to search for an explanation of the unhappy result. Did the factfinder "have it in" for you or your client? Did your adversary surprise you with a secret verbal tactic? Did you forget to practice what they taught you in "Advanced Acting Techniques for Litigators?"

The most likely explanation is that you failed to prepare and effectively present persuasive arguments. Arguments are persuasive packages that explain to a factfinder why the evidence in a case proves your desired factual conclusions. Arguments marshall evidence around the factual conclusions you want to prove. Thus, the term "arguments" connotes more than what you say during final summation. Arguments determine the evidence you offer and emphasize during direct and cross examination, as well as the content of opening statement and final summation. By developing arguments prior to trial and communicating them throughout trial, you maximize the likelihood that a factfinder will accept the accuracy of your factual conclusions.

1. THREE TYPES OF ARGUMENTS

In Part One of this book you will learn to prepare for trial by using an Argumentation Model. You will use the Argumentation Model to

1

construct and organize three types of arguments with which you can persuade a factfinder. The three types of arguments are:

- Arguments based on undisputed evidence.
- Arguments relating to disputed evidence.
- Arguments based on story inconsistencies.

No matter what area of substantive law a trial concerns and no matter what the evidence underlying a factual dispute, most of your effort at trial consists of presenting these three kinds of arguments.

These arguments are essential because at trial parties typically offer competing versions of past events to a factfinder (judge or jury). Each party seeks to convince the factfinder that its version of reality—its story—is correct and justifies a favorable verdict. And the three types of arguments are the principal organizational tools for persuading a factfinder that your client's version of events is accurate.

Of course, success at trial requires more than the development of persuasive arguments; you also have to communicate them effectively to a factfinder. Thus, Part Two examines and illustrates techniques for presenting evidence and communicating arguments at each phase of trial. By combining effective techniques with the content of the three types of arguments, you maximize the likelihood that a trial will produce a successful outcome for your client.

2. CIRCUMSTANTIAL EVIDENCE: THE STUFF THAT ARGUMENTS ARE MADE OF

The three types of arguments set forth above are all based on circumstantial evidence. Hence, it makes sense to organize a case around these types of arguments only if circumstantial evidence is in fact the dominant type of proof at trial. Consider therefore what circumstantial evidence is and why it predominates at trial.

a. Circumstantial vs. Direct Evidence

All evidence at trial is either direct or circumstantial. As you may already be aware, direct evidence, if accepted as accurate, proves a material fact [1] without the need for an inference. By contrast, circumstantial evidence, even if accepted as accurate, proves a material fact only if a factfinder draws one or more inferences from the evidence.

To take a simple example, assume that a material fact in an assault case is that, "Sam struck Cliff with a baseball bat." Carla testifies, "I saw Sam strike Cliff with a baseball bat." Carla's testimony is direct evidence. If the factfinder believes Carla, the material fact is established.

Next, assume that Norm testifies, "I saw Sam, who was holding a baseball bat, chase Cliff out of the bar." Norm's testimony is circum-

---

[1]. As used here, the term "material fact" means a fact which proves or disproves an element of a plaintiff's claim. See C. Wright & K. Graham, 22 *Federal Practice And Procedure* (Evidence) Sec. 5165 (1978).

stantial evidence. If the factfinder is to conclude that Sam struck Cliff, the factfinder must infer the material fact ("struck with baseball bat") from the evidence ("chased with a bat").

b. Why Circumstantial Evidence Predominates at Trial

The mere mention of circumstantial evidence may remind you of one of the hoariest criticisms of an adversary's evidence: "It's nothing but a bunch of circumstantial evidence." But this criticism has little basis in fact. As the next sections illustrate, virtually every case that reaches trial consists primarily of circumstantial evidence!

(1) Circumstantial Evidence Is Embedded in Stories

Witnesses typically testify in story form. That is, witnesses typically provide chronological accounts of what they have heard, seen, or otherwise perceived.[2] These chronological accounts consist primarily of circumstantial evidence. By way of illustration, assume that Alison has instituted an action against Ken for breach of contract. One material fact that Alison must prove is that Ken orally agreed to sell her 100 pounds of volcano ash on June 22; Ken denies entering into an agreement with Alison.

When Alison testifies, she will not limit her testimony to a June 22 conversation with Ken. In addition, she will provide an account of events leading up to and following the making of the contract. For example, she may describe her training as a volcanologist, her appointment as Director of the Lava's Lane Volcano Museum on June 1, her decision to create a tactile experience with volcano ash, how she came into contact with Ken, the negotiations culminating in the June 22 ash purchase agreement, the announcement in the July 1 edition of the Museum's Monthly "Flogram" of the planned exhibit, the resulting rise in Museum membership, the cancellations that resulted from Ken's failure to deliver the ash, and the purchase of volcano ash at almost twice the price from an alternate supplier.

Almost all of these story events constitute circumstantial evidence. For example, from the "before" evidence of Alison's becoming the director of the volcano museum on June 1, and the "after" evidence that Alison announced the exhibit in the July 1 program, a factfinder may infer that she agreed to buy volcano ash on June 22. Thus, when you couch testimony in story form, what you are really doing is providing circumstantial evidence of material facts.

(2) Credibility Evidence Is Circumstantial

Recall that typically parties go to trial because they have conflicting versions of historical events. An eyewitness claims that Sam struck Cliff

---

2. Expert witnesses are perhaps an exception. For a discussion of arguments based on expert testimony, see Chapter 15.

with a bat; Sam claims Diane struck Cliff. Alison says that Ken made a deal to sell her volcano ash; Ken says that he only promised to think about the deal.

To convince a factfinder of the accuracy of your client's version of material facts, evidence supporting the credibility of your version and attacking the credibility of your adversary's version usually plays a prominent role at trial. And because an inference is necessary to link credibility evidence with the accuracy of testimony about material facts, credibility evidence is by definition circumstantial.

For instance, Alison might attack Ken's credibility by proving that he has given conflicting accounts of what was said during the June 22 volcano ash conversation. From that evidence a factfinder might conclude that Ken's version of the conversation is inaccurate. This conclusion would probably be based on an inference that people who remember an event accurately are likely to describe it in a consistent way. Because a similar inferential process is necessary with all credibility evidence, credibility evidence constitutes a form of circumstantial evidence.

Thus, even when direct evidence is available to you, you need to rely on circumstantial evidence to convince a factfinder that the direct evidence is accurate. For example, if you are trying to prove that "Sam struck Cliff with a bat," you may have direct evidence from Carla, "I saw Sam strike Cliff with a bat." Nevertheless you will need to introduce circumstantial evidence to establish the accuracy of Carla's testimony.

(3) Direct Evidence Is Often Unavailable

A third reason that circumstantial evidence predominates at trial is that direct evidence of material facts is frequently unavailable. For example, in a criminal case the identity of the culprit is a material fact. But unless the prosecution has an eyewitness to the crime, the prosecution will have to prove identity through circumstantial evidence.[3]

Moreover, many material facts are unobservable. For example, only a witness who can bend spoons without touching them could testify to another's "state of mind," a material fact in so many legal claims. Thus, a will contestant may have to prove that a testator's will was the product of an insane delusion; a prosecutor may have to prove that a defendant intended to harm his victim. As direct evidence of another person's state of mind is unavailable, these parties would have to rely on circumstantial evidence to prove these material facts.

3. THE INFERENTIAL SIGNIFICANCE OF CIRCUMSTANTIAL EVIDENCE IS OFTEN UNCERTAIN

At this point, you may be thinking, "It shouldn't matter that most evidence is circumstantial and that its probative impact depends on

---

3. Of course, the defendant could provide direct evidence of identity, but the defendant is not available to the prosecu- tion as a witness and could hardly be counted on to provide proof of identity anyway.

inferences. Once I offer circumstantial evidence, a factfinder will readily see my desired inferences." Your point would be well taken if any given item of circumstantial evidence gave rise to only a single inference and if that inference was always obvious.

Unfortunately, neither supposition is correct. A single item of circumstantial evidence frequently gives rise to multiple and even conflicting inferences. Moreover, rules of evidence typically prevent a witness from testifying to your desired inference. The three types of arguments identified above will help you persuade a factfinder to accept your desired inferences.

a. Circumstantial Evidence Gives Rise to Multiple and Conflicting Inferences

The reason that circumstantial evidence typically gives rise to multiple and even conflicting inferences is that inferences are always based on generalizations. Generalizations are assertions derived from beliefs about how events normally occur.[4] For example, if you are told that, "Bob is crying in the kitchen," you are likely to infer that Bob is sad. This inference would be based on a generalization, drawn from everyday experience, that people often cry when they are sad. This simple graphic illustrates the link between evidence, generalization and inferred conclusion:

Evidence	Generalization	Inferred Conclusion
(Bob is crying)	(People sometimes cry when they are sad)	(Bob is sad)

As the diagram suggests, an item of evidence connects to an inferred conclusion via a generalization.

If a single item of circumstantial evidence gave rise only to a single generalization, you would not need to rely on arguments to persuade a factfinder to draw your desired inference. However, many generalizations can logically flow from any single item of circumstantial evidence. For example, consider the following possibilities based on the evidence, "Bob is crying in the kitchen:"

Generalization	Inferred Conclusion
(People sometimes cry when they are happy	(Bob is happy)
(People sometimes cry when peeling onions)	(Bob is peeling onions)

---

4. From a logician's perspective, generalizations are a form of premise—logical assumption—which is true less than one hundred percent of the time. Generalizations differ, of course, from premises typically found in hard sciences which are often true all the time. See C. Wright & K. Graham, *Federal Practice and Procedure* (Evidence) Sec. 5171 (1978). Although most of the premises (generalizations) used by factfinders arise from common experience, this is not always the case. When the inference to be drawn requires expert knowledge, common experience will not provide an adequate source. Rather, in such instances, resort to expert testimony will be required. Id. at Sec. 5165.

As these examples demonstrate, circumstantial evidence standing alone proves nothing. The inferred conclusion a factfinder chooses to draw will depend on what generalization the factfinder attaches to the evidence.[5]

Consider how multiple generalizations may make uncertain the inference a factfinder will draw from an item of circumstantial evidence in an actual case. Assume that Bussel is on trial for armed robbery of a convenience store. As the prosecutor, you introduce evidence that six months before the robbery, Bussel had been fired by the manager of the store that was robbed. Among the literally hundreds of inferences the factfinder could logically make from this single item of circumstantial evidence are:

1. Bussel knows what newspapers the store sells.

2. Bussel knows police patrol procedures in the area of the store.

3. Bussel knows how much money is typically in the cash register.

4. Bussel had trouble paying his bills during the six months prior to the robbery.

5. Bussel was a poor employee.

6. Bussel knows the layout of the store.

7. Bussel robbed the store in retaliation for his firing.

8. Bussel did not rob the store because he feared that he would be easily recognized.

Thus this single item of circumstantial evidence is linked to eight different conclusions by eight different generalizations. For example, the generalization for Conclusion # 2 is something like, "People who work at a convenience store often are aware of police patrol procedures in the area of the store."

More worrisome for you as prosecutor, the factfinder may reach Conclusion # 8. To draw that inference, the factfinder would rely on a generalization such as, "People who have been fired from a store six months earlier often do not rob the store because they realize that if they return to the store they are likely to be recognized." This generalization leads to a conclusion that Bussel was not the robber.

Of course, as the prosecutor you want to persuade the factfinder to reach Conclusion # 7. The generalization underlying this conclusion is something like, "Employees who have been fired by a store manager six months before a robbery sometimes rob the store as revenge against the manager."

5. Factfinders probably rarely explicitly articulate the generalizations underlying their inferred conclusions, just as you would probably not explicitly articulate a generalization when you conclude that someone you have seen crying is sad. Nevertheless, a generalization would underlie your conclusion.

Thus, when you offer the "Bussel was fired" evidence, you have no assurance that the factfinder will on its own draw your desired inference. The factfinder may not recognize your desired inference, may draw one that neither you nor the defense counsel care about (e.g., No. 1), or even draw one that is diametrically opposed to your desired inference.[6]

b. A Witness May Be Unable to Testify to Your Desired Inference

A second reason that a factfinder may be uncertain about your desired inferences is that rules of evidence often prevent a witness from testifying to those inferences.

Only when a witness testifies to her or his own behavior can the witness properly testify to your desired inference. For example, in the Bussel hypothetical above, Bussel could testify that he never considered retaliating against the store out of fear that he would be easily recognized if he did so.

But when, as is often the case, one witness testifies to the actions of another, you typically cannot elicit your desired conclusion. For example, the prosecution may offer the store manager's testimony that Bussel was angry when Bussel was fired six months before the robbery. But the store manager could not testify that Bussel probably robbed the store in retaliation for his discharge.[7] Thus, at least during manager's testimony, the factfinder may be uncertain about what inference to draw from testimony that Bussel was angry when fired.

4. PART ONE: CONSTRUCTING ARGUMENTS IN PREPARATION FOR TRIAL

You should now understand why circumstantial evidence predominates at trial, and why you cannot simply rely on a factfinder to recognize and accept your desired inferences. When preparing for trial, you need to anticipate the inferential uncertainty that will arise from your circumstantial evidence. Part One sets forth an Argumentation Model that helps you overcome inferential uncertainty in two major ways:

- The Model helps you to be thorough when identifying evidence supporting your arguments; and

- The Model helps you to organize that evidence into persuasive arguments that explain how the evidence proves your desired conclusions.

Thus, the preparation methods described in Part One identify much of the evidence you will offer at trial.

---

6. A factfinder's task will be even more difficult when, as is often the case, the parties dispute more than one material fact.

7. Such testimony would constitute an improper opinion under FRE 701.

It is important that you understand at the outset that the Argumentation Model consists of a *process* for developing arguments. As an organizational tool, the Model does not dictate what evidence to include in an argument. Rather, it responds to your individual judgment about what evidence a factfinder is most likely to find persuasive. Two different attorneys applying the Model to the same body of evidence may well produce distinctly different arguments, because they have different views about what evidence a factfinder is likely to find persuasive.[8]

The Model responds to the major premise of the adversary system, which is that truth is most likely to emerge when parties present what they see as their most persuasive arguments supporting their versions of historical events.[9] However, use of the Model does not necessarily guarantee that your arguments will lead a factfinder to "objective" truth. Neither this nor any other model can guarantee objective truth. As circumstantial evidence is always based on generalizations that by definition are true less than 100% of the time, any conclusions drawn from arguments based on such evidence will not necessarily accurately reflect the historical facts.

5. PART TWO: COMMUNICATING ARGUMENTS AT TRIAL

Part Two focuses on techniques for presenting evidence and communicating your arguments during each phase of the trial, from opening statement to closing argument. Part Two also explores how the arguments you constructed guide your examination of expert witness and your selection of jurors.

8. As you will see as you read through Part One, you have to evaluate the persuasiveness of your arguments to a likely factfinder.

9. L. Fuller, "The Adversary System" in *Talks on American Law* 30–43 (1961).

Part One—Section A

CONSTRUCTING ARGUMENTS IN PREPARATION FOR TRIAL—PREPARING YOUR AFFIRMATIVE CASE

Part One describes the pretrial process of constructing arguments. This Part assumes that you have completed pre-trial discovery.[1] That is, you have interviewed and/or deposed the likely witnesses, and examined the potentially relevant documents and tangible exhibits. It also assumes that you've prepared a chronological outline of your version of events. The chronology reflects the collective stories of all your witnesses, and forms the backdrop against which a factfinder will evaluate your arguments.[2] Finally, Part One also assumes that settlement negotiations have failed, so you need to prepare for trial.

Part One has two sections. This Section describes the process of preparing the arguments you will ask a factfinder to accept. Section B concentrates on preparing responses to an adversary's likely arguments and attacking the credibility of an adversary's witnesses.

---

1. In some senses pretrial discovery is almost never fully completed before trial actually begins. As you actually begin the process of thinking about what witnesses you will call and what evidence you will attempt to adduce from each, you invariably learn that you need still further information. Nonetheless, there does come a time during a lawsuit in which one's principal preparatory efforts focus primarily, if not almost exclusively, on organizing the results of one's discovery for presentation of the case at trial. It is this time, when one moves from a focus on discovery to a focus on presentation of testimony, that we have in mind when we use the phrase, "completed pretrial discovery."

2. This chronology will be quite useful when you construct arguments based on inconsistencies in witnesses' stories. See Chapter 8.

Chapter 2

IDENTIFYING FACTUAL PROPOSITIONS AND SUPPORTING EVIDENCE

Chapter 1 set forth your main trial preparation activity: constructing three types of arguments linking evidence to your desired conclusions. This chapter is fundamental to your understanding of how to prepare each type of argument, as it explains how to go about identifying the factual conclusions you must prove and the evidence that tends to prove them.

1. IDENTIFY "LEGAL ELEMENTS"

As you probably know, the legal claims that you attempt to prove or disprove at trial consist of discrete legal elements. For example, the elements of armed robbery consist of "identity," "taking of property," "by means of force and fear" and "intent to permanently deprive the owner of possession." And the elements of a garden variety negligence action consist of "duty," "breach," "causation" and "damages."

Before constructing any of the three types of arguments, you must identify the elements of the claims (aka, "causes of action") at issue. Sometimes you can readily ascertain the necessary elements through the use of court forms, jury instruction books and treatises. Other times, especially when a claim rests on a newly-created common law right or statute, you may have to do more extensive legal research to identify legal elements.

2. CONVERT ABSTRACT ELEMENTS TO FACTUAL PROPOSITIONS

If you look back at the legal elements in the previous section, you will see terms like "identity," "by means of force or fear," "duty" and "breach." Like all elements of legal claims and affirmative defenses, these terms are abstractions. The terms do not refer to any specific event or condition, but rather are labels that may attach to an infinite variety of events and conditions.

For example, if you are told that Munzer stole property "by means of force or fear," you have no idea what Munzer actually did. Similarly, if you are told that French "breached" her "duty" to Graham, you cannot tell what circumstances created a duty on French's part nor what she did to breach that duty. Finally, if you are told only that a bike was not of "merchantable quality," you cannot tell what condition made the bike non-merchantable.

The abstract terminology of legal elements is no accident. Elements must be abstract if they are to apply to a wide range of possible conduct and conditions. But as a consequence, you do not directly prove or disprove elements at trial. Rather, you prove specific events and conditions which in turn satisfy abstract elements. Thus, before constructing arguments you must convert abstract elements into "factual propositions." A "factual proposition" is simply an abstract element restated as the specific event or condition in your case which satisfies that element.

For instance, assume that you represent Curly, who has sued Moe for refusing to honor an agreement to pay Curly the contract price for 50,000 cinnamon raisin bagels and one pint of cream cheese. One element in dispute is whether Curly "performed" his obligations under the contract. Curly claims that on Aug. 31 he left a sack containing the bagels and cream cheese in Moe's backyard. Your factual proposition for the element of "performance" would be, "On Aug. 31, Curly left a sack containing 50,000 bagels and a pint of cream cheese in Moe's backyard."[3] The factual proposition defines the specific event you will actually prove, and that event in turn satisfies the abstract element of "performance."

You will find it easier to state factual propositions if you recognize that some elements refer to conduct, others to mental states, and others to conditions. Consider these examples:

a. Breach of care: "Sanna backed out of her driveway at a speed of about 85 m.p.h." Here, the factual proposition identifies *conduct*.

b. Mens rea: "Brutus stabbed Caesar with the intent to kill him." Here, the factual proposition identifies a *mental state*.

c. Not of merchantable quality: "The bike had square wheels." This factual proposition describes a *condition*.

d. Damages: "Mark had back pain every day for six months." This factual proposition also describes a *condition*.

As these examples illustrate, you can restate every element as a factual proposition no matter whether it refers to conduct, a mental state or a condition.

---

3. Factual propositions should always contain a date reference (e.g. Aug. 31) because you are trying to invariably prove what happened at a specific point in time.

3. BEGINNING TRIAL PREPARATION BY CONVERTING ELE-MENTS TO FACTUAL PROPOSITIONS

Beginning trial preparation by converting abstract elements to factual propositions is not simply an academic ritual; it is essential to thorough trial preparation. Attorneys often fail to present strong arguments because they neglect to clarify, either to themselves before trial or to the factfinder during trial, the precise conduct, mental state or condition that satisfies a legal element.[4] Converting legal elements to factual propositions forces you to identify exactly what you have to prove to satisfy a legal element. Since this conversion takes place as you prepare for trial, the process helps you clarify your arguments throughout the trial.

Moreover, preparing arguments in the context of factual propositions rather than abstract elements enhances the thoroughness of trial preparation. For example, return to *Curly v. Moe*, and assume that as Curly's counsel you are identifying evidence in preparation for trial. As you prepare for trial, you are less likely to overlook important evidence if you look for evidence that "On Aug. 31, Curly left a sack containing 50,000 bagels and a pint of cream cheese in Moe's backyard" than if you look for evidence that "Curly performed." [5]

4. A PLAINTIFF'S PERSPECTIVE ON FACTUAL PROPOSITIONS

As you know, to win at trial a plaintiff has the burden of proving all the elements of a claim. For example, if a plaintiff in a negligence action succeeds in proving "duty," "breach" and "causation," but fails to prove "damages," the plaintiff loses.

Thus, if you represent a plaintiff you should formulate a factual proposition for each element of a claim, and make sure you have some evidence to prove each proposition. Short of a defendant's stipulating to a proposition, you will have to offer evidence in support of each.[6]

---

4. For example, some trial advocacy books recommends that you prepare for trial by making a "trial chart." But the recommended trial charts are based on abstract elements, not on the specific events, conditions or states of mind you will prove. But cf. J. F. Nijboer, "The Law of Evidence in Criminal Cases (the Netherlands)." Referring to the rules about charging criminal defendants, the Dutch jurist and scholar notes that, "The text itself is a statement that goes into the details of the case. The prosecutor cannot describe the charge in the words of the law, since they are considered to be too abstract, too far away from the world of common people." Id. at 2, n.1.

5. Research suggests that most of us think more efficiently and creatively in a concrete rather than an abstract context. See, e.g., J. Pryor et al., "The Influence of the Level of Schema Abstractness Upon the Processing of Social Information," 22 J. of Experimental Soc. Psych. 312 (1986)(reporting results of experiments showing increased memory, improved classification skills, and better recall for concrete rather than abstract schema); C. Anderson, "Abstract and Concrete Data in the Perseverance of Social Theories: When Weak Data Lead to Unshakable Beliefs," 19 J. of Experimental Soc. Psych. 93 (1983)(empirical studies demonstrating that spontaneous causal processing of information is more frequent and theories persevere more strongly when data is concrete rather than abstract).

6. As you will see, however, you need only construct explicit arguments for the factual propositions that a defendant seriously contests.

On a plaintiff's behalf, you may sometimes develop more than one factual proposition for a single element. For instance, in a negligence action you may contend that the defendant breached his duty of care by driving 90 m.p.h. and by driving without maintaining the brakes. Since proof of either form of conduct satisfies the element "breach of care," you will develop a factual proposition for each form of conduct.

5. A DEFENDANT'S PERSPECTIVE ON FACTUAL PROPOSITIONS

a. *Developing Defense Factual Propositions*

Defendants too have to develop factual propositions for legal elements. Sometimes, a defendant's factual proposition will simply negate a plaintiff's proposition. For instance, if plaintiff Curly's factual proposition is that on August 31 he delivered 50,000 bagels to Moe, defendant Moe's countering proposition may be, "Curly never delivered 50,000 bagels to me."

In other instances, a defendant will have an affirmative story to tell that is inconsistent with the plaintiff's factual proposition. For example, assume that as the defendant in *Curly v. Moe* you contend that Curly mistakenly delivered the bagels to Vance, who lives three blocks from Moe. Your defense factual proposition for the element of "performance" would be something like, "On Aug. 31, Curly delivered bagels to Vance instead of to Moe." [7]

Of course, one important difference separates plaintiffs and defendants. Plaintiffs have to formulate and prove propositions that satisfy each element of every claim for relief. Representing a defendant, you have the option of formulating propositions only for elements you wish to contest.

b. *Affirmative Defenses*

With respect to affirmative defenses, a defendant's task is identical to a plaintiff's. Just like a plaintiff, a defendant must formulate factual propositions that satisfy each element of an affirmative defense.

For example, assume that Bill is sued on a promissory note, and contends that he was induced to sign the note through fraud. Fraud in this situation is an affirmative defense, and in order to prevail Bill must establish each element of the fraud defense. Accordingly, Bill will formulate factual propositions for each such element.

6. "NORMATIVE" FACTUAL PROPOSITIONS

You can satisfy most legal elements simply by proving that certain matters occurred in the past. For example, the proposition that "Curly

---

7. If you represent a criminal defendant, you may base your defense entirely on the prosecution's failure to sustain the burden of proof, doing nothing except attacking the prosecution's evidence. In such instances, you might not state defense factual propositions

delivered 50,000 bagels to Moe on August 31" may satisfy the element of performance in a breach of contract case.

But sometimes elements require a factfinder to do more than determine "what happened". Some elements require factfinders to evaluate the propriety of what happened according to social norms. For example, a plaintiff in a fraud case must prove that his reliance was "reasonable." In a police misconduct case, a prosecutor may have to prove that a police officer used "excessive" force. For a factfinder to determine whether reliance was reasonable or force was excessive, the factfinder must judge the propriety of the conduct according to its understanding of community norms. Such judgments are therefore called "normative." [8]

All of us make normative judgments regularly in everyday life. For example, assume that you are considering going to dinner at Cafe Rock Hard. But you do not go, either because you decide that the service is too slow or the noise level is too high. Such decisions are largely normative, as you would necessarily evaluate the Rock Hard's speed of service and noise level according to your personal judgment of reasonable restaurant standards for such matters.[9] Of course, whatever your subjective judgment, it may differ from someone else's.[10]

A factfinder cannot make normative judgments merely by deciding how events took place. For instance, an ex-employee claiming wrongful termination may have to convince a factfinder that the sacking was without "just" cause. A factfinder cannot resolve this case simply by deciding that, as a matter of historical fact, the ex-employee was fired because he twice reported late to work. In addition, the factfinder also has to make a normative judgment: Does twice reporting late for work constitute "just" cause for dismissal? [11]

---

8. See A. D'Amato, Jurisprudence: A Descriptive and Normative Analysis of Law 221–327 (1984).

9. Note that such decisions would also be partially historical, resting on "objective" data about how long it took you to be served and the decibels of sound the last time you were at the Cafe Rock Hard.

10. Indeed, your own subjective evaluation may differ from one occasion to another.

11. The law is filled with elements containing normative aspects. In contract law breaches of a contract are actionable only if they are "material." Many commercial matters are judged by a reasonableness standard. See, e.g., UCC [section] 2–607 (goods may only be rejected by buyer if acceptance was based on a reasonable assumption that a non-conformity would be cured); UCC [section] 2–608 (revocation of acceptance must be within a reasonable time). See particularly, UCC [section] 1–204 (defining "reasonable time" and "sea-

sonably"). Similarly, in the area of torts consider perhaps less obvious examples such as outrageous conduct in connection with the infliction of emotional distress. And such normative decisions are well established to be appropriate decisions for a jury. See *Pacific Mutual Life Insurance Co. v. Haslip*, 499 U.S. 1, 19, 111 S.Ct. 1032, 1043, 113 L.Ed.2d 1 (1991):

> The law is filled with normative elements for a variety of reasons. Principal among them, however, is the reality that rule makers cannot regulate action in a given area without such rules. If broad rules allowing for normative judgments were not adopted, the number of individual rules that would be necessary to regulate conduct in any area would be almost endless. For example, unless one were willing to say that any deviation from the terms of a contract, no matter how slight, would give rise to an action for breach of contract, one must adopt a broad rule

The upshot of all this is that when you prepare to prove or disprove a "normative" legal element, you should convert it to one or more factual propositions that reflect your factual contentions both as to what happened and the propriety of what happened. For example, assume that you represent a plaintiff, Orin, who alleges that police officer Casey used excessive force when arresting him at the scene of a political protest.[12] To establish the normative element of "excessive force," Orin will prove two factual propositions. One might be that Off. Casey struck him numerous times with a baton to effect the arrest; the other might be that the use of the baton was inappropriate because Off. Casey could have arrested him using the less harmful "drag and carry" method.[13]

7. IDENTIFYING CRUCIAL FACTUAL PROPOSITIONS

Not all factual propositions are created equal. In any trial, some propositions will be crucial to a case's outcome; these are the factual propositions at which you want to direct your arguments. This section describes how to begin preparing arguments by identifying crucial factual propositions.

a. Vigorously Contested Propositions

For the most part, crucial factual propositions are those which your adversary is likely to vigorously contest. When you and an adversary lock horns on the accuracy of a proposition, a factfinder will typically see resolution of the disagreement as central to its verdict.

Usually, whether you represent a plaintiff or defendant, you will know before trial which propositions an opponent is likely to vigorously contest. In many jurisdictions, court rules compel parties to specify the issues they will raise at trial during a pretrial conference. In addition, you can often determine what propositions an adversary will vigorously contest by the thrust of pretrial discovery as well as by statements made by counsel during settlement or plea bargaining negotiations.

b. Propositions the Factfinder Will Be Reluctant to Accept

You cannot automatically limit crucial propositions to those that an adversary is likely to vigorously contest. You should also treat a proposition as "crucial" if you think that a factfinder may be unsympathetic to it. For example, assume that in a jury trial you represent the plaintiff in a fraud case. The defendant concedes making the allegedly fraudulent statement, but contends that the statement was true. Since the defendant contends that the statement was accurate, you doubt that the defense can credibly contest your client's "reliance."

such as material breach. Once one turns to such standards, the opportunity for the factfinder to make its own judgment about what does and does not constitute compliance is unending.

12. This example is based on the case of *Forrester v. City of San Diego*, 25 F.3d 804 (9th Cir.1994).

13. Often identifying factual propositions for "normative" elements is more complicated than in the example described in the text. For a more detailed discussion of the process of converting normative elements to factual propositions, see Chapter 6.

But if you think that some jurors might blame the plaintiff for not making an independent investigation before relying on the statement, you might nevertheless treat the factual proposition for "reliance" as "crucial."

The need to treat a factual proposition as crucial despite the absence of a vigorous contest often arises in the damages context, when you represent a party about whom a factfinder may harbor a social prejudice. For instance, assume that you represent an older person who seeks damages for loss of consortium; or a person with AIDS seeking damages for lost future wages as a result of a discriminatory firing. In each situation, the defendant may be reluctant to vigorously contest the amount of damages. The defendant may fear that some factfinders will perceive an explicit argument attacking the value of older peoples' intimate relationships or the duration of an AIDS' patient's future employment prospects as callous or culturally unacceptable. Nevertheless, as some factfinders may secretly harbor those social prejudices, you may want to treat the damages propositions as crucial.

8. PREPARE EVIDENCE LISTS FOR YOUR CRUCIAL PROPOSITIONS

Having identified the crucial propositions, your next step is to prepare an Evidence List for each. When preparing Evidence Lists, examine a file thoroughly. Review depositions, answers to interrogatories, witness statements, interviewers' notes and other documents. Combine information from different witnesses into a single evidentiary list for each crucial proposition.[14] You will almost certainly want to offer the evidence on your Lists into the record at trial.[15]

An Evidence List should, of course, contain any direct evidence, since direct evidence if accepted as true by a factfinder establishes the accuracy of a factual proposition. For example, if the proposition you want to prove is that "Citron offered to sell Graubard his car for $10,000," you will surely list direct evidence from Graubard that "Citron said he would sell me his car for $10,000."

If a proposition is seriously disputed, however, your direct evidence

---

14. An evidence list is a typical component in what other texts refer to as a "trial notebook." Some authors advise you to organize evidence in a trial notebook on a witness by witness basis. See J. Brovins & T. Oehmke, The Trial Practice Guide: Strategies, Systems and Procedures For The Attorney 20 (1992); Going to Trial: A Step–By–Step Guide to Trial Practice and Procedure, 1989 ABA Sec. of Gen. Practice 76–77; D. Baum, Art of Advocacy: Preparation of the Case [section 11.41–42 (1989)]. While you may ultimately want to prepare for witness examination in that way, the conception in this text is different: before organizing testimony on a witness by witness basis, list evidence according to the factual proposition it tends to prove.

15. When representing a plaintiff, you will also need to make Evidence Lists for non-crucial propositions which you have the burden of proving at trial. Obviously, for such non-crucial propositions your lists need only contain sufficient evidence to make a prima facie showing that the proposition is true, since your adversary does not seriously dispute the accuracy of these propositions.

is by definition disputed.[16]   Thus, to complete an Evidence List you will necessarily have to search a file for circumstantial evidence. Often, you will readily identify circumstantial evidence by intuitively recognizing a link between the evidence and a factual proposition. For example, assume that the proposition that you are trying to prove is that "Citron knew that her statement that the car had a Maserati engine was false." Examining your file, you find information that Citron had been told that she was likely to be fired unless she increased her new car sales. You may simply "see" that this information supports an inference that Citron made an intentional misstatement in order to save her job, and therefore put it on your evidence list.

If your intuitive well is dry, two techniques may help you identify circumstantial evidence. One is to ask yourself, "Is there any evidence that indicates a *motive* or a *reason* that my proposition is accurate?" For example, if you are trying to identify evidence that "Citron knew that her statement that the car had a Maserati engine was false," you might ask yourself, "Is there any evidence indicating that Citron had a motive to falsely state that the car had a Maserati engine?" Similarly, if you are trying to prove that "Randy's blood alcohol level was .12," you might ask yourself, "Is there any evidence that suggests a reason for Randy to have a blood alcohol level of .12?"

A second technique is to examine what took place "before" and "after" the time period encompassed in a factual proposition. For example, if you are trying to prove that Citron made a false statement, you would ask yourself, "Did anything happen *before* or *after* Citron made the statement that tends to prove that she knowingly made it?"

What if a proposition spans a wide period of time? For example, what if your proposition is that "Peter had back pain for six months?" You could ask the same type of question: "Did anything happen *before* or *after* Peter's back began hurting that tends to prove that he was in pain?"[17] But you could add an additional question concerning what happened *during* the time span itself: "Did anything happen *during* the time that Peter's back hurt that tends to prove that he was in pain?"

When compiling your Lists, do not agonize over making sure to include each and every piece of evidence tending to prove a given proposition. The burden of trying to list all the evidence that happens to appear in a story is likely to outweigh any advantages. However, as

16. The reason that a factual proposition cannot be crucial if your direct evidence is undisputed is that undisputed direct evidence automatically proves the accuracy of a factual proposition.

17. For some factual propositions the techniques mentioned in the text will not be sufficient to enable you to identify circumstantial evidence. For example, assume you are trying to prove the proposi-

tion that "The brake lining in Stephanie's car ruptured just prior to the accident." Because our common experience does not tell us what evidence tends to prove this, you will need the help of an expert to identify the evidence tending to prove this proposition. Often you will have had an expert identify such evidence before you begin trial preparation.

Evidence Lists will become the basis of the evidence you offer and the arguments you make at trial, you want to be thorough.[18]

For an illustration of what an Evidence List might look like, assume that you represent a plaintiff who was a victim of an all-too-prevalent consumer fraud scheme. Your client is Nelson, who signed a Note secured by a second Deed of Trust in favor of Carlson in the amount of $25,000. Nelson received only $13,000 in cash. The lender, Carlson, deducted the rest as "loan fees," "broker's fees," "document fees" and "escrow charges." Carlson then sold the secured note to Goldway. When Nelson fell behind in his payments on the Note, Goldway threatened to foreclose on Nelson's property. You filed suit on Nelson's behalf to enjoin the foreclosure and rescind the deal, on the ground that Carlson engaged in fraudulent practices to induce Nelson to enter into the transaction.

Assume now (as is often true in such matters) that the principal issue in the case is whether Goldway was a bona fide purchaser of the note. One of your factual proposition for this element is, "Goldway should have known that Carlson obtained the loan through fraud." A list of evidence tending to prove this proposition might look like this:

Evidence List: "Goldway Should Have Known of Fraud"

- Goldway had a real estate broker's license.
- Goldway had been in the business of purchasing loans secured by second deeds of trust for over 5 years.
- Goldway admits that when purchasing loans secured by deeds of trust, a purchaser must be careful because often times people who borrow money on notes secured by second deeds of trust are in desperate financial condition.
- Goldway's normal business practice was to examine the note and deed of trust before purchasing them and to also examine the Truth In Lending disclosure statement signed by the borrower.
- Goldway had purchased notes secured by second deeds of trust from Carlson on 30 occasions during the two years before purchasing Nelson's note and deed of trust.
  - In these prior transactions Carlson sometimes called herself and signed her name as Johnson.
  - In these prior transactions Carlson sometimes called herself and signed her name as Olson.
  - In these prior transactions Carlson sometimes called herself and signed her name as Moor.
  - In these prior transactions Carlson sometimes called herself and signed her name as Jones.

18. Often, the same evidence is relevant to prove more than one factual proposition. No problem—that evidence will simply appear on more than one list.

- Nelson's note was made payable to Carlson but the deed of trust was executed in favor of IRAM corporation.
- Goldway purchased the note and deed of trust without seeing any Truth In Lending statement signed by Nelson.
- Goldway never inquired about the APR rate.
- Goldway made no independent check to determine whether Nelson had the ability to repay the loan.
- The loan application form signed by Nelson and which Goldway says he examined before purchasing the note and deed of trust:
  - Stated that Nelson was 68 years old and earned $52,000 as an RN at Memorial Hospital
  - Was signed by Nelson but filled out in a handwriting that was clearly different from that of Nelson.[19]

9. SELECT THE CRUCIAL PROPOSITIONS FOR WHICH YOU WILL CONSTRUCT ARGUMENTS

Because a trial's outcome is likely to turn on how a factfinder resolves crucial propositions, as a general rule this step is a simple one: you develop arguments supporting the accuracy of each crucial proposition.

You may be unable to adhere to this general rule if a case involves numerous crucial propositions. For example, assume that you represent a citizen's group suing a municipality for violations of a permit issued under the Federal Clean Water Act. You allege that the defendant municipality has violated 20 of its obligations under various sections of the permit, and have developed a factual proposition for each violation. You think it likely that the defendant will vigorously dispute each violation. But if you put forth arguments for all 20 crucial factual propositions, you may well overwhelm the factfinder.[20] In such a case, you may have to develop explicit arguments only for some of the propositions.[21] In exercising your judgment, consider factors such as the following:

- Which propositions is the factfinder likely to see as most significant? [22]

19. The Nelson v. Goldway hypothetical and the list of evidence set forth here are drawn from an actual case handled by students in the UCLA clinical program in Spring 1994.

20. Cognitive limitations prevent people from attending to a large number of arguments, especially when those arguments are presented orally. See Moore, "Trial by Schema" 37 UCLA law Rev. 273 (1989).

21. Though in some cases you may develop arguments only for some crucial propositions, at trial you will of course introduce the data on the Evidence Lists for all your crucial propositions.

22. When deciding what propositions you think a factfinder will see as significant, you should take into account the factfinder's background and likely social preferences and prejudices. For example, in the environmental example discussed in the text, you might focus on different propositions depending on whether the factfinder is a working class jury, a judge who is a conservative Republican and a former patent lawyer, or a judge who is a liberal Democrat and a former family law lawyer.

- Which propositions will support the remedy your client desires most? [23]

- Based on a rough assessment of the Evidence Lists, for which propositions can you make the strongest arguments?

10. BEGINNING TO CONSTRUCT ARGUMENTS FOR CRUCIAL FACTUAL PROPOSITIONS

Having decided to prepare an explicit argument for a crucial proposition, you begin the argument construction process with a single item of evidence. Just like the proverbial journey of a 1000 miles that begins with a single step, so a persuasive argument begins with a single piece of evidence.

The source of that single piece of evidence is almost always your Evidence List. In an ideal world, you might construct an argument based on each item on the list. Alas, the world is not ideal. In most cases, you will not have the time to prepare or deliver and a factfinder will not have the patience to listen to arguments based on every item on a list.[24]

Therefore, with a crucial proposition and Evidence List in hand, select an item or two that you consider to be the *most highly probative* of the proposition. That is, choose the one or two items that you think a factfinder will see as most clearly establishing the proposition. These are the items with which you will begin to construct explicit arguments.

When making your selection, do not worry about whether an item of evidence is disputed or undisputed by an adversary. Even if an item of evidence is disputed, assume for the moment that you will win the dispute. If you abandon highly probative evidence merely because an adversary disputes its accuracy, you will often forgo, without thorough analysis, an opportunity to convince a factfinder that your client's version of highly probative disputed evidence is accurate.

You will probably first rely on your own reaction in deciding what evidence is most highly probative: if you were the factfinder, what evidence would strike you as most significant? But do not be a prisoner of your own perspective. One person in the world guaranteed *not* to be the factfinder is you. And in the end, what counts is what the factfinder sees as highly probative. As the probative value of evidence depends on generalizations based on everyday experiences, and as a factfinder's everyday experiences may differ from your own, you need to consider who your factfinder is likely to be, and what that factfinder is likely to find highly probative.

---

23. For example, in the environmental case in the text some propositions may be more likely to result in an injunction to minimize future violations. You client may feel strongly that obtaining such an injunction is more important than recovering damages for past violations.

24. This is especially likely to be true when a case involves more than one crucial factual proposition.

For example, assume that you represent Kay Knapland, who is suing her former employer for sexual harassment. One proposition you will try to prove is that, "Knapland's supervisor made statements about her appearance that Knapland found offensive." One item of evidence available to you is the following statement made to her by her former supervisor: "You look really great when you wear that red dress." You might see such a comment as highly probative evidence, especially if you are a woman who has been offended by similar remarks made to you. But if your likely factfinder is a male who commonly makes comments such as these to people he works with, the factfinder might not see the supervisor's statement as highly probative. In such a situation, you might look to your Evidence List and select a different item as highly probative evidence. Alternatively, if the factfinder consists of jurors, some of whom may see the supervisor's statement as highly probative and others of whom may not, you may decide to stick with the statement as highly probative evidence and look for other highly probative items to serve as the bases of additional arguments. Whichever option you choose, only by viewing evidence from the standpoint of a factfinder can you make intelligent decisions about what evidence is highly probative.

Admittedly, you may sometimes be uncertain about whether the highly probative items you've selected will produce your strongest arguments. But unlike the builders of the Leaning Tower of Pisa, you can readily scrap a foundation if you don't like the way an argument is tilting. If in the course of preparing an argument you decide that an item of evidence is not as probative as you initially thought, or that other evidence is far more probative, abandon the initial argument. Or, if you decide that other evidence has equal appeal, you may make an additional argument. Where you finish is much more important than where you start, and prior to trial you may alter arguments a number of times before deciding on your strongest ones.

11. DECIDE WHETHER HIGHLY PROBATIVE EVIDENCE IS "DISPUTED" OR "UNDISPUTED"

When identifying highly probative evidence, you drew no distinction between disputed and undisputed evidence. However, you now have to make that determination because whether highly probative evidence is disputed or undisputed fundamentally affects the type of argument you prepare and deliver. If your adversary does not dispute an item of highly probative evidence, you can confine an argument to its inferential impact. But if it is disputed, you also have to argue why your version of the dispute is the credible one.

Obviously, you may regard an item of evidence as undisputed when you and an adversary have formally stipulated to its accuracy.[25] Similarly, you may stamp "undisputed" on evidence when your adversary admits it in response to a Request for Admissions, or the accuracy of the

---

25. Prior to trial, parties may formally stipulate to evidence as part of a pre-trial order.

item is accepted by virtually all witnesses in answers to interrogatories, pretrial statements or deposition testimony.

But in addition, no matter what the "paper" record, your judgment may be that an adversary is very unlikely to dispute an item, or that a factfinder will give short shrift to any dispute. In such instances, you may proceed as though the evidence were undisputed.

12. WHERE DO YOU GO FROM HERE?

The process outlined in this chapter enables you to identify highly probative evidence for crucial factual propositions. In the ensuing chapters, you will learn how to construct arguments persuading a factfinder that this evidence proves those propositions.

Chapter 3

ARGUMENTS BASED ON UNDISPUTED EVIDENCE

This chapter describes and illustrates how to construct arguments based on undisputed circumstantial evidence. When circumstantial evidence is undisputed, your principal concern is to prepare an argument that explains to a factfinder why the evidence proves a crucial factual proposition.[1] After describing the process of constructing persuasive arguments, the chapter concludes with a discussion of how to take a factfinder's likely differing life experiences into account when evaluating arguments.

1. EMBRYONIC ARGUMENTS

When you select an item of circumstantial evidence as "highly probative" of a crucial factual proposition, you create an "embryonic argument." You have an "argument" because you have linked evidence to a specific proposition; but it is only "embryonic" because the linkage fails to explain the basis for the inference connecting the evidence to the proposition. This chapter explains the process of carrying an embryonic argument to "full term" by identifying the generalization(s) linking the evidence to your factual proposition and strengthening the generalization(s) with additional evidence.

The following short hypothetical illustrates an embryonic argument. Assume that you represent Carson in a negligence action against Melinda. Carson claims that Melinda drove in excess of the 35 m.p.h. speed limit and as a result collided with him. An undisputed item of evidence that you uncovered during discovery and consider highly probative is that at the time of the accident, Melinda was 20 minutes late for a business meeting.

Your embryonic argument based on this evidence is: At the time of the accident Melinda was 20 minutes late for a business meeting (item of

---

1. Remember, you needn't prepare arguments regarding undisputed *direct* evidence because by definition undisputed direct evidence establishes that a factual proposition is accurate.

circumstantial evidence); therefore, Melinda was driving in excess of the 35 m.p.h. speed limit (factual proposition).

This embryonic argument has some validity. But you are not ready to say, "Bingo! That takes care of this factual proposition. Let's see what else I've got to prove, and maybe I'll have time to get down to the beach."

First, the evidence is hardly conclusive. Given that people often can be late for meetings without speeding, a factfinder may not be impressed by the argument. Before accepting your argument a factfinder will probably want to know more about such things as how important the meeting was, how long it was to last and how far away Melinda was from the meeting site when the accident occurred

Second, remember from Chapter 1 that circumstantial evidence typically gives rise to multiple and conflicting inferences. For example, a factfinder who is routinely late may generalize that "People who are only 20 minutes late are *not* likely to be in a hurry," and therefore conclude that Melinda was not speeding.

For both of these reasons, as Carson's attorney you would want to enter the courtroom with a stronger argument that Melinda was driving too fast.

2. IDENTIFYING GENERALIZATIONS AND "ESPECIALLY WHENS"

To strengthen an embryonic argument, you begin by identifying the generalization connecting the evidence to the factual proposition.[2] For example, as Carson's attorney in Carson v. Melinda, begin by identifying a generalization linking the evidence ("20 minutes late for a business meeting") to your factual proposition ("drove in excess of the 35 m.p.h. speed limit"). Such a generalization might be stated something like, "People who drive when they are 20 minutes late to a business meeting sometimes drive in excess of a 35 m.p.h. speed limit."

The generalization reminds you that when they draw inferences from circumstantial evidence, factfinders evaluate information according to their beliefs about how events typically unfold. That is, lacking a Time Machine, no factfinder could be certain of how Melinda behaved in response to being late for a meeting. But a factfinder may infer how she probably reacted based upon the factfinder's beliefs about how people generally behave.[3] Thus, arguments at trial typically consist of asking a

---

2. In the descriptions of argument construction, "you" are the lawyer who carries out each of the steps. But when you represent a client as part of a "litigation team," you normally need to consult with one or more of your colleagues at various times during the process.

3. The generalization in Carson v. Melinda refers to the behavior of people. But litigation can involve objects, machines or animals, and they too can be the subject of generalizations. For instance, assume that an embryonic argument links the evidence, "Dog barked" to the factual proposition, "Dion Tology broke into Toby's house in the middle of the night." The supporting generalization would be, "Dogs sometimes bark when a person breaks into a house."

factfinder to infer that what is true about "people like this" is also true about the party.

But as the very term implies, for any given occasion a generalization may not accurately capture what took place. For example, you can generalize that students often do assigned readings before coming to class and that people usually climb mountains because they are there. But whether such generalizations are applicable to *particular* occasions may depend on the unique circumstances of those occasions. For example, Mickey may not have done the assigned reading for Con. Law on March 12 because he was at a "call back" job interview on March 11. And Minnie may have climbed Mt. Enn on May 9 not because it was there, but because she wanted to see what was on the other side.

At trial, factfinders cannot be content to assess "how events typically occur." Instead, they have to decide how they believe specific events took place.[4] That is, a factfinder has to determine whether Minnie climbed Mt. Enn on May 9 because she wanted to see what was on the other side, regardless of whether the factfinder believes that most other people climb it just because it is there. Thus, to prepare effective arguments you typically cannot be content with identifying the generalization underlying an embryonic argument. Rather, you have to identify additional evidence suggesting that the generalization is especially likely to be true given the unique circumstances of a particular case.

Think of the unique circumstances of a particular case as "especially whens." "Especially whens" are items of evidence and reasons indicating why a generalization is especially likely to be accurate in the case at hand. Thus, to strengthen an argument add "especially when" to a generalization and examine a file to identify additional evidence suggesting that your generalization is especially likely to be accurate in the case at hand.

Returning to Carson v. Melinda, you would attempt to strengthen your argument by adding "especially when" to the generalization, "People who drive when they are 20 minutes late to an important business meeting sometimes drive in excess of the 35 m.p.h. speed limit." You ask yourself:

"People who drive when they are 20 minutes late to an important business meeting sometimes drive in excess of the 35 m.p.h. speed limit, especially when...."

Then examine your file for evidence tending to prove the accuracy of the generalization in this specific case.

To practice the process of strengthening embryonic arguments, assume that your file in this case is limited to the deposition of a single witness, Arvee Park. During your deposition of Park, he testified as follows: Park has been Melinda's administrative assistant for close to

---

4. See C. Nesson, The Evidence or the Event? On Judicial Proof and the Acceptability of Verdicts, 98 Harv. L. Rev. 1357 (1985)(public acceptance of verdicts depends on belief that factfinders decide what really happened).

four years. Melinda is President of Melinda's Metals, a company that produces finished aluminum parts for products such as tent poles, automobile moldings and window frames. On the day of the accident, Melinda had a 3:00 P.M. meeting with Sonny Shyne, the marketing director of Sonny's Sunroofs. Melinda had been attempting to arrange a meeting with Shyne for a few months because Melinda thought that her company could underbid Shyne's then-current supplier of aluminum sunroom parts. According to what Melinda told Park, Shyne's decision to meet with her was an about-face from his earlier reluctance. At the time of the meeting Melinda's company had unused manufacturing capacity. Melinda was late for the meeting with Shyne because just as she was about to leave, at around 2:30 she got a phone call from her son's kindergarten teacher. Melinda had told Park that her son had been having behavioral problems in school, and since Melinda had been having trouble getting in touch with the kindergarten teacher, Melinda said she would take the phone call. Park was unable to telephone Shyne to tell him that Melinda would be late because there was no phone where the meeting was to occur.

Based on the information in Park's deposition, you can identify a number of "especially whens" and write out an outline of your "full term" argument. In outline form, your argument that Melinda was speeding at the time of the accident might look like this:

Outline of "Late for Meeting" Argument

Item of Evidence: At the time of the accident, Melinda was 20 minutes late for a business meeting.

Generalization: "People who drive when they are 20 minutes late to a business meeting sometimes drive in excess of the 35 m.p.h. speed limit...."

Especially When:

1. They have arranged the meeting themselves.

2. The person they are going to meet has been reluctant to meet with them previously.

3. The meeting is with a potential new customer.

4. Their company has excess manufacturing capacity.

5. They are unable to let the potential new customer know that they will be delayed.

Therefore....

Factual Proposition:

At the time of the accident, Melinda was driving in excess of the 35 m.p.h. speed limit.

For illustrative purposes, Park's short story may be richer than many in its "especially when" content. But it demonstrates how "especially whens" strengthen a generalization by identifying the circumstances that make the generalization especially applicable in a specific case. Hence, the "especially whens" tend to persuade a factfinder that your factual proposition is correct.[5]

Note that "especially whens" are as grounded in a factfinder's everyday experience as your initial generalization. Just as common sense indicates that people who are late for a meeting sometimes drive too fast, so too does common sense suggest that people are even more likely to drive too fast when they have had difficulty arranging the meeting and the meeting is with a potential new customer. Your desired inference ("drove in excess of the speed limit") is still based on a generalization, but one strengthened to reflect the unique evidence in your case.[6]

This list of "especially whens" may enable you to better appreciate Chapter 2's advice not to agonize over what evidence to list or regard as "highly probative." When you go through the process of strengthening an argument with "especially whens," you may for the first time realize how various pieces of evidence may fit into an argument, whether or not you have previously included them in an Evidence List.

Moreover, you may decide that one of your "especially whens" is even more highly probative than the evidence that served as the basis of an embryonic argument. If so, you may construct a substitute argument with the former "especially when" at its center. For instance, assume that after identifying "especially whens" for the embryonic argument above, you decide that item (e) is more probative than "20 minutes late." No worries. Develop a substitute embryonic argument, this one linking item (e) to your desired inference. Then construct a new argument following the same procedure. Your generalization would be "People who are unable to let a potential customer know that they will be late for a meeting sometimes drive in excess of the 35 m.p.h. speed limit." You then marshal "especially whens" for this new generalization.

The new generalization may lead you to identify different "especially whens." But even if your list of "especially whens" remains largely unchanged, you may decide that you have strengthened your argument by using what you see as more probative evidence as its starting point.

3. USING "INTERMEDIATE GENERALIZATIONS" TO FURTHER STRENGTHEN ARGUMENTS

In the example above, you constructed a "full term" argument with a single generalization linking an item of highly probative evidence to a

---

5. Though the evidence which forms the basis of an embryonic argument may be undisputed, your adversary may well dispute the accuracy of one or more "especially whens." In this case, for example, Melinda might dispute the fact that her company had excess manufacturing capacity. As you will see when you read Chapter 4, this possibility is by no means fatal to an undisputed-evidence argument.

6. Like looking into mirrors which face each other, and dividing "6" into "20," the process of tailoring generalizations by adding "especially when" could continue indefinitely. For example, after tailoring the generalization above with the two additional items of evidence, you might search for additional evidence by folding the existing "especially whens" into the initial generalization and again adding "especially when." But assuming that you have a life and other cases to work on, one round of "especially whens" is generally enough.

factual proposition.   Often, however, you can further strengthen an argument by identifying more than one linking generalization before you turn to the process of identifying "especially whens."

The reason is that a single generalization may conceal unstated inferences.   When you use intermediate generalizations to surface the unstated inferences, you strengthen an argument by making it more likely that a factfinder will recognize and find persuasive the link between an item of evidence and a factual proposition.

To see how intermediate generalizations may help you strengthen an argument, change the facts in Carson v. Melinda just a bit.   On Carson's behalf your factual proposition remains that Melinda drove in excess of the 35 m.p.h. speed limit.   But this time your item of evidence is that at the time of the accident, Melinda's two young children were roughhousing in the back seat of her car.   Assuming that you regard this as highly probative evidence, you might prepare an argument by generalizing that "People who drive with young children roughhousing in the back seat of their car sometimes drive in excess of the 35 m.p.h. speed limit," and then searching for "especially whens."

But here, you may doubt whether a factfinder is likely to see the connection between the evidence and the factual proposition.   Implicitly at least, you recognized a link between "children roughhousing" and "speeding" when you selected the evidence as "highly probative," but simply juxtaposing the evidence and the conclusion may not make that link evident.   The reason is that the single generalization may obscure unstated inferences.   You may surface these unstated inferences and thereby clarify your argument by identifying intermediate generalizations.   Here, your intermediate generalizations may go as follows:

a.   People who drive with young children roughhousing in the back seat of their car sometimes are irritated.

b.   People who are irritated sometimes try to get out of the situation causing them to be irritated as quickly as possible.

c.   People who try to get out of the situation causing them to be irritated as quickly as possible sometimes drive faster than the speed limit.

Therefore, Melinda was driving in excess of the 35 m.p.h. speed limit.

Here, the single generalization concealed the unstated inferences made explicit in generalizations a-c.   By articulating those unstated inferences you make the link between the evidence and the factual proposition clearer, and thereby make your argument more persuasive.

Once you formulate intermediate generalizations, you may then review your file in pursuit of "especially whens" for each.   Here you would ask yourself,

a.   People who drive with young children roughhousing in the back seat of their car sometimes are irritated, especially when. . . .

   b.   People who are irritated sometimes try to get out of the situation causing them to be irritated as quickly as possible, especially when....

   c.   People who try to get out of the situation causing them to be irritated as quickly as possible sometimes drive faster than the speed limit, especially when....

For example, if your file or list of important evidence indicates that the children's roughhousing included the hurling of food or other objects, you might include that as an "especially when" for generalization (a) or (b).[7]

Note that when you subdivide a broad generalization into intermediate ones, *the inferred conclusion from the first generalization begins the second generalization, and so on.*   Starting each succeeding generalization with the conclusion of the preceding generalization is a *must* if you are to avoid a logical gap in the inferential process.

a.   The Beauty of Intermediate Inferences Is in the Eye of the Beholder

The purpose of using intermediate inferences is to enable you to articulate the inferences *you* implicitly recognize when you decide that evidence is highly probative.   Usually, you can use a variety of intermediate inferences to connect evidence to a factual proposition.   With the "roughhousing" evidence, for example, you might have adopted this set of inferences:

   a.   People who drive with young children roughhousing in the back seat of their car sometimes are concentrating on what their children are doing.

   b.   People who are concentrating on what their children are doing sometimes are inattentive to the road.

   c.   People who are inattentive to the road sometimes drive in excess of the speed limit.

In the abstract, neither this nor the previous argument is superior.[8] And you probably can identify still other possible arguments.   The key is to identify the connections that *you see* when you identify an item as highly probative.

b.   Do You Need Intermediate Inferences?

As you can see, one of the decisions you face when constructing arguments is whether to formulate intermediate inferences.   Unfortunately, you cannot fall back on the comfort of rules to guide your

---

7. When you use intermediate generalizations you may or may not have especially whens for each generalization.

8. Note, however, that you generally score no "Brownie" points for developing numerous intermediate inferences.   If an argument relies on a lengthy inferential chain (more than three intermediate inferences), you might look for a better argument.   See B.J. Calder, Cognitive Response, Imagery and Scripts: What Is the Cognitive Basis of Attitude?   5 Advances In Consumer Research 630 (1978).

decision. The question you have to ask yourself is whether the single generalization will enable a factfinder to readily grasp the link between an item of evidence and a factual proposition. If you think the factfinder will do so, be content with the single generalization. But if you are uncertain, consider whether intermediate generalizations might strengthen the link.

One technique that might help you make the decision is to look at the evidence which is the basis of your embryonic argument, and ask yourself, "What do I infer from this evidence?" If you can move right to the factual proposition, you probably do not need to develop intermediate generalizations.

Returning to Carson v. Melinda, for example, you would ask yourself, "What do I infer from the fact that two young children were roughhousing in the back seat?" If your answer is "speeding," go directly to "especially whens;" do not pass "Go."

But if your answer is something else (e.g., "concentrating on the kids;" "mad as hell;" "distracted"), then you probably should use intermediate inferences to construct a stronger argument. In that case, keep asking yourself, "What do I infer?" until your answer is the factual proposition. For instance, assume that you infer from "roughhousing" that Melinda was "mad as hell." You would then ask yourself, "What do I infer from the fact that Melinda was mad as hell?" and so on until you reach "speeding."

4. DON'T FORCE ALL OF YOUR ESPECIALLY WHENS INTO A SINGLE ARGUMENT

When constructing an argument, you may have a tendency to jam too many "especially whens" into a single argument. Resist the temptation. A long string of "especially whens" is often a sign that you have forced two or more potentially separate arguments into a single one. Thus, consider "spinning off" at least one of your "especially whens" and use it as the basis of a separate argument for the same factual proposition. At trial, multiple arguments for a single proposition are common and often persuasive. For example, assume that in Carson v. Melinda you prepare separate arguments that Melinda was speeding, one based on the undisputed evidence that she was late for a meeting and the other based on a second item of undisputed evidence that Melinda had received a very disturbing report about her child's behavior from the child's kindergarten teacher just before leaving her office for the meeting. Based on this second item, you will argue that Melinda was distracted and upset and therefore did not pay close attention to her speed. Using the second item as the basis of a separate argument may produce a stronger overall presentation than if you try to jam the "phone call" evidence as an "especially when" into the "late for a meeting" argument. Ultimately, you will have to rely on your judgment to decide how many separate arguments to prepare for a single factual proposition.

5. FROM PREPARATION TO PERFORMANCE: ARGUMENTS BASED ON UNDISPUTED EVIDENCE GO TO TRIAL

Part II of this book explores the techniques through which you present arguments at trial. However, at this early stage you might appreciate a "preview" of how preparing arguments directly affects what you do at trial.

Return to Carson's initial argument that Melinda was speeding, based on the evidence that she was 20 minutes late for a meeting. That argument, as you recall, is as follows:

Item of Evidence:

At the time of the accident, Melinda was 20 minutes late for a business meeting.

Generalization:

"People who drive when they are 20 minutes late to a business meeting sometimes drive in excess of the 35 m.p.h. speed limit...."

Especially When

a.   they have arranged the meeting themselves.

b.   the person they are going to meet has been reluctant to meet with them previously.

c.   the meeting is with a potential new customer.

d.   their company has excess manufacturing capacity.

e.   they are unable to let the potential new customer know that they will be delayed. Therefore....

Factual Proposition:

At the time of the accident, Melinda was driving in excess of the 35 m.p.h. speed limit.

Now assume that on direct examination, Melinda testifies that though she was late for a meeting, she drove carefully. Note how your "especially whens" may serve as the basis of your cross examination of Melinda:

Q: You are the one who arranged the meeting with Shyne, right?

A: Yes.

Q: Before this, you had tried to set up other meetings with Shyne?

A: That's true.

Q: But until this particular meeting, he had been unwilling to meet with you, isn't that right?

A: Well, yes, this was our first meeting.

Q: And you regarded this meeting as an important one?

A: Oh I don't know, I meet with people all the time.

Q: Yes, but Shyne was a potential new customer, right?

A: Yes.

Q: And you were looking for a new customer, at least in part, because your company had excess manufacturing capacity, isn't that right?

A: That's true.

Q: You were unable to let Shyne know that you might be late for the meeting, isn't that true?

A: That's true.

Q: And this was the meeting that you were late for when the accident occurred?

A: Yes.

Q: . . . . .

Here, your list of "especially whens" forms the basis for your cross examination questions eliciting evidence that Melinda was especially likely to speed given the unique circumstances of this particular case.

6. TAKING ACCOUNT OF A LIKELY FACTFINDER'S REACTION TO YOUR ARGUMENTS

Any argument will necessarily reflect your judgment about what evidence package is most likely to be persuasive. But remember, a factfinder's life experiences and values may be different than yours. What to you is persuasive may to other people be unconvincing or even offensive. Consequently, you should always explicitly consider who your factfinder is likely to be, and that factfinder's likely reaction to an argument.[9] And if you are uncertain of a factfinder's likely reaction, you may try out arguments on people whose life experiences more closely approximate those of the factfinder than do yours.

For example, assume that you represent Trimble, a police officer charged with manslaughter in the shooting of a motorist, Johnson, following a nighttime traffic stop. Trimble claims that he is not guilty, because he shot Johnson in the belief that Johnson was pointing a gun at him.[10] One argument that you've constructed on Trimble's behalf is as follows:

Item of Evidence:

Trimble saw Johnson holding a dark object in his hand when Johnson got out of the car.

---

9. In jury trials, evaluating a factfinder's likely reaction is particularly difficult when the jury will probably be composed of individuals with disparate life experiences and values.

10. You would also have to convince the factfinder that Trimble's belief was reasonable, which is a normative element. For a discussion of how to develop arguments for normative elements, see Chapter 6.

Generalization # 1:

Officers who see motorists getting out of a car holding dark objects in their hands sometimes believe that the motorists are holding a gun. . . .

Especially When

a. they have stopped the motorist for driving erratically.

b. the motorist initially refuses to comply with the officer's request to get out of his car.

c. the traffic stop occurred in what the officer believed was a high-crime area.

Generalization # 2:

"Officers who believe that a motorist is holding a gun when he gets out of a car sometimes believe that the motorist intends to shoot the officer."

Therefore . . . Trimble believed that Johnson intended to shoot him.

How persuasive this argument is may well depend on where the trial takes place and the experiences and values of a factfinder. For example, a factfinder living in an affluent suburban area may see the "especially when" that the stop occurred in a high crime area as strong evidence supporting Trimble's belief that Johnson was armed. But a factfinder residing in a high-crime area may have an opposite reaction, believing that such an "especially when" is tantamount to giving police officers a license to shoot unarmed motorists in their community. If you conclude (perhaps aided by input from a colleague or friend) that an argument or some portion of it may be unacceptable or offensive to a likely factfinder, your choices include maintaining the same argument and trying to secure a sympathetic factfinder through jury voir dire,[11] responding to the factfinder's likely concerns during final summation,[12] or modifying or even abandoning the argument.

Consider some other settings in which a factfinder's potential reaction may lead you to modify or abandon an argument. For example, assume that you represent a defendant charged with rape. Many factfinders would be highly offended by an argument that the alleged victim's provocative manner of dress tended to prove that she consented to sexual intercourse.[13] Or, assume that you represent an employer sued for wrongful termination who claims that a discharged employee, a mother of two young children, failed to mitigate damages. Some factfinders would be offended by an argument that the woman failed to seriously pursue other employment because she wanted to stay home with the children. Finally, assume that you represent an heir in a will contest case. Some factfinders might find unacceptable an argument that the deceased testator was unable to remember the natural objects of

---

11. For a discussion of voir dire techniques, see Chapter 18.

12. For a discussion of how you might do so, see Chapter 14, note 32.

13. Legislation in some jurisdictions forbids such an argument. See Proposed FRE 413.

his bounty because he was nearly 75 years old.[14] In each of these cases, you would need to ask yourself whether the likely factfinder will find the argument persuasive, or whether the factfinder's life experiences or values might produce a negative reaction.[15]

14. Even if you determine that an argument is tactically sound, you may well be concerned about its ethical propriety. For example, you may be reluctant to make an argument based on negative racial, ethnic, age or gender stereotypes, even if you think a factfinder will not be offended by them. For a discussion of how such concerns can arise in the context of credibility arguments, see Chapter 5, Section 5.

15. For ease of explanation, this chapter describes the development and evaluation of arguments as separate processes. In practice, of course, you will undoubtedly carry out both processes simultaneously.

Chapter 4

COUNTERING AN ADVERSARY'S LIKELY RESPONSE TO ARGUMENTS BASED ON UNDISPUTED EVIDENCE

Chapter 3 described how to construct arguments based on undisputed circumstantial evidence. However, your process along the preparatory path resembled that of Little Red Riding Hood, who skipped through the forest in blithe ignorance of possible enemies. But as you know, forests are inhabited by dangerous wolves and courtrooms by zealous adversaries. Therefore, trial preparation is not complete until you identify an adversary's likely response to an argument and consider your counter-response. Otherwise, you may first realize in the middle of trial, "My, what big responding arguments my adversary has!" If you expect your argument to carry the day against an adversary's response, you had best identify and think about your counter-response before trial begins.

1. TWO POTENTIAL RESPONSES TO YOUR ARGUMENTS BASED ON UNDISPUTED EVIDENCE

An adversary has two ways of attacking an argument based on undisputed evidence.[1] One way is to offer additional evidence weakening the link between the undisputed evidence and your desired conclusion. The second way is to attack the credibility of one or more of the "especially whens" on which your argument relies. To prepare for trial you need to consider whether an adversary is likely to make either or both of these responses and to consider a counter-response.

A simple hypothetical will help you think through this part of trial preparation. The hypothetical is *Prager v. Dolinko*, a wrongful death case.[2] Plaintiff Robert Prager alleges that his wife Pauline was struck

---

1. These ways are not mutually exclusive; an adversary may make both responses to the same argument.

2. The case is straightforward in that the evidence is quite limited, and you are likely to be very familiar with the substantive law of negligence.

and killed by a truck driven negligently by the defendant Steve Dolinko. Dolinko admits to driving the truck that killed Ms. Prager, but claims that he was not negligent.

The entire case file consists of the statements of Cynthia White, (a witness for Prager) and the defendant Dolinko, together with a diagram of the intersection where the accident occurred. As you read through the file, assume that you represent the plaintiff, Prager.[3] After reading the file, think about the factual proposition that you might formulate for the legal element, "breach of duty of care." Then consider the evidence you might rely on to prove your proposition.

To assist your understanding, please refer to the following diagram as you read through the file:

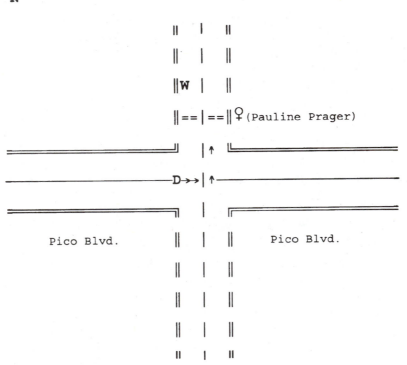

a. Witness Statement of Cynthia White

I am 22 yrs. old and single. For the past two years I have been a Clinical Psychology student at Duke & Duchess University.

At about 3:00 p.m., on January 6th last year, I was stopped for a red light at the intersection of Westwood and Pico Blvds., heading south. My car was immediately north of Pico, in the lane closest to the west

3. Assume that Dolinko's statement is a summary of his deposition testimony.

curb of Westwood. There was no car in the lane to my left. Traffic in general was extremely light and I had a clear view of the northeast corner of Pico and Westwood.

As I was stopped at the light, I looked to my left and saw a woman, who I later learned was Pauline Prager, step off the curb on the northeast corner into the crosswalk and begin walking towards me across Westwood. I noticed that she was wearing designer jeans, because I was looking for a pair to buy for myself. Just before Ms. Prager stepped off the curb, I saw a car that was eastbound on Pico make a left on Westwood and go north. This car was a blue, late model sedan, and part of the license plate number was "NOM." I watched Ms. Prager for a second and turned to look at the light. It was still red for traffic on Westwood.

I then noticed a pickup truck marked "Dolinko Construction Co." going eastbound on Pico begin to make a left turn to go north on Westwood. I only saw the truck for a few moments, but I'd say it was going at least 25–30 m.p.h. I noticed that the driver seemed to be looking to his right toward the corner that Ms. Prager had stepped off of, where two or three young children were playing. Then I turned to see if the traffic light was still red for traffic on Westwood. It was. Then I heard a woman's voice screaming and a thud. I turned my head and saw the Dolinko pickup truck stopped about 50 feet north of the crosswalk on Westwood. Ms. Prager's body was about 10 feet in front of the truck, all crumpled. I saw the driver of the pickup truck get out and run over to Ms. Prager and I heard him say, "My God, I'm sorry, I didn't see you."

Lots of cars stopped to try to help Ms. Prager, so I decided to continue on to my 3:15 hairdresser appointment. After my appointment, I drove back to Pico and Westwood. The police were still there and I told them that I had witnessed the accident.

b. Witness Statement of Steve Dolinko

I am 27 years old, married with three children. For the past four years I have been the sole owner of Dolinko Construction Co., which specializes in remodeling single family homes. Besides myself, the company has 13 full time employees.

On January 6th last year around 3:00 pm, I was on my way back to the office when I got a call on my car phone that there was a problem with a large remodeling job I was doing on Sawyer Street. At the time of the call, I was going east on Pico. But since I was in the vicinity of the job and we had missed an inspection that needed to be done before we could continue with the job, I decided to check out the job site. Therefore I decided to turn left on Westwood. As I approached Westwood, I slowed down to about 10 m.p.h., but I never actually came to a complete stop. I saw that there were no cars coming west on Pico, and then I saw that the crosswalk on the north side of Pico was clear. I know I was not speeding, because I had some kitchen cabinets in my truck the road there is very bumpy and I did not want to damage them. I had my eyes on the road at all times.

As I completed my left turn and went through the crosswalk, I resumed normal driving speed. Suddenly, about 20 feet north of Pico, on Westwood, a woman ran out from between 2 parked cars. One of the parked cars was a Toyota, the other was a Mazda. When I saw the woman I immediately yelled, honked my horn, turned off the engine, turned the steering wheel sharply to the left, and slammed on my brakes. The woman stopped running, turned toward me and just stood there motionless. The truck hit her and stopped almost at the same time. When it stopped, the woman's body was under the truck, with her legs sticking out. I got out of the truck and went to help the woman. I didn't say anything. When I saw that she was badly hurt, I ran immediately to a store to call an ambulance.

On the day of the accident, I had been working on a construction site all day, and I had had no alcoholic beverages to drink.

c. Plaintiff Prager's Argument Based on Undisputed Evidence

Representing Prager, one factual proposition that you may select for the element "breach of the duty of care" is, "On January 6th around 3:00 P.M., Dolinko was momentarily inattentive to the road just before he struck Prager."[4] As Dolinko's main claim is that he was not negligent, this proposition is undoubtedly crucial.

Listing important evidence for this proposition, you may include the following:

1. Dolinko's construction company is small.
2. Just before the accident, Dolinko was looking in the direction of three children on a street corner.
3. Dolinko is the father of three young children.
4. Just before the accident, Dolinko got a phone call informing him of a problem with one of his remodeling projects.
5. The problem was significant enough to cause a work stoppage.
6. Just after the accident, Dolinko said, "My God, I'm sorry, I didn't see you."
7. Prager stepped off the curb at the corner into the crosswalk.

Looking at this list, you realize that Dolinko disputes Nos. 2, 5, 6 and 7.[5] But No. 4 is undisputed, and you consider it highly probative of your factual proposition. Your intuitive judgment is that such a phone

---

4. There is no "magic" to this phrasing; you might well phrase yours differently. In addition, you might identify other factual propositions satisfying this same element. For example, you might assert that "On January 6 around 3:00 P.M., Dolinko was driving at an excessive rate of speed when he made the left turn." The point is to use the information in a file to develop factual assertions which, if proved, satisfy an abstract legal element.

5. Chapter 5 discusses how to develop arguments about disputed evidence.

call is likely to distract or disturb a building contractor. Thus, your embryonic argument based on this undisputed item of evidence is, "Just before the accident, Dolinko got a phone call informing him of a problem with one of his remodeling projects (item of evidence); therefore, Dolinko was momentarily inattentive to the road just before he struck Prager (factual proposition)."

To strengthen this embryonic argument, you add a connecting generalization(s) and "especially whens." Based on the file in *Prager*, your argument might be as follows: [6]

Generalization: "Building contractors who receive a call on their car phone informing them of a problem with one of their remodeling jobs are sometimes inattentive to the road."

Especially when:

1.   The problem has to be dealt with before the job can continue.

2.   The job is a large one.

3.   The contractor receiving the call is the owner of the company.

4.   The contractor receiving the call is in the vicinity of the job site.

5.   The contractor receiving the call changes his route to go the job site.

6.   The contractor was also looking in the direction of children on a nearby corner.[7]

Experience suggests that each of these "especially whens" tends to increase the probability that the call would have caused a building contractor like Dolinko to become inattentive.

Now that you have fleshed out one of your arguments based on undisputed evidence, examine how to identify and counter your adversary's likely response.

2.   ADVERSARY'S POTENTIAL RESPONSE # 1: UNDERCUTTING THE GENERALIZATION(S) LINKING EVIDENCE TO YOUR DESIRED CONCLUSION

One response that Dolinko may make to your argument is to offer evidence undercutting your generalization(s) by pointing to possible exceptions to it. Dolinko will in effect respond, "The plaintiff's evidence may be true. But there's some other evidence that the plaintiff didn't

---

6. For illustrative purposes, only one connecting generalization is used in the text. You might, however, use more than one connecting generalization. For example, your generalizations could be: *Generalization 1* "Building contractors who receive a call on their car phone informing them of a problem with one of their remodeling jobs are sometimes concerned about the problem." *Generalization 2* "Building contractors who are concerned about a remodeling job are sometimes inattentive to the road." As discussed in the preceding chapter, whether you use one or more generalizations to flesh out an embryonic argument depends on whether you think the added generalizations will make the argument clearer for the factfinder.

7. Note that "especially whens" need not be limited to items on a list of important evidence.

tell you about. When you look at this other evidence, you'll see that the plaintiff's argument isn't persuasive."

To identify the undercutting evidence that Dolinko may offer, employ the mirror image of the "especially when" technique. Using each generalization that you used to construct your argument, add "except when" instead of "especially when." The "except whens" you identify are potential responses that Dolinko may make. You can then check your file to see if there is evidentiary support for any of the potential "except whens."

Thus as Prager's counsel, to identify Dolinko's likely response you will ask yourself, "People who receive a call on their car phone informing them of a problem with one of their remodeling jobs sometimes are inattentive to the road, except when...." Plausible evidence that Dolinko might point to that would weaken the force of this generalization *in this very case* includes:

a. *Except when* they routinely receive such phone calls.

b. *Except when* they are not responsible for taking care of the problem.

c. *Except when* they already expect the problem to arise.

Each of these items is a potential response that Dolinko might make to your argument. For example, relying on the item in "a," Dolinko's counsel may argue, "The fact that Dolinko got a phone call just before the accident telling him about a problem on one of his remodeling jobs is no evidence at all that he was inattentive. He routinely gets such phone calls, and people who routinely get phone calls informing them of problems are not distracted by the calls." [8]

Undoubtedly, you can come up with additional responses that Dolinko may make. Because all generalizations are by definition subject to exceptions, you will always be able to identify *potential* responses. [9] But you want to prepare for real concerns, not imagined ones. Hence, the issue you have to focus on during trial preparation is, "What response is Dolinko *likely* to make?" [10]

---

8. As should be apparent, a rebuttal response based on circumstantial evidence is grounded in generalizations, just as any other argument based on circumstantial evidence.

9. For the notion that generalizations are by definition less than 100% accurate, see Wright & Graham, *Federal Practice & Procedure* Sec. 5171 (1978).

10. If your argument relies upon intermediate generalizations (described in Chapter 3, sec. 2(c)), you will have to consider potential "except whens" for each generalization. For example, assume that in this case you had developed this inferential chain in place of the single generalization supporting your embryonic argument: Gen. # 1: "People who receive a call on their car phone informing them of a problem with one of their remodeling jobs sometimes are thinking about the problem." Gen. # 2: "People who are thinking about a problem sometimes think about solutions to and potential ramifications of the problem." Gen. # 3: "People who are thinking about solutions to and potential ramifications of a problem sometimes are momentarily inattentive to the road as they drive." You might look for an adversary's likely response by adding "except when" to each of these generalizations.

The most obvious starting point for an answer to this question is the file itself. Does the file suggest the existence of any "except whens?" [11] If so, and if your adversary has prepared as carefully as you, you can assume that a response based on that evidence will be made.

However, do not be too quick to dismiss the possibility of a response just because your review of a file reveals no "except whens." Nobody's pretrial fact investigation is perfect. For example, if you had taken Dolinko's deposition and he had testified to getting the "problem" phone call, would you necessarily have thought of and asked Dolinko about all plausible explanations for why he might not have become inattentive as a result? Probably, the answer is "no." Thus, the chance almost always exists that an adversary will undercut a generalization with evidence that you do not know about. But if you use the "except when" technique to identify plausible responses an adversary *is likely to* make, you at least give yourself a chance to think about how you might counter a response once it is made. [12]

3. COUNTERING AN ADVERSARY'S "EXCEPT WHEN" RE-SPONSE

You do not go to the trouble of identifying an adversary's likely response just so you can turn smugly to an adversary during trial and say, "I predicted all along that you were going to try to undercut my argument with that except when." Rather, you do so in order to plan your counter to whatever evidence an adversary puts forward.

Your planning should recognize that often an adversary will come up with "except whens" that you cannot dispute. For example, you may have to concede that Dolinko often does receive phone calls informing him of job problems. But this is certainly no reason to abandon an argument. In the Land of Generalizations, responses and counter-responses are common. Thus, you may simply continue to argue that notwithstanding an except when or two, your argument is convincing. For example, even if Dolinko offers evidence that he routinely gets phone calls informing him of job problems, and argues that he therefore did not become inattentive, you can nevertheless argue that he was distracted by this phone call because it related to a large remodeling job, and the problem was a significant one.

A second common way of countering an adversary's undercutting evidence is to put the adversary's evidence in the form of a generalization and look for your own "except whens." For instance, if you expect Dolinko to claim that he wasn't distracted by the phone call because he

---

11. Whether in thinking through the file you would need to actually return physically to the various documents which comprise it would, of course, depend on factors such as how recently you had reviewed the file and how voluminous the file was.

12. Consistent with the "cyclical" nature of trial preparation, you might follow up your identification of "except whens"

with additional fact investigation, even if it consists only of informal interviews or of "information bargaining" with the adversary during negotiation. For a discussion of "information bargaining," see G. Bellow & B. Moulton, The Lawyering Process: Materials For Clinical Instruction In Advocacy 508–16 (1978).

routinely receives such calls, ask yourself, "Contractors who routinely receive problem phone calls are not distracted by them, except when...." This ploy may point you towards evidence in your file that you hadn't previously recognized as important, but which undercuts your adversary's desired inference.

A final common way of countering an adversary's "except whens" is to dispute its accuracy. For example, if you think it likely that Dolinko will claim that problem phone calls are routine, you might examine your file for evidence on which to base an argument disputing the accuracy of Dolinko's assertion.[13]

4. ADVERSARY'S POTENTIAL RESPONSE # 2: DISPUTING THE ACCURACY OF YOUR "ESPECIALLY WHENS"

The second way an adversary can reply to an argument based on undisputed evidence is to dispute the accuracy of your "especially whens." The adversary may argue that if one or more of your "especially whens" is inaccurate, then so is your argument as a whole.

For example, one of your "especially whens" in the "problem phone call" argument comes from White's testimony that when Dolinko made the left turn, he was looking toward two or three children playing on a nearby corner. Dolinko may challenge the credibility of this "especially when" by attacking White's ability to observe and remember where he was looking, and by offering his own testimony that he was watching the road at all times.[14] He may then respond to your argument with his own argument that as one of the underpinnings of your argument has failed, your whole argument fails.

5. COUNTERING AN ADVERSARY'S ATTACK ON THE CREDIBILITY OF YOUR "ESPECIALLY WHENS"

Assume that both from looking through a file and from your adversary's pretrial conduct, you believe that an attack on the credibility of one or more of your "especially whens" is likely.[15] One counter-move you can make is to drop those "especially whens" from your argument. This option is especially attractive if you have a number of "especially whens" to support an argument, and the credibility of one or two of them is doubtful. To follow this option, simply do not offer the "especially when" into evidence.[16] And if a witness unexpectedly volunteers the disputed "especially when" during your direct examination, or if it comes in through cross examination, do not rely on it during your final argument.

---

13. For an examination of the arguments you may use to dispute the accuracy of an adversary's evidence, see Chapter 5.

14. See Chapter 5 for a "checklist" of factors that affect credibility.

15. You have probably noticed that trial preparation often requires you to "examine the file." But in practice these will not be separate visits. Particularly as you gain experience, you will perform many of these "file examining tasks" at the same time.

16. Neither ethical considerations nor evidentiary rules require you to offer every potential item of evidence.

For example, assume that you think it likely that Dolinko can effectively attack the credibility of White's testimony that she noticed Dolinko looking at young children playing on the corner. Since you have other "especially whens," you may decide not to ask White about where Dolinko was looking just before the accident.[17]

By contrast, if you think that your adversary's attack on an "especially when's" credibility is unlikely to impress a factfinder, by all means rely on your "especially when." This option is particularly attractive if you have few "especially whens" to support an argument and you think the "especially when" is important.

Thus, if you think that White's testimony about Dolinko's looking towards the children is important and she can credibly explain how she was able to observe and recollect this fact, plan to include this information in White's testimony.[18]

---

17. You could not of course prevent Dolinko from eliciting evidence from White that she saw him watching children on the side of the road. In practice however, Dolinko may be reluctant to bring up additional harmful information, just to attack its credibility. And if you choose not to rely on the evidence, a factfinder may disregard Dolinko's credibility attack.

18. Your argument might then have two parts: one emphasizing the inferential significance of Dolinko's watching the children, the other emphasizing the credibility of White's testimony. Chapter 5 describes the process of constructing the latter type of arguments.

Chapter 5

CONSTRUCTING ARGUMENTS SUPPORTING YOUR VERSION OF DISPUTED EVIDENCE

Thus far you have learned how to construct arguments emphasizing the inferential strength of undisputed, highly probative circumstantial evidence. But often an adversary will dispute your version of highly probative evidence, whether it be circumstantial or direct. When a dispute arises, you typically need to prepare an argument that seeks to persuade a factfinder to resolve the dispute in your favor. This chapter describes how to prepare such an argument.

For example, assume that as Carson's attorney you want to rely on Park's testimony that Melinda was 20 minutes late for a meeting to prove that she was speeding. Melinda, however, contends that she was on time for the meeting. Before you can ask the factfinder to infer from Park's testimony that Melinda was speeding, you first need to convince the factfinder that Park's testimony is correct.

This chapter sets forth a Credibility Checklist, consisting of factors that routinely affect a lay witness' credibility with respect to a disputed item of evidence. The chapter then illustrates how to use the Checklist to construct arguments bolstering the credibility of a witness' testimony.[1]

Using the Checklist can help ensure that you do not overlook potential credibility arguments. When you review a file with its individual factors in mind, you will often recognize pertinent information that you may miss if you only looked broadly for "evidence bearing on credibility."

1. A CREDIBILITY CHECKLIST

Despite the uniqueness of individual disputes, the factors tending to affect the credibility of witnesses' assertions are relatively constant from

---

1. For a discussion of credibility relating to expert witnesses, see Chapter 15.

one case to another.[2] These factors are the following:

Credibility Checklist

1. Physical Ability

2. Reason or Motive to Engage in Disputed Conduct

3. Internal Consistency

4. Consistency With Other Witnesses and Documents

5. Authority to Engage in the Disputed Conduct

6. Neutrality

7. Reason or Ability to Recall

The following subsections illustrate how each of these factors may affect a witness' credibility with respect to a specific disputed item of evidence.

a. *Physical Ability*

You may bolster the credibility of disputed evidence with an argument that a witness had the "physical ability" to do what he asserts that he did.[3] The argument may pertain either to factors in the outside environment or to a witness' physical or emotional condition.

For example, assume that your evidence is Frank's testimony that "I heard June say that she was going to meet Jack at 5:00 o'clock." June disputes this testimony; she denies that she made this statement. In an argument supporting Frank's credibility, you might point to evidence supporting his physical ability to hear what June said, such as his being alert, his close proximity to her and the absence of noise in the area where the statement was made.

Sometimes you can make a physical ability argument by pointing to a witness' experience. For instance, assume that Neil testifies that he saw Lorene driving 95 m.p.h. You might point to Neil's 20 years of driving experience to bolster your argument that Neil was able to estimate a car's speed.

b. *Reason or Motive to Engage in Disputed Conduct*

People have always believed strongly in "cause and effect." Few events are seen as random. For example, ancient peoples attributed floods to the vengeful wrath of a Rain God. Today, people wanting explanations for the daily gyrations in stock prices typically attribute them to factors such as, "Stock prices went down today on news that Federal Reserve would raise interest rates." Since the search for causal

2. This point was made many years ago by Dean Wigmore. See J. Wigmore, The Principles of Judicial Proof Or The Process of Proof: As Given By Logic, Psychology, and General Experience 267 (1931).

3. For the sake of brevity, the discussion of each portion of the Checklist refers to what a witness says she did. Of course the Checklist is not limited to assertions about what a witness did. It applies equally to all testimonial assertions, including those relating to what a witness said, thought, saw, heard, touched or smelled.

explanations is so rooted in human nature, you may bolster the credibility of disputed evidence with an argument based on evidence that a witness had a reason or motive to do what she asserts she did.

For example, return to Neil's testimony that he saw Lorene driving 95 m.p.h. To support the credibility of this testimony, you might point to evidence indicating that Neil had a specific reason to pay attention to Lorene's car. Perhaps he noticed it because he was thinking of buying the identical model.

c. Internal Consistency

Believable stories typically "hang together;" they are consistent from beginning to end. Thus, you may bolster the credibility of disputed evidence with an argument based on evidence that the witness' disputed testimony is consistent with other parts of the witness' story.

For example, assume that the disputed evidence is Jason's testimony that, "On March 31, I entered into an oral agreement with McCalla to manufacture 1000 floor mops." To support the credibility of this testimony, you may point to Jason's additional testimony that he ordered 1000 mop handles on April 2. Experience suggests that after people enter into manufacturing contracts, they often order the supplies and equipment needed to fulfill the contract.

d. Consistency With Other Witnesses and Documents

Believable stories are generally not only "internally" but also "externally" consistent. Thus, you may bolster the credibility of disputed evidence with an argument based on evidence that the witness' assertion is consistent with the testimony of other witnesses and documents.

For instance, you might support the credibility of Jason's testimony that he entered into an oral agreement to make 1000 mops on March 31 with a purchase order executed by Jason's company on April 2 for 1000 mop handles.

e. Authority to Engage in the Disputed Conduct

People often limit their activities to those that they have the authority to perform. Thus, you may bolster the credibility of disputed evidence with an argument based on evidence that the witness had authority to do what she asserts she did.

For instance, assume that Brette is being prosecuted for stealing three rings from the jewelry store where she works. Your disputed evidence is Brette's testimony that she took the rings home in order to repair them after the store closed. You may bolster Brette's credibility with the shop owner's testimony that Brette had the authority to do ring repairs at home.[4]

4. This section of the checklist will often be important when your witness is an agent acting on behalf of a principal. For example, if there is a dispute about whether a corporate agent made an offer of employment to a plaintiff, whether the agent was

f. Neutrality

People's recollections are often influenced by motivations such as love, jealousy and friendship.[5] Thus, you may bolster the credibility of disputed evidence with an argument based on evidence that it comes from a witness who is neutral and has no ax to grind.

For example, assume that a witness, Andy, testifies that he saw Brette repairing the allegedly stolen rings. Andy noticed this when he went to Brette's apartment soliciting contributions for Tree People, an environmental organization, and saw Brette with a jeweler's magnifying glass in one hand and a ring and a sharp tool in the other. You may bolster Andy's credibility by arguing that he is neutral and has nothing to gain by his testimony.

g. Reason or Ability to Recall

Unlike fine wines, people's memories usually do not improve with age. In the absence of evidence suggesting why a witness is able to recall something that took place long before trial, a factfinder may not believe the witness' testimony. Thus, you may bolster the credibility of disputed evidence with an argument based on evidence indicating how a witness is able to recall past events.

For example, return to Andy's testimony that he saw Brette repairing rings. You may bolster his credibility with evidence explaining that Andy is able to recall what Brette was doing because on that evening he and Brette had a lengthy discussion about the "greenhouse effect."[6]

h. Using Sub–Categories to Personalize the Checklist

The Checklist categories are necessarily broad; you will probably develop sub-categories of your own as you gain trial experience and perhaps read the trial practice literature written by and for practicing lawyers. For example, when cross examining a prosecution witness, some criminal defense attorneys routinely ask about any meetings the witness had with the prosecutor prior to trial, and whether the prosecutor rehearsed the witness' testimony during these meetings.[7] Such a cross examination might suggest that the witness' memory needed refreshing, or that the witness is no longer neutral. Hence, if you decide to follow this practice, your Checklist might include the sub-category of "Rehearsal" under the broader categories of "Neutrality" or "Reason or

---

"authorized" to make such offers would be relevant to resolve the dispute.

5. For a more complete list of factors tending to give rise to distortion, watch one week of any television soap opera.

6. This example also demonstrates how evidence that is admissible for one purpose may also support a "silent" argument that Brette is a "good" person. (See Chapter 9 for a discussion of silent arguments.) Here, the testimony about Andy and Brette dis-

cussing the "greenhouse effect" is admissible to bolster Andy's credibility. But this conversation about the "greenhouse effect" may also show that Brette is knowledgeable and concerned about environmental dangers, and may lead a factfinder to like her. Of course, this evidence may have the opposite effect if the factfinder sees "environmentalists" as "pointy headed do-gooders."

7. See D. Reed, *Automatic Cross–Examination* pp. 56–59. (1992).

Ability to Recall." Similarly, under the broad category of "Physical Ability," you might include such sub-categories as "Distance," "Obstructions," and "Competing Events." The purpose of a Checklist is to help you make a thorough search for evidence supporting credibility arguments, and you should personalize the Checklist to reflect the nature of your practice and your experiences.

i. Conclusion

In Dickens' famous *A Christmas Carol*, Scrooge asks the Ghost of Christmas Future, "Are these the shadows of things that might be or that must be?" In like manner, recognize that the Checklist identifies credibility arguments which you *might* make, not that you must make. Unless the witness whose credibility you support is Mother Teresa, you will undoubtedly not make arguments based on evidence from all the categories and sub-categories in your Checklist for a single item of disputed evidence. Moreover, the fact that an argument is potentially available does not mean that you have to make it; you can easily undermine a witness' credibility by putting forth arguments that are weak or strained. The Checklist's purpose is to remind you of potentially available sources of credibility arguments, not to compel you to make any specific argument.[8]

2. USING THE CREDIBILITY CHECKLIST: PEOPLE v. DIXON.

To understand how to use the Checklist to construct arguments bolstering the credibility of disputed highly probative evidence, consider *People v. Dixon*.[9] The defendant Donna Dixon is charged with shoplifting. The events take place in Small Town, Anywhere.

a. Summary of the Prosecution's Evidence

James Embree is the owner and manager of the Oak Hills Supermarket. On Saturday, December 9th at approximately 12:15 P.M. Embree saw the Defendant Donna Dixon enter the supermarket. Embree's attention was initially drawn to Dixon because she had a very large purse which she opened when she placed it in the kiddie seat of her shopping cart. Embree thought that Dixon might be a potential shoplifter so he went to the meat department where he could watch her without obstruction through the store's one-way mirror. While watch-

---

8. Of course, all the arguments from the Checklist rely on circumstantial evidence, and therefore are premised on generalizations. For example assume that you argue that a witness did not have the "physical ability" to accurately hear what was said because he was 20 feet away from the conversation. This argument relies on a generalization such as, "People who are 20 feet away from a conversation often cannot accurately hear all that is being said." As set forth in section 3 *infra*, sometimes you can surface these generalizations to help you buttress an argument. But at the outset there is typically no need to expressly articulate underlying generalizations.

9. The *Dixon* case is based on an actual criminal trial in which our former colleague, Graham Strong, represented the defendant. We have changed the names of the people involved and modified the facts of the original case slightly, but the basic scenario remains unchanged.

ing Dixon through the one-way mirror, Embree saw her put a cheese ball, two cans of chili peppers and a can of chili powder in her purse. Embree then went to the security room to observe Dixon on the television monitor and to record her on videotape. In the security room, Embree videotaped Dixon taking a bottle of Anacin from the shelf and apparently placing it in her purse. He then left the security room and went to the register to see if Dixon would pay for the items he had seen her place in her purse. She paid for two six-packs of soda, a gallon of milk, toothpaste, two boxes of crackers and a cheese dip. Embree stopped Dixon as she was leaving the store and asked her if she had forgotten to pay for what was in her purse. She said she had nothing from the store in her purse and refused Embree's request to search it. Embree detained Dixon in his office and called the police.

Officer Brian Morey arrived at the market at approximately 1:15 P.M. Embree told Morey, "I caught a woman shoplifting. I've got a tape of her stealing a bottle of Anacin. I'll show it to you." Embree and Morey reviewed the tape while a sales clerk stayed with Dixon. After reviewing the videotape, Morey told Embree that he wasn't sure if it showed Dixon placing the Anacin in her purse or in the cart. Embree said he thought the tape showed her putting the Anacin in her purse. Embree and Morey then returned to Embree's office. Morey advised Dixon of her rights and asked her if she had bought any Anacin while she was in the store. Dixon said that she had put some Anacin in her shopping cart but had later decided it was too expensive and put it back on the shelf in another aisle of the store.

Morey, Dixon and Embree then went to look for the Anacin she said she had placed back on the shelf; they were unable to find it. They returned to Embree's office. Morey searched Dixon's purse and found a cheese ball, two cans of chili peppers and a can of chili powder, but no Anacin. Dixon admitted that the items were from the Oak Hills market but said she had bought them on a trip to the market earlier that day and had inadvertently left them in her purse. Embree said he had been working in the market all day and was quite sure that Dixon had not been in the store earlier. Morey arrested Dixon for shoplifting. Dixon has never produced a receipt for the cheese ball, chili peppers or chili powder.

b. Summary of Dixon's Evidence

Donna Dixon is a 23 year old receptionist. She and her husband Richard live in an apartment complex about a mile from the Oak Hills Market. On December 9th, Dixon was having a few friends over for a party in the late afternoon, and had decided to cook chili for the party. At about 10:00 A.M. on the morning of the 9th, Dixon went shopping at Oak Hills. There she met and spoke briefly with a neighbor, Janet Jones, who lives in the Dixons' apartment complex. (Jones was questioned a week later and verified Dixon's statement.) Dixon then bought some groceries for the coming week. For the party that afternoon she bought two 12–packs of beer, chili beans, chili powder, chili peppers, a cheese ball and potato chips. All the groceries save the beer fit into two large paper bags.

Dixon's car was an older model Volkswagen convertible with a tear in the back part of the roof. Richard had removed the back seat to make more room for his carpenter's tools. Dixon put the beer on the front seat and the bags on the floor in the back and drove home. When she arrived home she took the beer into the kitchen and then returned to the car for the groceries. When she picked up the first bag the bottom broke and the groceries spilled out. She put several items in her large straw purse, carried some of the other items into the house and got some dry bags to bring in the remaining groceries. The bottom of both bags had gotten wet on the drive home because rain from the day before had leaked through the roof into the back of the Volkswagen. She put the groceries away but forgot about the items in her purse.

At 11:30 Dixon put the chili beans on to cook. She doesn't add the chili peppers and powder until the beans have cooked for a couple of hours. Around noon, Dixon began to get ready for the party and discovered that she needed a few more items, so she returned to the Oak Hills Market. She grabbed her purse without realizing that it still contained some of the groceries from her first trip. At the market, she bought some additional items for the party and some toothpaste. After she went through the register the manager stopped her and asked her if he could look in her purse. Dixon was insulted and offended by his accusation, told him she had nothing in her purse from the market and refused his request to search it. The manager told her he had it all on videotape and took her to his office and called the police.

A police officer came, talked with the manager and a short while later advised Dixon of her rights and asked her if she had bought any Anacin while she was in the store. She told them she had put some Anacin in her shopping cart but had later decided it was too expensive and put it back on the shelf in another aisle of the store. They all went to look for the Anacin but it was no longer in the place where she thought she had left it. They returned to the manager's office and the Officer told her he would have to search her purse. He did and found a cheese ball, two cans of chili peppers and a can of chili powder, the items she had left in it earlier; he found no Anacin in her purse. She explained what had happened, but was arrested.

Dixon has been unable to find the receipt for the groceries she bought on her first trip to the market. In fact she is not even sure she picked up the receipt. Dixon's husband had gone to a construction job early in the morning of the 9th and he did not see his wife until late in the afternoon when she had been released from jail. Four of Dixon's friends will testify that they were invited to an afternoon party at the Dixons' on December 9th.

c. Using the Checklist to Develop Credibility Arguments Supporting Your Version of a Disputed Item of Evidence

Assume that you are the prosecutor in *Dixon*. You would first identify the crucial factual propositions. Here, one such factual proposition corresponding to the abstract element, "took property of another," is: "On the afternoon of Dec. 9th, Dixon put a cheese ball in her purse and went through the market checkstand without paying for it." [10] Examining this proposition, you realize that a portion of it is undisputed; Dixon admits not paying for the cheese ball in the afternoon.[11] Thus, the only portion of the factual proposition for which you have to construct an argument pertains to Dixon's putting a cheese ball in her purse. Embree's testimony provides important direct evidence of this proposition. But his testimony is disputed: Dixon maintains that she already had the cheese ball in her purse when she arrived at the market in the afternoon.

To persuade a factfinder that Embree's assertion is credible, construct an argument based on the factors in the Credibility Checklist. Record the argument in a "Disputed Evidence Argument Outline," which will help you structure witness examinations and final summation. Based on the summaries of the evidence set forth above, your "Disputed Evidence Argument Outline" for this item of disputed evidence may read as follows: [12]

Argument Outline, "Embree Saw Dixon Take The Cheese Ball"

1. *Physical Ability*: Embree observed Dixon from an area specially designed to permit store employees to watch customers without being noticed, and his view was unobstructed.

2. *Reason or Motive to Engage in Conduct*: Embree had a reason to observe Dixon because one of his responsibilities is to monitor potential shoplifters. His suspicions were aroused when he saw Dixon enter the market with a large, open purse.

3. *Internal Consistency*: Embree's story about what happened is consistent with his having seen Dixon put the cheese ball in her purse. He went to the videotape room to tape Dixon after he saw her take the cheese ball; he stopped her at the register and called the police; and he asked to search her purse.

4. *Consistency with Other Witnesses and Documents*: Embree says he saw Dixon take a cheese ball, and Morey saw the cheese ball in Dixon's purse when he arrested her. Also, she had no receipt for it.

5. *Authority*: Not applicable.[13]

---

10. For ease of discussion, the factual proposition in the text refers only to the cheese ball. In an actual case, you would typically include the other items in the same proposition.

11. As the prosecutor, you would have to offer evidence that Dixon failed to pay for the cheese ball that afternoon, but you would not have to construct an argument to prove it.

12. In an actual case your Argument Outline might be more detailed than the one in the text, as you would have available more detailed information.

13. In an actual case your outline would not refer to this factor because Embree is obviously "authorized" to see whatever he claims to have seen and no argument is appropriate.

6. *Neutrality*: Embree has no ax to grind in saying that he saw Dixon put the cheese ball in her purse. He does not know Dixon and was not on the "lookout" for her.

7. *Reason to Recall*: Embree's experience as a store owner supports an inference that he knew he would be called as a witness to testify at trial about the events.[14]

This Outline furnishes a ready guide to the evidence you may offer and the final summation you deliver at trial.[15] For example, during direct examination of Embree, you may emphasize the evidence establishing his physical ability to observe Dixon, his reasons for focusing on her and his never having seen her previously. And, a portion of your final summation supporting the credibility of Embree's testimony may go as follows:

"Embree clearly had the physical ability to observe Dixon; he had an unobstructed view of her taking it. Also, he was watching from an area that was specially built to allow employees to observe customers' activities inside the store. In addition, Embree was specifically watching Dixon; he became suspicious of her when he saw her enter the market with a large, open purse. Moreover, Embree's subsequent behavior is consistent with his having seen Dixon put the cheese ball in her purse: he waited until Dixon paid for her other items, then asked to look inside her purse. And Embree's testimony is supported by Officer Morey: Morey found the cheese ball in Dixon's purse, just where Embree says that he saw her put it. Finally, Embree's testimony is unaffected by any hostile feelings towards Dixon: he had never seen her before, and he took action based only on what he saw. Based on all this evidence, you should believe Embree's testimony that he saw Dixon put the cheese ball in her purse that afternoon."

3. STRENGTHENING CHECKLIST ARGUMENTS

Use of the Checklist helps you to identify evidence supporting credibility arguments. But when a credibility argument is particularly crucial to a case's outcome, you may want to take the argument construction process one step further. This additional step may allow you to strengthen an argument by identifying generalizations and "especially whens" linking an item of evidence to the credibility conclusion you are trying to establish.

For example, assume that you want to argue that an eyewitness had the "Physical Ability" to accurately identify a robber. Using the Check-

---

14. Unless the defense contends that Embree's testimony is the product of a failure of recollection, you will probably not make this argument. It does little to distinguish Embree from most of the rest of the population, as most people, store owners or not, realize that if they witness a crime they may have to testify about what they saw. Thus, if you were the prosecutor you would probably not bother to develop an argument for the factor, "reason to recall."

15. Remember that at trial you need not make every argument in the checklist. You can pick and choose from the arguments bolstering Embree's testimony.

list, you have identified the following item of evidence to support this argument: the witness observed the robber from a distance of 20 feet. The generalization linking this evidence to the credibility conclusion you are trying to establish is something like, "People who see someone at a distance of 20 feet can usually accurately see that person's face." Identifying this generalization and then adding "especially when," may lead you to further evidence supporting this argument. For instance, people who see someone at a distance of 20 feet can usually accurately see that person's face, especially when . . . their view is unobstructed, they see the robber's face for several seconds, and they have a full-face view of the robber. Sometimes, taking this extra step will lead you to evidence you had not previously seen. But even if you identify no additional evidence, you have been thorough and given yourself an opportunity to construct the strongest possible argument.

4. TAKING ACCOUNT OF A LIKELY FACTFINDER'S REACTION TO CREDIBILITY ARGUMENTS

Just as you have to consider the potentially different life experiences and values of a likely factfinder when you develop arguments based on undisputed evidence, so too must you do so when developing credibility arguments.

For example, assume that you are prosecuting Gutierrez, a Mexican–American who is charged with assaulting another customer in a shop run by a Korean–American. The shopkeeper claims that Gutierrez struck the first blow; Gutierrez contends that he acted in self-defense. According to the police report, one reason the shopkeeper gives for having seen Gutierrez start the fight is that, "I was watching him closely because I've had trouble with Mexican people taking things from the store." This statement potentially bolsters the shopkeeper's credibility by suggesting that he had a "motive" to observe the defendant. However, many potential factfinders (minorities and non-minorities alike) are likely to be offended both by the shopkeeper's explanation and your argument based on it. The argument perpetuates negative stereotypes both of Mexican–Americans and Korean–Americans, and may cause some factfinders to disbelieve the witness. Hence, you might be extremely reluctant to elicit such evidence or make such an argument, even though it comports with a Checklist factor.

Suppose now that you are the defense lawyer, and that you are representing Gutierrez. The Korean–American shopkeeper is now prepared to testify on Gutierrez's behalf that the other customer struck Gutierrez first, and that Gutierrez acted in self-defense. Again, the shopkeeper's "motive" for noticing that the other customer attacked first emanates from his statement to the police that, "I was watching him closely because I've had trouble with Mexican people taking things from the store." Do these changes affect your evaluation of a likely factfinder's reaction? That is, do you think a factfinder might react differently to an argument based on a negative racial stereotype if you are making it as a defense attorney rather than as a prosecutor, and if you are making it to support the innocence of a member of the maligned minority rather than to convict him? Does your answer change depending on whether the likely factfinder is a jury that may have no minority group members?

Apart from an argument's potential effect on a likely factfinder, you also need to consider the ethical propriety of making arguments based on negative racial, ethnic, gender or religious stereotypes. For example, assume that you conclude as the prosecutor in the example above that your likely factfinder would not be offended by your argument about the shopkeeper's reason for noticing that Gutierrez was the aggressor. Nevertheless, you may well be concerned about the ethical propriety of such an argument, especially when as a prosecutor you represent the broader community which has as one of its goals the elimination of racism. Might you overcome your concerns by maintaining the argument, and acknowledging during summation that while it is unfortunate that the shopkeeper had a biased attitude, the attitude nonetheless provided a genuine basis for concluding that your version of the disputed evidence is accurate? Are your ethical concerns any different if you are the defense attorney, arguing that the shopkeeper's biased attitude supports an argument that Gutierrez acted in self-defense? Whatever your answers in these criminal contexts, would they be different if the case were a civil action for assault and battery? While such questions may not be capable of a universal answer, their existence demonstrates that you may often have to go outside the Checklist to decide what arguments you will actually put forward.[16]

5. IDENTIFYING AND COUNTERING AN ADVERSARY'S PO-TENTIAL CREDIBILITY ARGUMENTS

Just as you consider how an adversary may undermine the probative impact of undisputed evidence by offering "except whens,"[17] you should also think about the arguments your adversary may make to attack the credibility of your witness' testimony.

To identify an adversary's likely responses to your credibility arguments, consider each Checklist factor regardless of whether you have developed an affirmative argument based on it.[18] But this time look for evidence negating each factor. For example, go through the whole Checklist and examine your file for evidence indicating that your witness did *not* have the requisite "physical ability," did *not* have a "reason or

---

16. Many offensively stereotypical arguments that affect factfinding at trial are "silent." That is, they infest a case even though they are never explicitly made. For a discussion of how to identify and counter "silent arguments," see Chapter 9.

17. See Chapter 4.

18. You need to consider each checklist factor without regard to your affirmative arguments because your adversary may make independent use of any of the factors. For example, regardless of whether you prepare an argument that your witness *did* have physical ability to do what she asserts she did, your adversary may prepare an

motive to engage in the conduct," etc.[19]

In *Dixon*, for example, consider whether your adversary can develop an argument that Embree's testimony that he saw Dixon take the cheese ball is not credible because it is internally inconsistent with other portions of his story. (Factor No. 3) Based on the witness statements above, Dixon may have a plausible argument that Embree's testimony that he saw Dixon put a cheese ball in her purse is internally *inconsistent*. Dixon may point out that Embree did not tell Morey that he saw Dixon put a cheese ball in her purse when Morey first arrived; he only told Morey about the Anacin.[20] This supports an inference that Embree's testimony is not credible, because everyday experience suggests that if Embree had seen Dixon take the cheese ball, he would have immediately mentioned it to Morey.

Having identified your adversary's potential credibility arguments, you can then assess how to counter them. One common response is to provide an explanation undermining the adversary's argument. For example, assume that Dixon will argue that Embree's story is internally inconsistent because he failed to mention to Off. Morey that he saw Dixon put the cheese ball in her purse. You may seek to counter this argument by seeking out from Embree an explanation for his failure to do so. For instance, you may have the following dialogue with Embree:

> You: Mr. Embree, is there any reason why you failed to tell Morey about seeing Dixon take the cheese ball?

> Embree: As a matter of fact, there is. I was so sure that the tape would show Dixon taking the Anacin that I just didn't bother saying anything about the cheese ball.

Identifying this evidence may enable you to successfully counter this attack on the credibility of Embree's testimony.

The second way to counter an adversary's credibility arguments is to dispute the accuracy of the evidence on which your adversary relies. This counter is not available to you in *Dixon*, since Embree admits not telling Off. Morey about seeing Dixon take the cheese ball. But it is a common type of response. For instance, if an adversary claims that your eyewitness did not have the "physical ability" to observe an automobile accident because he had just been drinking martinis, you may develop

argument that your witness *did not* have the requisite physical ability.

19. For purposes of illustration, the text suggests you consider each factor on the checklist twice, once to identify your argument and once to identify the adversary's potential response. Of course, in practice you could identify your arguments and the adversary's response during a single review.

20. You may identify the apparent inconsistencies your opponent might exploit by reenacting, either in your imagination or physically, what happened according to Embree's story. As you reenact Embree's story, you look for things that he did that you would not expect him to have done if he had seen Dixon put the cheese ball in her purse. You also look for things he did not do, but that you would have expected him to have done if he had seen Dixon put the cheese ball in her purse. For a more detailed description of this reenactment process, see J. Davidson & M. Lytle, After The Fact: The Art of Historical Detection (2nd ed. 1985).

arguments disputing the accuracy of that evidence. To do so, of course, you would again use the Checklist.[21]

6. COUNTERING AN ADVERSARY'S CHARACTER EVIDENCE–BASED CREDIBILITY ARGUMENTS

An additional type of credibility argument that an adversary might make is one based on character evidence. As you probably know, character evidence relating to credibility focuses on a witness' honesty or trustworthiness.[22] For example, from evidence that a witness has been convicted of perjury, a factfinder may infer that the witness' testimony is inaccurate.[23] Though character evidence may be a source of credibility arguments, it is not a part of the Checklist for several reasons:

- Under the statutory policy requiring "bad before good," [24] you cannot bolster a witness' credibility through character evidence; you can only respond to an adversary's attack.

- Character evidence typically does not relate to a specific disputed item of evidence. Rather, it pertains to everything a witness says.

- Particularly in civil cases, parties rarely offer character evidence.

When character evidence is offered at trial, it can take one of the following forms:

- Opinion or reputation evidence that a witness is not trustworthy.[25]

- Evidence that a witness has previously been convicted of a crime.[26]

- In some jurisdictions, evidence that a witness has engaged in nefarious conduct of some sort not resulting in a conviction which suggests that the witness may not be trustworthy.[27]

If you become aware prior to trial that an adversary intends to attack a witness with character evidence, you will want to prepare a response. Sometimes, your response will take the form of evidence. For

---

21. Even if your judgment is that the factfinder on balance is more likely to conclude that your witness' testimony on a highly probative item of evidence is *not* true, you will sometimes still offer that evidence and "take your best shot" at persuading the factfinder. You pursue this alternative when you think that you will almost certainly lose the case if you do not offer the evidence.

22. The admissibility of character evidence to attack credibility is the subject of much controversy, particularly when it is admitted against criminal defendants. See FRE 404(b), Committee Notes; C. McCormick et al., Cases and Materials on Evidence 43–109 (7th ed. 1992). See also, E. Gainor, Character Evidence by Any Other Name . . .: A Proposal to Limit Impeachment by Prior Conviction Under Rule 609, 58 Geo. Wash. L. Rev. 762 (1990); E. Imwinkelried, The Right to "Plead Out" Is-

sues and Block the Admission of Prejudicial Evidence: The Differential Treatment of Civil Litigants and the Criminal Accused as a Denial of Equal Protection, 40 Emory L.J. 341 (1991); Calvin W. Sharpe, Two–Step Balancing and the Admissibility of Other Crimes Evidence: A Sliding Scale of Proof, 59 Notre Dame L. Rev. 556 (1984).

23. The legitimacy of offering evidence of prior convictions against a defendant in a criminal case is a subject of controversy. For an entry into the debate, see H. Richard Uviller, Credence, Character, and the Rules of Evidence: Seeing Through the Liar's Tale, 42 Duke L.J. 776 (1993).

24. FRE 608(a).

25. See FRE 608(a).

26. See FRE 609.

27. See FRE 608(b).

example, if an adversary offers opinion evidence that a witness is not trustworthy, you can offer opinion evidence to the contrary. Other times, you probably will be limited to making a response during final summation. Thus, if an adversary offers "prior bad act" character evidence, you may argue that its probative impact is so slight that the factfinder should disregard it.

7. WHEN DISPUTED EVIDENCE IS CIRCUMSTANTIAL, CREDIBILITY OFTEN IS ONLY HALF THE BATTLE

Direct evidence which is believed by a factfinder conclusively establishes a factual proposition. For example, assume that you convince the factfinder that Embree's testimony that he saw Dixon put the cheese ball in her purse and walk through the counter without paying for it is true. You need make no further argument to establish the factual proposition satisfying the element "taking property of another."

By contrast, establishing the accuracy of circumstantial evidence is often only half the battle. Even if the factfinder accepts the accuracy of circumstantial evidence, you typically still have to persuade the factfinder to infer from the evidence that the factual proposition is true.

For example, return to the example of Carson v. Melinda, involving the claim that Melinda was 20 minutes late for a meeting and therefore likely to be speeding, and assume that you represent Carson. Melinda disputes the claim that she was late for a meeting. Even if you prevail and convince the factfinder that she was late for a meeting, you probably will have to make a further argument persuading the factfinder to infer from the evidence of "late for a meeting" that Melinda was speeding.[28] As you probably recognize, this further argument treats the disputed evidence as undisputed and follows the argument construction process described in Chapters 3 and 4.

8. CONCLUSION

The Credibility Checklist described in this chapter is a tool for making trial preparation less painful and more thorough. The Checklist breaks down a very broad issue into a series of manageable ones. Thus, during trial preparation you do not ask yourself the broad question, "What are all the arguments I can make to show that my witness is right?" Instead, you make a series of focused inquiries, e.g., "Did the witness have the physical ability to hear what he says he heard?" "Is the witness' testimony internally consistent?" The narrower inquiries should enhance your ability to identify, evaluate and articulate credibility arguments about disputed items of evidence.

---

28. In some situations, the probative impact of circumstantial evidence may be so great that winning the credibility argument is tantamount to winning the battle. For example, the late Dean William Prosser once asserted that "There is still no person who would not accept dog tracks in the mud against the sworn testimony of a hundred eyewitnesses that no dog had passed by." W. Keeton, et al., Prosser and Keaton On the Law of Torts 243 (5th ed. 1984).

Chapter 6

SATISFYING NORMATIVE ELEMENTS

As noted in Chapter 2, many elements of claims and defenses require factfinders to determine more than what happened in the past. Some elements also require factfinders to evaluate the propriety of a party's conduct.[1] Elements which require this additional determination contain a "normative" standard.

For example, an element containing a normative standard was the focus of the much-publicized 1993 trial of the four Los Angeles police officers who were charged with violating Rodney King's civil rights. One crucial proposition the prosecution had to prove was that the officers used "excessive" force by kicking and striking King while effecting his arrest. To reach a decision the jury had to determine not only what force the officers used (a historical fact), but also whether the force used was "excessive" (a normative conclusion).[2]

This Chapter explores techniques for developing factual propositions to satisfy elements with normative standards. Fortunately, once you have developed factual propositions for normative elements, you use the same types of arguments you have already learned to prove those propositions.

1. IDENTIFYING AN ELEMENT'S NORMATIVE STANDARD

An element's normative standard is one that requires a factfinder to act as the "conscience of the community" and evaluate the appropriateness of a party's conduct in the light of surrounding circumstances.

---

1. See, e.g., F. Harper, F.James Jr., & O. Gray, 3 *The Law of Torts* Sec. 17.1 (2d ed. 1986). Thus normative elements have both an "historic" and a "normative" aspect. For example, when determining whether conduct is "reasonable" (making a normative judgment) a factfinder has to decide what it believes happened (a historical judgment) and then decide whether what happened was appropriate (a normative judgment.)

2. In some cases even though an element has a normative aspect, arguments will been confined to the historic facts. For example in a case where a plaintiff contends a defendant was negligent in rear ending a plaintiff because the defendant took his eyes off the road, typically no argument will be advanced concerning the propriety of defendant's conduct. Absent special facts, the defendant will concede that if defendant did take his eyes from the road, the defendant's conduct was inappropriate.

Sometimes, the word "reasonable" acts as an explicit signal that an element contains a normative standard. Consider these examples:

In a negligence case, a plaintiff must prove that the defendant's conduct was "unreasonable."

In a warranty action, the buyer must prove that he gave "reasonable" notice of breach to the seller.

In a real estate action, a subletting tenant must prove that the landlord "unreasonably" withheld approval of a lease assignment.

Each of these elements contains a normative standard because the factfinder must evaluate the reasonableness of a party's behavior. For example, the factfinder cannot find in favor of the buyer in the warranty action simply by concluding that the buyer gave notice of a breach to the seller two days after receiving defective goods. The factfinder must also determine whether, in the light of all the circumstances, the buyer's giving two days notice was reasonable.

But no single verbal formula exists for identifying an element's normative standard, and terms other than "reasonable" also signify that an element contains a normative standard. For example:

In a contract action, a plaintiff must prove that a breach was "material."

In a wrongful termination case, the employee must prove that she was fired without "just cause."

In a Rodney King-type case, the prosecution must prove that a police officer used "excessive" force when making an arrest.[3]

Again, in each situation the factfinder must evaluate the propriety of whatever the factfinder believes took place.

2. FORMULATING NORMATIVE PROPOSITIONS

Just as when you prepare arguments in support of non-normative elements, begin preparing arguments to satisfy normative standards by formulating factual propositions. The specific circumstances in your case which you contend satisfy an element's normative standard will be your normative factual propositions.

For example, assume that you represent the plaintiff in a fraud case, and that the law requires you to prove that your client "reasonably relied" on the defendant's misrepresentations. As described in Chapter 2, you have already identified the factual proposition that establishes your client's reliance. To prepare for trial you must now formulate one or more normative factual propositions. That is, you must identify the specific circumstances in an individual case that you contend establish that the plaintiff's reliance was "reasonable."

---

3. As this list perhaps suggests, normative elements typically focus on the propriety of a defendant's behavior. However, this is not always the case. For instance, an element requiring a buyer to give notice of breach within a reasonable time is concerned with the appropriateness of a plaintiff's behavior.

To identify such specific circumstances, examine a file with the four questions set forth below in mind. These questions typically will prove useful regardless of the normative standard with which you are dealing. Answering these questions should help you to identify a wide range of factors that factfinders commonly consider when assessing the appropriateness of a party's conduct. Thus, the answers to these questions will be normative factual propositions supporting your argument that a normative standard has been satisfied.[4]

a. Was the Party's Conduct Fair, Just or Reasonable?

Frequently, factfinders evaluate the appropriateness of a party's conduct by determining whether the conduct was fair, just or reasonable. Consequently, by identifying reasons suggesting that a party's conduct was fair, just or reasonable, you will identify normative propositions.

For example, assume that in an action for misrepresentation, your factual proposition for the element of "reasonable reliance" is that your client, the plaintiff, relied on certain representations by the defendant stockbroker in deciding to purchase shares in Good Mutual Fund. To identify your normative propositions for the "reasonable" aspect of this element, ask yourself: "What circumstances indicate that it was fair, just or reasonable for my client to rely on the stockbroker's representations?" Assume that your review of the file uncovers the following reasons:

Plaintiff's reliance was reasonable in that:

1. Plaintiff was not acquainted with mutual funds;

2. Plaintiff had never previously purchased stock;

3. Plaintiff knew that defendant was a licensed broker.

These reasons are your normative propositions. As in this example, you will frequently identify multiple normative propositions for an element's normative standard.[5] Just as you often look at more factors than "price" to determine whether you consider a restaurant to be "good", so will a factfinder's judgment about the fairness, justice or

---

4. In some cases your client or experts may be able to help you develop a more complete set of answers to these questions.

5. Of course, the substantive law in a particular jurisdiction may limit the normative propositions you are allowed to prove in any particular case. For example, assume you represent a defendant charged with murder because he shot and killed two people who accosted him on a subway. Defendant admits that he shot the victims but claims self defense. To establish this defense, you must prove your client "reasonably" believed he was in fear of great bodily harm at the time of the killings. To show your client's belief was reasonable, you might want to prove the following normative proposition: two weeks before the shooting your client saw someone severely beaten in similar circumstances. Whether you will be allowed to prove that proportion may depend on the extent to which the substantive law limits you to the circumstances that a hypothetical "objective" reasonable person would have considered at the time of the killing. See Richard Singer, The Resurgence of Mens Rea: Honest But Unreasonable Mistake of Fact in Self–Defense, 28 B.C.L. Rev. 459 (1987).

reasonableness of your position typically depend on a number of circumstances.[6]

b. What Positive or Negative Consequences Resulted or Might Have Resulted From the Conduct?

A factfinder may also evaluate the appropriateness of a party's conduct according to its actual or potential consequences. For example, assume that as the prosecutor of police officers for using excessive force to effect an arrest, your historical factual proposition is that the officers struck the victim 15 times with a baton after he was down on the ground. To identify normative propositions that this force was excessive, examine the file to identify the positive and negative consequences of the police conduct. If you can show that as a consequence of the baton blows the arrestee risked permanent brain damage, one of your normative propositions may be, "The force was excessive in that the blows created the risk of permanent brain damage."

Similarly, assume that an employee sues for wrongful termination. The fired employee, whose duties included opening up the store, was fired for being 30 minutes late for work. As counsel for the employer, you want to prove that the termination was for "just cause". Your normative propositions may refer to the negative consequences resulting from the employee's tardiness. For example, you may try to prove that the employee was terminated for just cause in that 20 other employees were unable to start work on time, and that the store may have lost business because it opened late.

In many cases, you will also want to prove knowledge of potential positive or negative consequences and the likelihood of potential consequences coming to fruition. For example, in the excessive force case discussed above, you might want to prove normative propositions such as: "The police officers knew that they were creating a risk of brain damage when they struck the plaintiff in the head with their batons."

c. Were Less Restrictive Alternatives Available?

A factfinder may also consider the availability of other alternatives when evaluating the appropriateness of a party's conduct. The *availability* of less restrictive alternatives suggest that a party's conduct was inappropriate, while the *lack of availability* of such alternatives suggest that it was appropriate. For example, return to the case alleging excessive force by police officers to effect an arrest. If there were six officers present at the arrest the alternative that you may identify as your normative proposition might be: "The force used by the officers was excessive in that the six officers present at the arrest could have

---

6. While the text is written from a plaintiff's perspective, defense counsel too often have to identify factual propositions for normative elements. For example, in the Good Mutual Fund case, defense counsel would want to identify circumstances indicating that the plaintiff's reliance was unreasonable.

effected the arrest by holding down and handcuffing the arrestee." [7]   Of course, you also need to establish that this alternative is "less restrictive" than the conduct engaged in by the police. To do so, you need to identify the benefits of your suggested alternative course of action. Those benefits are also normative propositions. In this example, your normative proposition might be: "Holding down and handcuffing the arrestee reduces the risk that the arrestee will be seriously injured."

Consider an example in which the lack of reasonable alternatives made your client's conduct appropriate. For example, assume that your client, a defendant in a negligence case, allegedly acted unreasonably in driving 60 m.p.h. at 2 p.m. on a residential street when taking her child to the hospital because of a medical emergency. To identify normative propositions consider whether any reasonable alternatives were available. For example, if your file indicates that your client unsuccessfully tried to call for an ambulance, your additional normative proposition may be, "My client's driving 60 miles per hour was appropriate in that her attempts to arrange for an ambulance were unsuccessful."

d. Did the Conduct Conform to Custom and Practice?

Finally, a factfinder may evaluate the appropriateness of a party's conduct according to whether it conforms to custom and practice. For instance, assume that in a malpractice case a plaintiff wishes to establish that a doctor's failure to order a blood test prior to surgery was unreasonable. The plaintiff's normative proposition may be, "The doctor's failure to order a blood test was unreasonable in that it violated standard medical practice." [8]

Similarly, assume that in an accident case, a plaintiff wishes to establish that the manner in which the defendant loaded his truck was unreasonable. The plaintiff's normative proposition may be, "Using a "two-wheeler" to unload the truck was unreasonable in that it violated the custom and practice for loading such trucks." [9]

3. TAKING ACCOUNT OF A LIKELY FACTFINDER'S REACTION TO NORMATIVE PROPOSITIONS

As you know, the touchstone of success at trial is how a factfinder reacts to your arguments. And what seems fair to you may be irrelevant

---

7. Of course, you might have identified this alternative in response to the prior question about why the officers' conduct was unfair, unjust or unreasonable. Some overlap in the responses to the questions you ask to identify normative propositions is inevitable. Nonetheless, sometimes the different questions will produce different answers. Thus, using each the four questions will tend to make you more thorough.

8. As you may have surmised, when you seek to formulate normative propositions by asking a question about conformity with custom and practice, you will often need to employ an expert to help you answer the question. And at trial you will typically need an expert to testify to compliance or non-compliance with custom and practice. Chapter 15 discusses how to prepare arguments supporting the credibility of expert testimony.

9. Note that in responding to an argument based on custom and practice, a party may concede the existence of the current custom and practice. Nonetheless, the responding party may argue that the standard practice is too lax and therefore should not be relied upon to determine the appropriateness of a party's conduct. See Prosser & Keeton, Torts § 32 (5th Ed.) 1984.

or even offensive to a factfinder. Thus, when formulating normative propositions you have to consider a likely factfinder's reactions to them.

For instance, assume that you represent Correy Ander, a 78 year old investor who claims that she was defrauded by a stockbroker into purchasing a company's largely worthless securities. Ander claims that she "reasonably" relied on the stockbroker's representations concerning the company's past earnings. To satisfy the normative aspect of this element, you have formulated the following proposition: "Ander's reliance was reasonable, because as a 78 year old person Ander was unable to conduct her own investigation into the company's financial strength." If you are considerably younger than your client, you may find this proposition a powerful one. But it is based on a stereotype of the diminishing abilities of older people, a stereotype that a factfinder who is in Ander's age bracket or who views older people as vital and active may find offensive. If your likely factfinder is such a person, you may not want to rely on such a proposition.[10]

4. PREPARING ARGUMENTS TO SUPPORT NORMATIVE PROPOSITIONS

After formulating normative propositions, your next step is to prepare arguments that they are accurate. Fortunately, you construct arguments to prove normative propositions just as you did to prove other factual propositions. Focus on the crucial normative propositions and identify highly probative evidence that they are accurate. Depending on whether your highly probative evidence is disputed or undisputed, use the techniques described in Chapters 3 through 5 to construct arguments that your propositions are accurate.

For example, assume that your crucial normative proposition is that, "My client's driving 60 miles per hour was appropriate in that she was unable to arrange for an ambulance." You will identify highly probative evidence that the proposition is correct, determine whether or not the evidence is disputed, and proceed accordingly. Thus, assume that your client says that when she called "911," the operator informed her that no ambulance would be available for half an hour. If the adversary disputes your client's testimony, you would use the Credibility Checklist to identify arguments supporting her version.

5. VALUE JUDGMENTS AND ARGUMENTS ABOUT NORMATIVE STANDARDS

When a crucial issue is whether an element's normative standard has been met, both you and your adversary will typically attempt to prove the accuracy of one or more normative propositions. And in many instances a factfinder will conclude that both of you have in part succeeded. For example, return to the "driving 60 m.p.h. to take the child to the hospital" case. The factfinder may find that both of the

---

10. Alternatively, you might try to inoculate against the factfinder's resistance to your proposition in closing argument. See Chapter 14 Sec. 4 D.

following propositions are accurate: (1) Your client was unable to get an ambulance and sincerely believed that her child might lose the use of her left hand if the child did not get to the hospital immediately; and (2) Your client's behavior resulted in a serious accident and created a risk of serious injury to bystanders.

How can a factfinder resolve this normative dilemma? The factfinder has to make a value choice. A conclusion that the plaintiff's driving was reasonable reflects a value choice that it is more important to try to save a child's hand than to avoid the risks of injury or death created by such driving. A conclusion that the plaintiff's driving was unreasonable reflects the opposite value choice.

Logically, you cannot "prove" that one of these values is more important than another.[11] Therefore, formulating and constructing arguments for multiple normative propositions as suggested above will maximize the chance that the factfinder will strongly agree with at least some of the values underlying your normative propositions.

---

11. Some might argue that this conflict can be resolved in a neutral "objective" way. The argument might be that theoretically, at least, the factfinder might resolve this dilemma by determining which set of risks had a greater chance of coming to fruition. Thus in the driving case, the question would be were the risks that the child would lose use of her left hand greater than the risks that the driving would cause serious injury. The neutrality argument would continue by asserting that after that determination is made, the factfinder would then decide the case by adopting the choice that is least likely to come about. Deciding the issue on this basis, however, would not be making a choice on a neutral basis. To choose to determine which set of social risks the society ought to chance on the basis of which set is least likely to occur is itself to make a value judgment. The value being advanced under this principal is simply the value of being risk adverse. Many people, of course, would reject the idea that such a criterion should be used to make important social decisions. After all aren't some risks more worth taking than others?

Part One—Section B

CONSTRUCTING ARGUMENTS IN PREPARATION FOR TRIAL —PREPARING RESPONSES TO AN ADVERSARY'S CASE

Thus far you have studied how to prepare one side of a case: yours. You have learned both how to prepare arguments supporting your factual propositions, and how to respond to an adversary's likely counter-arguments. Now it is time to turn the analysis around by learning how to undermine an adversary's case by identifying an adversary's likely affirmative arguments and preparing your responses to them.

Chapter 7

PREPARING RESPONSES TO AN ADVERSARY'S AFFIRMATIVE ARGUMENTS

To this point, you have developed your arguments, an adversary's likely responses, and your counter-arguments to those responses. But an adversary almost always presents an affirmative case in addition to responding to yours, and thorough preparation requires that you also prepare to respond to an adversary's affirmative case. How to prepare such responses is the topic of this and the next chapter.

1. IDENTIFY AN ADVERSARY'S CRUCIAL FACTUAL PROPOSITIONS

Recall from Chapter 2 that an adversary, even if a defendant, is likely to present its own version of past events. Thus, an adversary's factual propositions often are not simply a negation of your own. Rather, an adversary is likely to develop arguments supporting factual propositions which set forth the adversary's own version of what happened.

For example, return for a moment to *People v. Dixon*.[1] Recall that as the prosecutor, one of your crucial factual propositions was that during the afternoon visit to the supermarket, defendant Dixon put a cheese ball in her purse and tried to leave the market without paying for it. In response, Dixon will probably do more than try to undermine this proposition. Dixon is also likely to try to prove a proposition setting forth her own version of what happened. Given her story, the factual proposition supporting her version would be something like, "Dixon already had the cheese ball in her purse when she entered the market."

One possible method of preparing to undermine an adversary's case would be to pretend that you are the adversary and to prepare the adversary's case with the same thoroughness that you prepared your own.[2] This would entail formulating all of an adversary's likely factual

---

1. For the facts of this case, please see Chapter 5.

2. Modern litigation gives you the potential wherewithal to do all this. With the

66

propositions, constructing arguments for them, and then preparing your responses.

But rarely will you do this. Except in unusual circumstances,[3] you will have neither the time nor the resources to prepare an adversary's case as zealously as you prepare your own. Many clients are unwilling to pay for you to fully develop both sides of a case. And in most cases clients are wise not to do so. When you do offer an affirmative case, a successful outcome is likely to rest more on the strength of that case than on your attacks on an adversary's case. Thus, you will typically follow a more limited approach to preparing responses to an adversary's case described in this chapter.

Using this more limited approach, you begin by identifying only an adversary's likely *crucial* factual propositions. This approach is limited because you do not have to formulate an adversary's factual proposition for every element in a case. Instead, focus on your own crucial factual propositions and then formulate the adversary's version of them. To do so, you will probably rely on information gained through the normal pretrial processes of discovery, pretrial conferences, settlement discussions and the like.[4]

For example, recall *Prager v. Dolinko*.[5] As the plaintiff, one of your crucial factual propositions for the element of "negligence" is that Prager was in the crosswalk when Dolinko's truck struck her. Like most adversaries, Dolinko will probably not simply deny that Prager was in the crosswalk. Instead, he will have a corresponding factual proposition setting forth his own version of what happened. Given Dolinko's story, his corresponding factual proposition in this case might be something like, "Prager was struck because she suddenly ran into the street from between two parked cars." As it corresponds to your crucial factual proposition, you would regard this as one of Dolinko's crucial factual propositions.

2. IDENTIFY AN ADVERSARY'S HIGHLY PROBATIVE EVIDENCE

Having identified an adversary's crucial factual propositions, you outline the arguments the adversary is likely to make so that you can prepare responses to them. To do that, select the items of evidence that the adversary is likely to regard as highly probative of its crucial factual propositions. While you may not be certain of what evidence an adver-

---

pretrial emphasis on broad discovery, informal negotiation and mandatory pretrial conferences, you often have access to much of the same information as an adversary.

3. If you represent a criminal defendant who will neither testify nor present witnesses in his or her behalf, your *only* means of success is to undermine the prosecutor's arguments.

4. Traditionally, the prosecution in a criminal case has had the least means of

gaining access to an adversary's factual propositions. However, modern statutes afford prosecutors a greater window into a defendant's anticipated factual propositions than in years past. For example, in federal prosecutions defendants have to notify the prosecution if they will rely on the defenses of "alibi" or "insanity."

5. For the facts of this case, please see Chapter 4.

sary will see as most probative, discovery, settlement negotiations and pretrial conferences usually give you a good idea.

How you then proceed depends on whether or not you dispute an adversary's highly probative evidence.

3. ATTACK THE PROBATIVE STRENGTH OF AN ADVERSARY'S UNDISPUTED EVIDENCE

If you are *not* going to dispute the accuracy of an item of an adversary's highly probative evidence, your response will have to attack its probative strength. To develop that type of response, link the adversary's highly probative evidence to the adversary's crucial factual proposition with one or more generalizations. Then examine a file for "except whens" to the generalizations.[6] All of this is familiar to you; you did the same thing in Chapter 4 when identifying an adversary's potential "except whens" to your arguments based on undisputed evidence. Your "except whens" will be the evidentiary basis of your response to the adversary's argument.[7]

4. ATTACK THE CREDIBILITY OF AN ADVERSARY'S DISPUTED EVIDENCE

If you do dispute the accuracy of an item of your adversary's highly probative evidence, use the Credibility Checklist set forth in Chapter 5 to develop arguments that your version of the dispute is accurate. Each of the factors on the Checklist "works both ways." That is, by turning each factor around you can develop arguments attacking the accuracy of adverse testimony.

For example, assume that in *People v. Dixon*, the highly probative evidence that you dispute is Dixon's assertion that she already had the cheese ball in her purse when she entered the market. To attack this evidence, you would review the file with the Checklist factors in mind. The credibility arguments you prepare might include:

1. *Internal Inconsistency*: Dixon's other activities are *inconsistent* with her entering the market in the afternoon without realizing that she had the cheese ball in her purse. Your argument based on this factor might go as follows:

> If Dixon had the cheese ball in her purse when she returned to the market, she would have noticed the added weight. Everyday experience suggests that she would have noticed the cheese ball in her purse when she took the car keys out of her purse to drive to the market, or when she got out of her car.[8] Also, Dixon refused to

---

6. This approach assumes that the highly probative evidence which you do not dispute is circumstantial evidence. But it must be, for if you concede the credibility of direct evidence you concede the accuracy of your adversary's factual proposition.

7. Note that unlike when you prepare you own undisputed evidence arguments,

when preparing to respond to an adversary's undisputed evidence you typically do not have to identify the adversary's "especially whens."

8. As you undoubtedly recognize, this argument is based on an inference from evidence that Dixon drove to the market.

allow Embree to search her purse. If she did not realize that she had the cheese ball in her purse, she would have agreed to the search.

2. *Lack of Neutrality*: Dixon has a motive to lie; she does not want to be convicted.[9]

5. SHOULD YOU IDENTIFY AN ADVERSARY'S LIKELY COUNTER–ARGUMENTS?

Once you have prepared your responses to an adversary's disputed and undisputed evidence, should you continue on to ferret out the adversary's potential responses in order to counter them as well? You may be relieved to learn that generally you need not do so. You will never run short of potential counter-arguments; that is the nature of circumstantial evidence.

For example, assume that you are prepared to argue that Dixon's testimony that she already had the cheese ball in her purse when she entered the market is not credible because she would have noticed the extra weight in her purse and removed it. In theory, you could identify potential responses that Dixon could make to undermine your argument.[10] However, given that you are responding to an adversary's likely arguments, preparing to this extent is not normally worthwhile. If a file reveals an obviously damaging riposte to an argument, of course you should search for better arguments. But you rarely will have the resources to prepare for all possible adversarial counter-arguments.

6. FURTHER CURTAILING THE RESPONSE PROCESS

While this chapter suggests that you prepare a limited response to your adversary's case, even that response may be too time consuming in some cases. If you find yourself potentially having to respond to numerous factual propositions of an adversary, or if your resources and preparation time are curtailed, you may choose to truncate the process even further. For instance, you may choose to develop responses only for the adversary's factual propositions which you *most vigorously* contest.

---

9. Note that in preparing to attack the credibility of Dixon's assertion, you need not first develop Dixon's own credibility arguments.

10. For instance, whether you or Dixon first offers testimony about the added weight, Dixon may explain that the reason that she failed to notice the extra weight is that the purse she was carrying was very heavy, or that she was too rushed to notice the added weight. And she may explain that she refused to allow Embree to examine the purse because she suddenly recalled that the cheese ball was in there, and she knew she would be arrested even though she hadn't stolen it. Then for each of Dixon's potential responses you could prepare a counter-argument. For instance, you may reason, "If Dixon says that she refused to open her purse when Embree asked her to because she was afraid she'd be arrested, I'll offer evidence that at the time she didn't tell Embree that she had made a mistake." Of course, then you may imagine Dixon's potential responses to your counter-argument. And so on.

Chapter 8

ATTACKING AN ADVERSARY'S CASE THROUGH STORY INCONSISTENCIES

This Chapter describes a second method of attacking an adversary's case. Rather than focusing on arguments concerning individual items of evidence, you focus on the credibility of an adverse witness' overall story. Thus you switch from a "factual proposition" perspective to a "story" perspective.[1] You make this switch by preparing an argument that all or a substantial part of an adverse witness' story is unreliable, based on inconsistencies in that story.[2]

After briefly describing the three primary ways in which a witness' stories may be inconsistent, the chapter sets forth techniques for using story inconsistencies to construct arguments attacking credibility. It concludes by discussing your options when you recognize that an adversary might attack one of your own witnesses' stories as inconsistent.

1. THREE TYPES OF INCONSISTENCIES

A story may be inconsistent because it is inconsistent with common experience, internally inconsistent, or inconsistent with established facts. Before examining how to construct arguments based on inconsistencies, briefly consider each of these three types.[3]

1. Though we describe this method of preparing credibility arguments last, in an actual case you might decide to begin argument preparation by searching for inconsistencies in adverse witnesses' stories. We have tried to organize the discussion in a way that clarifies the types of arguments you may prepare, and have not tried to prescribe a fixed order of preparation.

2. When you argue that "all" of a witness' story is unreliable, you do not contend that literally every statement the witness says on the stand is untrue. You would probably not, for example, challenge the accuracy of a witness' testimony about her personal background, employment history or other facts that are of only minimal relevance to the disputed issues in the case. An argument that challenges "all" of a witness' story only suggests that the significant evidence the witness testifies to is unreliable.

3. You will readily recognize that one of the types of inconsistencies described below (internal inconsistency) is also part of the Chapter 5 Checklist. The reason is simple: this factor relates both to arguments about the accuracy of specific evidentiary disputes and to arguments about the credibility of a witness' overall story.

a. Inconsistencies With Common Experience

In daily life, people routinely assess the credibility of stories according to their everyday experience. For example, a parent will not believe a child's claim that he didn't eat the last cookie if the child explains that the cookie monster ate it. A reader of a mystery novel may conclude that the character who "did it" is the one who claimed not to be at the scene of the 3 A.M. murder because at that very moment she was on her way to the library to drop off an overdue book. And a school teacher may not accept a student's story that the student was unable to turn in his homework because his dog had eaten it. In each of these situations, a listener is likely to doubt the credibility of the story because "it doesn't make sense, things just don't happen that way."

A failure to act may also be seen as inconsistent with common experience. For example, assume that a police officer testifies that the defendant's breath smelled strongly of alcohol at the time of his arrest for driving under the influence. If the police officer's written report of the arrest does not mention that fact, the factfinder may find that omission inconsistent with common experience.

b. Inconsistencies With Established Facts

"Established facts" are those that a factfinder will almost certainly accept as true. A story which is in some way inconsistent with established facts is generally not credible.

For example, assume that you are prosecuting Syd for a convenience store robbery. Syd claims that he attended Mass at 11 P.M., the time of the robbery. But Father Mordechai, the local parish priest, is prepared to testify that he celebrated the only Mass on the night of the robbery and that it took place at 9 P.M. A factfinder will almost surely accept Father Mordechai's testimony about the time of the Mass, making Syd's story inconsistent with an established fact.

c. Internal Inconsistencies

Internal story inconsistencies are of two types. One type concerns an inconsistency in the story of a single witness. For example, assume that Jason is a manufacturer who claims that he entered into an oral agreement with McCalla to manufacture 1000 floor mops. If Jason at one time stated that his Vice President Jaleen was present when the contract was finalized and at another time stated that no one other than he and McCalla were present when the contract was finalized, Jason's story is internally inconsistent.[4]

---

4. Sometimes when you uncover an internal inconsistency you will want the factfinder to accept as true one of the witness' conflicting statements. In such a situation, you use the Credibility Checklist to construct arguments supporting the credibility of the statement you contend is true. For example, assume that you represent a proponent of a will. Carla Bell, a witness to the execution of the will, told your investigator that the decedent appeared rational and alert when signing the will. At deposition, Bell said that the decedent appeared confused and disoriented when the will was executed. Because Bell's initial statement is highly probative disputed evidence for

A second type of internal story inconsistency arises when disagreement exists between two or more witnesses for the same party. For example, assume that plaintiff Bob has sued Jones, his former employer, for wrongful discharge. Jones claims that at a meeting two weeks before discharging Bob, Jones warned Bob about Bob's repeated failure to report for work on time. Jones' assistant, who was present at that meeting, says that Jones warned Bob about poor record keeping, but that Jones said nothing to Bob about reporting late to work. The stories of Jones and Jones' assistant conflict, making the defendant's overall story internally inconsistent.

2. IDENTIFYING STORY INCONSISTENCIES

The following example illustrates how to go about identifying story inconsistencies.[5] Assume that you represent the defendant, Steve Dolinko, in *Prager v. Dolinko*. As you may recall, Prager claims that Dolinko's careless making of a left turn caused him to strike her in a crosswalk. Cynthia White, a witness for the plaintiff, is prepared to testify that she saw Prager in the crosswalk, and that Dolinko was going too fast when he made the left turn. You want to identify any inconsistencies in White's story. Put aside for the moment thoughts of factual propositions and highly probative evidence that White's testimony provides. Simply look at her story and consider whether you find any of the three types of inconsistency described above.[6] Please take a moment or two to examine White's story, which is set out at page 36, and write down any inconsistencies you see.

Slow down; that wasn't even a complete moment, let alone two! All right—did anything in her story strike you as inconsistent? If you said, "I don't think the three sisters will ever make it to Moscow," you have inadvertently looked at a Checkhov play by mistake. But if you focused on White's leaving the scene of the accident to keep her hair appointment, reward yourself with a pat on the back.[7] Everyday experience suggests that people who see someone cause a serious accident usually don't then leave the scene to keep a hairdresser's appointment. Of course, White may have an explanation for why she behaved this way, and you will have to consider possible explanations when constructing

your client, you might complete the Credibility Checklist to support the accuracy of her initial statement. And because Bell's testimony at deposition is highly probative disputed evidence for your adversary, you would also complete a Credibility Checklist attacking the accuracy of Bell's deposition testimony.

5. An adverse witness' "story" should not be limited to what you expect the witness to testify to at trial. You can not be certain what an adverse witness will testify to and often the most damaging inconsistencies will be deleted from the witness' trial testimony by opposing counsel.

Therefore, you should consider the story told by the witness in pretrial depositions, interviews and documents. At this point you want to identify all potential inconsistencies. You can decide later whether you will actually use them at trial.

6. Remember, in an actual case with more witnesses, you would also compare White's story to the stories of other witnesses.

7. Unless you live in California, in which case you can reward yourself with an iced cappuccino made with decaf and nonfat milk.

your argument.[8]   But if you fail to list inconsistencies for which a potential explanation may exist, you will almost never develop inconsistency arguments.

The next section describes how to construct arguments based on the inconsistencies you see in adverse witnesses' stories.

3. CONSTRUCTING CREDIBILITY ARGUMENTS BASED ON STORY INCONSISTENCIES

An argument based on a story inconsistency typically consists of two parts.   In the first part, you convince a factfinder that an adverse witness' story is in fact inconsistent.   In the second part, you set forth the inference to be drawn from the inconsistency.

a.   Part One: Convincing a Factfinder That a Story Is Inconsistent

Before you can attack a witness' credibility based on a story inconsistency, a factfinder of course has to recognize the inconsistency. Sometimes an inconsistency will be glaringly apparent, and you will need do nothing more than point out the testimony creating the inconsistency before moving on to part two.   For example, assume that plaintiff Pam testified at deposition that her associate, Robert, was present at an April 18th meeting when the terms of the "Jackson" contract were agreed upon.   But at his deposition Pam's witness, Robert, testified that he never attended a meeting concerning the "Jackson" contract.   Here, an internal inconsistency is apparent; Pam and Robert cannot both be right.   In this situation, as defense counsel you would simply point out the internal inconsistencies between Pam's and Robert's stories before arguing what conclusion to draw from the inconsistency.

Often times, however, inconsistencies with common experience will not be readily apparent, for what strikes one person as flying in the face of common sense may initially appear to another to be normal.   For example, recall the previously-mentioned inconsistency in Cynthia White's story: White says that she saw Dolinko cause a serious accident, but also says that she immediately drove off to keep a hairdresser's appointment.   Perhaps White's conduct immediately leaps out to you as strongly inconsistent with everyday experience.   But a factfinder may not have the same reaction, either because the rest of White's story obscures the inconsistency or because the factfinder's experience differs from yours.   Whatever the reason, you may need to construct an argument making the inconsistency explicit before asking the factfinder to draw your desired inference.

To develop an explicit argument that an inconsistency exists, use the "If ... Would Not. . . . Because ..." technique.   To use this technique, begin by juxtaposing the two aspects of a story that strike you as inconsistent.   Then, explicitly identify the reasons why the two aspects

8.   See Sec. 4 *infra*.

of the story are inconsistent. In the example from White's story you would write out the following:

If: White had seen Dolinko cause a serious accident. . . .

We *would not* expect White to have immediately gone to her hairdresser appointment. . . .

Because:

> (1) White would have stayed at the scene to see if she could help the victim.

> (2) White would have stayed at the scene to call an ambulance.

> (3) White would have stayed at the scene to leave her name and phone number with the authorities.

> (4) White would have stayed at the scene because she would have wanted to see how badly the victim was injured.

Therefore, White's story is inconsistent with everyday experience.

In the example above, the "If" and the "Would Not" statements juxtapose the two aspects of White's story that give rise to the inconsistency with common experience. The "Because" statements are the reasons that you would not expect the second aspect to have occurred if the first aspect is true. Of course these reasons must be supported by evidence in the file, or must be reasonable inferences from such evidence.[9]

The "If . . . Would not. . . . Because . . ." technique should help you to explicitly identify the evidence you will rely on to argue that an adverse witness' story contains inconsistencies.[10] For instance, during the cross examination of Ms. White you might ask questions such as these to illustrate the argument that her story is inconsistent with common experience:

Q: Ms. White, you saw the accident where Ms. Prager was run over, correct?

Q: After seeing this accident, you continued on to your hairdresser's appointment, right?

---

9. Because of these limitations in the "Because . . ." portion of the White example in the text you could *not* list "(5) White would have stayed at the scene because she was trained as a nurse." This statement is not supported by evidence in the file or any reasonable inference from such evidence.

10. There are other techniques you can use to help you explicitly identify such evidence. For example, you could use the generalization and "especially when" approach described in Chapter 3. Using this approach you might say "People who see someone cause a serious accident usually do not immediately leave the scene of the acci-

dent to go to a hairdresser appointment. Especially when—(1) They want to stay at the scene to see if they can help the victim," etc. With a generalization approach, the two aspects of the story creating the implausibility are incorporated into the generalization and the "especially whens" are the same as the "Because . . ." statements. Regardless of which approach you use to identify the evidence tending to establish the inconsistency, you should recognize that your argument, just like arguments based on undisputed and disputed evidence, is premised on generalizations drawn from people's common experience.

Q: You left the scene without helping Ms. Prager, right?

Q: You left without calling an ambulance?

Q: You left without giving your name to anyone at the scene?

Q: You left without knowing whether Ms. Prager had been killed by the truck, isn't that correct?

Q: You didn't know exactly how badly she had been injured when you left, right?

b. Part Two: Explaining the Significance of the Inconsistency

Generally, it is not enough merely to argue that a witness' story is in some way inconsistent. A factfinder's reaction may well be, "O.K., so what?" For instance, assume that you argue that "White's story is inconsistent; it doesn't make sense that somebody would have seen a truck run down a pedestrian in a crosswalk and then driven off to the hairdresser." If you stop there, a factfinder may react, "That's a bit odd, but so what?" Thus, you should prepare to explain the significance of an inconsistency.

Frequently, you will argue that an inconsistency shows that an adverse witness is incorrect with respect to important testimony. For example, having established the above inconsistency in White's story, you might prepare the following argument:

"What's the significance of her having driven off to the hairdresser? It shows that she didn't really see Mr. Dolinko speed through the intersection and strike Ms. Prager in the crosswalk. If she had, surely she would have stayed at the scene, at the least to talk to the police." [11]

In this example, you don't prepare an argument that White's entire story is false or unreliable. Rather, you focus on her important testimony, and argue that the inconsistency destroys the reliability of that testimony.

A second option you have is to prepare an argument that an adverse witness' story as a whole is unreliable, without focusing on any particular testimonial assertion. For example, in this same example this alternative form of argument would go something like this:

"What's the significance of Ms. White having driven off to the hairdresser? It shows that her story is unreliable. Things just don't happen like that, and you just can't put much faith in what she says."

---

11. Note that if you were a "perfect thinker" you might well have developed this argument when completing the Credibility Checklist. White's testimony that Prager was in the crosswalk is a highly probative item of disputed evidence for your adversary. When using the Credibility Checklist to prepare your response to this item of disputed evidence, a perfect thinker would have taken note of this inconsistency. But as most of us are not perfect thinkers, examining a story as a whole for inconsistencies often surfaces credibility arguments that you might overlook when completing the Checklist.

Because the argument does not tie the seeming inconsistency in White's testimony to any specific testimonial assertion, the second alternative is a more general form of argument than the first. You will find this type of argument especially useful when several inconsistencies appear in a single witness' story.

Whichever option you choose, the second part of the argument construction process serves as a check on the link between an inconsistency and your desired inference. Making this link explicit enables you to evaluate the strength of your argument.[12]

4. IDENTIFYING AN ADVERSARY'S LIKELY RESPONSES TO ARGUMENTS BASED ON INCONSISTENCIES

As always, thorough preparation of an argument includes consideration of an adversary's likely response. Here, you want to examine a file for likely explanations that may vitiate the impact of an inconsistency.[13] For example, above you attacked Cynthia White's testimony with an argument that her leaving the scene of an accident to keep a hairdresser's appointment is inconsistent with common experience. But before deciding to make this argument at trial, you need to examine your file for an explanation that might eliminate the seeming inconsistency.

Here, assume that the file indicates that White has stated that she regrets leaving the scene, and did so only because seeing Prager run down left her temporarily in shock. This explanation tends to vitiate the inconsistency by tapping into another part of our experience: seeing a serious automobile accident can be shocking and people who are in shock often behave in an unusual fashion.

Having identified this explanation, you may nevertheless choose to maintain your argument. That is, you may decide to develop the inconsistency during cross of White, and argue during final summation that it renders her story unreliable. Alternatively, you may think that the explanation so undercuts the impact of your argument that you abandon it even before trial. Finally, you may opt for a middle ground: offer the evidence giving rise to an inconsistency during cross examination, but if your adversary offers the anticipated explanation during redirect, abandon the argument in closing.

5. INCONSISTENCIES IN ADVERSARIES' OVERALL STORIES

Just as you can use inconsistencies in an individual witness' story to attack credibility, so too may you attack an adversary with inconsisten-

---

12. In some instances, of course, you may decide that an inconsistency is so insignificant that you will make no argument at all based on it.

13. As in earlier chapters, the text describes a linear process of argument construction: first construct an argument, then consider an adversary's likely response. In practice, you will find that the tasks are simultaneous: you consider an adversary's likely responses as you construct an argument.

cies in the adversary's overall story.[14]

For example, assume that you represent Franco, who is charged with murdering his ex-wife. The prosecution will call a medical examiner who will testify that the victim died around 9:30 A.M. from a cut throat. The prosecution will also call Detective Sherman, who will testify that he found a bloody glove in Franco's backyard about seven hours after the murder. At the preliminary hearing, Sherman testified that the blood on the glove was wet and sticky when he first picked it up. The prosecution will also call a forensic expert, who will testify based on DNA test results that the blood found on the glove at Franco's home matched the victim's blood.

When preparing for trial you identified the following inconsistency with common experience in the prosecution's overall case:

If: The murder occurred around 9:30 A.M. as the medical examiner said. . . .

We *would not* expect blood on the glove to be wet and sticky seven hours later. . . .

Because:

Blood normally dries in less than seven hours.

Therefore, the prosecution's story is inconsistent with common experience.

Based in part on this inconsistency, you have prepared an argument that Detective Sherman framed Franco for his ex-wife's murder.[15] Your argument is that the blood remained wet and sticky after seven hours because Sherman put the glove in a plastic bag when he found it at the crime scene, and then removed it from the bag several hours later and "planted" it at Franco's house.

How you develop this argument at trial will depend in part on whether you think the prosecution is aware of the inconsistency. If the prosecutor is aware of the inconsistency, you have nothing to lose by communicating the argument explicitly during cross of Sherman and by calling an expert to testify that blood typically dries within two to three hours, especially in the open air. Aware of the inconsistency, the prosecutor will probably be prepared to offer evidence explaining it away, perhaps through its own expert testimony that although blood usually dries within two to three hours in the open air, under the circumstances that existed in the Franco case the blood could well have been wet and sticky after seven hours. To communicate your argument during the cross examination of Sherman, you might proceed as follows:

Q: Detective Sherman, the blood on the glove was wet and sticky when you found it, correct?

14. Preparing a chronological outline of an adversary's version of events will help you spot inconsistencies in overall stories.

15. Assume that you have other evidence tending to prove that Sherman had a motive to frame Franco and an opportunity to do so.

A: Yes.

Q: As a well-trained detective, you notice such details?

A: I certainly try to.

Q: Now, you found the glove outside, next to Mr. Franco's house, is that your testimony?

A: It is.

Q: And the victim was killed at approximately 9:30 A.M., right?

A: Yes, that's about right.

Q: And you went to Mr. Franco's house at about 4:30 P.M., seven hours later?

A: Yes.

Q: In your experience, wouldn't you expect blood found on a glove that's been in the open air for seven hours to be dry, and not wet and sticky as you claim?

A: All I know is that it was wet and sticky.

Q: Wasn't the glove wet and sticky because you put the glove in a plastic bag and put it outside Mr. Franco's house to implicate him in his ex-wife's murder?

A: That's preposterous.

If you think that the prosecution is unaware of the inconsistency, you might decide to delay communicating your argument until final summation, when it will be too late for the prosecution to offer explanatory evidence. To follow this strategy, on cross you would simply have Sherman testify in accordance with his preliminary hearing testimony that the blood on the glove was wet and sticky when he found it. And you would establish through the prosecution's forensic expert that blood normally dries within two to three hours. Then, during summation, you would present your argument based on the inconsistency.[16]

6. EXAMINE YOUR OWN CASE FOR INCONSISTENCIES

Just as you examine adverse stories for inconsistencies, your crafty adversaries are likely to do the same thing with respect to both your individual witnesses' stories and your overall story.[17] Thus, your preparation should include searching your stories for apparent inconsistencies. If you recognize that one of your own stories seems in some way inconsistent, look for an explanation that obviates the seeming inconsistency. A reasonable explanation typically blunts the force of your adversary's attack. If a witness does not provide a plausible explana-

16. Generally, you want to communicate arguments throughout a trial, and not wait until closing argument. If you delay, a factfinder may already have made an adverse tentative decision. However, as the Franco example suggests, you may sometimes opt not to communicate an argument until closing to minimize the likelihood that your adversary will introduce evidence undermining your argument.

17. Your chronological outline of your version of events will be particularly helpful in identifying inconsistencies in your overall story.

tion, you may delete the testimony giving rise to the inconsistency unless doing so creates even greater problems.[18]

To prepare for an attack on an individual witness' story, point out to your witness the potential inconsistency and ask the witness for an explanation. For example, return again to *People v. Dixon* and assume that you represent the defendant Donna Dixon. As advised, you have examined her story for possible inconsistencies. Not surprisingly you have found the same inconsistency as the prosecutor. You think it possibly implausible that Dixon would have carried around a cheese ball in her purse without noticing the extra weight or feeling it when she reached for her car keys. So, see if your client can explain away the seeming inconsistency.[19] You might ask her,

> "Donna, there's something about your story that I expect the prosecution to ask you about when you testify, so we should talk about it now. You've told me that you forgot that the cheese ball was in your purse when you went back to the market. But it seems like a cheese ball is pretty big and heavy, and you'd notice it when you lifted up your purse or reached for your keys. So is there any reason why you didn't realize that the cheese ball was in your purse?"[20]

Dixon may well be able to explain the seeming inconsistency. For example, assume that Dixon replies that, "I didn't notice it because that day I was carrying a roomy duffel-bag type of purse, and I just didn't notice the extra weight." Especially if Dixon has a Mary Poppins-like satchel that you can offer as an exhibit, your argument would encompass both the testimony that she wasn't aware of the cheese ball in her purse and her explanation. On the other hand, if a witness' explanation is not satisfactory (e.g., Dixon says, "I didn't know it was in my purse because I'm used to carrying around my pet bowling ball.") and you cannot prevent the factfinder from hearing the implausible explanation, you will have to accept that a potential weakness exists in your case.

---

18. For example, deleting testimony creating an inconsistency may deprive you of highly probative evidence or render a witness' story difficult to understand.

19. Be warned that you may be overly prone to offering explanations. Some advocates are likely to see many more weaknesses in their own case than a factfinder will. And if you spend too much time explaining away seeming inconsistencies you may lose much of your case's affirmative impact. To paraphrase The Bard, the factfinder might believe that, "Thou dost explain too much." See also, R. Klonoff and P. Colby, *Sponsorship Strategy: Evidentiary Tactics For Winning Jury Trials* 61–81 (1990), which advises an advocate to put on only evidence that materially advances her case, provided that

the evidence is equally available to both sides. If neither introduces the evidence, the jury will assume it would not have materially aided either side.

20. If Dixon is unable to come up with any explanations on her own, can you ethically suggest possible explanations to her? Similarly, can you ethically bring together two witnesses whose stories differ and suggest potential explanations to them? Generally the answer to both these questions is yes, provided you do not suggest that the client or witness fabricate testimony. See e. g. J. Applegate, "Witness Preparation," 68 Tex. L. Rev. 277 (1989); see also, ABA Model Rule of Professional Conduct 3.4(b), 1.2(d).

Chapter 9

SILENT ARGUMENTS

Previous chapters have described methods of constructing and responding to arguments that you or an adversary can explicitly make to a factfinder. You can make these arguments explicit because they conform to the legal system's definition of a rational connection between evidence and factual propositions or credibility issues.

But factfinders are not computers (at least not yet), and they cannot be programmed to consider only the arguments that the law defines as rational. Silent arguments are arguments the legal system does not regard as rationally valid. They are "silent" because legal rules prohibit you or your adversary from explicitly articulating the inferences and generalizations underlying the evidence supporting such arguments. Nevertheless, a factfinder often may be consciously or unconsciously influenced by silent arguments.[1] For example, in a breach of contract case, a factfinder might be adversely influenced by the fact that your client has Asian facial features or talks with a non-U.S. accent. However, your opponent would be prohibited from explicitly arguing that these factors support a verdict against your client because the legal system does not recognize a rational connection between a person's facial features or accent and the likelihood of breaching a contract.

Sometimes silent arguments are based on information that is apparent from a witness' appearance, e.g. race or ethnicity. Other times, testimony supports silent arguments. For example, evidence that your client is a homosexual may cause a factfinder to feel hostility toward him.

Because of the frequent impact of silent arguments, this Chapter examines the most common silent arguments and how to prepare responses to an adversary's silent arguments. Finally, it explores how you might, when appropriate, introduce evidence to support silent arguments you want a factfinder to accept.

---

1. As is true with any other argument, the likelihood that a factfinder will be influenced by a specific silent argument depends on the personal experiences and background of the factfinder.

1. COMMON TYPES OF SILENT ARGUMENTS

The two most common types of silent arguments are "good person/bad person" arguments and those based on sympathy or empathy. These categories should help you identify the specific silent arguments that might arise in a case.

a. "Good Person/Bad Person" Arguments

Common experience suggests that factfinders are often influenced by the degree to which they like or dislike witnesses. Consequently, your adversary will often attempt to offer evidence to support silent arguments suggesting that his witnesses are "good" and your witnesses are "bad."

For example, assume that Gary Turner, a legal secretary, alleges that he was wrongfully discharged by your client Bill Blasi, the lawyer who employed him. To show that Turner is a "good" person, your adversary may try to admit evidence that two months before he was fired, Turner turned down an opportunity to work elsewhere at a higher salary. Turner decided not to accept the other job because he knew Blasi was getting ready for trial on a big case and he didn't want to leave Blasi in the lurch. And to show that your client is a "bad" person, your adversary may attempt to introduce evidence that three weeks before Turner was fired, he was late to work on one occasion because he had to take his child to the doctor. Blasi reprimanded Turner for being late and said, "I don't give a damn about your family's medical problems. Just get to work on time." By introducing this evidence, your adversary hopes to highlight Turner's admirable loyalty and expose Blasi's insensitivity.

A common and extremely pernicious type of "good person/bad person" argument relies on negative stereotypes relating to race, ethnic background, sexual orientation and the like.[2] Of course, a witness' race or ethnic background may appear obvious to the factfinder from a person's appearance or surname. But your adversary will often attempt to introduce additional evidence to draw on a negative stereotype. For example, believing that a factfinder might harbor negative feelings toward interracial couples, a prosecutor might attempt to elicit evidence that your witness, an African–American man, is married to a Caucasian women. Or thinking that a factfinder might be offended by homosexuals, your adversary may try to establish that your witness is a gay man who has had several male sexual partners.

b. "Sympathize or Empathize With My Witnesses."

Common experience also suggests that, apart from whether factfinders like or dislike a witness, they are often influenced by the degree to

---

2. Counsel often attempt to elicit evidence to tap into negative stereotypes based on race or sexual orientation. See e. g. S. Johnson "Racial Imagery In Criminal Cases" 67 Tulane Law Rev. 1739 (1993).

which they empathize or sympathize with a witness.[3] For instance, factfinders often sympathize with those they believe to be innocent victims of circumstances. And factfinders often empathize with someone when they can see themselves (or their spouses, children or friends) in the same situation as that person. For example, assume that you are prosecuting a defendant charged with attempting to illegally purchase drugs late at night in a poor, crime-infested area of a city in which drug dealing is common. His defense is that when on his way to catch a bus to take him to his job as a night watchman was he was walking by the corner where a drug sale was taking place, and was swept up along with those actually engaged in drug transactions.

To generate sympathy for the client, defense counsel might offer evidence suggesting that he was an innocent victim of circumstances. Such evidence might emphasize that the arrest occurred on the corner where he had to catch his bus to work. Moreover, the entire neighborhood is unsafe and riddled with drug trafficking. Consequently, any route he takes to the bus requires him to walk by an area where drug transactions are common.[4]

2. RESPONDING TO SILENT ARGUMENTS YOU DO NOT WANT A FACTFINDER TO ACCEPT

This section discusses approaches you may use to prevent a factfinder from adopting a silent argument favoring an adversary. At the outset, however, recognize that in many cases, you will not be able to exclude all the evidence supporting silent arguments favoring an adversary. As noted above, sometimes evidence supporting such arguments is apparent from a witness' appearance (e.g. skin color) or manner of testifying (e.g. accent). Other times evidence supporting silent arguments will be admissible background testimony. For example, an adversary's witness may be the president of the local university or a well known charitable organization, or your witness may be a drug user seeking a lesser sentence by acting as a police informant. In still other cases, the facts of the case may make the admission of evidence supporting silent arguments inevitable. For example, in a case where a female defendant is charged with murdering the woman with whom she had a sexual relationship, evidence of the defendant's sexual orientation may well be admissible to establish motive. Similarly, a case involving what

---

3. There is obviously some overlap between the evidence that will support this type of silent argument and the "good person/bad person" silent argument discussed above. But these two types of silent arguments are not co-extensive. For example, a factfinder may be sympathetic toward a plaintiff who has lost his arm in an auto accident, even though the plaintiff may not be a particularly likeable person.

4. Sometimes your adversary will try to generate sympathy or empathy by the form in which evidence is offered. For instance, assume you are defending a case involving a severely injured plaintiff. Your adversary may not limit his presentation to oral testimony describing the plaintiff's injuries. Your adversary may also attempt to arouse sympathy through a "Day in the Life" videotape graphically illustrating the effect of the injury on the plaintiff's life. Similarly, pictures showing the bruises on a party's face may generate more sympathy than an oral description of the same injuries.

happened at a welfare office will inevitably indicate that a witness is a welfare recipient or a welfare bureaucrat.

Nonetheless, even where the introduction of evidence supporting a silent argument favoring your adversary is inevitable, you may be able to use the approaches described below to minimize the likelihood that a factfinder will adopt such arguments.

a.   Make a Motion in Limine Prior to Trial

As you prepare for trial, you want to identify evidence an adversary is likely to offer that might support an adverse silent argument.[5] When you anticipate such evidence being offered at trial, consider making a pretrial motion in limine to prevent the adversary from offering or referring to the evidence.[6] Such a motion typically asks the judge to exclude the evidence because it is irrelevant, is inadmissible character evidence, or because its probative value is outweighed by its unduly prejudicial impact (i.e., its tendency to support a silent argument). If the motion in limine is successful, the factfinder will never hear the evidence supporting the silent argument.

For example, assume that an African–American plaintiff seeks civil damages against your client, a Caucasian police officer who allegedly used excessive force to effect an arrest. Your client claims that he struck the plaintiff when the plaintiff tried to escape from custody. The plaintiff denies trying to escape and says your client struck him without provocation.

John Wallace, a defense witness, will confirm your client's version of the dispute. But seven years prior to trial, when he was 18 years old, Wallace was a member of the Ku Klux Klan for six months. You anticipate the plaintiff cross examining Wallace about his previous Klan membership to establish bias against the plaintiff. You believe that Wallace's distant Klan membership is of minimal relevance, and likely to give rise to the silent argument that Wallace (and by association the defendant) is a "bad person." Thus, you might make a motion in limine arguing that any probative value of the Klan evidence is outweighed by its unduly potential prejudicial impact. Your motion would ask the judge to forbid plaintiff's counsel from making any reference to Wallace's Klan membership.

If you do not make a motion in limine the following exchange may take place on cross:

5. To identify such evidence you might review a file with the following questions in mind: What information might lead the factfinder to like my adversary's witnesses? Are they, for example, friendly, honest, sensitive, loyal, trustworthy or hard working? What was there about the opposing party's conduct that makes it fair or just to decide the case in the opposing party's favor?

Why might the factfinder dislike my witnesses? For example, is there evidence that might make my witnesses look unfriendly, dishonest, insensitive, disloyal, untrustworthy or lazy?

6. See Chapter 17 for a further discussion of Motions in Limine. In some courts, such pretrial evidentiary disputes may be addressed in pretrial conferences.

Opposing counsel Q: Mr. Wallace, isn't it true that you have been a member of the Ku Klux Klan?

You: Objection your Honor, irrelevant.

Court: Will counsel approach the bench. (Argument by counsel about the admissibility of the evidence).

Court (to counsel at the bench): I will sustain the objection and instruct the jury to disregard the question. But defendant's motion for a mistrial is denied.

Although the judge sustains your objection, the jury hears the question. As jurors are likely to have difficulty "unringing the bell," the question may influence the jurors regardless of the judge's instruction. Had the judge sustained your objection as a result of a motion in limine, the jury would never have heard the question.

In cases where some evidence supporting a particular silent argument will obviously be admissible, you may still make a motion in limine to exclude other evidence which might support the same silent argument. For example, assume that you represent a female defendant charged with murdering the woman with whom she lived and had a sexual relationship. The prosecution has evidence that your client committed the murder in retaliation for physical abuse inflicted on her by the decedent. Your client denies committing the crime. Evidence of your client's sexual orientation and sexual involvement with the decedent may well be admissible to establish motive. But you still might move to exclude such evidence as your client's routinely dressing in male attire,[7] frequenting lesbian bars with the deceased, and belonging to lesbian social and political organizations. Your motion would argue that such evidence is either irrelevant or more prejudicial than probative because it seeks to play on the factfinder's potential dislike of lesbians. Even if the judge decides to postpone ruling on your motion, you have highlighted the potential admissibility problems if the prosecutor attempts to introduce the evidence at trial.[8]

b. Object at Trial

If you do not secure a pretrial ruling excluding evidence supporting a silent argument favoring an adversary, you will often object when such evidence is offered at trial. The disadvantage of objecting is that your objection may call the factfinder's attention to the evidence or the adversary's questions supporting the silent argument. On the other hand, if you do not object you may be barred from raising the improper admission of such evidence on appeal.

---

7. Although this evidence might resonate with a common stereotype that lesbians routinely wear male attire, research suggests that the stereotype is inaccurate. See M. Fajer "Can Real Men Eat Quiche Together, Story Telling, Gender–Role Stereotypes, and Legal Protection For Lesbians and Gay Men," 46 U. Miami L. Rev. 511, 612 (1992).

8. For a discussion of the shortcomings of the motion in limine as a device to prevent counsel from making silent arguments based on racial stereotypes, see Johnson, *supra*, note 2.

c. Establish "Except Whens" to the Generalization(s) Supporting a Silent Argument

Like all arguments, silent arguments are based on generalizations. Thus, sometimes you can successfully respond to a silent argument by establishing "except whens" to the generalization(s) supporting a silent argument you do not want the factfinder to accept.

For example, assume that you represent an Iranian–American plaintiff in a personal injury suit. From comments made in pretrial conferences, you suspect that the judge trying the case subscribes to the following generalization: "Iranians are often engaged in schemes to stage auto accidents and recover fraudulent damage awards." You can respond to this silent argument by assuming for the sake of argument that the generalization is valid and looking for "except whens." For example, "except whens" to the generalization might include:

- They have never been involved in a lawsuit before.

- They have never made a claim on their auto insurance.

- They have worked steadily at the same job for several years.

If you can introduce evidence to establish these "except whens," you can undercut the judge's silent argument by taking your client out from under the judge's racist generalization.[9]

Consider another example. Assume that you represent a tenant who withheld rent because of the landlord's failure to maintain the leased premises in a habitable condition. At the unlawful detainer trial, you believe that the judge is likely to adopt a silent argument that tenants who assert habitability defenses are "deadbeats who can't pay rent and trump up habitability claims." To respond to this argument, look for exceptions to the generalization supporting it:

Generalization: Tenants sometimes withhold rent and then raise spurious claims of breach of the covenant of habitability....

Except when:

- They complained about the problems with the apartment long before they began to withhold rent.

- They had the resources to pay the rent.

- They have lived at the same apartment for a long period of time.

Again, introducing evidence tending to prove the "except whens" will tend to get your client out of the stereotypical "box" into which this factfinder drops "these sorts of cases."

---

9. Although the evidence establishing the "except whens" in this example might be technically inadmissible, this factfinder might well admit the evidence because it responds to his racist sense of relevance. Indeed, the example in the text comes from the personal experience of a colleague of the authors, and the colleague was able to introduce this sort of "except when" evidence at trial.

d. Select Favorable Factfinders

You will sometimes be able to select a factfinder who is unlikely to adopt a silent argument favoring an adversary. For a discussion of the techniques for doing so, see Chapter 18.

e. Discuss Silent Arguments In Closing Argument

Although you can not explicitly make silent arguments during closing argument, you can discuss why the factfinder should not be influenced by silent arguments favoring your adversary. For a discussion of the techniques for doing so, see Chapter 14 Sec. 4 C.

3. THE ETHICS OF INTRODUCING EVIDENCE TO SUPPORT SILENT ARGUMENTS YOU WANT THE FACTFINDER TO ADOPT

Just as your adversary can introduce evidence to support silent arguments, so can you. Thus, in trial preparation you can identify evidence tending to support "good person/bad person" and "sympathy/empathy" silent arguments that would make a factfinder more likely to find for your client.[10] You may reasonably ask, however, "Is it ethical to try to introduce evidence that encourages a factfinder to find for my client on a basis which the law defines as improper?" The answer is "Sometimes yes, sometimes no."

When you can make a good faith argument that the probative value of evidence supporting a favorable silent argument exceeds its prejudicial impact, evidence rules permit you to offer the evidence at trial.[11] Indeed, your obligation to zealously represent your client may require you to do so. For example, return to the *Turner v. Blasi* wrongful termination example discussed earlier in the chapter. As you recall, Gary Turner, a legal secretary, alleges that he was wrongfully discharged by Bill Blasi, the lawyer who employed him. Assume that you now represent Turner. To show that Blasi is a "bad" person, you might offer evidence that on one occasion three weeks before Turner was fired, Turner was late to work because he had to take his child to the doctor. Blasi reprimanded Turner for being late and said, "I don't give a damn about your family's medical problems. Just get to work on time."

By recognizing the silent argument this evidence tends to support, you have identified its potential prejudicial impact. To determine if you can offer the evidence at trial you need to consider its probative value, i.e. how it tends to prove a factual proposition or resolve a credibility dispute. In this case, assume that you can argue that the evidence is relevant to bolster Turner's assertion that after this comment he was particularly careful to follow all of Blasi's instructions to the letter. Blasi's "don't give a damn" comment put Turner on notice that Blasi

---

10. To identify evidence supporting your silent arguments you would review the file with questions in mind similar to those discussed in note 5 *supra*.

11. See FRE Sec. 403.

would not tolerate even minor infractions. Thus the evidence would tend to support Turner's testimony that he performed well during the last three weeks of his employment and rebut Blasi's testimony that Turner did not. Given these circumstances, you can make a good faith argument for the evidence's admissibility.

In other instances, good faith arguments for the admissibility of evidence supporting silent arguments will be unavailable. For example, assume that a witness for the opposing party observed an auto accident involving your client. You typically can not seek to introduce evidence that the witness had been at the welfare office 30 minutes before the accident. Such evidence has nothing to do with the accident or the witness' capacity to observe what happened.[12]

When your evidence tends to support a silent argument based on a negative racial, ethnic, or strongly held social stereotype, you should always make a motion in limine to obtain a pretrial ruling that the evidence is admissible unless you are certain that the probative value of the evidence outweighs its potential prejudicial impact. Silent arguments based on such stereotypes are pernicious and may deny, or appear to deny, a party a fair trial. Making a pretrial motion in limine to have the court rule on the admissibility of such evidence ensures that the jury will hear no mention of it unless the court concludes that its probative value outweighs its potential prejudicial impact.[13] In addition to the ethical propriety of such a motion, you may well save a client time and money if a judge rules during trial that the evidence you offer to support a silent argument is inadmissible and so highly prejudicial that a mistrial is necessary.

4. NON-TESTIMONIAL SILENT ARGUMENTS

Prior sections have primarily discussed silent arguments based on evidence elicited from witnesses. This section briefly identifies the common types of non-testimonial silent arguments that you or an adversary may make.[14]

---

12. Some lawyers might argue that the "welfare office" evidence tends to show that the witness needs money, and therefore might be testifying in hopes of receiving payment from the adverse party. If such a strained argument constitutes "good faith," in our view there would be no meaningful limitation on the evidence that could be offered in support of silent arguments.

13. Even when evidence supporting a silent argument favoring a decision for your client is admissible, your client may be offended by the appearance that she is relying on such an argument and decide not to introduce the evidence at trial. See D. Binder and P. Bergman, *Lawyers as Counselors* 261–265 (1991). And even if your client is willing to introduce admissible evidence supporting a silent argument, you

may be unwilling to do so and may need to seek permission to withdraw from the case. See *Ibid.* at 286 and 358–359 and ABA Model Rules of Professional Conduct, 1.16 (b)(3).

14. Many jurisdictions define anything presented to a factfinder's senses as "evidence." See Cal. Evid. Code sec. 140 ("'Evidence' means testimony . . . or other things presented to the senses . . ."). Federal courts are divided over the question of whether such information qualifies as substantive evidence (see 2 McCormick, *Evidence* Sec. 216 at 27), but clearly a factfinder is likely to take non-testimonial information into account when making a decision.

A common type of non-testimonial silent argument involves the presence of family members at trial. For example, you may generate sympathy for a client if the factfinder knows that the client's spouse and children are regularly in court and supporting the client.

Your demeanor may also give rise to silent arguments. For example, as a lawyer you want not only to mouth the appropriate arguments but also demonstrate to a factfinder that you are a competent, honest professional and you personally believe in the merits of a client's case. Use a sincere tone of voice and interact with your client during recesses in a way that suggests that you respect and believe the client. Similarly, while you should always act professionally towards opposing parties and witnesses, if you contend that they defrauded your client, you should not joke around with them in the factfinder's presence.

Factfinders are also likely to draw inferences from your client's demeanor off the stand. As a general rule, remind your clients to observe courtroom decorum. A factfinder may take offense at obvious physical reactions to testimony. Factfinders may even draw inferences from a client's dress. While clients commonly wear ordinary business attire to court, you and a client may want to consider whether different attire will be more consistent with the overall image of the client that you want to project.[15]

Note that it is always possible that factfinders will draw negative inferences about the merits of your case from factors such as the way you interact with your client ("her lawyer doesn't even seem to believe her, so why should I?") or from your client's dress ("he dresses like a wheeler-dealer, he probably did defraud the plaintiff"). Such negative inferences are always possible because you cannot interact "neutrally" with a client, nor can a client dress "neutrally." Therefore, non-testimonial silent arguments are unavoidable. Consequently, you have no choice but to try to benefit from non-testimonial silent arguments.[16]

5. SILENT ARGUMENTS CAN BACKFIRE

Like any other form of circumstantial evidence, evidence pertaining to silent arguments can "cut both ways." A factfinder may react with hostility to evidence that you had hoped would promote sympathy. For example, one factfinder's heart may be touched by evidence in a "Day in the Life" video depicting a plaintiff's disabling injuries or the presence of a client's family in the courtroom, while another regards these as unconvincing and desperate emotional ploys.

---

15. For example, in one widely-publicized case, two young brothers were charged with the murder of their parents. They admitted killing the parents, but claimed they acted in self-defense. Throughout the trial the brothers appeared in court in the preppie attire of college students.

16. Although this chapter is limited to silent arguments made in the courtroom, in cases receiving media coverage counsel often make silent arguments to potential jurors through the media.

Thus, think carefully about the likely effect of evidence promoting a silent argument. As always, you need to consider who your factfinder is, and how that specific factfinder is likely to react. If you do decide to offer such evidence, try not to gild the lily. Evidence supporting silent arguments can be like salt: a pinch can improve the taste of a bowl of soup, but too much can ruin it altogether.

Chapter 10

FINAL ASSESSMENT
OF ARGUMENTS

When you complete the steps described in the previous chapters, you will typically have produced a number of arguments through which you will attempt to convince a factfinder of the accuracy of your factual propositions and the inaccuracy of your adversary's. These arguments will form the backbone of your trial presentation. For example, decisions about what factfinder to prefer, what evidence to emphasize during direct and cross examination, and what to say to the factfinder during opening statement and final summation all grow directly out of your arguments.

Before implementing such decisions, however, you need to make an overall check on your arguments. One part of an overall check is simply to be sure that your arguments produce a coherent overall version of events. A second part is to obtain feedback on the persuasiveness of your case. This chapter addresses these tasks.

1. MAKING YOUR OVERALL CASE COHERENT

When constructing arguments, you typically focus on one argument at a time. You may have little opportunity to consider all of your arguments as a package. As a result, while any individual argument may be coherent and internally consistent, apparent or actual inconsistencies may appear when you examine your package of arguments. In order to present a coherent overall case, you should review your arguments and try to eliminate any inconsistencies that appear.

For example, assume that an important issue in a breach of contract case is the terms of an agreement reached during a Dec. 31 meeting. You have prepared an argument attacking the adversary's version of what was said about washing machines during the meeting. You base this argument in part on evidence suggesting that Mr. Frank, a witness who will testify for your adversary, does not have a good reason to recall the discussion of washing machines. You have also prepared a second argument, this one supporting your client's version of what was said about big screen TV's during the meeting. You base this argument in part on the same Mr. Frank, except that this time you will argue that Mr. Frank has a good reason to remember the discussion of big screen TV's.

Here, an apparent inconsistency appears when you examine the two arguments together. They seem to be incoherent—you attack one portion of Frank's story, yet support a different portion. When such a problem appears, try to eliminate it. Here, for example, perhaps one of the arguments is strong even without reference to Frank's testimony. If so, you might simply drop the reference to Frank out of the argument. Or, you might have an explanation for Frank's ability to recall one subject but not the other. Whether you decide on one of these or a different option, examining your arguments as a package is the key to presenting a coherent overall version of events.

In addition to making arguments coherent, revisit your overall chronology.[1] You may have identified evidence when preparing arguments that you overlooked when initially putting together your overall chronology. Since the main goal of your arguments is to convince a factfinder that your overall chronology is accurate, add any new items of evidence to your overall chronology and make sure that it too is coherent.

For example, check an overall chronology for clarity. Have you identified as accurately as your witnesses' memories allow the times when events took place? Are there gaps between events which you need to explain or fill in?

In addition, just as you comb an adversary's overall chronology for inconsistencies, check your own. Is it susceptible to an argument that it is inconsistent with everyday experience or with established facts, or that it is internally inconsistent? If you uncover seeming inconsistencies, how can you respond? Can you explain them away, or can you eliminate the evidence giving rise to them?[2]

No matter how thorough a final check, you may be unable to eliminate every possible inconsistency. But do not automatically despair. Tying up every loose end may be possible for mystery writers, but it is not always possible for lawyers. As chaos theory has taught us, at the end of the day incoherence may be all that is coherent.

2. WHO KNOWS WHAT EVIL LURKS IN THE MINDS OF FACT-FINDERS? THE "SHADOW" KNOWS....

When formulating arguments, you always have in mind their appeal to a likely factfinder. But once you've completed argument preparation

---

1. Remember, development of an overall chronology typically precedes preparation of arguments. See Chapter 1.

2. Of course inconsistencies, like all circumstantial evidence, "cut both ways." Social science researchers tell us that rarely will two people perceive and recall events in exactly the same way. See E. Loftus, *Eyewitness Testimony: Civil and Criminal* 1992. Thus, two honest witnesses may well disagree about some details. And should you try to conceal conflicts by trying to tightly control their testimony, you may reduce rather than add to their credibility. Often, you are better off displaying a conflict openly and promoting it as a badge of honesty.

and made your arguments as coherent as possible, you'll still want to determine how people other than yourself and adoring family members react to those arguments. Since all of us are to one degree or another prisoners of our own experiences, arguments that seem persuasive to us may not appeal to people with different experiences. Consequently, evaluate your story and arguments by presenting your case to outsiders, or "shadows," and obtaining their feedback.

Shadows are simply mock factfinders. You can obtain a shadow cheaply and informally by calling on office personnel unfamiliar with the case or social acquaintances. Or, if a client is willing and able, you may hire a professional jury research service which will in turn hire people to serve on a mock jury. However much time or money you invest, you want shadows to give you meaningful feedback on your arguments. Therefore, try to obtain shadows whose backgrounds and attitudes mirror as closely as possible the factfinder who is likely to decide a case.[3]

You may choose among a variety of methods of presenting a case to a shadow. You may ask a shadow to read a description of each party's story and arguments, present them orally yourself, ask witnesses to "testify," or simply deliver a mock closing argument for both sides.[4] If time or money is short, you may need to limit yourself to the one or two critical arguments in the case. Whatever option you choose, try to present each side's case as fairly as possible. Because "garbage in" produces "garbage out," a shadow will be of little help if you hide harmful information that is certain to emerge at trial.

When debriefing a shadow, try to find out what is appealing or unappealing about each side's case. What precisely makes an argument appealing or unappealing? Does a shadow's sense of the strength and weakness of the arguments match yours? If not, can you modify your presentation to take account of the shadow's feedback?[5]

With these steps, you have done all you can to produce arguments that are persuasive and coherent. In Part 2, you'll see how to present a case in a way that gives prominence to these arguments.

---

3. In a judge tried case, therefore, you may want to present your case to other lawyers.

4. Depending on how you present your case to a shadow, you may also be able to obtain feedback on inconsistencies in the overall story of both sides.

5. For a further discussion of mock juries see R. Hastie, S. Penrod, and N. Pennington, *Inside The Jury* (1983) pp. 236–40.

Part Two

COMMUNICATING ARGUMENTS AT TRIAL

When you complete the argument construction process described in Part One, you will have produced the following:

- A chronological outline of your overall story,

- A list of your factual propositions and the evidence supporting them.

- The arguments for each of your crucial factual propositions.

- The arguments responding to an adversary's case.

These documents identify the most important evidence that you will offer at trial. For example, one typical trial task is to prepare outlines of each witness' direct and cross examination testimony. And when preparing an individual witness' testimony, you turn to these documents and include in your outline the evidence in these documents to which the witness can testify. Thus, the preparation methods described in Part One help you identify much of the evidence you will offer at trial.

Part Two describes techniques for persuasively organizing and communicating your evidence during each phase of trial, from opening statement to final argument.

Chapter 11

OPENING STATEMENTS

Spencer Tracy as Colonel Henry Drummond addresses the jury in the "Scopes Monkey Trial" as Fredric March and Gene Kelly look on. "Inherit the Wind," © 1960 United Artists Pictures, Inc. All rights reserved.

Opening statement is your first formal opportunity to present your case to a factfinder. Often downplayed as simply an "outline" or a "roadmap" of the evidence to follow, opening statement is not a forerunner to, but rather an integral part of, the persuasive process. An effective opening statement provides the factfinder with a chronological picture of your version of events, communicates your most important arguments, and also paints your client in a sympathetic light.

An opening statement typically has three principal parts. The Introduction consists of your theme and a succinct summary of your most important arguments. Then, in a brief Overview you summarize the evidence you will offer in support of the principal arguments justifying a verdict in your client's favor. Finally, in a Conclusion you explicitly identify the result you want the factfinder to reach.

1. INTRODUCTION

Even in a short trial, a factfinder (even a judge) is likely to have difficulty remembering testimony and sorting it according to the argument that it tends to prove or disprove.[1] This is especially true since most arguments rest on evidence that will be supplied by multiple witnesses. Moreover, the important evidence provided by even a single witness may be spread throughout the witness' testimony, and that testimony is commonly interrupted by objections, conferences at the bench and recesses. Consequently, an Introduction can help mold a factfinder's final assessment about what evidence is most important by setting forth your theme and summarizing your one or two most important arguments.[2]

a. Setting Forth Your Theme

A theme is a persuasive device that provides a focal point around which a factfinder can organize your arguments and supporting evidence. A theme also implicitly suggests that it would be fair and just to find for your client. By setting forth a theme of no more than four to five sentences at the outset of an opening statement, you seek from the outset to incline a factfinder in the direction of a story that favors your client.

Typically, an effective theme has two attributes:

- A succinct, general description of your version of what happened and why.

1. Moore, "Trial By Schema: Cognitive Filters In The Courtroom," 37 UCLA law Rev. 273 (1989).

2. This rationale assumes that factfinders evaluate evidence as it is offered, rather than (as they are routinely instructed to do) waiting until the case has been submitted to them. However, both common sense and jury research suggest that factfinders begin to develop hypotheses about what really happened early in the trial in order to decide what testimony to pay attention to and remember as the testimony unfolds. See Moore, *supra*, note 1.

● A characterization that paints your client in a positive light and/or the adversary in a negative light.

Combining a succinct description of what happened with an explanation of why it happened typically is persuasive because people have profound beliefs in cause and effect. That is, people in our society tend to believe that events are not random; they have underlying causes. Therefore, a theme that alludes to the cause of events usually is rationally appealing.

Characterizing your client as a "good person" and/or the opponent as a "bad person" usually increases a theme's persuasive impact. As Aristotle noted about factfinders centuries ago,

"When they feel friendly to the (person) who comes before them for judgment they regard (such person) as having done little wrong, if any; when they feel hostile they take the opposite view." [3]

Admittedly, no formula for determining what may cause a factfinder to view a party as a "good person" or a "bad person" exists. The best you may be able to do is to ask yourself whether, considering contemporary standards and values and the evidence you will offer at trial, can you formulate a characterization that is likely to cause a factfinder to think well of your client and/or poorly of the adversary.[4]

The following examples illustrate how you might develop an effective theme. Assume that a fired employee, Thelma Louise, sues the Grand Canyon National Bank for wrongful discharge. Louise admits that she did not fully carry out a financial investigation of Scott Productions, a prospective borrower, and claims that other assigned job duties prevented her from doing so. Relying on Louise's incomplete investigation, Grand Canyon made the loan to the borrower and wound up with a substantial loss when Scott declared bankruptcy a couple of months later. Grand Canyon then terminated Louise's employment.

In this case, you might state your theme on behalf of Louise as follows:

"My client, Thelma Louise, was a good and loyal five year employee of the defendant, Grand Canyon National Bank. She was fired because her supervisor, Harvey Pitt, gave her too much work to do. Because she couldn't do everything, the bank made a bad loan. By firing her, Mr. Pitt is trying to shift the blame for the bad loan to her." [5]

---

3. Aristotle, *Rhetoria* Book II.1.

4. Sometimes it has been suggested that a description that will cause a factfinder to view a person positively is a description that evokes sympathy for such person. However, as noted by Kalven and Zeisel, "Sympath[y] is but a collective term for many very different sentiments...." See, H. Kalven and H. Zeisel *The American Jury* 1966 at 218 n. 38.

5. Occasionally, you may need to augment your introductory remarks to include a bit of background information such as your name, who you represent and who your witnesses will be. In most cases, however, the factfinder will already be aware of this information prior to your opening statement. In a jury trial, such information will emerge through the voir dire process. Similarly, in a judge-tried case, the judge will almost always have gleaned such

This theme succinctly identifies what happened (the bank made a bad loan) and why (your client was given too much to do), and the emotional center of your case (a nasty supervisor is trying to shift the blame to an employee who was trying the best she could).

Of course, the Bank's attorney will also want to set forth a theme during opening statement. Here, that theme might be something like this:

> "My client, the Grand Canyon Bank, depended on the plaintiff to carry out an important financial investigation. She decided that she knew more than her supervisor, Mr. Pitt, and that she would do things her way rather than carry out his instructions. As a result of her insubordination the bank lost nearly half a million dollars and she was rightfully terminated."

This statement too has the essential ingredients of a theme. It sets forth what happened (the bank lost nearly a half million dollars on a bad loan) and why (an employee didn't follow her supervisor's instructions) and incorporates an emotional appeal (the employee was insubordinate).

Both themes represent an attempt to shape a factfinder's mindset as the evidence unfolds. The plaintiff hopes that the factfinder will pay particular attention to arguments that the plaintiff was overworked, while the defendant hopes that the factfinder will concentrate on the plaintiff's willful failure to carry out a supervisor's instructions.

Obviously, the evidence supporting your theme has to be prominent throughout a case if a theme is to accomplish your rhetorical purpose. For example, assume that you represent a state agency suing a contractor for alleged defects in the construction of a bridge. You will attempt to prove that the bridge had at least 17 material defects. In your theme, you want to explain that the reason for the defects was that the contractor was not personally present on site to supervise the construction. But if your evidence will link the contractor's absence to only two or three of the 17 material defects, evidence supporting your theme will not be prominent throughout the case. In this instance, you should seek an explanation that will be better echoed in the evidence.

b. Summarizing Your Strongest Arguments

The second part of an Introduction affords you an opportunity to summarize your strongest arguments.[6] Like a theme, you intend the summary as a succinct guide to the arguments and supporting evidence as they unfold at trial.

In the wrongful termination case, assume that plaintiff Louise's strongest arguments pertain to her claim that she was unable to perform

---

information from pretrial briefs and conferences.

6. The arguments to which you refer may include both your affirmative arguments and your responses to an adversary's likely arguments. The latter are especially likely to predominate if you are a criminal defense counsel who will primarily attack weaknesses in the prosecution's case.

a complete financial investigation because she was overworked. Your argument summary on her behalf might go as follows:

"Ms. Louise was an overworked employee. She will explain to you that a week after Mr. Pitt assigned the Scott job to her, she asked him to assign another employee to help her with the investigation, but he ignored her request. And another employee, Susan Davis, will tell you that Ms. Louise asked her to help with the Scott investigation. Also, bank records will show that at the time this investigation was in progress, Ms. Louise had more investigations assigned to her than any of her co-workers. You will also hear that the first time that Mr. Pitt claimed that Ms. Louise was in any way responsible for the bad loan was when Mr. Pitt's supervisor asked him to explain why the loan was made in the first place."

Here, you first emphasize the argument that Ms. Louise was overworked. The argument rests on the generalizations that "people who ask for help often believe that they have too much to do," and "people who have heavier case loads than their co-workers are often overworked." You also highlight the argument that Pitt fired Louise to shift the blame to her.

Again, the defendant will want to counter with a summary of its strongest arguments. Recall that the bank's theme is that Louise was insubordinate, in that she intentionally ignored Pitt's instructions. On the defendant's behalf, you might summarize your arguments as follows:

"The plaintiff intentionally refused to carry out Mr. Pitt's instructions. On several occasions the plaintiff told co-workers that Mr. Pitt was a nit-picker who laid down lots of unnecessary requirements that made it almost impossible for good loans to get approved. And Mr. Pitt will testify that Ms. Louise never asked him for additional help to complete the Scott investigation, and bank records will show that Ms. Louise never worked overtime during the time she was doing the investigation. As plaintiff's counsel said, bank records will show that Ms. Louise had been assigned more investigations than her co-workers, but you will see that the memo assigning her the Scott investigation stated that it was top priority."

Here, the defense emphasizes three arguments. One is a defense argument that the plaintiff was insubordinate (the "nit-picker" statement to co-workers). Disputing the plaintiff's evidence that she asked for help, a second defense argument supports its version of the dispute (plaintiff never asked for help or worked overtime). And in response to plaintiff's argument that she had more work than other employees, a third defense argument is that the plaintiff was told that the Scott job had top priority.

2. PROVIDE AN OVERVIEW OF YOUR EVIDENCE

You will typically follow an Introduction with a brief Overview of the evidence you intend to offer. You may include in your Overview not only evidence from the direct examination of your own witnesses, but also evidence you are confident of eliciting during cross examination of the adversary's witnesses. Thus, opening statement is a good opportunity to provide a factfinder with a relatively uninterrupted picture of your version of the events. During witness examinations, by contrast, your version will almost always be scattered throughout the testimony of different witnesses and will be interrupted by cross examinations, objections and recesses.

a. Provide a Chronology

Your Overview will usually be organized as a chronological story of your version of what happened.[7] Such an organization responds to the way that judges and jurors typically approach decision-making, which is to make sense of the testimony by developing a story about what they believe really happened.[8]

Just as looking at a picture on a boxtop helps one piece together a jigsaw puzzle, so a chronological Overview makes it easier for a factfinder to understand and remember your evidence. Whether what is being explained is the plot of a movie, how car keys were lost and then found or the events culminating in litigation, chronology is our basic method of communication. Indeed, the meaning of events is inherently tied to chronology. Compare these skeletal stories:

(1) I went to a party, I had a few drinks, I got in an auto accident.

(2) I went to a party, I got in an auto accident, I had a few drinks.

As you see, change chronology and you change meaning.[9]

The principal decision you have to make when preparing your Overview is how detailed to make it. An exhaustive detailing of all your expected evidence is ineffective. Just like an overly detailed preview may destroy any interest you have in seeing a film, so is excessive detail likely to flatten a factfinder's interest in your evidence and obscure the evidence supporting your arguments on the crucial factual propositions. Moreover, the more specific details you include in your Overview, the more likely a witness' testimony will vary, allowing your adversary to point out during closing argument that you promised more than you could deliver.[10] Finally, too much detail may cause your witnesses to

---

7. Alternatively, you may present a "witness by witness" summary of events. This may enable you to offer a more complete picture of each witness' testimony, but it is likely to obscure the chronology of events.

8. See Bennett & Feldman, *Reconstructing Reality in the Courtroom* (1981); Holstein, "Jurors' Interpretations and Jury Decision Making", 9 Law & Hum. Behav. 83 (1985); Pennington & Hastie, "Evidence Evaluation in Complex Decision Making," 51 J. Personality & Soc. Psychology 242 (1986); Pennington & Hastie, "A Cognitive

Theory of Juror Decision Making: The Story Model," 13 Cardozo Law Rev. 519 (1991)

9. Though chronology aids factfinder understanding, you needn't always proceed sequentially from earliest event to latest during an Overview. If you think later-occurring events are more important, you may begin an Overview by describing those events chronologically and then describing earlier events, again in chronological order. For example, as the prosecutor in a murder case, you may first give a chronological account of the killing and then relate the events giving rise to the defendant's motive.

10. During final summation, your ad-

sound like they are parroting your story rather than telling their own, leading the factfinder to conclude that you have told the witnesses what to say.

Thus an effective Overview has to consist of something less than all the evidence you will elicit. But how can you decide what to put in and what to leave out? First, you will want to include the evidence necessary to enable a factfinder to understand your version of how events unfolded. Second, you will typically want to include the evidence supporting the arguments you constructed prior to trial to prove your crucial propositions. In a complex case, however, including the evidence supporting all your arguments on the crucial propositions may make the Overview too long and boring. In the end, you must exercise your judgment and try to tell an interesting story that focuses the factfinder's attention on your most important arguments.[11]

b. Use Concrete, Everyday Language

As you know from listening to stories in social settings, a memorable story is more than just a chronological narrative. Engrossing stories help a listener form a mental image of what took place. Typically they briefly describe the scene of important events, identify the principle characters and use concrete language. These are the qualities of well-told stories, whether you are around the dinner table or in trial.

For example, assume that you represent a bicycle rider who was injured when the allegedly defective quick-release mechanism on the front wheel of his bike malfunctioned and caused the bike to collapse. Compare the following Overviews:

> Excerpt A—"I expect the evidence to show that my client rode his bike at a normal speed and in a normal manner across railroad tracks. The evidence will further show that the uneven surface loosened the quick-release mechanism on the front wheel. The front wheel came loose, so that the bike gave way under my client and he fell to the ground."

> Excerpt B—"Joey was out for a bike ride on a typical late August day. School was about to begin, but Joey and his two friends had a few more days to relax and enjoy summer vacation. They decided to see a movie matinee, and headed down Bolas St. towards Beloit Ave. They were pedaling at a normal rate of speed, as they had plenty of time to get to the movie. Michael rode across the tracks, and then David. Of course they bumped up and down a bit, but they had no problem at all. Then Joey pedaled across. Suddenly his bike began

---

versary can permissibly contrast the evidence you produced with that you promised to deliver.

11. In some jurisdictions, the opponent may ask for a directed verdict for the defense if plaintiff does not refer to evidence establishing a prima facie case on each element of a cause of action. However, plain-

tiff will be given a second opportunity to include any necessary additional evidence before such a motion is granted. See *United States v. Donsky*, 825 F.2d 746 (3d Cir. 1987); *Best v. District of Columbia*, 291 U.S. 411, 415, 54 S.Ct. 487, 489, 78 L.Ed. 882 (1934).

to shake and bounce. Just as Joey got across the tracks, the quick-release mechanism on the front tire came loose and the front wheel fell off loose. Joey's bike collapsed, and he was thrown to the ground.''

Excerpt A has few characteristics of a memorable story. The chronology is unclear and the language is abstract, flat and legalistic. The lawyer refers to what ''the evidence will show'' and the injured rider is referred to as ''my client''. Excerpt B, by contrast, briefly sets the scene, concretely describes what happened and refers to ''Joey'' by name, helping the factfinder to see him as a person rather than a legal entity. The language in excerpt B is conversational and vivid, further helping the factfinder to picture what happened.

c. Overview Emphasis Technique # 1: "Changing the Pace"

As you provide an Overview, you can emphasize the evidence supporting your most important arguments by employing the ''changing the pace'' technique. To ''change the pace'' is simply to describe some events in more detail than others. Slowing the pace naturally provides emphasis.

For example, assume that in a breach of contract case your client, Matt, will testify that he met with Beth on March 1 to discuss the purchase of a shopping center. You want to mention this event during the Overview to keep the chronology clear, but none of your arguments refer to this event and you therefore do *not* want to emphasize it. You may cover this meeting at a fast pace, saying something like:

''On the first of March, Matt and Beth met to talk about the sale. They discussed the purchase price and other terms. A week later a second meeting took place. . . .''

By contrast, assume that what took place during this event is important evidence for one of your arguments. As a result, you want to emphasize it. To do so, slow down the pace by adding additional details:

''On the first of March, Matt and Beth met to talk about the sale. The meeting began in the morning at Matt's office and lasted most of the day. The first thing they discussed was the purchase price. Matt began by offering $1,550,000 and Beth responded by saying that she couldn't take less than two million. This discussion lasted for over an hour, and Beth provided Matt with lease agreements from all the tenants as well as financial statements for the three previous years . . .'' [12]

Like any other technique, changing the pace is not foolproof. If you add too much detail, you may drown important evidence in a sea of minutiae. As usual, you must exercise your best professional judgment to decide when ''enough detail'' slops over into ''too much detail.''

---

12. Of course, your slow pace needn't pertain to the entire meeting. You may want to emphasize only a portion of what took place.

d. Overview Emphasis Technique # 2: Marshalling Evidence Supporting a Particular Argument

Though you normally relate an Overview chronologically, a second way you can emphasize important evidence is to digress from chronology and marshall, or juxtapose, several items of evidence supporting a particular argument.

For example, assume that you represent the plaintiff in the case of *Carson v. Melinda*. Carson and Melinda were involved in an auto accident, and Carson alleges that Melinda's speeding caused the accident. Melinda has admitted that at the time of the accident she was 20 minutes late to a business meeting. Based on this undisputed item of evidence you have prepared the following argument:

Undisputed Item of Evidence: At the time of the accident, Melinda was 20 minutes late for a business meeting.

Generalization: People who drive when they are 20 minutes late to a business meeting sometimes drive in excess of the 35 m.p.h. speed limit....

Especially When

1. they have arranged the meeting themselves.

2. the person they are going to meet has been reluctant to meet with them previously.

3. the meeting is with a potential new customer.

4. they are unable to let the potential new customer know that they will be delayed.

Factual Proposition: At the time of the accident, Melinda was driving in excess of the 35 m.p.h. speed limit.

If you were to relate these events in the order of their occurrence, the evidence supporting this argument would be scattered throughout your Overview. For instance, you would inform the factfinder of Especially When # 1 ("arranged the meeting themselves") well before Especially When # 4 ("will be delayed"). This chronology would obscure your point that both items of evidence support the same argument.

To emphasize that several items of evidence support a particular argument, you can briefly digress from chronology to marshall the evidence supporting that argument. For example, returning to *Carson v. Melinda*, assume that you have summarized Carson's version of what happened prior to the accident. Your Overview might then continue as follows:

... And as Carson was driving down Sunset Blvd., Melinda's car approached him from behind.

At this moment, Melinda was on her way to a business meeting with a Mr. Cutter. And Melinda was not on time for the meeting. She was twenty minutes late. Mr. Cutter will tell you that he had been reluctant to meet with Melinda, but that at Melinda's request he agreed to meet to discuss whether his company would agree to purchase a substantial amount of machine parts from Melinda's firm. Mr. Cutter will also tell you that Melinda did not tell him she would be late for the meeting until an hour after the accident.

And as Melinda was on her way to this meeting, she passed Carson's car at a speed of approximately 60 miles an hour. She then suddenly swerved into Carson's lane and the two cars collided....

Here, you briefly digress from the chronology and marshall the evidence supporting your "late for a meeting" argument. You thereby make it easier for the factfinder to understand the significance of testimony that will come out piecemeal over three different witness examinations (Carson's and Cutter's Direct and Melinda's cross).[13]

Just as you can marshall evidence to emphasize an argument based on highly probative undisputed evidence, so too can you marshall evidence emphasizing arguments drawn from the Credibility Checklist. For example, assume that you represent the defendant in *Platt v. Darwin*. Platt alleges that Darwin, a police officer, used excessive force when arresting him. Platt says that when he was arrested, Darwin knocked him to the ground and then struck him in the head with his baton. Darwin admits knocking Platt to the ground but denies striking Darwin in the head. When completing your Credibility Checklist, you identified the following arguments supporting Darwin's testimony that he did not strike Platt in the head with his baton:

Reasons or Motives Not to Engage in Conduct: (a) After Platt was knocked to the ground he complied with Darwin's instruction and was no longer resisting arrest. (b) Darwin knew that striking an arrestee in the head violated police department regulations, unless such action was absolutely necessary to subdue a suspect. (c) Darwin knew that another officer had been suspended and demoted for striking a suspect in the head with his baton.

Consistency with Other Witnesses and Documents: Dr. Kauffman examined Platt at the hospital after his arrest and his opinion is that the bruise on Platt's head was not the result of a baton blow but rather occurred when Platt's head struck the ground.

Again, you can briefly depart from chronology to marshall the evidence supporting Darwin's version of the disputed evidence of whether Darwin struck Platt in the head with his baton. For example, assume that you have summarized Darwin's version of what happened up to the time Platt was knocked to the ground.

... When plaintiff was on the ground officer Darwin told him to put his hands behind his back and the plaintiff complied and was handcuffed.

---

13. The more you digress from chronology to emphasize an argument, the more you lose the advantages of chronology. Thus, you will have to exercise careful judg-ment when deciding how many arguments to emphasize and how long to make those digressions.

In her opening statement, plaintiff's counsel told you that after the plaintiff was on the ground, Officer Darwin struck plaintiff in the head with his baton. That is not true. Officer Darwin never struck plaintiff in the head with his baton. Officer Darwin will tell you that after plaintiff was on the ground he obeyed orders and there was no need to strike plaintiff at that time. Officer Darwin will also testify that he knew that it was against department regulations to strike a suspect in the head with a baton, unless it was absolutely necessary to subdue the suspect. And several weeks prior to this arrest, Officer Darwin was told by the Captain of Internal Affairs that a fellow officer had been demoted and suspended for violating this regulation prohibiting baton blows to the head. Dr. Kauffman, who examined plaintiff shortly after his arrest, will tell you that in his expert opinion, the bruise on plaintiff's head resulted not from a baton blow to the head, but from plaintiff's head hitting the curb when he was knocked to the ground.

After plaintiff was handcuffed, Officer Darwin....

By marshalling the evidence supporting your client's version of disputed evidence, you emphasize the argument and help a factfinder appreciate the evidence supporting it. And if you choose to make your opening statement right after the plaintiff's, you provide this emphasis within minutes rather than waiting days or even weeks until you get to present the defense case in chief.

3. CONCLUSION

The Conclusion to an opening statement is typically quite simple and straightforward: Explicitly inform the factfinder of your desired result. Disclosing your bottom line in advance of the evidence provides closure for your story and is another way of helping a factfinder understand the significance of testimony. In civil matters, a plaintiff's Conclusion often specifies the type and amount of damages sought. For example, a personal injury plaintiff may say, "At the conclusion of the case, we'll ask you to award Ms. Jones the sum of $400,000 to compensate her for medical expenses, pain and suffering and lost wages." A bottom line is possible even when a plaintiff chooses not to specify the amount of damages being sought: "At the conclusion of the case, we'll ask you to award damages in the amount you think fair to compensate Ms. Jones for her medical expenses, pain and suffering and lost wages." Similarly, a civil plaintiff seeking injunctive relief will ordinarily specify the terms of the sought relief: "The terms of the injunction which the Environmental Council seeks are to require the defendant City to file an EIR (Environmental Impact Report) before embarking on the construction of the new highway."

Obviously, your Conclusion will be different if you represent a civil defendant or a criminal litigant. For instance, a criminal defense attorney's Opening Statement may conclude with a bottom line such as, "At the conclusion of the evidence, we will ask you to find Ms. Jones not guilty." But whatever its precise contents, your Conclusion should make explicit to the factfinder the relief you seek.

4. AN ILLUSTRATIVE EXAMPLE—PEOPLE v. DIXON

By way of illustration, examine a hypothetical opening statement you might deliver as the prosecutor in *People v. Dixon*, involving the attempted shoplifting of a cheese ball and other items from a supermarket.[14] The Opening Statement goes as follows:

1   "Ladies and Gentlemen, this is a straightforward case of petty
2   theft. On the afternoon of December 9 of last year, James
3   Embree, the owner of Oak Hills Supermarket, saw the defen-
4   dant Donna Dixon put a cheese ball, a can of chili peppers and a
5   can of chili powder in her purse. The defendant went through
6   the checkout line without paying for them, and then lied about
7   whether she had taken them when confronted by Mr. Embree.
8   At the time of the theft, Mr. Embree had an unobstructed view
9   of the defendant's actions, and the arresting officer, Officer
10   Morey, found the items in the defendant's purse but was unable
11   to find a receipt for them.

12   "To help you follow the testimony you will hear shortly, let me
13   briefly summarize the evidence the State will offer to prove Ms.
14   Dixon's guilt beyond a reasonable doubt. On Saturday, Decem-
15   ber 9th, shortly after noon, Mr. Embree was working in the
16   manager's office on the second floor of the market. The office
17   has wrap-around windows which allow Mr. Embree to see the
18   floor of the market.

19   "Mr. Embree first noticed the defendant when he saw her with
20   a large open purse in her cart. Mr. Embree had never talked
21   with or met the defendant before, and he knew from past
22   experience that shoplifters often use an open purse to steal
23   items. To keep an eye on her, he went downstairs to the one-
24   way mirror that runs behind the back of the meat department.

25   "While watching the defendant through the one-way mirror,
26   Mr. Embree saw her put a cheese ball into her purse. At this
27   time he was no more that 20 feet from the defendant, she was
28   in a well-lit area of the store and there were no other patrons or
29   objects to obscure his view. He continued to watch her both
30   from behind the one-way mirror and later from the store's
31   security room, which is equipped with videotape equipment. As
32   he videotaped her, he saw the defendant place other small
33   items in her purse. He then saw her go through the checkout
34   line without paying for the items, at which time he detained her
35   and called the police.

36   "Officer Morey, the police officer who responded to the call, will
37   tell you about the grocery items he found in the defendant's

14. The statement of facts in *Dixon* is set forth in Chapter 5 at pgs. 48–50.

38   purse and the fact that he saw no receipt for them.   At the
39   conclusion of the trial, we'll ask you to find the defendant guilty
40   of petty theft.''

Analysis

a.   Introduction

This Introduction consists of a theme and a summary of your
principal arguments.   The theme (lines 1–7) briefly summarizes what
happened and characterizes the defendant unsympathetically as a liar.
Note that this theme does not explain why the defendant shoplifted.
Because of a prosecutor's limited discovery privileges and inability to call
the defendant as a witness, a prosecutor sometimes cannot explain why
things occurred as they did during opening statement.   Finally, your
Introduction summarizes your strongest arguments (lines 7–11).

b.   Overview

The Overview conveys your version of what happened chronologically.   It briefly sets the scene (lines 14–18), and uses concrete language
from beginning to end.   The Overview consists primarily of the evidence
supporting your important Credibility Checklist arguments.   That is,
you refer to the evidence suggesting that Embree had the "physical
ability" to see Dixon steal the items, and that he had a "reason and
motive" to see her take the items (lines 19–23; that his testimony is
"consistent with other witnesses and documents" (lines 36–39); and
that Embree is "neutral" (lines 20–21).

Finally, the Overview also incorporates emphasis techniques.   You
slow the pace when discussing Embree's ability to see Dixon take the
cheese ball by providing details bolstering his opportunity to observe the
theft (lines 25–29).   You also briefly digress from chronology to marshall
evidence supporting one of your most important arguments from the
Credibility Checklist (lines 20–21).

c.   Conclusion

As is usually the case, your Conclusion is short and sweet, consisting
only of a request that the jury find the defendant guilty of petty theft
(lines 38–40).

5.   RULES AND STRATEGIC DECISIONS

a.   The Rule Against Arguing During Opening Statement

The principle rule governing opening statement is the one forbidding argument.[15]   In general, what this means is that you can refer to
the evidence that a witness or document will provide, but not to the
inferences and conclusions you will ask the factfinder to draw from

---

15. See, Tanford, *An Introduction to
Trial Law* 51 Missouri Law Rev. 623, 649
note 131.

testimony. For example, you may say that "Embree saw Dixon from a distance of only 20 feet" if you expect Embree to so testify. But you cannot say that "Embree's identification of Dixon is accurate," because a witness is not allowed to testify to this conclusion. Similarly, in a case involving an auto accident, you can properly tell the factfinder that "moments before the accident the defendant received a call on his car phone informing him of a missed inspection on an important job." But during opening statement you cannot say "this phone call distracted the defendant and caused him to be inattentive to the road," because that is the inference you will ask the factfinder to draw from the evidence.[16]

Be aware that judges have wide discretion when it comes to enforcing the rule against arguing during opening statement. For example, consider this potential Introduction to an opening statement:

> "Pauline Prager's tragic death was caused by Mr. Dolinko's inattention to the road. Because he wasn't watching the road closely he struck Ms. Prager while she was in a crosswalk. This case revolves around whose version of events you believe. The defendant will tell you that Ms. Prager was not in the crosswalk. But Ms. White will testify that Ms. Prager was in the crosswalk when she was struck by the defendant. And the evidence will show that Ms. White is a neutral, unbiased witness who had a clear view of the accident."

In line with this Chapter's recommendations, this Introduction describes what happened and why, suggests that Dolinko is a "bad guy," and summarizes your credibility argument. But a judge could view it as argumentative: for example, no witness will testify that "Dolinko wasn't watching the road," or that White is "neutral and unbiased." However, most judges will permit such comments during an Introduction, and some judges will permit a considerable amount of argument throughout the opening statement.

In an attempt to avoid the "argumentative" label, some attorneys preface argumentative remarks with the opening statement mantra, "the evidence will show." But this phrase does not magically convert argument into evidence. Thus, the phrase, "Ms. White is neutral and unbiased" is no less argumentative simply because it is prefaced by the comment that "the evidence will show that...." The test of argument is whether remarks of counsel refer to evidence that will emanate either from witnesses or documents. What the "evidence will show" is a matter for final summation.

b. *Do Not Refer to Evidence of Doubtful Admissibility*

It is both legally and tactically unwise to refer during opening statement to evidence unless you are confident that you will elicit it at trial, either on direct examination of your witnesses or cross examination

---

16. You may object during an opponent's opening if you think the opponent is engaging in improper argument. When you do so, you can point out to the judge that no witness or document will provide the improper argument stated by your opponent.

of the adversary's. From a legal standpoint, referring to important evidence that does not become part of the record may lead a judge to declare a mistrial (especially in a jury trial). In addition to the added burden and expense of starting over, a judge may also impose sanctions on you and your client for causing the mistrial to occur.[17]

From a tactical standpoint, during closing argument your adversary may ask the factfinder to infer from your failure to produce what you promised that you intentionally misled the factfinder or tried to paper over a weak case by making assertions that you knew you could not fulfill. Thus, it is almost always unwise to refer to evidence if it is of doubtful admissibility, or if you are uncertain about what a witness will say.[18]

c. Opening Statements by Defense Counsel

When representing a defendant, you typically have a choice about the timing of your opening statement. You can deliver it immediately after the plaintiff's opening, before the plaintiff begins her case-in-chief. Or, you can wait until after the plaintiff rests and deliver an opening statement just before the defense's case-in-chief. In both civil and criminal cases, defense attorneys almost always choose the former alternative. Doing so enables defense counsel to offer a factfinder a competing view of the case, before the factfinder can become mentally locked into the plaintiff's version of events. Moreover, an immediate response to the plaintiff's opening statement may help a factfinder understand the arguments that you develop during cross examination. The primary disadvantage of this common option is that the delay between the defense opening statement and the defense case-in-chief may cause a factfinder to forget some of your remarks. This may take away from an opening statement's effectiveness as a guide to your evidence and arguments.

In a criminal case, the disadvantages of a defendant presenting an immediate opening statement are perhaps greater. Since defendants often have to plead only "not guilty," and a prosecutor often has very limited discovery, an immediate opening statement may reveal a defense argument of which the prosecution was unaware, allowing the prosecution time to develop a response to it. In addition, what you say during opening statement is likely to depend heavily on whether your client will testify, and you may be reluctant to make this decision until after the prosecution has presented its evidence.

d. Sandbagging

No, you don't request the judge's permission to deliver your opening statement from behind a protective shield of dirt-filled sacks. "Sandbag-

---

17. See, e.g., *Barnd v. City of Tacoma,* 664 F.2d 1339 (9th Cir.1982); *People v. District Court of the 2nd Judicial District,* 664 P.2d 247 (Colo.1983).

18. When admissibility is uncertain, consider making a "motion in limine" be-

fore the time for opening statement to seek a pretrial ruling on admissibility. When your opponent mentions evidence you believe is inadmissible you may object during the opponent's opening.

ging" refers to the practice of intentionally neglecting to mention favorable evidence—either affirmative evidence for your version of events or evidence undercutting your adversary's version. Assuming that your adversary does not already know about the concealed evidence, sandbagging may reduce an adversary's opportunity to respond to the evidence when you reveal it during testimony.

Because the scope of modern discovery is so broad, and because extensive negotiations and pretrial conferences precede most trials, an adversary is likely to be aware of significant evidence. Thus, omitting significant evidence from an opening statement may serve only to sandbag a factfinder. However, you may want to consider this tactic if you think that an adversary is ignorant of an important argument you intend to advance. By not mentioning the evidence you intend to produce to support the argument, you minimize the likelihood your adversary will prepare a response. And failing to mention evidence during opening statement does not preclude you from offering it at trial.

e. Volunteering Weaknesses

An issue that may confront you on opening statement is whether to reveal information that undermines a client's claim. As a general rule, you do not want to include unfavorable evidence in an opening statement. Including unfavorable information will detract from the favorable first impression you hope to make on a factfinder. Hence, you typically want to put your strongest version of events before a factfinder and leave it to your adversary to try to undermine it. However, this general rule is subject to an important exception. If you conceal unfavorable information that seriously calls into question your client's version of events and your adversary elicits that information at trial, a factfinder may conclude that your opening statement was misleading and thus that you and your client lack credibility.

For example, assume that you represent the plaintiff in a slip and fall case. The plaintiff claims that he stumbled over a concrete abutment in the defendant's unreasonably dark parking lot; the defendant's claim is that the lot was sufficiently lit and that the plaintiff's own carelessness caused him to fall. Assume that Wilma Johnson is prepared to testify on your behalf that about a week before the plaintiff's fall, she too stumbled over a concrete abutment in the same parking lot.

Assume that the weakness in your case is that Wilma Johnson is a close friend of the plaintiff. If you omit mention of this information during opening statement, the factfinder may infer that you have been less than candid in an effort to conceal a serious weakness. If you include the information in opening, the factfinder's first impression of your case may not be as favorable. Once again, the ultimate decision is a matter of judgment.

Chapter 12

DIRECT EXAMINATION

In courtroom dramas, direct examination routinely takes a back seat to cross examination and closing argument in determining the outcome of a trial.[1] But in real life, direct examination is usually your primary opportunity to convince a factfinder that your arguments are accurate.[2]

---

1. For example, the cross examination by George C. Scott (playing a prosecutor) of Lee Remick (playing defendant's wife, Lau-ra Manion) in "Anatomy of a Murder" is a true classic.

2. The archetypal instance in which this is not true is when a criminal defendant

This chapter describes techniques for eliciting clear and persuasive direct examinations, and for emphasizing the arguments you've prepared prior to trial.

1. GENERAL PRINCIPLES

Effective direct examinations generally adhere to three basic principles.

a. Testimony Emerges Chronologically

As in the Overview of an opening statement, you typically elicit testimony during direct examination in chronological story form. A chronology tends to help factfinders understand and accept what witnesses say. Moreover, a chronology responds to the way that judges and jurors usually approach decision-making, which is to develop a story about what they believe really happened.[3] Finally, a chronology tends to stimulate a witness' recall of past events and therefore to help a witness testify more completely and accurately.[4]

The chronology principle does not require you to slavishly determine the earliest event to which a witness will testify, and proceed sequentially from there. You may choose other starting places, reflecting your judgment about what portions of a story are most important or what a factfinder is most anxious to hear. But wherever you break into the story, the events should usually unfold chronologically.

For example, assume that you represent a defendant charged with murdering his former girlfriend; the defendant claims that her death was an accident. The prosecution case describes the couple's rocky two month relationship and culminates with the alleged murder. Assume that the defendant will present a much rosier version of the relationship and describe the killing as a tragic accident. Here, you might well choose to break into the story with the defendant's description of what happened on the night of the victim's death, and then move to a description of the couples' relationship.[5] This order might respond to the factfinder's likely agenda, as your client's version of how the victim died is the central issue in the case. Nevertheless, you can take advantage of chronology. Elicit the circumstances of the night of the killing chronologically, and then do the same for the relationship.

b. Testimony Emphasizes Arguments

An effective direct examination is not simply a chronological run-through of everything a witness knows about a case. Such testimony

offers no affirmative evidence, but instead relies on cross examination and the burden of proof. In most cases, however, defendants too offer affirmative versions of what happened through direct examination.

3. See W. Bennett & M. Feldman, *Reconstructing Reality In the Courtroom* (1981).

4. See D.A. Binder, P. Bergman & S.C. Price, *Lawyers as Counselors: A Client-* *Centered Approach* 118 (1991), citing L.W. Barsalou, *The Content and Organization of Autobiographical Memories in Remembering Reconsidered: Ecological and Traditional Approaches to the Study of Memory* 213–14, 222–24 (1988).

5. This is an example of "frontloading" the most important part of a story. See Sec. 3 b below.

would be tedious, and the irrelevant details would eclipse the important evidence supporting your arguments. Thus, the stories you elicit must be selective ones, with the selection process largely governed by pretrial argument preparation. You will want to emphasize the evidence supporting your arguments, and touch lightly on or even ignore other portions of a story.[6] To do this, you will occasionally need to digress briefly from chronology.

As an example of how arguments shape the content of direct examination, assume that you represent the plaintiff in a fraud case. The plaintiff claims that the defendant's false statements induced him to redo all the plumbing in his house. If the defendant denies making the statements attributed to her by the plaintiff, your direct examination of the plaintiff will emphasize the evidence bolstering the plaintiff's version of this evidentiary dispute. By contrast, if the defendant admits making the statements but denies that the plaintiff relied on them, your direct will center on evidence demonstrating plaintiff's reliance.

c. Questions Are Both Open and Closed

To elicit a story which is both chronological and emphasizes your arguments, you will need to use a combination of open and closed questions.

(1) The Spectrum From Open to Closed Questions

Open questions give witnesses freedom to decide what topics to discuss and what words to use when discussing them. Consider this question: "What happened after Joan said she couldn't sell it for less than $15,000 a unit?" The question is open because it allows the witness substantial freedom to choose what to talk about and what words to use. The witness may discuss any person, time, place, activity or subject. For example, the witness could responsively say: "We went to Bob Hamlin's office where he showed us a large chart that outlined projected sales figures." The open question allows the witness to select the actor (Bob), the scene (Hamlin's office), the activity (reviewing a chart), and the subject (projected sales figures).[7]

As questions become more closed, they circumscribe these freedoms. For instance, examine the following question: "After Joan mentioned that she couldn't sell the unit for less than $15,000, what was the next thing she said?" This question allows the witness some degree of

---

6. By intentionally deleting some information you do not therefore produce untruthful stories. A story may be accurate yet still be less than complete. By analogy, consider two maps of the United States, one depicting the states according to their size and the other according to their population. Both delete some information and both are "accurate;" they are designed for different purposes.

7. If an open question allows a witness too much freedom of response, it is often objectionable as "calling for a narrative." For example, a question such as, "Tell us everything that happened" sets so few parameters on the response that it violates the question-answer norm, and thus is likely to be objectionable.

freedom: it is up to the witness to describe what was said. But the question is less open than the previous one, as it limits the witness to a specific actor (Joan), a particular time (next thing said), and a particular activity (what she said).

Questions become closed when they limit witnesses to one or two word or "yes" or "no" responses. For example, consider these questions:

- "After Joan mentioned that she couldn't sell the unit for less than $15,000, what did she say the price to install each unit would be?"

- "After Joan mentioned that she couldn't sell the unit for less than $15,000, did she say that the price to install each unit would be $800?"

These questions are closed. The first limits the witness to a one word answer, the installation price; the second calls only for a "yes" or "no" answer. In neither case can the witness choose what to talk about, and in the second example the witness can only confirm or deny the information in the question.

The ultimate closed question is one which suggests a desired answer; such a question is "leading." For example, assume that you phrase the previous question in this manner: "After Joan mentioned that she couldn't sell the unit for less than $15,000, the next thing she said was that the price to install each unit would be $800, right?" This question is leading because it does more than ask the witness to give a one or two word answer or a "yes" or "no response;" it suggests that your desired answer is "yes."

(2) Advantages of Open Questions

The primary advantage of open questions is that they encourage witnesses to relate events in their own words.[8] Doing so tends to enhance a witness' credibility, because they foster the idea that the testimony is coming from the witness and not the lawyer.[9] Moreover, open questions typically allow you to elicit stories efficiently. With a single response to an open question, a witness can cover territory much more quickly than if you elicited the same testimony point by point with a series of closed questions. As factfinders tend to have relatively short attention spans, the responses to open questions maintain their interest

---

8. If an open question calls for a witness to relate a *series* of events, arguably it is subject to objection as "calling for a narrative." Such objections are sometimes sustained because they permit a witness to tell too much of a story in a single answer, thereby foreclosing opposing counsel from a reasonable opportunity to identify and object to inadmissible evidence. For a further discussion of this objection and how to overcome it, see Section 5 c *infra*.

9. See W. O'Barr, *Linguistic Evidence: Language, Power, and Strategy in the Courtroom* 76–83 (1982)(Studies on styles of courtroom speech indicate that narrative testimony, as opposed to fragmented testimony, enhances witness credibility because it makes a more favorable impression on the jury. Narrative testimony was considered to be long and full responses, whereas fragmented testimony was brief, incisive, nonelaborative responses.)

in your witnesses' stories.[10] Finally, in combination with closed questions, open questions allow you to emphasize evidence pertaining to arguments. When you probe important events by alternating open with closed questions, you can emphasize those events without drawing an objection that your questions have been "asked and answered."

(3) Advantages of Closed Questions

Direct examiners cannot live on bread and open questions alone. In response to open questions, witnesses frequently neglect to mention evidence to which they can properly testify and that you consider to be important.[11] Moreover, you may want to give additional emphasis to evidence that a witness does provide in response to an open question. As closed questions target specific evidence, they allow you both to elicit omitted testimony and emphasize important evidence.

(4) An Illustrative Example

The following sample dialogue illustrates the interplay of open and closed questions to elicit a chronological narrative and emphasize important evidence. Assume that you represent Mr. Haver, the plaintiff in a fraud case involving alleged misstatements about the plaintiff's need to redo all the plumbing in his house. You are conducting the plaintiff's direct examination. In this portion you want to tell the story of the defendant Lonnie Smith coming to plaintiff's home to talk with Haver about the condition of water in his house and to emphasize statements made by Smith during that visit about the condition of Haver's water. A portion of the questioning goes as follows:

1. Q. Mr. Haver, please tell us if Lonnie Smith, the woman seated at counsel table, came to your house last November?

2. A. Yes, that's her.

3. Q. Please tell us what happened when Ms. Smith came to your house?

4. A. She rang the doorbell and introduced herself. She said she was with 7–12 Water Company and that she would like to talk with us about a survey the company had done in our area. She said it wouldn't take but a few minutes. She went into the living room and sat down.

5. Q: What happened after Ms. Smith sat down?

---

10. S. Hamlin, *What Makes Juries Listen* 212–13 (1985)(using open-ended questions to stimulate direct and full witness responses helps the jury stay interested and follow the examination); see also J. Tanford, *The Trial Process: Law, Tactics and Ethics* 268–69 (2d ed. 1993).

11. In fact, witnesses who do include every bit of evidentiary detail in response to open questions tend to have little credibility, as it sounds as though the lawyer has thoroughly scripted their testimony.

6. A: She pulled out some papers that she said was the results of a sample analysis that her company had done on my neighborhood's tap water. She said that the tests indicated that my water had a dangerously high mineral content, and that to take care of it properly I should redo all the plumbing in the house.

7. Q: Did she mention any minerals in particular?

8. A: Yes; she talked about lead a lot.

9. Q: Please tell us what she said about lead.

10. A: She said the high lead content was very dangerous because recent government studies showed that it could cause brain problems and birth defects.

11. Q: Did she tell you what the lead content of your tap water was?

12. A: Yes, she said over ten parts per thousand.

13. Q: What if anything did she say about that?

14. A: She said that this was dangerously high, that anything over three parts per thousand was running a big risk of illness.

15. Q. After she discussed the amount of lead in your water and the dangers of lead, what happened next?

16. She brought out a . . . .

Analysis: Questions 3, 5 and 15 are open questions that keep Haver's story on a chronological track. Note that they allow him to describe events in his own words. Questions 9 and 13 are somewhat less open. They focus Haver on specific subjects, but allow him some freedom to use his own words. Questions 7 and 11 are "yes" or "no" questions. They focus Haver on specific evidence that you want to emphasize. Typically, you will use such a combination of questions to orchestrate direct examinations which flow chronologically and which emphasize the evidence supporting your arguments.

2. CONDUCTING PERSUASIVE DIRECT EXAMINATIONS

This section explains how to combine the general principles described above with other helpful questioning techniques to produce direct examinations that emphasize the arguments you prepared prior to trial. The section sets forth and analyzes two direct examinations, the first in a criminal and the second in a civil context.

a. *Illustrative Example No. 1: Criminal Case*

Assume that you are the prosecutor in State v. Holland.[12] You seek to prove that the defendant Roy Holland raped and murdered Maryann Matthews on August 15.

---

12. This hypothetical is drawn from the case of *People v. Rowland*, 4 Cal.4th 238, 14 Cal.Rptr.2d 377, 841 P.2d 897 (Sup. Ct. CA, 1992).

Your evidence will show that on the night Matthews was killed, she was a patron in the Wild Idle Lounge. The defendant Holland came into the lounge sometime around 9 P.M. and tried to strike up a conversation with Matthews, but she ignored him. Holland left the lounge around 10 P.M.; Matthews left around 10:30 P.M. You also have information from Bunny Haro, Matthews' friend, that Matthews was ill when she left the bar. The next morning Matthews' body was found in a deserted area, a victim of rape and strangulation. Additional evidence that you plan to offer tying Holland to the murder consists of fingerprints, bloodstains on Holland's clothing, and a statement Holland made to police officers.

Your information about Holland's probable defense comes from a statement he gave to the police shortly after he was arrested and "Mirandized." In it, he admitted that he had sexual intercourse with Matthews on the night she was killed, but claimed that it was consensual. He said that he met Matthews in the lounge, and they agreed to meet later that evening. He picked her up in his truck when she left the lounge. They drove out of town, went for a walk and made love. The blood on his clothing came from a cut that Matthews suffered when she fell and hit her arm on a rock while walking. He dropped Matthews off at her car and drove home. The last he saw of Matthews, she was getting into her car.

(1) The Prosecution's Argument

As the prosecutor, one of the factual propositions you want to prove is that Matthews did not have consensual intercourse with Holland.[13] An item of evidence that you have identified as highly probative of this proposition is Haro's statement that Matthews said that she was ill when she left the lounge on the night of her death.[14] Since the defense has not admitted that Matthews made this statement, you treat Haro's testimony as disputed.[15] Based on your discussions with Haro prior to trial, you have completed the following Credibility Checklist to support Haro's testimony:

Credibility Checklist for Disputed Testimony:

Haro says that on the night of her death Matthews said she wanted to go home early because she was ill.

---

13. In the real world a witness' story often encompasses several arguments directed toward a variety of factual propositions. However, in this case, the focus is on this single argument concerning a single factual proposition. When a witness' testimony pertains to a greater number of arguments and/or factual propositions, the process of preparing for and eliciting direct examinations remains the same as in the illustrations in this section.

14. Assume that even if the statement is hearsay, it would be admissible as a "declaration of state of mind." See Fed. R. Evid. 803(3).

15. You often need to take this position when you are uncertain about whether an adversary will challenge credibility, as well as when you think a factfinder is likely to debate credibility regardless of whether your adversary makes an issue of it.

Physical Ability: Haro was sitting only a few feet from Matthews when the statement was made. Matthews and Haro were the only ones at the table, and there was no background noise that prevented Haro from hearing what Matthews said.

Reason to Recall: When she found out the next day that Matthews was dead, Haro initially thought that Matthew's death might have been connected to her illness.

Of course, Haro's testimony that Matthews said she wanted to go home early because she was ill is circumstantial evidence of lack of consent to sexual intercourse. As a result, prior to trial you did more than use the Credibility Checklist to identify evidence bolstering your version of the dispute. Based on your discussions with Haro, you have also constructed the following argument that Matthew's statement, if true, indicates that she would not have had consensual intercourse with the defendant.

Item of Evidence: On the night of her death, Matthews told Haro that she wanted to go home early because she was ill.

Generalization No. 1: "People who say they are feeling ill often are genuinely ill."

Especially When . . . .

* They look ill.
* They sound ill.

Except When . . . .

* They are making up an excuse to leave their friend.

Your Response to "Except When" . . . . As Matthews and Haro often discussed people they were seeing socially, Matthews had no need to make up an excuse to conceal a plan to meet the defendant.

Generalization No. 2: "People who are genuinely ill do not engage in consensual sexual intercourse."

Especially when . . . .

* The other person is a stranger.
* They have to be at work early the next morning.
* They have a particularly heavy work schedule the next' day.

Therefore, Matthews did not have consensual intercourse with Holland on the night of her death.

This argument identifies the "especially when" evidence that you will want to emphasize during Haro's direct. In addition, the "except when" anticipates a possible defense argument: Matthews told Haro she was sick to conceal the fact she was leaving the bar to meet the defendant. Your response identifies additional evidence you may include in Haro's direct to undercut this potential defense argument.[16]

16. Sometimes, a judge will not allow you to offer evidence anticipating an adver- sary's rebuttal until after the rebuttal has been offered. You may have to wait until

Realizing that the defendant is also likely to dispute Haro's testimony that Matthews appeared to be ill, you also prepared a separate Credibility Checklist for that disputed testimony. This Checklist looked like this:

Credibility Checklist for Disputed Testimony of Haro That Matthews Appeared Ill

> *Physical Ability*: Haro was close enough to hear that Matthews sounded ill, and the bar was well enough lit to enable Haro to see Matthews' eyes and overall physical appearance.[17]

(2) Response to the Defendant's Arguments

So far you have considered only your side of the case. But as you know from Part I, you must also consider the defendant's likely arguments. So doing enables you to consider whether your direct of Haro should include evidence responding to any of those arguments.[18] Here, the defendant's most likely argument in response to Haro's testimony will be that Matthews was not genuinely ill on the night of her death, regardless of what she may have told Haro. That is, the defense is likely to argue that her claim of illness was an excuse to leave early and meet Holland. This argument depends on the defense attacking Haro's testimony about Matthews' looking and sounding ill. To respond to this argument, you prepared the *defense's* Credibility Checklist for Haro's disputed testimony Matthews appeared ill, *and* your potential response.

Defense Credibility Checklist for Disputed Testimony of Haro That Matthews Appeared Ill

> *Lack of Physical Ability*: The lounge was not brightly lit, and there was background noise from music and talking. Also, Haro had consumed alcohol before talking with Matthews. *Your Response*: Haro was sitting close enough to observe Matthews accurately and the alcohol did not affect her physical ability to observe.

> *Motive or Reason Not to Engage in Conduct*: As Matthews' close friend, Haro would not have been suspicious of Matthews' statement

---

redirect or even until after your adversary completes her case-in-chief. However, often such evidence is admitted during direct simply because the evidence is part of the story, or because opposing counsel fails to object. In addition, evidence which rebuts your adversary's case may be admissible on direct when it is also affirmative evidence to support your case. Here, for example, your direct of Haro could properly include evidence that she and Matthews commonly talked about people they were seeing socially because the evidence is relevant circumstantial evidence tending to prove that Matthews did not willingly meet with the defendant. 6 Wigmore, Evidence (Sections)

1869, 1873 (Chadbourn rev. 1976). See also Fed. R. Evid. 611(a).

17. Obviously, the credibility arguments that pertain to Haro's testimony that Matthews said that she was sick also pertain to this testimony. You need not repeat those arguments on this Checklist.

18. You will not automatically include evidence supporting your responding arguments in a direct examination. For example, so doing may reveal a weakness in your case that the adversary had not previously recognized. For a discussion of the strategic considerations that can help you decide when to include evidence supporting your responding arguments in a witness' direct examination, see Sec. 8 *infra*.

and thus Haro had no reason to look closely for symptoms to confirm Matthews' statement. *Your Response*: Haro knew that Matthews had been ill recently and observed Matthew's appearance closely because she was concerned about her health.

(3) Eliciting Haro's Direct Examination

The foregoing arguments identify the evidence which is the backbone of Bunny Haro's direct examination. Following the general principles of direct examination discussed above, your direct examination of Bunny Haro may go as follows:

1. Q: Ms. Haro, what is your occupation?

2. A: I'm the manager of the Top Value hardware store over in Byron.

3. Q: How long have you been employed there?

4. A: For about 11 years, the last four as manager.

5. Q: Can you briefly describe your duties as manager?

6. A: I'm in charge of just about everything. I have 10 people working for me, and I do all the hiring and work schedules. I also do all the regular and special ordering and take care of any customer complaints about the merchandise.

7. Q: Ms. Haro, you were in the Wild Idle Lounge on the evening of August 15, is that right?

8. A: Yes, I was.

9. Q: What time did you arrive there, approximately?

10. A: I think it was right around 8:15.

11. Q: Did you see Maryann Matthews in the lounge that same evening?

12. A: Yes, she was already there when I got there.

13. Q: Did you think that Ms. Matthews would be at the lounge that night?

14. A: I figured she'd probably be there because I knew it was her night off.

15. Q: Did you two often meet at the Wild Idle?

16. A: Yes. It was always a nice place where we felt comfortable and could meet friends and relax.

17. Q: Did you see the defendant, Mr. Holland, in the lounge on that evening?

18. A: I didn't notice him when I first got there, but I did see him later.

19. Q: How is it that you noticed him?

20. A: It's just that most of the people are pretty regular customers, and he was someone I'd never seen before.

21.   Q: Did you speak to the defendant?

22.   A: Not really. He walked by me once shortly after I got there and said "hi" or something like that, that's about it.

23.   Q: Did you talk to Ms. Matthews at all on that evening?

24.   A: Not till just before she left. I was playing darts with some friends, and I hadn't really sat down until around 10:00.

25.   Q: Let's talk about what happened at around 10:00. Did you have a conversation with Ms. Matthews at about that time?

26.   A: Sometime around then, yes.

27.   Q: Ms. Haro, can you tell us where in the lounge your conversation with Ms. Matthews took place?

28.   A: Well, as I said, I had just finished playing darts, so I was sitting at a table in the little raised part of the lounge off to the left of the darts.

29.   Q: Do you recognize the diagram over there which has previously been marked State's Exhibit 5?

30.   A: Yes, that's the inside of the lounge.

31.   Q: Could you please approach the diagram and place the letter "H" at the table where you were sitting at the time Ms. Matthews spoke with you.

32.   A: All right.

33.   Q: And while you are there, could you place an "M" to indicate where Ms. Matthews was sitting?

34.   A: Yes.

35.   Q: Actually, let me clarify an assumption I may have made. Was Ms. Matthews seated or standing when she spoke to you?

36.   A: She sat down at the table with me.

37.   Q: Ms. Haro, did you have any trouble hearing what Ms. Matthews told you during this conversation?

38.   A: None whatsoever.

39.   Q: You testified that she came to your table and sat down. How far from you was she?

40.   A: Oh, not too far. I guess like from me to him (indicating the court reporter).

41.   Q: For the record, the witness has indicated a distance of about three to four feet.

42.   Q: Was there anyone else sitting with you at the table?

43.   A: No. Just the two of us.

44.   Q: What was the noise level in the lounge at the time?

45. A: The jukebox was on and I think a couple of people were dancing, but it wasn't so loud that we couldn't hear each other.

46. Q: Was there anything about your own physical condition which made it difficult for you to understand or remember what she said to you?

47. A: No, not a thing.

48. Q: Had you had anything to drink that night?

49. A: Just a couple of beers while I was playing darts, light alcohol ones at that.

50. Q: Had the drinks affected you in any way?

51. A: Not a bit. I'd been snacking on pretzels and popcorn too, and the light beers in no way affected me.

52. Q: All right, please tell us as much as you can about the conversation you had with her.

53. A: Well, after I sat down she walked over and said, "what's up" or something like that. She didn't look well. She said that she was feeling really sick, that she had a headache and she had to go home because she had a busy day at work the next day and had to be there early.

54. Q: Now, when she spoke to you, can you remember exactly what she said about her headache?

55. A: I think she said that she felt like her head was splitting open.

56. Q: You said that she mentioned something about a busy day at work the next day. What did she say about that?

57. A: Maryann worked with her mom at the Ranch House restaurant. She said that the next day was a really bad day to feel sick because her mom was not going to be there and she'd have to do all the cooking.

58. Q: What meals did the Ranch House serve, if you know?

59. A: Breakfast, lunch and dinner.

60. Q: What specifically did she say about when she'd be starting work the next day?

61. A: She said she had to be in by 6 A.M. And she was dreading getting up that early because she didn't usually start work until 10 A.M.

62. Q: After Ms. Matthews told you she'd have to do all the cooking the next day, what happened?

63. A: I said something like, "Luv, it sounds like you've got a big day ahead of you tomorrow. You should go home and get some sleep. I'll call you tomorrow and see how you're feeling." Then she told me that something disturbing had

come up at work that she wanted to get my opinion on, but that it could wait. After that she left.

64. Q: When you had this conversation with Ms. Matthews did you think that she was ill?

65. A: Yes. I did.

66. Q: Would you tell us what, if anything, about her appearance made you think she was ill?

67. A: Well, even in the lounge light I could see that she was pale, and her eyes looked watery and droopy. And she sounded sick. Her voice was weak and husky.

68. Q: How far away from her were you when you noticed that she looked and sounded ill?

69. A: I was sitting only a couple of feet away from her at the table.

70. Q: You testified that Ms. Matthews looked pale and sounded ill. Did the symptoms you noticed that night concern you in any way?

71. A: Yes.

72. Q: Why?

73. A: Because I knew she'd just gotten over a terrible case of the flu a couple of weeks earlier. When I saw how she looked I was afraid that she might be having a relapse.

74. Q: Aside from what you've already told us, did anything else happen to lead you to believe that she was feeling ill?

75. A: Yes, she left early. Ordinarily we stay and listen to music until around midnight, but that night she left right after she talked to me.

76. Q: Ms. Haro, is there any particular reason that you can remember that it was this particular night that Ms. Matthews was ill?

77. A: I remember it because when I found out she had died, at first I thought it was somehow connected to how sick she had been the night before.

78. Q: Did Ms. Matthews ever mention the name of Roy Holland to you that night?

79. A: No.

80. Q: Did she indicate in any way that she had met someone that night?

81. A: No.

82. Q: Did she say she was going to see someone after she left the lounge?

83. A: No.

84. Q: Prior to that night, had you and Ms. Matthews discussed people you were seeing socially?

85. A: Sure. If we met someone interesting we'd almost always talk to each other about him.

86. Q: Just to conclude, what time was it that Ms. Matthews left the lounge that evening?

87. A: Just a little after 10, right after talking to me.

88. Q: Did you ever see your friend again?

89. A: No.

(4) Transcript Analysis

(a) The Questioning Elicits a Selective, Chronological Story

Haro's testimony provides an overall chronology of events. The story begins when she arrived at the lounge (Nos. 7–10), refers briefly to events that occurred before she spoke to Matthews (Nos. 17–24), sets the scene for the important conversation between the friends (Nos. 25–51), recounts the conversation, Matthews' departure from the lounge, and Haro's opinions and concerns about Matthews' health (Nos. 51–75).

Yet, the story is far from a "complete" story of Haro's activities on that evening. For example, you pass over the details of the dart game because they have nothing to do with your argument.

At the same time, you occasionally depart from chronology. For example, after Haro arrives at the lounge, you offer testimony that she and Matthews had met there previously (Nos. 15–16). You also show that the friends' common past practice was to discuss interesting social acquaintances. (Nos. 84–85) But these digressions are minor, and are unlikely to interfere with the factfinder's understanding of what happened.

(b) The Questioning Combines Open and Closed Questions

As is common, you utilize different forms of questions when eliciting Haro's testimony. For example, No. 5 is an open question permitting Haro to expand on her duties as manager. Numbers 52, 56 and 60 are also open questions, encouraging Haro to use her own words to describe the friends' conversation.

Many of the questions are of the closed variety. For instance, Nos. 1 and 3 are closed questions pertaining to personal background; Nos. 37 and 42 help you to set the scene for the conversation; and Nos. 78 and 80 emphasize Matthews' apparent lack of contact with Holland. A number of the other questions are also closed; you might identify them and consider their role in developing the evidence relating to your argument.

Even leading questions play a role, albeit a small one, in the direct. Number 7 is a permissible leading question because it is preliminary, as there is no dispute that Haro was in fact in the lounge on the night of the murder.

(c) The Questioning Emphasizes Evidence Supporting Your Arguments

The story you elicited is weighted to emphasize your arguments that Haro did hear Matthews say that she was ill, and that Matthews was genuinely ill and thus unlikely to engage in consensual sexual intercourse.

To demonstrate that Haro's testimony about Matthews' statement that she was ill is accurate, you emphasize Haro's ability to hear what Matthews said (Nos. 31–51), and establish the reason that she can accurately remember the events of that evening (Nos. 70–77).

The direct also incorporates the evidence that Matthews was genuinely ill (Nos. 52–55; 62–71; 74–75).[19]

The direct also emphasizes evidence suggesting that Matthews was unlikely to have engaged in consensual sexual intercourse with Holland that night (Nos. 19–20; 52–53; 56–61; 78–83).[20] Throughout the examination, your emphasis is derived principally, albeit not exclusively, from closed questions. (For example see Nos. 37, 39, 42, 44, 46, 48, 50.)

As you can see, communicating arguments sometimes requires that you depart slightly from chronology. Evidence that Matthews had been ill two weeks earlier (Nos. 72–73) would be meaningless if elicited in its proper chronological sequence, at the outset of Haro's testimony.[21]

(d) Additional Story Telling Techniques

As illustrated in the above transcript, a persuasive direct examination typically relies on questioning techniques in addition to those described by the three basic principles of direct examination. The following sub-sections explore these additional techniques.

(1) *"Introduce" the Witness.* At the outset you introduce Haro by eliciting testimony about her personal background. (Nos. 1–6) While such testimony is not strictly relevant, judges commonly allow brief personal testimony to give a witness a chance to settle in and the factfinder a chance to learn a little bit about the witness.[22] Keep it short; too much introduction can quickly become improper character

---

19. Note that Haro can offer her opinion that Matthews was ill, as the opinion is based on personal knowledge and everyday experience. See Fed. R. Evid. 701.

20. Haro would probably not be permitted to testify to an opinion that Matthews did not willingly engage in sexual intercourse. She is in no better position than the factfinder to draw this inference. See Fed. R. Evid. 701.

21. For a more detailed discussion of questioning techniques that help you emphasize your arguments, see Sec. 3 *infra*.

22. Personal background questioning will be far more extensive if you have to qualify a witness as an expert. See Chapter 15.

evidence. Moreover, a factfinder's attention is often strongest at the outset of a witness' testimony and you therefore want to move quickly to the heart of a direct.[23]

(2) *Set the Scene.* To make her story more concrete and vivid, and therefore more memorable, you use a number of scene setting questions as you move Haro through her story. Numbers 7–16 provide evidence that sets the scene for where the events took place, and Numbers 27–51 set the scene for the critical conversation.[24]

As a general rule, include scene-setting testimony whenever the scene of events changes. For example, assume that you want to offer evidence that a couple of minutes after Matthews left the bar, Haro went out to make sure Matthews was all right. You should preface questions about what happened by asking scene-setting questions such as the time of the second meeting, its physical location and the presence of any other persons.

(3) *Include Evidence Supporting Silent Arguments.* Finally, note that your questioning elicits testimony supporting a silent argument.[25] Nos. 56–61, which emphasize evidence indicating that Matthews would be unlikely to engage in consensual sex, also depict her as a hard working person with strong ties to her mother. As such, the story portrays the victim as an individual toward whom the factfinder should feel sympathy.

b. Illustrative Example # 2: Civil Case

For a second illustration of direct examination questioning techniques, assume that you represent defendant Marilyn Bollinger, who sold a house to plaintiff Don Evans. Evans has sued your client for fraudulent concealment, claiming that Bollinger intentionally neglected to disclose that the house had a leaky roof.

Your client tells you that her house had a leak in the roof the first week in January, and she had the roof patched by Dave Lopez of Elegant Roofing. Ms. Bollinger had bought the house new 15 years earlier, and had never previously had trouble with the roof. After Lopez patched it, the roof again leaked a little bit during a very heavy rainstorm in the middle of February. After the leak in mid-February, Bollinger called Elegant Roofing, but discovered it had gone out of business. The roof did not leak during several rainy days after mid-February. After receiving a large inheritance from an aunt in March, Bollinger decided to sell the house and move into a larger one. She put the house on the market on the first of April. Since she was in no hurry to sell the house she did not use a real estate broker.

---

23. Personal background questioning beyond the minimum allowable is objectionable as "irrelevant" or "improper character evidence."

24. As part of scene-setting, you might offer a photograph or other illustrative exhibit.

25. To review silent arguments, see Chapter 9.

During April and May, Bollinger met with a couple of people who seemed interested in the house, but neither made an offer to buy it. Evans, who ultimately purchased the house, visited it twice in June and made an offer to purchase it during his second visit. During the second visit, Bollinger told Evans about the repair and subsequent leak in the roof, but assured him that the house was otherwise in excellent condition. Evans agreed to buy the house, contingent on securing a loan and the house receiving a favorable report from Evans' inspector. These conditions were met, and Evans completed the purchase and moved in.

When you took Evans' deposition, he stated that he visited the house twice in June before purchasing it in July. He asked your client whether she had had any problems with the house, and she replied that she had not and that the house was in excellent condition. She never mentioned any problems with the roof. Evans then agreed to buy the house, subject to the two conditions mentioned above. The inspector that Evans hired gave the house a "clean bill of health," so Evans completed the purchase and moved in. Four months later, during the season's first heavy rain in November, water came pouring into the second bedroom, the ceiling collapsed and Evans had to put a new roof on the house. The lawsuit followed, seeking actual and punitive damages for Bollinger's fraudulent concealment of the problems with the roof.

(1) Bollinger's Arguments

One of the crucial factual propositions the defendant will attempt to prove in this case is:

"During Evans' second visit to the house, Bollinger told Evans that the roof had leaked after an earlier repair."

This proposition, if proven, will negate the element of "Concealment" in plaintiff's fraudulent concealment claim. After listing the evidence supporting this proposition, you decided on the following as an item of highly probative undisputed evidence:

During Evans' second visit to the house, he told Bollinger that Evans intended to hire an inspector to check out the house before he agreed to purchase it.

Based on the information in your file, you constructed the following argument based on this evidence:

Undisputed Item of Evidence: During Evans' second visit to the house, he told Bollinger that he intended to hire an inspector to check out the house before he agreed to purchase it.

Generalization: Sellers who are told by a prospective buyer that the buyer intends to have the house inspected prior to purchase often disclose problems with the roof to the prospective buyer.

Especially when:

- They believe the inspector will recognize the problems during the inspection.

- They want to deal fairly with the prospective buyer.

Except when:

- They think an inspection by the prospective buyer relieves them of any obligation to disclose problems with the roof.

Therefore, Bollinger told Evans that the roof had leaked after an earlier repair.

In addition to the above evidence tending to prove Bollinger's factual proposition, Bollinger asserts that she told Evans about the leaky roof problem. This is direct evidence, as no inference is necessary to move from the evidence to the factual proposition Bollinger is attempting to prove ("told Evans that roof leaked after earlier repair"). The evidence is of course disputed: Evans claims that Bollinger said nothing about the roof. With the aid of the Credibility Checklist you produced the following arguments that Bollinger's testimony is accurate:

Credibility Checklist for Disputed Testimony: Bollinger told Evans that the roof leaked after an earlier repair.

Reason or Motive To Engage in Disputed Behavior: Bollinger was unsure about whether the leaky roof problem had been fixed, and felt compelled to disclose it.[26]

Consistency of Disputed Behavior With Other Witnesses and Documents: Bollinger met with two other prospective purchasers, Bob Hatfield and Julie Montague, and they will testify that she told them about the leaky roof problem.

Reason To Recall Disputed Behavior: Bollinger recalls talking about the leaky roof problem with Evans because it had been raining heavily earlier that day and she walked into the spare bedroom to make sure the ceiling was dry.

(2) Response to Plaintiff Evans' Arguments

To this point, you have prepared your side of the case. But again, you must also identify Evans' likely arguments in order to consider whether your direct of Bollinger should include evidence responding to any of them.[27] Here, for example, assume that you think it likely that Evans' strongest argument will be that the undisputed evidence that the

---

26. Note that in this section of the Checklist you could also have included the following motive or reason: "Bollinger knew that Evans intended to have the house inspected, and assumed that the inspector would see that the roof had been recently patched. She disclosed the problem in advance so that Evans wouldn't think that she was trying to conceal problems with the house and walk away from the deal." But since you have already developed an explicit argument to establish this motive based on an undisputed item of evidence, you need not include that motive in the Checklist.

27. Remember, you will not necessarily include evidence supporting all of your responding arguments in a direct examination. See Sec. 8 *infra*.

roof was patched in January and leaked in February proves that she did not mention the roof problems to Evans prior to the sale. Evans' argument would probably go something like this:

Undisputed Item of Evidence: Bollinger knew that the roof was patched in January and leaked in February.

Generalization # 1: Sellers who know that a roof has leaked one month after being patched sometimes think that the house needs a new roof.

    Especially when:

- They think the house might need a new roof before being patched.
- They know that the roof is 15 years old.

    Except when:

- The roof does not leak in subsequent rains.
- A roofer who has looked at the roof has not suggested that the roof needs replacing.

Generalization # 2: Sellers who think that a house needs a new roof sometimes don't tell a prospective purchaser about repairs to or problems with the roof.

    Especially when:

- They don't want the prospective purchaser's inspector to examine the roof carefully.
- They don't want to pay for a new roof before selling the house.

Therefore, Bollinger did not tell Evans that the roof had leaked after an earlier repair.

    In addition, using the Credibility Checklist, you identified other arguments that you think Evans' attorney is likely to make that Bollinger did *not* tell Evans about the problems with the roof, and your potential responses to those arguments.[28]

    Adversary's Credibility Checklist for Disputed Testimony: Bollinger did *not* tell Evans that the roof leaked after an earlier repair.

    Reason or Motive To Engage in Disputed Behavior:

        (a) Bollinger was anxious to close the sale with Evans because Bollinger had been unable to sell the house for over two months, and withheld the information about the roof to make sure the sale would go through. *Your responding argument:* Bollinger was not anxious to sell the house because her recent inheritance made her financially secure and she expected it would take a long time to sell the house when she decided not to use a real estate broker.

        (b) Bollinger mentioned the roof to other prospective purchasers and they decided not to buy the house. Consequently, she decided not to mention it to Evans so the sale would go through.

---

28. Because this dispute relates to direct evidence of a crucial factual proposition, Evans attorney will have to attack Bollinger's version of the dispute.

Your responding argument: She doesn't know why the other prospective purchasers decided not to buy the house.

Consistency of Disputed Behavior With Other Witnesses and Documents: When the sale of the house closed, Bollinger signed a document indicating that the house "had no defects in the plumbing, floors, roof...." *Your responding argument:* Bollinger did not consider the condition of the roof a "defect" and she had already told Evans about the leaky roof problem.

(3) Eliciting Bollinger's Direct Examination

Once again, the arguments you have prepared will form the backbone of your direct examination. Here, your direct of Bollinger might go as follows: [29]

1.   Q: Ms. Bollinger, what is your occupation?

2.   A: I'm a Senior Supervising Accountant with the firm of Ernst and Olde.

3.   Q: How long have you been employed there?

4.   A: For a little over 19 years.

5.   Q: Can you please briefly describe your job duties?

6.   A: I oversee the training and review the work of all accountants who have been with the firm for two years or less. I also do accounting for a few clients that have been with me for a long time.

7.   Q: Ms. Bollinger, do you know the plaintiff, Don Evans?

8.   A: Of course. He bought my house a year ago last July.

9.   Q: This is the house at 1520 Sawyer Street?

10.   A: That's correct.

11.   Q: Ms. Bollinger, did you hear the plaintiff testify that he had problems with the roof on the house after you sold it to him?

12.   A: Yes, I did.

13.   Q: Did you say anything to him about the roof before you sold him the house?

14.   A: I sure did.

15.   Q: What did you tell him about the roof?

16.   A: I told him that the roof had leaked in January and that I'd hired a roofing company and had it patched. I told him that I thought it was OK, but that it had leaked a bit after a very heavy rain.

---

29. For purposes of illustration, we assume that the parties' arguments are limited to those described in the text. Recall that in a more complex case a direct may include evidence relating to many more arguments, but your process of preparation will be the same.

17. Q: Ms. Bollinger, let's go back to the time before you sold the house. When did you first have a problem with your roof?

18. A: I had a leak in the roof in early January about six months before I sold the house to Mr. Evans.

19. Q: When you say a leak, what do you mean?

20. A: I had some water dripping in through the ceiling in a corner of the spare bedroom.

21. Q: What did you do when you noticed the leak?

22. A: I called a roofing company, Elegant Roofing, and someone from the company came out the next day and repaired the roof.

23. Q: Do you remember who did the repair?

24. A: It was a guy named Dave Lopez. I checked it on the receipt.

25. Q: Did Mr. Lopez tell you anything when he repaired the roof?

26. A: He just said he'd found the place where the leak was, and that he'd patched it. He told me to call again if I still had a problem.

27. Q: Did Mr. Lopez say anything about your needing a new roof?

28. A: No, he didn't say anything at all about that. He just said he'd patched the leak and that should take care of the problem.

29. Q: And what did you pay for this repair?

30. A: It cost me $1000.

31. Q: What then happened?

32. A: Well, there were some heavy rains about a month later, in mid-February. After the first rainy day, I came home to find a small drip in the spare bedroom. I immediately tried to call Elegant Roofing, but found that the phone number had been disconnected.

33. Q: Did you do anything else to try to take care of the problem?

34. A: No, not really.

35. Q: Why not?

36. A: We had several days of rain in February and into March, and after that first time the ceiling didn't drip again. So I thought the roof was probably OK.

37. Q: When did you decide to sell the house?

38. A: I really decided to sell about a year before I did, when I found out I was to receive a fairly large inheritance from an aunt and wanted to move to a larger house. But I

didn't put it on the market until the beginning of April, after I actually received the money.

39. Q: Did you use a real estate broker?

40. A: No.

41. Q: And why not?

42. A: I wasn't really in a hurry to sell. I didn't have a new place picked out yet, and I didn't want to be pressured by a broker to sell.

43. Q: After you put it on the market, what happened?

44. A: Quite a few people came by, but I only had serious discussions with three of them.

45. Q: Who were the people you had serious discussions with?

46. A: With Mr. Evans, of course. And before that, there was a Bob Hatfield and a Julie Montague.

47. Q: When did you first meet with the plaintiff?

48. A: I think I met with him the first time in early June.

49. Q: Where did this meeting take place?

50. A: We met at the house. I was having an open house, and he came by.

51. Q: Please tell us what happened at this first meeting.

52. A: I remember he was the only person looking at the time. We walked through the house together, and he asked me things like how long I'd lived in the house, how old the house was, why I was selling, and what the neighborhood and the schools were like.

53. Q: How long did the meeting last?

54. A: Not long, really. I'd say about 15–20 minutes.

55. Q: Did he offer to buy the house at that time?

56. A: Oh, no. He said he was just starting to look, getting an idea of prices and different neighborhoods and what houses were available.

57. Q: Did you discuss the price of the house?

58. A: A little bit. I had it advertised at $220,000. He wanted to know if the price was negotiable, and whether I was willing to take back a second mortgage.

59. Q: What was your response?

60. A: I said that I thought the price was a fair one, and that I wanted to get something in that range, but that of course I'd consider any reasonable offer. I also told him that I didn't necessarily have to have an all-cash deal, and under the right circumstances I'd take a second.

61. Q: Was there any discussion during this meeting of the leaky roof problems you had had?

62. A: No, I don't think so.

63. Q: And why is that?

64. A: We just never got down to specific details at that time. Mr. Evans said he was interested in things like yard space, number of bathrooms and bedrooms, and the size of the kitchen. I had given him an information sheet describing the features of the house, and he said he just wanted to look at the general layout. At that time I didn't know if he was a serious purchaser.

65. Q: Did you have a second meeting with Mr. Evans?

66. A: Yes.

67. Q: And when did this meeting occur?

68. A: Between two and three weeks later. I'm not sure of the date, but I'm pretty sure it was still in June.

69. Q: How did this meeting come about?

70. A: Mr. Evans called me at my office wanting to know if the house was still on the market. I said it was. He told me that he'd seen a lot of houses and that he was very interested in mine, and asked if we could get together. We made an appointment for the next evening.

71. Q: Please tell us what happened during this second meeting.

72. A: We walked through the house again. He said he really liked it and was interested in buying it. I said that was great, because I had enjoyed living there and he seemed to really like it too.

73. Q: After he said he was interested in buying the house, what happened?

74. A: We sat down in the kitchen and started to talk about the price. We eventually agreed on a price of $205,000. The sale was contingent on his getting a loan for $175,000, and I agreed to take a second for the rest.

75. Q: After you agreed on the price, what happened?

76. A: He said he wanted to have his inspector examine the house before the deal could be final.

77. Q: Can you tell us in more detail what was said about the inspector.

78. A: I remember him saying that his sister-in-law had told him that it was important to have the house inspected. I told him that was a good idea, and it would be no problem at all. I also told him that the neighbors to the right of me had moved in about six months earlier and were very happy with the person who'd inspected their house, and I offered to find out that person's name. He said that wasn't necessary, that he had a friend who would do it, and that his friend could come by within the week. I said

that was fine, to let me know and I'd make arrangements for the inspector to have access to the house.

79. Q: After the discussion about the inspector, what happened?

80. A: He asked me about any problems I'd had with the house. I told him that basically the house was in excellent condition—a few stopped up drains now and again but nothing major. I also told him that I'd had a problem with the roof, but that I was pretty sure it was fixed.

81. Q: To the best of your recollection, what was said about the roof?

82. A: I said that back in January I'd had a leak in the roof above the spare bedroom. I told him that I'd gotten the roof patched right away and that I thought it was OK. I mentioned that it hadn't leaked when it rained the last few months, though I had had a small drip during a very heavy rain in February just after the roof had been patched.

83. Q: After you told him about the roof, did Mr. Evans reply in any way?

84. A: Yes, he said that it didn't sound like a big problem, that he'd get it checked out.

85. Q: If you thought the roof had been fixed, why did you mention it to Mr. Evans?

86. A: For one thing, I wasn't absolutely positive that the leak had been taken care of so I thought it was only fair to mention it to him. Also, I figured the inspector would recognize that a patch had recently been put on the roof, and even assuming everything was OK I didn't want Mr. Evans thinking I was trying to hide something from him.

87. Q: Ms. Bollinger, is there any reason in particular you can recall telling Mr. Evans about the roof?

88. A: Yes, because it had been raining heavily earlier that day and I walked into the spare bedroom to make sure the ceiling was dry.

80. Q. You mentioned earlier that you thought that Bob Hatfield and Julie Montague were serious purchasers. Did you also discuss the roof with them?

90. A: I'm sure I mentioned it to them because I wanted to be upfront with everyone.

91. Q: What did you say to them, as best you can recall?

92. A: I told them the same thing I told Mr. Evans, that the roof had leaked at one time and that I'd had it patched, and that I thought the problem had been taken care of but I couldn't be sure.

93. Q: Did Mr. Hatfield and Ms. Montague ever tell you why they did not buy the house?

94. A: No, they never told me.

95. Q: Did Mr. Evans ultimately send an inspector to your house?

96: (Remainder of direct examination, dealing primarily with the inspection, the details of the closing and contacts with Evans after sale of the house omitted)

Again, examine this transcript with particular attention to how successfully it carries out the three basic principles of direct examination.

(a) The Questioning Elicits a Selective Story With a Clear Chronology

Bollinger's story generally emerges chronologically. Beginning with No. 18, Bollinger describes the leaky roof problem which began in January and continued into March (Nos. 18–36). She then recounts her actions in April of putting the house on the market and her subsequent contacts with prospective purchasers other than plaintiff. (Nos. 37–46.) Next she discusses her initial contact with plaintiff in June and the events leading up to Evans' purchase of the house, describing her first and then her second meeting with Evans (Nos. 47–88). In the omitted final portion of Bollinger's direct, she testifies to the visit by Evans' inspector, the transfer of the property to Evans and his ensuing complaints. (See Nos. 95–96)

Despite the direct's overall chronological format, you do occasionally depart from it. For example, following brief background testimony, the story starts somewhere in the middle with Bollinger's testimony that she told Evans about the leaky roof prior to the sale of the house (Nos. 11–16). Since the factfinder has already heard the plaintiff's story that nothing was said about the roof, pulling this important testimony out of the chronology tends to emphasize Bollinger's contradictory claim.[30]

Finally, note that Bollinger's story is a selective one. For example, it does not include everything that occurred during the first meeting between Evans and Bollinger. For instance, there is no description of everything that occurred when the parties walked through the house. (See Nos. 51–54) This kind of selectivity is also present with respect to the second meeting. (See Nos. 71–73.) Again, including all details would tend to obscure the evidence you wish to emphasize.

(b) The Questioning Combines Open and Closed Questions

You again rely on different forms of questions when eliciting Bollinger's testimony. For example, No. 5 is an open question permitting Bollinger to describe her duties as an accountant. Among the numerous

---

30. You further emphasize this testimony by eliciting it again in its proper chronological sequence (Nos. 78–82). Given the importance of the testimony and the recital of the intervening events, a judge is unlikely to prevent you from eliciting the information twice.

other fairly open questions, No. 41 invites Bollinger to describe why she chose not to employ a broker, No. 51 asks her to describe the first meeting, No. 81 asks her to relate what she told Evans about the roof, and No. 85 seeks the reason for her telling him about a possible roof problem. Such questions ensure that testimony pertinent to your arguments comes first from the witness, not from your questions.

Nevertheless, you also rely on closed questions throughout the testimony. You often use closed questions to elicit details that Bollinger neglects to mention in response to an open question. Here, for example, Nos. 53, 55, and 57 elicit additional details about the first meeting. And, you often employ closed questions to elicit specific evidence pertaining to an argument (See for example Nos. 13, 39, 83 and 89).

Leading questions figure hardly at all in this example. However, No. 9 asserts that the house that Bollinger is talking about is the one on Sawyer Street, a matter not in dispute.

(c) The Questioning Emphasizes Evidence Supporting Your Arguments

Bollinger's story emphasizes the two crucial items of evidence supporting your argument that she told Evans that the roof had previously leaked.

As you recall, one of your crucial items is that Bollinger knew that the house was to be inspected prior to the sale. You emphasize for example Bollinger's knowledge of this through an open question encouraging her to describe in detail what the parties said about the inspector (No. 77). You also later elicit the "especially whens" tying Bollinger's awareness of the inspection to her disclosure of the potential roof problem (No. 85).

The direct also includes the evidence you identified when you completed the Credibility Checklist to support the direct evidence that Bollinger told Evans about the roof problem. She testifies that she wanted to be upfront with all prospective purchasers (No.90) and that she told others about the problem (Nos. 89–90), and indicates how it is she can specifically remember telling Evans about the roof (Nos. 87–88).

The direct also emphasizes some of the evidence you identified when using the Credibility Checklist to plan your responses to Evans' likely credibility arguments. For instance, you elicit testimony that Bollinger did not employ a real estate broker because she was in no hurry to sell (Nos. 41–42), and that she was unaware of why neither Hatfield nor Montague purchased the house (Nos.93–94).[31]

You also achieve emphasis by at times deviating from a strict chronological presentation. Note, for example, that the testimony that

---

31. For a more detailed discussion of questioning techniques that help you em- phasize your arguments, see Sec. 3 *infra*.

Bollinger also told earlier prospective purchasers about the leaky roof emerges in the context of her conversation on this subject with Evans even though Bollinger made those statements before she ever met Evans. (Nos. 86–92). So doing tends to emphasize your credibility argument that Bollinger dealt consistently with all prospective buyers. At the same time, this departure probably does not muddle the overall chronology since the testimony in general moves in clear temporal order.

(d) Additional Story Telling Techniques

In eliciting a clear story that emphasized the arguments you intended to make, you again used the additional story telling techniques stressed above. Through Nos. 1–6 you introduced your witness by briefly covering her professional background. And once again you use scene-setting testimony to increase the story's clarity by providing the factfinder with a visual image of events. Here for example, Nos. 47 and 49 set the scene for the first meeting between Bollinger and Evans and Nos. 65–70 set the scene for the critically important second meeting.

3. ADDITIONAL TECHNIQUES FOR EMPHASIZING EVIDENCE

Focusing direct on evidence supporting your arguments is a primary method of emphasizing important testimony. The subsections below explore additional emphasis techniques.

a. Incorporate Important Evidence Into Subsequent Questions

A common emphasis technique involves incorporating evidence from a previous answer into a subsequent question. For example, assume that Mr. Dennis is charged with second degree murder. The State alleges that Dennis drove a car while drunk, and struck and killed a pedestrian. As prosecutor you call Larry Wendt, a passerby who witnessed the collision. On direct, Wendt testifies that after the accident, he walked over to the defendant's car and noticed a bottle of whiskey on the front seat. To emphasize Wendt's testimony about the whiskey, the direct continues as follows:

1. Q: You say you saw a bottle of whiskey on the front seat of the car. What made you think it was whiskey?

2. A: It was a clear bottle and the liquid inside was the color of whiskey, and the car smelled of whiskey.

3. Q: When you first saw the whiskey bottle in the defendant's car, where were you standing?

4. A: I was right next to the window on the passenger's side of the car.

5. Q: Was this whiskey bottle on the driver's side of the front seat of the defendant's car?

  6.   A: Yes, it was.

  7.   Q: How big was the bottle of whiskey you saw in the defendant's car?

  8.   A: It looked like it was a quart bottle.

  9.   Q: After you saw the whiskey bottle in the defendant's car what did you do?

10.   A.   I went. . . .

Once Wendt testifies to seeing the whiskey, you emphasize that evidence by incorporating it into your subsequent questions. The technique allows the factfinder to hear about the whiskey bottle evidence several times, and reduces the possibility the factfinder will "miss" this important evidence if he or she is momentarily inattentive during the direct.[32] But take care not to overgild the lily. If you persist in repeating testimony, the factfinder may resent what is seen as an implication either that they are not paying attention to the testimony or are not smart enough to understand it.

b. *Front Load the Most Probative Evidence*

A factfinder's attention is typically at its height when you begin a witness' examination. Therefore you will often want to begin a direct by quickly highlighting a witness' most significant testimony. For example, assume that you represent a tenant seeking to establish that his apartment was uninhabitable. One of your witnesses is a building inspector who inspected the apartment on three separate occasions and found housing code violations each time. After introducing the witness and establishing that she is a building inspector, you continue as follows:

  1.   Q: Now, did you inspect Apartment 3 at 11359 Bolas Street during the months of February and March of this year?

  2.   A: I did, three different times.

  3.   Q: And did you find violations of the building code during those inspections?

  4.   A: Yes, I did.

  5.   Q: Please briefly summarize the violations you found.

  6.   A: All right. They consisted of an unvented heater, a cockroach infestation and no hot water.

  7.   Q: Did you notify the owner, Leona Trump, of these violations?

  8.   A: Yes, I did.

---

32. If you return to *Evans v. Bollinger* and *State v. Holland*, you can see other examples of this incorporation technique. For instance, Nos. 75–80 *in Evans* illustrate incorporating evidence into subsequent questions with respect to evidence that Evans told Bollinger that Evans wanted to have the house inspected. Nos. 63–75 in *Holland* illustrate the technique with respect to evidence that Matthews was ill when she left the bar.

9. Q: OK. Now, I'd like to take you back to the first time you visited the apartment. When was that?

10. A: . . . .

Here, you emphasize the witness' key evidence at the outset of the direct. Because you limit the witness to a brief summary of her observations, you will be able to elicit the information again as you go through her chronology.

c. Limit Stories of Redundant Witnesses

When previous testimony has already made a story clear, you can often emphasize important evidence by focusing the testimony of succeeding witnesses on the important testimony. For instance, assume that in an automobile accident case, previous testimony has already described the events that took place after the accident. You want to emphasize the current witness' testimony that he smelled alcohol on the defendant's breath following the accident. To do so, you would focus the witness' testimony on the witness' perceptions of the defendant's breath. You would not need to elicit a complete description of everything the witness observed after the accident.

d. Emphasis Through Multiple Chronologies

To this point the discussion has assumed that a witness has but one story to tell. However, to emphasize evidence supporting an argument, you may sometimes choose to have a witness relate multiple chronologies, each focused on a different topic. For instance, assume that you represent an employer who is defending a claim for illegally firing an employee on the basis of age. The employer will testify that firing resulted from the employee's work-related deficiencies, including improper work attire, acts of insubordination and drinking on the job. Here instead of using one chronology to bring out the evidence supporting each deficiency, you might have three chronologies: one focusing on improper work attire, another bringing out the evidence on insubordination and the last describing the instances of drinking. By proceeding in this way, you emphasize the evidence supporting each of your arguments.

This technique is effective when there is little or no factual overlap among the chronologies. When the chronologies overlap, using this technique results in substantial redundancy and risks boring and perhaps confusing the factfinder.

e. Use Examples to Illustrate Conduct or Conditions Over Time

Frequently, witnesses testify about either conditions or behaviors over time. For example, in a personal injury case, you may want the plaintiff to testify about how her back felt during the six months following surgery. Or in a will contest case, you might want to call a neighbor of the deceased to testify about how the deceased was continually forgetting things during the last two years of his life.

Typically, such witnesses will not be able to recall and you would not want to take the time to elicit the day to day happenings during the entire time period. For instance, the neighbor is likely to be unable to recall each and every time during the two year period that she noticed that the deceased was forgetful.

To make testimony about behaviors and conditions over time vivid and credible, take a "stop action" approach and focus on specific examples of the behavior or condition. In the will contest case, for instance, assume that you have introduced the neighbor and elicited testimony regarding his relationship with the deceased. You might then proceed as follows:

1. Q: Mr. Lopez, during the last two years of Mr. Wilson's life did you ever observe him to be forgetful?
2. A: He was always forgetting things.
3. Q: When is the first time you recall his being forgetful?
4. A: It was sometime in April, two years ago.
5. Q: (Set the scene and elicit the details of this event.)

. . .

15. Q: After the April incident in which he forgot he had invited his son for dinner, do you recall another instance in which Mr. Wilson was forgetful?
16. A: There was the time he got lost coming home from the market.
17. Q: When did that occur?
18. A: Around the middle of that summer.
19. Q: (Again, set the scene and elicit the details.)

. . .

33. Q. After the time that Mr. Wilson became lost, do you remember another occasion on which he was forgetful?
34. A. Yes,....

Here, the examination makes vivid and concrete the witness' conclusion that Wilson was "always forgetting things." In this examination you proceed chronologically through the illustrative examples. However, you needn't always do so. For instance, you may want to begin with the most vivid example, regardless of when in the chronology it occurs.

f. Use Exhibits

No discussion of emphasis would be complete without calling to mind the adage "a picture is worth a thousand words." Techniques for offering and using pictures and other exhibits are described in Chapter 16.

g. Elicit a String of Denials

Often, you can emphasize your client's version of what happened by focusing a series of questions on what did *not* happen. For example, assume that you represent Hurt, who is suing Dempsey for injuries suffered in a barroom brawl. Hurt claims that he did nothing to provoke Dempsey's attack. To emphasize Hurt's version of events, you might ask the following series of questions:

Q: And then what happened?

A: That guy (pointing to Dempsey) just walked over and started shoving me.

Q: Before the defendant started shoving you, did you touch him?

A: No.

Q: You didn't touch him at all?

A: No.

Q: Before he started shoving you, did you say anything to him?

A: No.

Q: Were you even looking in the defendant's direction before he started shoving you?

A: No.

Q: All right, after he started shoving you, what then happened?

A: . . . .

4. ADDITIONAL QUESTIONING TECHNIQUES

This section examines questioning techniques which will enable you to successfully cope with situations that commonly arise during direct examination.

a. Helping Forgetful Witnesses

No matter how well you've prepared them, under the pressure of testifying in open court witnesses routinely forget or neglect to mention evidence you want to elicit. Examine several techniques for dealing with such a situation.

(1) Follow a Closed/Open Questioning Sequence

As you know, asking open questions is a useful way of enhancing witnesses' credibility. But open questions often do not cue a witness to the precise evidence you want to elicit. Consequently, when responding to open questions witnesses often neglect to mention evidence you desire. To elicit the omitted evidence, you may employ a "closed/open" sequence of questions. Consider the following example:

1.   Q: What happened after your car came to a stop?

2.   A: The plaintiff, Mr. Sander, got out of his car and came over to talk to me.

3.   Q: What did Mr. Sander say at that time?

4.   A: He said I shouldn't have tried to make a left turn until all the traffic had cleared. Then he said that he wanted the name and telephone number of my insurance agent.

Assume that in response to No. 3, you expected the witness to testify that Sander also said that he didn't think that he had been hurt in the accident. To elicit this omitted evidence, follow a closed/open sequence:

5.   Q: When he came over to talk to you, did Mr. Sander say anything about how he was feeling?

6.   A: Yes.

7.   Q: What did he say?

8.   A: He said that he felt fine and he didn't think he had been hurt.

Here, the closed question (No. 5) gently reminds the witness of the omitted subject matter, which you then elicit through an open question (No. 7). Note that the closed question should not include the substance of the desired testimony. That is, you do not ask in No. 5, "When he came over to talk to you, did Mr. Sander say he didn't think he had been hurt?" The question is arguably leading and therefore improper. Even were a judge to permit it, the important testimony would come from the lawyer's mouth rather than the witness' and thus might lack credibility.

It may take more than one simple closed/open combination to elicit omitted testimony. For example, assume that from pretrial witness interviews you know that three topics were discussed at a meeting in early January between your client and the defendant: (1) installation dates for a new computer system, (2) the price of the system and (3) the software programs that would be included with the computers. Assume further that with respect to installation dates the defendant made three representations at this meeting: (a) the electrical wiring for the computers would be installed by February 15; (b) three of the computers would be installed and ready to use by March 1; and (c) all ten of the computers would ready to use by March 15. On direct, you want your client to testify to all of the above information. At trial, the testimony about this meeting proceeds as follows:

1.   Q: At the meeting in early January, what did you and the defendant Ms. French discuss?

2.   A: We talked about what we'd be getting and how much each of the computers would cost. And Ms. French told me that if we made a down payment of $5,000 right then we could get everything for a total price of $42,000. I thought that was a fair deal so I agreed and wrote her out a check at the meeting.

3.   Q: During this January meeting, did Ms. French say anything about software programs?

4.   A: Yes, she did.

5.   Q: What did she say about software programs?

6.   A: She said that the computers would have an Easy Rite software program loaded into the hard drive of each computer when they arrived.

7.   Q: Was anything mentioned at this meeting about when the computers would be ready for you to use?

8.   A: Yes. We discussed that.

9.   Q: What did Ms. French say about when the computers would be ready?

10.   A: She promised me that they'd have three of the computers installed and ready to go by March 1 and the rest of them would be ready by March 15.

11.   Q: At the January meeting was there any discussion about work that Ms. French's company would be doing before the computers arrived?

12.   A: Yes. She said that they would have to put in some additional electrical wiring for the computers. She told me they would put the wiring in on a weekend so they wouldn't disrupt our business.

13.   Q: Did she tell you when the electrical wiring would be installed?

14.   A: Yes, she gave me a specific date. She told me the wiring would be finished by February 15.

Here, you employ a series of closed/open questions to elicit testimony that the witness fails to provide in response to the initial open question. Note that each closed question calls the witness' attention to the omitted subject matter, but does not include the desired evidence.

(2) Refresh Recollection

Sometimes a witness will not recall omitted testimony despite your use of the closed/open technique. You may then try to explicitly refresh the witness' recollection. Consider the following example:

1.   Q: What happened after your car came to a stop?

2.   A: The plaintiff, Mr. Sander, got out of his car and came over to talk to me.

3.   Q: What did Mr. Sander say at that time?

4.   A: He said I shouldn't have tried to make a left turn until all the traffic had cleared. Then he said that he wanted the name and telephone number of my insurance agent.

5. Q: When he came over to talk to you did he say anything about how he was feeling?

6. A: I don't remember.

7. Q: Might I approach the witness to refresh his recollection, your Honor?   Please read to yourself the document I'm giving you.[33]

(After the witness finishes reading the document, you return with it to counsel table or the lectern.) [34]

8. Q: Is your memory now refreshed as to what else, if anything, Mr. Sander said to you?

9. A: Yes. Sander also said that he felt fine and he didn't think he had been hurt.

Once a witness has testified to an absence of recollection (No. 6.) you can use a document, or anything else,[35] to attempt to refresh recollection.[36]

Recognize that this technique has limitations. Often, you may not want to make a document available to the opposition by using it to refresh recollection. Moreover, even if successful, this technique interrupts the flow of the direct examination and, if used extensively, can call into question your witness' credibility.

(3) Use Leading Questions

You can also elicit omitted evidence with leading questions, though some judges may insist that you first obtain the court's permission to lead. For example:

1. Q: When he came over to talk to you, did Mr. Sander said anything about how he was feeling?

2. A: I don't remember.

3. Q: Your Honor, may I refresh the witness's recollection with a leading question?

   Court: Go ahead.

4. Q: Did Mr. Sander tell you that he felt fine and he didn't think he had been hurt?

33. Remember, your adversary has the right to examine what you show to the witness, and to introduce it in evidence. See FRE § 612.

34. You should remove the document from the witness before you elicit the desired information. This is required, as the assumption (undoubtedly sometimes fictional) is that the witness is testifying from present recollection refreshed, not to whatever the document happens to say.

35. For example, you could play a song to help refresh a witness' recollection. This is seldom done, but it illustrates the point that anything may be used to refresh a witness' recollection. For a humorous account of the possibilities, see *Baker v. State* 35 Md.App. 593, 371 A.2d 699 (M.D. 1977).

36. If the witness has insufficient memory to answer your question fully after you have shown him the document, you may offer the document into evidence as the witness' "past recollection recorded" if you can meet the stringent requirements of that hearsay exception. See FRE 803 (5).

5. A: Yes. I remember now, that's what he said.

Although this technique for refreshing recollection is quick and easy to use, it may well detract from a witness' credibility. It creates an impression that the witness is merely a conduit for the story that you are telling.

b. Steering Around Unfavorable Evidence

Because information may be unfavorable or of marginal relevance, you often want witnesses to omit it from their testimony.[37] Since you cannot give a witness a script telling them what to say and what not to say, you'll have to fall back on questioning techniques to steer around the unwanted information. Again, you can use the closed/open questioning sequence.

For example, assume that your client is a plaintiff in a wrongful termination matter. The client had a meeting with her supervisor a week before she was discharged. At this meeting, they discussed the strengths and weaknesses of your client's work performances and your client's goals for improvement during the next review period. You want the client to testify about what took place during the meeting, but do not want her to talk about the discussion of goals for improvement. If you ask an open question, such as "What did you and your supervisor discuss at this meeting?" or "What happened at this meeting?" the client's answer may include the information you want to delete. Examine how the closed/open sequence can steer the client around the unwanted information:

1. Q: Did you and your supervisor have a meeting shortly before you were discharged?

2. A: Yes.

3. Q: And at that meeting, did your supervisor tell you what he thought were the strengths and weaknesses in your work performances?

4. A: Yes.

5. Q: Let's take the strengths first. Tell us what was said during this meeting about your strengths as an employee.

6. A: Well, he said that. . . .

7. Q: And tell us what he said he felt your weaknesses were?

8. A: He told me. . . .

In this sequence the second closed question (No. 3) defines the topics you want the witness to describe. The question is permissible since it is not leading; i.e., it does not refer to the substance of what was said, but refers only to whether a discussion of a particular topic took place. The open questions (Nos. 5 and 7) then ask the witness to talk only about the

---

37. You can not, of course, prevent the opposition from bringing out the harmful evidence on cross examination.

defined topics. Testimony about other unwanted topics is thus excluded from the direct.

You can also use the closed/open sequence to steer around specific time periods which you want witnesses to ignore. For example, examine the following portion of a direct examination of a witness to an assault:

1. Q: After the two men arrived, what happened?

2. A: There was a fight.

3. Q: Could you tell us what happened during the fight?

4. A: ... [witness narrates].

5. Q: Now, after the fight was over did you call anyone on the telephone?

6. A: Yes. I called the police.

7. Q: Please tell us what happened after you called the police.

8. A: Well....

Here you use the closed/open sequence (Nos. 5 & 7) to steer the witness around what happened between the end of the fight and the time the witness called the police.[38]

c. Resuming Testimony After a Break

A witness' testimony is frequently interrupted by such matters as objections and ensuing arguments, offers of proof and recesses. Following such breaks in the action, the factfinder and the witness may well have forgotten where the testimony left off. To remind them of the chronology, use leading questions that repeat testimony the witness gave immediately prior to the interruption.[39] For example, assume that argument over an objection has consumed several minutes. Both the witness and the factfinder will appreciate a reminder as to where in the story they are:

1. Q: Sorry for the interruption Ms. Johnson. You had just told us that you designed the accounts receivable computer program, correct?

2. A: Yes.

3. Q: And you prepared the manual which is Defendant's Exhibit B, right?

4. A: That's right.

5. Q: And you trained Mr. Houston as to how to use the program?

    A: Yes.

    Q: All right. Now let me ask you....

38. In addition to using the closed/open questioning sequence, you might think of witness preparation as an opportunity to instruct witnesses what not to mention during direct. However, there are a number of pitfalls with this latter approach. See Sec. 10 *infra*.

39. Judges normally will allow you to ask leading questions for this purpose.

d. Clarify Gestures and Courtroom Estimates

Witnesses often illustrate testimony with physical gestures and courtroom estimates. For example, you ask, "How far away from Mr. Dumpty were you when he fell?" The witness answers, "About the same distance as I am from you," or holds her hands in front of her and says, "I'd say we were this far apart."

Answers such as these may be understandable to anyone observing the testimony, but they are a muddle for someone reading the trial transcript. As one of your obligations as a trial attorney is to maintain a clear record, you have to verbally translate the witness' testimony.

Thus, following the first answer you might say, "For the record, the distance indicated by the witness is approximately 15 feet." [40] Following the second, you might say, "For the record, the witness has indicated a distance of approximately two feet." In neither case are you testifying; you are simply clarifying testimony the witness has already given.

Another option you have is to ask the witness to clarify the record:

Q: How far away from Mr. Dumpty were you when he fell?

A: About the same distance as I am from you.

Q: Can you estimate that distance for us please?

This second option can be risky. Many witnesses have difficulty translating visual distances into precise numbers. For example, though your actual distance from the witness in this example may be about 15 feet, the witness may give an estimate of 30 feet. Now you have unmuddled the record, but created a conflict in the testimony. Which is correct, the visual estimate or its numerical counterpart? To avoid creating false conflicts, better practice is to clarify the witness' answer yourself.

The business of maintaining a clear record becomes slightly more complex when you ask a witness to illustrate what happened during a dynamic event. For instance, you ask a witness to demonstrate what took place during a barroom brawl. The record will probably be filled with testimony like, "Joe went like this," and, "The other guy swung around this way."

Usually, it is neither feasible nor necessary to verbally describe all of the participants' movements. Instead, again take a "stop action" approach. Ask a witness to demonstrate a participant's position at one or two critical moments, and then clarify that position for the record. The record will look something like this:

1. Q: Ms. Tobias, please demonstrate for us again the position of
     the defendant's arm just before he struck the first blow.

(Witness demonstrates)

---

40. Many judges have diagrams which
indicate the distance from the witness box
to various locations in the courtroom.

2. Q: All right, for the record the witness is holding her right arm parallel to the floor, directly to the right side of her body. Her arm is cocked at about a 45 degree angle at the elbow. Her right hand is clenched into a fist.

3. Q: Next, Ms. Tobias, please demonstrate how the defendant was holding the broken bottle of beer. All right, for the record....

e. Examples of Questioning "Do's" and "Don'ts"

● *Do Ask: "Can you explain what you mean by....?"*

Example:

Q: What was the living room like when you next saw it?

A: There was a terrible musty smell and the ceiling had lots of water damage.

Q: Can you explain what you mean by lots of water damage?

A: Well, there were brown spots....

The "can you explain" question has many benefits. It is open; it permits you to repeat testimony in a question; and the additional details will be vivid and provide emphasis.

● *Do Ask: "What happened next?"*

Example:

Q: After you walked through the living room, what happened next?

This is perhaps the archetypal direct examination question. It is open and provides chronology. Because it limits the witness to the "next thing" that happened, it is not unduly narrative.

● *Do Ask: "How do you know that....?"*

Example:

Q: What's the next thing that happened?

A: I saw the robber reach into his pocket and pull out a gun.

Q: How do you know that what he pulled out was a gun?

A: It was in his left pocket, and I was standing to his left and the light reflected right off the barrel.

Like "can you explain" questions, "how do you know" questions afford you an opportunity to repeat a portion of an answer in an open question, and to elicit details which add vividness and credibility to a story.

● *Don't Ask: Questions Beginning With "So...."*

Example:

Q: So the living room ceiling had lots of dark brown spots?

Questions starting with "so" almost always turn out to be leading. The "so" is a dead giveaway; try not to use it.

• *Don't "Echo" or "Thank" a Witness*

Example:

Q: What was the living room like when you next saw it?

A: There was a terrible musty smell and the ceiling had lots of water damage.

Q: *Lots of water damage.* Can you explain what you mean by lots of water damage?

A: Well, there were brown spots covering about a third of the ceiling.

Q: *I see. Thank you.* About how many brown spots did you see?

A: . . . .

Prefacing questions with comments such as these is both annoying and improper. Attorneys tend to throw them in to buy time to think of a question. But you don't have to constantly fill the courtroom with chatter. A moment or two of silence while you think about how to phrase a question is perfectly appropriate.

5. RESPONDING TO COMMON OBJECTIONS

This section discusses how to avoid or overcome the most common objections made during direct examination.[41]

a. *Leading Questions*

As a general rule, leading questions are prohibited on direct examination. Recall that a leading question typically calls for a "Yes" or "No" answer, and suggests which one the questioner wants. Consider the following examples:

"Isn't it true that you never saw that document before?"

"You wanted Mr. Hanks to buy your house from you, didn't you?" As these examples demonstrate, leading questions are questions in form only. They are really counsel's assertion, which the witness is asked to confirm as accurate.

A judge may consider a closed question to be leading when it seeks important information and calls for a "yes" or "no" answer. For example, assume that a car's color is important. You ask, "Was the car red?" Though the question does not literally suggest your desired answer, a judge may sustain a leading objection. Important evidence should come from the witness, not the questioner.

If you inadvertently violate the rule, you may overcome the objection by eliciting the testimony with a non-leading question. If, for example, your "red car" question is deemed leading, you may then ask, "What color was the car?"

---

41. For a more comprehensive discussion of objections, see Chapter 17.

Courts generally recognize several exceptions to the "no leading questions on direct" rule. For example, you may use leading questions to elicit testimony on "preliminary matters," such as personal background. ("Ms. Allison, you are a weapons acquisitions specialist at the Central Intelligence Agency, is that right?") Subsidiary aspects of events are often non-controversial, and therefore typically qualify as preliminary matters. For example, assume that while a dispute exists as to what took place at a meeting, there is no dispute that the meeting took place. You may choose to cover the undisputed subsidiary matters quickly with leading questions:

Q: You attended a meeting on the 26th of August, correct?

Q: Menkel and Meadow were also at that meeting?

Q: The purpose of the meeting was to discuss the buyout proposal, isn't that right?

Q: Now, please tell us what took place ......

b. *Lack of Foundation*

A lay witness is permitted to testify to only two things: (1) her perceptions (i.e. what she did, saw, heard, smelled, touched, tasted or thought) and (2) conclusions and opinions which are rationally based on those perceptions and helpful to the factfinder.[42]

If you attempt to have a witness testify to opinions or conclusions without first having the witness testify to the perceptions on which they are based, your adversary may object on the grounds of "lack of foundation."

For example, consider the following testimony in an action brought against Mr. Edel:

1. Q: Now, do you know of a meeting that Mr. Edel attended on the afternoon of August 6?

2. A: I do.

3. Q: Please tell us what Mr. Edel said during that meeting.

4. Opposing counsel: Objection, lack of foundation.

5. Court: Sustained.

6. Q: Do you have personal knowledge of what Mr. Edel said during the meeting of August 6th?

7. A: Yes.

8. Q: Please tell us what Mr. Edel said during that meeting.

9. Opposing counsel: Objection, lack of foundation.

10. Court: Sustained.

The court properly sustains the objections to questions number 3 and 6. Each asks for a conclusion without your having first elicited the

---

42. See Fed. R. Evid. 701.

perception on which it is based. That is, you fail to disclose a proper basis for the witness' knowledge about what Mr. Edel said at the meeting, or a proper basis for the witness' claim of personal knowledge. For all the judge knows, someone told the witness what Mr. Edel said; in that case, the witness would be testifying to hearsay. In any event, it's up to you to lay a proper foundation of personal knowledge. Consider how to do so:

1. Q: Now, do you know of a meeting that Mr. Edel attended on the afternoon of August 6?

2. A: Yes.

3. Q: Did you attend this meeting?

4. A: I did. It took place in my office.

5. Q: Did anyone else attend this meeting?

6. A: No, it was just the two of us.

7. Q: Please tell us what Mr. Edel said during that meeting.

Here, you establish the witness' presence at the meeting, thereby demonstrating that he has personal knowledge of what Mr. Edel said.

Sometimes, laying a foundation requires you to do more than have your witness testify to the perceptions on which a conclusion or opinion is based. You may also have to establish that the witness' opinion or conclusion is rationally based on her perceptions. Consider the following example:

1. Q: Mr. Spillenger, were you at the corner of 3rd and Maple at around 10 A.M. on June 22?

2. A: I was.

3. Q: What did you see?

4. A: I saw a white car drive past at a speed of about 55 m.p.h.

Opposing counsel: Your Honor, I move to strike everything after the witness said he saw a white car drive by because counsel has not laid an adequate foundation for the witness' opinion with respect to the speed of the car.

Court: Sustained.

Judges normally permit witnesses to state opinions about the speed of cars, and the witness' opinion regarding the speed of the car is based on the witness' perception (i.e. he saw the car). Nevertheless the court may grant the motion to strike because the burden is on you to show that the witness' opinion is rationally based on his perceptions, and you have not established that the witness had an adequate opportunity to judge the speed of the car. To lay additional foundation assume you ask the following questions:

5. Q: Mr. Spillenger, what were you doing at the corner of 3rd and Maple at around 10 A.M. on June 22?

6. A: I had just left a sales rep meeting and was walking back to my office.

7. Q: What happened as you were walking back?

8. A: A sudden gust of wind blew most of the papers I was carrying on to the ground. So I quickly bent down to pick them up and asked passersby to help.

9. Q: As you were picking up your papers did you notice any cars driving past in the street?

10. A: Yes, I noticed a white car drive past me.

11. Q: How were you able to see this white car if you were picking up your papers?

12. A: I just managed to catch a glimpse of it out of the corner of my eye as I was collecting the papers.

13. Q: How long did you have to observe the white car?

14. A: Just a split second, I'd say.

15. Q: Based on what you saw, can you give us an estimate of how fast the white car was going?

Opposing Counsel: Objection, lack of foundation.

This objection would probably be sustained because you have still failed to lay a proper foundation for the witness' opinion. Catching a momentary "glimpse" of a car out of the "corner of my eye" is not the stuff out of which an estimate of speed can be "rationally" made.[43] To demonstrate an adequate foundation, the witness' answer to No. 14 would have to be something like, "A few seconds, at least." Such an answer would show that the witness had a legitimate basis on which to make an estimate of speed. Possible problems with the witness' perceptions would go to the probative weight of the opinion, not to its admissibility.

During direct you will often ask witnesses to testify to opinions or conclusions without first "laying the foundation" i.e. eliciting the perceptions on which they are based. This is especially so when the opinions or conclusions are not disputed by the adversary and are not critical to your case. By omitting foundational questions you can often make the direct faster paced and less tedious. However, when opinions or conclusions are critical to your case, or when the adversary objects, you must be prepared to lay a proper foundation.[44]

Finally, recognize that sometimes opposing counsel may object to your questions on the grounds of "lack of personal knowledge." This

---

43. Obviously, whether the witness' opinion is "rationally" based on his perceptions will be a judgment call for the court in close cases.

44. For a discussion of laying the foundation for tangible exhibits see Chapter 16.

objection should be treated the same as an objection based on "lack of foundation." You overcome the objection by establishing the perceptions on which the witness' testimony is based.

c. Calls for a Narrative

Sometimes opposing counsel objects to an open question because it calls for a "narrative." Judges are most likely to construe questions as calling for a narrative when the questions ask witnesses to describe an entire *series* of events. Consider these questions:

- "What happened on the day of the accident?"
- "Describe what happened from the time the two men entered your store until the police arrived."
- "Please tell us how you went about selecting the equipment for the new factory?"

Such questions are sometimes considered objectionable because they permit a witness to tell too much of a story in a single answer, thereby arguably foreclosing opposing counsel from a reasonable opportunity to identify and object to inadmissible evidence.

When a narrative objection arises, you can usually overcome it rather quickly by narrowing the focus of your open question. For example, consider the following direct:

1. Q: Would you tell us what happened from the time the two men entered your store until the police arrived?

2. Objection; calls for a narrative.

3. Sustained.

4. Q: What is the first thing that happened after the two men entered your store?

5. A: Well they went to the back of the store and spoke to the clerk.

6. Q: What happened at that point?

No. 4 focuses on the "first thing" that happened when the two men entered the store and is thus narrower than No 1. Nos. 4 and 6 are permissible because they are confined to a specific point in time. Such questions should allow you to overcome the narrative objection while still realizing the benefits of open questions.

6. EXAMINING LESS THAN PERFECT WITNESSES

The discussion to this point has assumed that for the most part a witness is friendly and responsive. The techniques below will help you deal with witnesses who do not fit this description.

a. Rambling Witnesses

You will frequently encounter witnesses whose answers continually contain far more information than you intend to elicit. Of course, when you get such responses the evidence you wish to emphasize often becomes lost.

If you spot a rambler when preparing the person to testify, you can sometimes overcome the problem by going over the person's testimony several times before trial and emphasizing the importance of giving responsive answers. However, in the end no sure fire method for controlling a rambling witness exists, because rambling is probably the result of a witness' lifelong way of responding to inquiries.

At trial, often the best you can do is to try to minimize a witness' tendency to ramble. One technique is to restrict open questions to the most important testimony. Then, if critical evidence has been swamped in a sea of ramble, emphasize it with closed questions. When eliciting non-crucial information, rely primarily on closed questions. These techniques may carry a double reward: You enhance a rambler's credibility by cutting off his opportunities to ramble, and both judge and jury are likely to silently applaud your efforts.[45]

b. Adverse and Hostile Witnesses

An adverse witness is one who is, or who is associated with, an opposing party. You will often call adverse witnesses during your case. A primary reason to do so is that the adverse witness can provide a significant amount of helpful evidence. Indeed, as a plaintiff you may be unable to sustain your burden of proof without calling an adverse witness. Other times, you may decide to call an adverse witness simply because you think she or he will make a terrible impression on the jury, and as the plaintiff you hope to get your case off to a rousing start by demonstrating that the opposing party is not credible.

Regardless of your reason for calling an adverse witness, evidence rules in nearly all jurisdictions permit you to ask leading questions of adverse witnesses.[46] You do not have to demonstrate that the witness demonstrates actual hostility towards your client. For example, assume that you represent a plaintiff suing a bank for improper lending practices. If you call one of the bank's branch managers as a witness during your case, the branch manager will be an adverse witness of whom you could ask leading questions.

Sometimes, you will be allowed to treat a witness as adverse even though the witness is not associated with the opposing party. If a witness is hostile—that is, a witness appears to be unwilling to testify or demonstrates bias against your client—a judge will often permit you to treat the witness as adverse and ask leading questions.[47] If you are aware of a witness' hostility in advance, you should approach the bench, indicate that the witness is hostile and ask for permission to use leading questions. Also, make an "offer of proof" describing the basis for the

---

45. Another option is to follow a rambling answer on direct with a polite request to listen carefully to your questions and respond only to what is asked. If your effort fails, the judge may give this instruction in a manner that is not as polite.

46. See FRE 611 (c).

47. Ibid.

hostility. The judge may accept your offer without more, and permit you to lead. Alternatively, and especially if the adversary objects, the judge may delay ruling until you establish the hostility through testimony.

For example, assume that you represent a defendant in an automobile accident case. Plaintiff alleges that your client suddenly pulled away from the curb into the path of the plaintiff's car. Your investigator has talked to Ms. Ambrose, the defendant's next door neighbor, who has partly contradicted the plaintiff's version of the accident. However, Ms. Ambrose does not want to testify; she has had misunderstandings with the defendant and does not want to be of any help. Ms. Ambrose has even told your investigator that if she is subpoenaed, she will claim inability to recall what happened. Nevertheless, you consider her testimony important and you do subpoena her.

At trial, you have explained to the judge that Ms. Ambrose is hostile and asked permission to use leading questions. The judge has granted permission, on the condition that you first demonstrate Ambrose's hostility.[48] Thus, you might question Ambrose as follows:

1. Q: Ms. Ambrose, you spoke to an investigator about two weeks after the accident, correct?

2. A: That's true.

3. Q: And you told the investigator what you had seen?

4. A: Yes.

5. Q: Some time later, the investigator contacted you again and told you that you would be subpoenaed, right?

6. A: Yes.

7. Q: And you told the investigator that you didn't want to testify, and that if you were subpoenaed you would claim that you couldn't remember anything?

8. A: I might have said something like that.

9. Q: And you also said that you didn't want to testify because you've had some misunderstandings with the defendant, and didn't want to do anything to help him, didn't you say that?

10. A: Maybe I did.

11. Q: Your Honor, I believe that I have sufficiently established the witness' hostility, and I request permission to examine her as an adverse witness.

12. The Court: That request will be granted. You may proceed, counsel.

---

48. As this is a foundational issue, you can normally use leading questions to es-   tablish hostility. See FRE 104(a).

c. *Turncoat Witnesses*

A turncoat witness is one who says one thing before trial and at trial says something totally contradictory. A turncoat witness can be quite jarring; you expect favorable testimony, but receive something quite different. In this situation, you have two primary response options.

First, you can impeach the witness with his pretrial statement.[49] This option is available if the witness' pretrial statement is contained in a writing signed by the witness or in the witness' deposition, or if the pretrial statement was made to someone other than you.[50] Your second option is to explain to the judge that the witness has changed his testimony and become hostile, and ask permission to complete the direct with leading questions.

7. ORDER OF WITNESSES

You typically want to choose an order of witnesses that facilitates factfinder understanding of your overall story and your most important arguments, and makes a strong first impression. These goals are easily accomplished if you have a very credible witness who can tell a story from beginning to end. For example, a plaintiff in a garden variety automobile accident case is often such a witness.

But the situation is often stickier. The witness best able to tell the overall story may be unlikely to create a favorable first impression. You may not have a single witness who can tell the overall story, and you may decide to begin with a witness who can only tell the portion of your story you think the factfinder is most anxious to hear. Your best witness may be your client, who wants to testify last in order to have the benefit of hearing the rest of the testimony. Or, your best witness may be unavoidably absent until the third day of trial. In any of these situations, you may have to compromise on your goals. For example, you may have to make a judgment about which is more important— starting with a witness who can tell the overall story, or starting with your most credible witness.

8. ANTICIPATING AN ADVERSARY'S ARGUMENTS

As you know, argument preparation includes identifying an adversary's likely arguments and your responses. During direct, a tactical decision you often have to make is whether to elicit the evidence giving rise to an adversary's arguments, and your responding evidence.

For example, assume that you are prosecuting Jones for robbing a liquor store. Your witness Smith will testify that she was in the liquor

---

49. For a discussion of impeachment techniques see Chapter 13.

50. When a witness' pretrial statement is only made orally to you, you typically can not personally take the stand and impeach the witness. See e.g. Rule 3.7 ("Lawyer As Witness") ABA Model Rules of Professional Conduct. You might, however, ask the witness if he made the inconsistent statement with a question such as, "Prior to trial didn't you tell me....?" You will not, however, be able to impeach a witness' unfavorable answer.

store and that Jones was the robber. However, the defense is almost certain to argue that Smith is not believable, because shortly after the robbery Smith told a police officer, "I didn't see a thing." On direct of Smith, after eliciting her identification of Jones, you might proceed as follows:

1.   Q: Ms. Smith, did you speak with Officer O'Reilly after the robbery?

2.   A: Yes.

3.   Q: What, if anything, did you tell Officer O'Reilly about the robbery?

4.   A: I told him that I didn't see what happened.

5.   Q: Is there any reason that you told him that?

6.   A: At the time, I was scared to death of getting involved, so I just said I didn't see anything. After I thought about it for a couple of days, I decided I had to tell the truth.

Here, you first elicit the inconsistency giving rise to the almost certain defense argument that Smith is not credible (No. 4), and then your responding explanation (No. 6). Alternatively, you might have waited to see if the defense developed this argument when cross examining Smith, and if so then offered the explanation on redirect. The conventional wisdom is to "take the sting out" of cross by pursuing the first alternative.

You should not mechanistically follow the conventional wisdom. Before anticipating an adversary's arguments, you have to consider factors such as:

- Is the adversary aware of and likely to develop the argument?

- Do you have a satisfactory response to the argument?

- Are your responses so numerous and complex that they both suggest that there must be force to the adversary's arguments and detract from the affirmative story you want to elicit?

Taking all of these factors into account, you may sometimes decide that you are better off giving the devil his due. That is, do not anticipate an argument until it has been made, and postpone any decision about a response until after the adversary puts in the evidence supporting the adversary's argument.[51]

9. REDIRECT EXAMINATION

As you probably know, the purpose of redirect examination is to respond to issues raised during cross examination. You may not use

---

51. Some conventional wisdom advises you to include harmful evidence in a direct even if you don't have a satisfactory response. By "volunteering a weakness," the argument goes, you demonstrate to a fact-finder that you have nothing to hide. In general, you are better off considering the factors discussed in the text than in slavishly following anyone's conventional wisdom.

redirect merely to have the last word or to rehash testimony previously covered on direct.

For example, if a cross examiner obfuscates the order of events, on redirect you may review the proper chronology. Or if opposing counsel develops an apparent implausibility during cross, during redirect you might ask the witness for an explanation.

Whatever the purpose of your redirect, remember that the same rules that apply to direct examination also apply to redirect. Perhaps influenced by questions asked on cross, some attorneys cannot resist turning redirect into a series of improper leading questions. And recognize that redirect is within a judge's discretion;[52] ask the court's permission before launching into it.

Finally, sometimes an opponent's cross of your witness could have been much more damaging than it turned out to be. In such cases, you may want to forego any redirect and allow the witness to be excused immediately. If you instead conduct a redirect examination, you give your opponent another opportunity to bring out damaging testimony during recross.

10. WITNESS PREPARATION

Direct examination usually falls somewhere between a witness' spontaneous recollection and a carefully rehearsed Broadway drama. Direct is rarely completely spontaneous, as you generally go over your direct before a witness testifies. However, preparation should not be so thorough that a witness seems to be reciting lines from a script.

Perhaps the best way of achieving an effective balance between spontaneity and thoroughness is to conduct a mock direct. Ask the questions you plan to ask at trial. Help a witness recognize that open questions invite expansive answers, whereas narrow questions focus on specific testimony. As you practice, you can explain that the witness should answer only the question that you have asked, and not volunteer information not called for by the question. With practice, the witness will become more responsive to your questions. With a responsive witness, you have maximum control over content and emphasis during direct. In contrast, when the witness is not responsive to your questions, the witness is, in effect, controlling the content of the direct.

When practicing direct you will also get a feel for a witness' vocabulary and ability to testify succinctly and clearly. For example, if you realize that a witness has a strong tendency to digress and give nonresponsive answers in response to very open questions (e.g., "What happened next?"), you may plan to ask more focused questions (e.g., "What did you do after the robbery?" "What did he say about the complaints from clients?") should the witness continue to digress at trial. You are the professional, and it is easier for you to adjust to a witness than to expect a witness to adjust to you.

---

52. FRE 611.

Having the witness practice giving responsive answers during a mock examination will help you avoid relying on the kind of abstract advice that is rarely helpful. It does little good to tell someone to "be clear" or "make the jury have confidence in you." Such statements echo the advice to "Buy low and sell high;" they are correct, but useless except in the abstract. By illustrating for a witness how giving responsive answers allows you to organize the testimony during direct, you show a witness how to "be clear" without even having to use that abstract label.

If abstract advice is the "Scylla" of witness preparation, then overly specific advice is the "Charybdis." Assume you tell a witness, "When I ask you about his physical appearance, make sure you mention his reddish nose, his long pointy red hat with the white tassel on the end and the wide black belt. But don't say anything about the way he was laughing; I don't want that to come out yet." Most witnesses are nervous enough about the prospect of answering questions under oath and remembering what they observed. A plethora of specific instructions will tend only to add to their nervousness.[53] If the witness gives responsive answers during direct, you should be able to control the content of the direct with your questioning techniques.

Always invite a witness to discuss with you any concerns they may have. It is all too easy to sit "on high" and dispense wisdom based on the concerns you think the average witness may have. But witnesses vary tremendously in their level of sophistication, courtroom experience, anxiety levels and the like, and you want to respond to their unique concerns. For example, one witness may be worried about what to do if he does not understand a question: "If you don't understand a question just tell me that you don't understand and I'll rephrase it." Another witness may be concerned about forgetting certain information; you can explain that you will be permitted to ask questions to refresh the witness' recollection and show the witness how you would do so. Another witness may want to know how to dress: "You could wear either a coat and tie, or your nurse's uniform. Let's talk about it." Because witnesses will commonly have such concerns you may want to raise them as a matter of course during preparation.

Lastly, consider the situation of preparing a witness who you meet for the first time at the courthouse shortly before the witness is about to testify. Typically you will have at least some knowledge of the witness' basic story. For example, if you are a prosecutor about to call a witness on whom the police served a subpoena, the police report probably will have given you an idea of the witness' basic story. Under this extreme

---

53. In addition, if a witness is not your client, what you say to her when preparing for trial is not privileged. If you tell a witness that you will inquire about some topics but not others during direct, your opponent may reveal those instructions during cross examination. Such instructions may seriously undercut your credibility and the witness'. Consequently, when preparing witness you will typically emphasize that you want them to answer your and opposing counsel's questions truthfully and responsively. Then, if opposing counsel suggests on cross that you improperly prepared a witness, you can have the witness testify to your instructions.

time constraint, you will probably first want to confirm the accuracy of the most important testimony you expect the witness to provide and then briefly explain to the witness the areas you expect to cover during direct. Any additional time can be spent conducting a mock direct.

11. HOW MUCH DO I WRITE DOWN AHEAD OF TIME?

Like symphony conductors, some attorneys take the entire "score" of a direct examination with them to the podium. Their questions are all written out, perhaps with the expected answers sandwiched in between. While this technique may enhance peace of mind, it also tends to detract from the persuasiveness of direct.

For one thing, no matter how much you tell yourself that the questions are only a guide, you may quickly resort to reading them to a witness verbatim. And whether you are asking questions or arguing, reading cannot help but flatten out your presentation.

Second, you may focus on your written script rather than on your witness. When you ask a question, both common courtesy and your interest in giving an air of spontaneity to testimony suggest that you look at the witness and take in the answer. Yet, a written script often becomes a magnet which pulls your eyes irresistibly downward to the printed page.

Finally, slavishly following a written script can produce embarrassing moments when, enmeshed in your script, you fail to notice that a witness has given an unexpected answer. A dialogue such as this may ensue:

Q: And at that time, did you notice a bicycle?

A: I'm not sure.

Q: And what color was it?

To avoid these gaffes, substitute an outline for a written script. Write down events you plan to cover, and key testimony you expect a witness to give. Make a note of exhibits you plan to offer, and foundational evidence you need to elicit. You might even include a question or answer on those infrequent occasions when exact words are critical. The outline technique may produce poor symphonies, but it can promote both peace of mind and direct examinations that sound fresh and unrehearsed.

Chapter 13

CROSS EXAMINATION

George C. Scott as Claude Dancer cross examines Ben Gazzara as Lt. Manion as Joseph N. Welch presides. "Anatomy of a Murder," © 1959 Carlyle Productions, Inc. All rights reserved. Courtesy of Columbia Pictures.

Your usual role on direct examination is to be a foil for a witness. You are the subservient member of the team, helping a witness to provide the evidence supporting your arguments. By contrast, think of cross examination as role reversal. You want to be the dominant speaker and have a witness act as a foil for you. Rather than permitting adverse witnesses to rehash the unfavorable evidence they've already given on direct, you typically want to focus cross examination on specific items of evidence supporting your arguments and undermining the adversary's. The arguments you've prepared prior to trial will point you to most of the evidence you attempt to elicit on cross examinations. This chapter focuses on techniques for eliciting that evidence effectively.

1. GENERAL PRINCIPLES

Cross examination connotes drama and mystique. Every cross is seemingly a chance to use your verbal powers to mesmerize a witness into testifying to exactly what you want said. But this is an unrealistic goal. Even Attila the Hun didn't always extract the information he desired, and he had more weapons at his disposal. Thus, just as with direct examination, effective cross examinations typically depend not on verbal trickery but rather on the content of your arguments and questioning techniques that limit a witness to the evidence pertaining to these arguments.

a. Use Leading Questions.

Leading questions are your primary cross examination tool. So tied to cross examination are leading questions that the late Dean and Judge Irving Younger, whose lectures about evidence and trial techniques were legendary, regularly threatened to return from wherever he was and haunt any inexperienced counsel who asked a non-leading question on cross examination. While Younger may have been exaggerating, his point should make you think at least twice about asking a non-leading question.

As explained in Chapter 12, leading questions often are no more than assertions in question form. They limit a witness to an answer of "yes" or "no," and leave no doubt as to which of those answers you expect to receive. Consider the following examples:

"The first time you saw Exhibit 7 was when Mr. Franks showed it to you, isn't that right?"

"You didn't want Mr. Hanks to buy your house from you, did you?"

"The car was red?"

As these examples demonstrate, leading questions are not really questions at all. They are assertions of counsel put in the form of questions.

Leading questions are a cross examination staple because they allow you to determine the content of testimony. For example, assume that you represent a former employee who claims that he was wrongfully discharged. Cross examining Emerson, a company vice-president, you want to show that Emerson had given your client a satisfactory evaluation. Compare the following two cross examinations:

Example #1–Leading Questions

Q: Mr. Emerson, when you completed Ms. Phelan's evaluation on December 1st, you believed she was doing a satisfactory job, isn't that right?

A: Yes.

Q: And you checked off "satisfactory" on Exhibit 7, Ms. Phelan's December 1st evaluation, didn't you?

A: Yes, I did.

Q: And on this December 1st evaluation you didn't write anything indicating Ms. Phelan had been insubordinate to her supervisor, did you?

Q: No.

Example #2–Open Questions

Q: Mr. Emerson, when you completed the evaluation for Ms. Phelan on December 1st, tell us how you thought she was performing on her job?

A: She had had some problems dealing with some of our customers when they called to check on the status of their orders, and she had had one run-in with her supervisor, but overall she was doing a satisfactory job.

Q: I'm showing you Exhibit 7 which you testified is the evaluation you filled out for Ms. Phelan on December 1st, could you tell us why you checked "satisfactory" on that evaluation?

A: Sure. A few days before filling out the evaluation, I'd had a conference in my office with Ms. Phelan to discuss her run-in with her supervisor and I told her that the company could not tolerate her behaving that way toward her supervisor. She said she was very sorry and that it would never happen again. So, I decided to give her a "satisfactory" on her written evaluation and not mention the insubordination in the written comments.

Both examples focus on a December 1 performance evaluation. In the first, leading questions limit Emerson to confirming three specific details about the evaluation which you want to emphasize. In the second, open questions invite Emerson to explain multiple aspects of your client's job performance. While both stories may be "the truth," only the leading questions allow you to emphasize that part of the truth that consists of the evidence supporting your arguments.[1]

b. Use One–Item Leading Questions

Dividing an event into a series of one-item questions tends to increase a factfinder's comprehension, add persuasiveness, and to discourage a witness from offering explanations that dilute the impact of your story. Compare these sequences of questions:

Sequence No. 1:

"You went into your supervisor's office, correct?"

"Once inside the office, you told her that you didn't care what she wanted you to do?"

---

1. Of course, the witness' explanations may be brought out by opposing counsel during redirect. But you will be better able to communicate your arguments to the fact- finder if your cross is not interrupted by explanations and other extraneous testimony from the witness.

"You also said that she was a sorry excuse for a manager, isn't that right?"

"You then walked out of the office?"

"And you slammed the door, right?"

Sequence No. 2:

"When you went into his office, you were upset with your supervisor and you told her that you didn't care what she wanted you to do, you thought she was a sorry excuse for a manager and then you walked out of her office and slammed the door behind you, isn't that right?"

The second question covers the entire event with a single question. Faced with such a complex question, a witness is likely to qualify or explain an answer. Moreover, multiple fact questions may draw an objection as argumentative or compound. Both outcomes interrupt the emphasis and smooth flow that the first sequence of questions tends to produce.

Another benefit of one-item questions is that they allow you to string together a series of short favorable questions that a factfinder can easily follow. For example, assume that you were allowed to ask and the witness simply answered "yes" to the complex question above (Sequence # 2). Compared to this single "yes," the series of positive responses that you elicit with Sequence No. 1 may be easier for the factfinder to follow and have more impact.

c. *Ask Safe Leading Questions.*

Leading questions are not so powerful that they can bend a witness to your will no matter what the truth. Imagine this possible cross examination:

Q: What did you tell the police officer about the color of the light?

A: I said that it was green.

Q: What did you say about the color of the light when reciting your marriage vows?

A: I said that the light was green.

Q: What were your last words to your dearest great-grandmother as she lay on her deathbed?

A: I told her that the light was green.

Q: But in fact the light was red, wasn't it?

A: Gee, yes it was. Since you asked me a leading question, I guess I'll have to change what I said before.

Of course, this examination is *totally fictitious*. Leading questions do not inveigle hapless witnesses into contradicting earlier statements or giving false testimony. Thus, to conduct an effective cross you have to identify leading questions which are likely to advance your client's cause regardless of how a witness answers them. To identify questions that help you regardless of response, you needn't rely on parlor magic, but on developing questions that are *safe*. A safe question is one which requires the witness to either provide your desired response or allows you to impeach (contradict) a response other than your desired one. Look to the following sources for safe questions:

(1) Witness' Prior Statement

A question is safe if your desired answer is consistent with a witness' prior statement. The question is safe because if the witness does not provide your desired answer, you can impeach the witness with the prior statement.[2]

There are many sources of prior statements. A witness' prior statement may consist of testimony given earlier in court (say, during direct examination) or during a deposition. It may consist of an assertion in a letter or a memo. It may be an oral statement made to your investigator or to a friend or neighbor. Or it may consist of a message the witness bannered on a blimp during halftime of the Super Bowl. Whatever the source, a question is typically safe if your desired answer is consistent with a witness' prior statement.[3]

For example, assume that you represent plaintiff Pitts in a wrongful termination case. A defense witness, Greer, testified at his deposition that he "thought Pitts' work during the first quarter of the year was exemplary." Cross examining Greer, you ask, "You thought Ms. Pitts' work during the first quarter of the year was exemplary, correct?" If Greer says "yes," you've elicited your desired evidence; if Greer says anything other than "yes," you can impeach him with his inconsistent deposition statement. Therefore, your question is safe.

Before deciding that a question is safe, make sure that it is genuinely consistent with a witness' prior statement. Subtle variations in terminology or time can affect an answer and leave you unable to discredit an undesired answer. For example, in the same wrongful termination case, assume that Greer wrote a letter on April 18th stating that "Ms. Pitts is a good salesperson for our firm." On cross examination you ask Greer, "As of April 18, you considered Ms. Pitts to be an excellent salesperson, right?" The question is not fully safe. Greer can say "no," because your desired answer ("Pitts is excellent") is different from Greer's prior statement ("Pitts is good").

Or, assume that you ask Greer, "In April, you considered Ms. Pitts to be a good salesperson, right?" Again, the question is not fully safe. The letter reflects Greer's opinion as of April 18; your desired answer pertains to the entire month. Thus, if something happened later in

---

2. We discuss the mechanics of impeachment *infra* at Sec. 3 c.

3. You may not be able to impeach the witness when the prior statement relates to a "collateral" matter. See D. Louisell & C.

Mueller, 3 Federal Evidence, Sections 343, 356 (1985); 2 Federal Evidence, Section 129 (1985) for a discussion of impeachment on a collateral matter.

April to change Greer's opinion, you may not be able to use the letter to discredit a "no" answer. Whenever possible, then, phrase questions so that your desired answer is fully consistent with a witness' prior statement.[4]

(2) Consistency With "Established Facts"

A question is also safe if your desired answer is consistent with established facts (typically a document or the testimony of a more believable witness).[5] If the witness does not give your desired answer, you can later impeach the witness through the document or more believable witness.

For example, in the Pitts' wrongful termination case, assume that Newman, an important customer of the defendant, has told you that she never complained to Greer about Pitts' work. Newman is a neutral witness, with no ax to grind on behalf of either party. On cross, you may safely ask Greer, "You never got a complaint about Ms. Pitts' work from Ms. Newman, did you?" Greer will either supply your desired response ("No"), or you will later call Newman to discredit Greer's response.

(3) Consistency With Common Experience

Finally, a question is safe if your desired answer is consistent with common experience. You can thus discredit a witness' undesired response as inconsistent with common experience.[6] For example, assume again that you are cross examining Greer, who testified on direct that he decided to terminate Pitts' employment because Greer had received complaints from customers that it took Pitts too long to fill their orders. Your argument is that this reason is a pretext, and that your client was fired illegally because she was a union organizer. On cross of Greer, you want to elicit evidence that Greer should have but did not investigate Pitts' work with two of the biggest customers she worked with. Your cross proceeds as follows:

1. Q: Before deciding to terminate Ms. Pitts' employment, you made some investigation of the complaints about her work, right?

2. A: Yes.

3. Q: I'm sure that you didn't want to let Ms. Pitts go if those complaints were totally unfounded?

---

4. Whether a witness' in court testimony is sufficiently inconsistent with a prior statement to permit impeachment is a question for the court to decide.

5. Here as in other aspects of the trial process, you cannot avoid judgment calls. The answer to the question of whether one witness is more believable than another is sometimes less than obvious.

6. Here again, the safety of a question is often a judgment call. What seems unlikely to you may seem sensible to a factfinder.

4. A: That's true.

5. Q: And you were concerned about Ms. Pitts' work for your important customers?

6. A: That's right.

7. Q: Generally, the more volume of business a customer gives you, the more important to have an employee who has a good relationship with that customer?

8. A: Usually, yes.

9. Q: And for the last three years, Mr. Rice has been your largest customer, correct?

10. A: Yes.

11. Q: Yet before firing Ms. Pitts, you didn't talk to Mr. Rice, did you?

12. A: No. I didn't.

13. Q: And Ms. Pitts handled the Rice account, correct?

14. A: Yes, she did.

15. Q: And for the last three years, Ms. Pilaf has been your second largest customer?

16. A: According to our records, yes.

17. Q: And Ms. Pitts handled the Pilaf account, right?

18. A: Yes.

19. Q: Yet you didn't talk to Ms. Pilaf before letting Pitts go, right?

20. A: No.

Here, everyday experience suggests that a company will be more concerned about its larger customers than about its smaller ones, and that anyone wanting to be seen as a competent supervisor will claim to have looked into problems before sacking an employee. Thus, questions 1, 3, 5 and 7 are safe because any answers other than your desired ones are seemingly inconsistent with common experience. Therefore, you could attack the credibility of undesired answers with the argument that they are implausible.[7] Of course, the safety of the remaining questions would have to be based on some other source. For instance, they may be safe because they are based on Greer's pretrial deposition, or on testimony that Rice and Pilaf are prepared to give.

d. Focus Questions on Arguments

Typically, your primary goals on direct and cross examination are the same—to elicit evidence bolstering your arguments or undermining an adversary's arguments. Direct examination, however, carries with it

---

7. Of course, you must wait until closing argument to comment explicitly on the   implausibility.

a good deal of baggage that tends to make it difficult for a factfinder to recognize how evidence links to arguments. This baggage includes personal background evidence, the story form of testimony, scene setting testimony, and foundational evidence. While such testimony usually provides clarity and bolsters a witness' general credibility, it can obscure your important evidence.

On cross examination, by contrast, you are freed of the baggage that comes with direct. For example, on cross you are typically not concerned with a witness' overall story. Instead, you want to tell *your own story* on cross by honing in on the evidence pertaining to your arguments. Elicit that evidence with safe leading questions and *sit down*. Whereas on direct examination you have to take special pains to emphasize important evidence, on cross you automatically emphasize important evidence by using safe, leading questions to focus on that evidence. Do not dilute this advantage by probing every bit of testimony a witness gave on direct examination, or by asking unsafe questions. If you do, you not only obscure your important evidence, but also you allow a factfinder to repeatedly hear evidence favoring your adversary.

e. Avoid "Cross" Examination

The term "cross" examination, reinforced by innumerable dramas depicting cross examiners belligerently snarling questions at witnesses from a distance of three inches,[8] connotes a very misleading image. As an officer of the court you must question all witnesses, your own and your adversary's, in a professional manner. Even if you think that everything an adverse witness says is an abject lie, your manner of questioning should show respect to the court and the institution of trial.

Typically, this means standing at a podium when asking questions unless you have the judge's permission to do otherwise, and using essentially the same personal manner during cross as on direct. True, situations have undoubtedly arisen in which a witness has been so obviously mendacious that a factfinder has relished counsel's angry, hostile cross examination questioning style. But such situations are rare. You can be firm and insist on an answer to which you are entitled. But you should not take such advantage of your power to ask leading questions that you belittle a witness. In most cases, all you would accomplish is to generate a factfinder's sympathy for the witness.

f. Unanticipated Answers and Unsafe Questions

Because safe questions generally allow you to impeach an answer other than your desired one, your ideal cross examination would be limited to safe questions. However, even safe questions cannot eliminate the risk of unanticipated or undesired answers. For instance, a witness may volunteer an explanation that suggests a plausible reason

---

8. Perhaps the most famous example is the cross examination of Mary Pilant (Kathryn Grant) by Prosecutor Claude Dancer (George C. Scott) in "Anatomy of a Murder."

for having made an inconsistent statement. The risk of explanation is particularly high when you rely on inconsistency with common experience, because witnesses can often see the point you're trying to make. For example, in the Pitts matter above, Greer may well recognize that you are suggesting that his testimony is implausible and in the middle of your cross blurt out an explanation for why he did not contact his largest customers. Section 3 below examines techniques for responding to unanticipated or undesired answers to safe questions.

Moreover, sometimes you will consider asking unsafe questions in an effort to fully develop your arguments, and Section 4 below explores situations in which you can ask unsafe questions while minimizing the risk that you will rehash direct or unearth unfavorable information. However, before worrying about explanations and unsafe questions, examine how to communicate your arguments with safe questions.

2. CONVERTING ARGUMENTS TO SAFE CROSS EXAMINATION QUESTIONS

As with direct examination, prior to trial you typically plan most of what will happen during cross examination when you construct arguments supporting your case and undermining your adversary's. To plan for the cross of a specific adverse witness, review those arguments and identify which ones (if any) depend on evidence from that witness. Then list, for each witness, safe questions which will help you to communicate these arguments to the factfinder during cross. Sometimes, you will be able to communicate an entire argument through the cross of an adverse witness. Other times you may have to be content to elicit a lone "especially when" or an isolated item of evidence that you identified through the Credibility Checklist and wait until final summation to connect the item with an argument. This section illustrates how to convert different types of arguments into safe cross examination questions.

a. Arguments Based on Highly Probative Undisputed Evidence

First, examine how to use cross examination to communicate an argument based on highly probative undisputed evidence. Return to the case of the ill-fated roof on the house sold by the defendant Marilyn Bollinger to the plaintiff Don Evans.[9] As you recall, Evans bought a house from Bollinger and has brought suit for breach of contract and fraud, claiming that Bollinger knew but failed to disclose that the house had a leaky roof. Assume that you now represent the plaintiff Evans and that you are trying to prove the crucial factual proposition:

"Bollinger never told Evans that the roof of the house had leaked."

---

9. The statement of facts in *Evans v. Bollinger* is contained in Chapter 12, Sec. 2 b.

This proposition, if proven, satisfies the element of "Concealment" in Evans' claim for fraudulent concealment in connection with the house sale.

To prove this proposition, you have constructed the following argument based on highly probative undisputed evidence: [10]

Undisputed Highly Probative Item of Evidence: Bollinger knew that the roof was patched in January and leaked in February.

Generalization # 1: Sellers who know that a roof has leaked one month after being patched sometimes think that the house needs a new roof.

    Especially when:

- They thought the house might need a new roof before it was patched.

- They know that the roof is 15 years old.

Generalization # 2: Sellers who think that a house needs a new roof sometimes don't tell a prospective purchaser about repairs to or problems with the roof.

    Especially when:

- They don't want the prospective purchaser's inspector to examine the roof carefully.

- They don't want to pay for a new roof before selling the house.

Therefore, Bollinger did not tell Evans that the roof had leaked.[11]

During cross of Bollinger you want to communicate this argument to the factfinder. To do so, examine the evidence supporting your argument and determine what you can safely put to Bollinger in the form of leading questions. In this case, as Evans' lawyer you might prepare the following cross of Bollinger to communicate the above argument:

1.   Q: You had owned the house for about 15 years before you sold it to Mr. Evans, is that right?

2.   Q: And during the 15 years you'd owned the house you never put a new roof on it, did you?

3.   Q: So when the roof first leaked in January it was 15 years old?

4.   Q: When your roof leaked in January, you had a roofer come out to look at it?

---

10. Note that this argument was also developed by Bollinger's counsel when preparing for Bollinger's direct examination. See Chapter 12, Sec. 2 b. Bollinger's counsel constructed the argument to identify evidence supporting the "except whens" for inclusion in Bollinger's direct. You will emphasize the evidence supporting the "especially whens" during Bollinger's cross.

11. To thoroughly assess the strength of this argument, during pretrial preparation you would have identified the adversary's "except whens". For example, you might have identified the following "except when" for the first generalization: The roof does not leak in subsequent rains. However, you would not want to undercut your own argument by introducing "except when" evidence during your cross.

5. Q: Before the roofer came out to look at the roof in January, you were not positive that the leak in the roof could be fixed with a patch, isn't that right?

6. Q: Before the roofer came out, you thought your old roof might have to be replaced, isn't that correct?

7. Q: Now after the roof was patched, it leaked again in February, right?

8. Q: And that was just a month after you'd had the roof patched?

9. Q: And when the roof leaked only a month after being patched, you thought that perhaps the patch on the roof had not completely corrected the problem, isn't that right?

10. Q: And you thought that if the patch hadn't completely corrected the problem, you might need a new roof, isn't that true?

11. Q: Mr. Evans told you that he wanted his inspector to inspect your house before he bought it, isn't that correct?

12. Q: You didn't want to pay to replace the roof of the house if it wasn't necessary, isn't that correct?

13. Q: Ms. Bollinger, when Mr. Evans said he wanted to have someone inspect the house, weren't you a little concerned that the inspector would recommend you pay for a new roof?

Analyzing this list of questions, note that all are leading. In addition, all are one-item questions. For example, you could combine Nos. 1–3 into a single longer question such as "You had owned the house for about 15 years before you sold it to Mr. Evans and never replaced the roof, so it was 15 years old when it first leaked in January?" By breaking this long question into three smaller ones, you make the testimony easier to follow and emphasize the age of the roof.

Moreover, the questions are all safe. Questions 1–4, 7, 8, and 11 emanate from Bollinger's prior statements, made during either a pretrial deposition or direct examination. By contrast, the safety of Questions 5, 6, 9, 10, 12, and 13 derive from common experience. For example, common experience suggests that Bollinger will admit that she could not be positive that her 15 year old roof could be fixed with a patch. (No. 5) A factfinder is likely to regard any answer other than an admission as implausible.[12]

---

12. Although undesired answers to many questions based on common experience create implausibilities, you often can not be sure the factfinder will see an undesired answer as implausible. For example, some people might not think a negative answer to question #9 in the Bollinger cross above would be implausible. There- fore when relying on safe questions derived from common experience you will often have to qualify your questions. For example, questions # 5 ("positive"), # 6 ("might"), #9 ("thought perhaps"), #10 ("completely" and "might"), and #13 ("little") all contain qualifiers intended to make an undesired answer seem implausible.

As you can see, safe questions often do more than simply parrot the language of generalizations and "especially whens." For example, Nos. 5, 9, 10 and 13 tend to strengthen the argument by emphasizing additional details suggesting that "especially whens" are accurate.

Of course, by planning to ask only safe questions you may have to forego some questions you would otherwise want to ask. For example, you do not ask Bollinger: "You didn't want Evans' inspector to examine the roof carefully, did you?" This question is not safe.[13] Bollinger can credibly say that she had no objection to the inspector closely examining the roof.

Because converting an argument to questions for cross is not a mechanical process, there is no single "correct" series of cross examination questions for any argument. Because of safety concerns, you may even choose not to ask any questions supporting one or more parts of an argument. Similarly, the order in which you ask questions, how many questions are necessary to emphasize the most important portions of the argument, and even the safety of a question is often a matter of judgment. You owe a client the benefit of your best professional skill and judgment, and in fulfilling that obligation you will have to exercise creativity to produce a cross that most effectively communicates your arguments.[14]

b. *Arguments Based on Credibility Checklists*

Use your credibility checklists to plan cross examinations supporting the credibility of your version of disputed evidence and undermining the credibility of an adverse witness' version.

(1) Arguments Supporting Your Witness' Version of Disputed Evidence

When you review a credibility checklist for evidence supporting your version of disputed evidence, you will often find that an adverse witness is the source of at least some of that evidence. In such situations, planning consists of making a list of the safe questions that will elicit that credibility evidence.

For example, assume again that you are counsel for Evans. You have direct evidence tending to prove your factual proposition that Bollinger did not mention the leak in the roof: Evans says that Bollinger never mentioned the leak to him. As Evans' testimony is disputed, you prepared a Credibility Checklist to help you identify arguments supporting Evans' version of this dispute. Assume that your Credibility Checklist included the following arguments:

---

13. In some instances, you choose to ask unsafe questions during cross. See *infra* Sec. 5 for a discussion of the risks and benefits of doing so.

14. During cross you can also undermine an adversary's argument based on undisputed evidence. When doing so, your questions focus on "except whens" rather that "especially whens." See Chapter 4.

Credibility Checklist for Evans' Disputed Testimony: Evans was never told by Bollinger that the house had a leaky roof.

Physical Ability: Evans was sitting very close to Bollinger at the time she claims to have told him about the leaky roof and Evans would have been able to hear the statement had it been made.

Reason or Motive to Listen: Evans would have paid attention to a statement about a leaky roof because buying the house was a major financial investment and he was very concerned about its condition.

Consistency with Other Witnesses and Documents: Evans' not being told about the roof is consistent with the testimony of Mr. Naila, Evans' inspector. Naila says that Evans did not tell him to look closely at the roof when inspecting the house or to check the roof to make sure that it no longer leaked. Also, Evans' not being told about the roof is consistent with the testimony of Bollinger, who admitted during her deposition that Mr. Naila did not say anything to her about the roof or the leak when he came to inspect the house.

Can you communicate any of these arguments during the cross of Bollinger? Certainly, you might plan to point out during her cross that Evans' version of this dispute is consistent with Naila's behavior when he inspected the house. Your planning might produce the following list of questions:

1. Q: You were at your house when Mr. Naila came to inspect it for Mr. Evans, correct?

2. Q: And when he arrived, you and he had a brief conversation?

3. Q: When Mr. Naila came to inspect the house, he did not say that Mr. Evans had told him about a leak in the roof, did he?

4. Q: And he didn't say that Mr. Evans had told him to be sure to check out the roof, did he?

5. Q: He didn't ask you for any records relating to a repair of the roof?

6. Q: And when Mr. Naila came to inspect the house, he didn't come up to you and say something like, "Ms. Bollinger, show me where the rain came in when the roof leaked in February", did he?

7. Q: And Mr. Naila never asked you how bad the leak in the roof had been, did he?

8. Q: In fact he didn't ask you anything about a leaky roof?

9. Q: When Mr. Naila came to inspect the house, he never mentioned the roof to you at all, did he?

All of these leading questions are safe. If the witness does not agree with the assertion in the question, she can be impeached with her deposition testimony. As in the earlier example, you communicate your argument by converting a single item on the checklist into multiple questions. That is, you do more than simply ask, "Mr. Naila said nothing to you about a leaky roof when he came to inspect the house, right?" Using multiple questions slows down the pace and thus emphasize Naila's unawareness of a roof problem. However, this is not the single "correct" series of questions to communicate this argument. Your judgment might have led you to ask more or fewer questions to communicate the argument.

(2) Arguments Undermining Your Adversary's Version of a Disputed Item of Evidence

In addition to bolstering your witness' version of disputed evidence, typically you also complete a Credibility Checklist to identify arguments attacking an adverse witness' version of disputed evidence. And you will often be able to communicate those arguments during your cross examination of that witness.

For example, as Evans' counsel you are attempting to prove that Bollinger did not mention a leaky roof to Evans. You have already identified your arguments supporting Evans' version of this dispute. Next, examine a Checklist you might have prepared to attack Bollinger's version.

Credibility Checklist Attacking Adversary's Version of Disputed Testimony: Bollinger told Evans that the roof leaked after an earlier repair.

Reasons or Motives for Not Engaging in Disputed Behavior:

(a) Bollinger was anxious to close the sale with Evans because Bollinger had been unable to sell the house for over two months, and withheld the information about the roof to make sure the sale would go through.

(b) Bollinger mentioned the roof to other prospective purchasers and they decided not to buy the house. Consequently, she decided not to mention it to Evans so the sale would go through.

Inconsistency of Disputed Behavior With Other Witnesses and Documents: When the sale of the house closed, Bollinger signed a document indicating that the house "had no defects in the plumbing, floors, roof...."

Again, during planning you might convert one or more of these arguments into cross examination questions. For example, the two arguments in the "Reasons or Motives" sections of the Checklist might produce the following safe, leading questions for Bollinger: [15]

1. Q: You first put your house on the market in April?
2. Q: You held open houses in April, isn't that right?
3. Q: No one made a written offer to purchase your house in April, did they?

---

15. Assume that the questions are safe because they are based either on Bollinger's deposition or on testimony that will come from more believable sources.

  4. Q: You held open houses in May?

  5. Q: And no one made a written offer to purchase your house in May, did they?

  6. Q: Mr. Hatfield came to look at your house before Mr. Evans did, correct?

  7. Q: And at some point, you thought Mr. Hatfield might be interested in purchasing your house, isn't that right?

  8. Q: You mentioned the problems you'd had with the roof to Mr. Hatfield, correct?

  9. Q: Mr. Hatfield never made an offer to buy your house, did he?

 10. Q: Ms. Montague also came to look at your house before Mr. Evans did, correct?

 11. Q: And at some point, you thought Ms. Montague might be interested in purchasing your house, isn't that right?

 12. Q: You mentioned the problems you'd had with the roof to Ms. Montague, correct?

 13. Q: Ms. Montague never made an offer to buy your house, did she?

You can likewise convert the "Other Witness and Documents" argument into cross examination questions. Consider, for example, the following series of questions:

  1. Q: Ms. Bollinger I'm showing you what has been marked as Exhibit # 30, would you look at it please?

  2. Q: That's your signature on the bottom of Exhibit #30, isn't it?

  3. Q: The sale of your house was a significant financial transaction, wasn't it?

  4. Q: And you realized that a document describing the condition of your house might be important?

  5. Q: And Exhibit #30 is a document you signed in connection with the sale of your house to Mr. Evans, correct?

       Your Honor, I have a transparency of Exhibit #30 which I would like to place on the overhead projector while I am examining this witness about the document.

       Court: You may proceed.

  6. Q: Now, Ms. Bollinger do you see the section of the document entitled "Seller's Representations Regarding Condition of the Property"?

  7. Q: And do you see the sentence that begins "Are there any defects in the plumbing, floors, roof"?

8. Q: And do you see the next sentence where it says "If there are any such defects, please explain the nature of each defect in the space below"?

9. Q: In the space below on this document you didn't indicate that your roof had leaked after it had been patched, did you?

10. Q: You didn't write down anything about the roof, did you?

11. Q: You did check the box that said there were no defects in any of the areas of the house listed on this document, isn't that right?

12. Q: And before you checked the box indicating that there were no defects in any of those areas of the house, you did read the sentence before the box, didn't you?

Again, notice how you can use safe questions to emphasize the evidence supporting an argument. Here, you could have limited your cross of Bollinger on this point to admitting the exhibit into evidence. But the additional questions highlight the importance of the document and its failure to mention the roof problem.

Problem for Analysis

In the examples above, your Credibility Checklists related to an item of disputed direct evidence. But the planning process is identical for witnesses who testify to important items of disputed *circumstantial* evidence.

To further your understanding of the cross examination planning process, return to the case of *State v. Holland* discussed in the previous chapter. As you recall, Holland is charged with the rape and murder of Maryann Matthews on August 15. You represent Holland, who denies committing the murder but admits having consensual intercourse with Matthews on the night of her death. Your client says that he met Matthews in a lounge and agreed to meet her later that evening. He picked her up in his truck when she left the lounge. They drove out of town, went for a walk and made love. He dropped Matthews off at her car and drove home. The last he saw of Matthews, she was getting into her car.

One of the prosecution witnesses will be Bunny Haro, Matthews' friend. According to Haro's statement, just before Matthews left the lounge she told Haro that she was feeling ill and was going home. Matthews also told Haro that she had a heavy schedule at work the next day and had to start work early. Haro noticed that Matthews looked pale and her voice sounded like she was sick. Based on this anticipated testimony of Haro you have constructed the following argument which you think the prosecution will make:

Item of Evidence: On the night of her death, Matthews told Haro that she wanted to go home early because she was ill.

Generalization No. 1: "People who say they are feeling ill often are genuinely ill.

> *Especially When* . . . .

- They look ill.
- They sound ill.

> *Except When* . . . .

- They are making up an excuse to leave their friend."

Generalization No. 2: "People who are genuinely ill usually do not engage in consensual sexual intercourse.

> *Especially when* . . . .

- The other person is a stranger.
- They have to be at work early the next morning.
- They have a particularly heavy work schedule the next day."

Therefore, Matthews did not have consensual intercourse with Holland on the night of her death.

Your response to this anticipated argument is to concede that Matthews told Haro that she was ill,[16] but to argue that Matthews' statement was a ruse to conceal from Haro that Matthews was going out with a man she had just met that night at the lounge. To support your response, you will dispute Haro's testimony that Matthews looked and sounded ill that night. And you have prepared the following Credibility Checklist arguments to discredit her testimony.

Credibility Checklist for Adversary's Version of Disputed Testimony: Haro says that Matthews appeared ill.

Lack of Physical Ability: The lounge was not brightly lit, and Haro had consumed some alcohol before talking with Matthews.

Motive or Reason Not to Engage in Conduct: As Matthews' close friend, Haro would have believed Matthews' statement that she was ill and thus Haro had no reason to look closely for symptoms to confirm Matthews' statement.

Now, prepare a list of safe questions that you might put to Haro to communicate these Checklist arguments. The evidentiary source of your safe questions should be the direct examination of Haro in Chapter 12 Sec. 2 A.[17]

---

16. You might make such a concession because you have completed Credibility Checklists regarding Haro's assertion that she heard Matthews say she was ill and concluded that the factfinder will almost certainly accept Haro's testimony that Matthews made such a statement.

17. If you're having difficulty converting a Checklist argument into specific questions, one technique you might use is to identify generalizations and especially whens linking an item of credibility evidence to your desired conclusion. Here, for instance, you might set out the following:

> a. "People usually believe close friends who say they are ill."

> b. "People who believe that a close friend is ill often neglect to closely inspect the friend, especially when . . . the lighting is bad, they are in a bar, etc."

(c) Arguments Based on Inconsistencies in an Adversary's Witness' Story

Another kind of argument you often communicate during cross is based on an inconsistency in an adverse witness' story. The following sections describe the planning process for this type of argument.[18]

(1) Arguments Based on Inconsistencies With Common Experience

First, examine how to communicate an argument that a story is inconsistent with common experience. Assume that you represent the defense in the well publicized rape prosecution of William Kennedy Smith. As you may recall, in 1991, William Kennedy Smith was a member of one of America's most powerful families. In that year, while in a bar, he met a young woman by the name of Patricia Bowman. Bowman claimed that Kennedy Smith raped her after she gave him a ride home from the bar to the lavish Kennedy Palm Beach estate. Smith's defense was consent.

Prior to trial, Ann Mercer, a close friend of Bowman's, gave a statement to the police. According to Mercer, Bowman telephoned Mercer from the Kennedy estate and said she had been raped. Mercer went at once to the Kennedy estate to pick up Bowman. When she arrived at the estate, Bowman was distraught and standing on a landing just outside the house. Bowman asked Mercer to find Bowman's shoes. Mercer then went through the house and down to the beach with Kennedy Smith looking for Bowman's shoes but was unable to find them. It was dark in the house and Mercer was alone with Kennedy Smith when looking for the shoes. When they were unable to find Bowman's shoes, Mercer returned to her friend and they left the estate.

Based on Mercer's pretrial statement to the police, you identified the following inconsistency with common experience in Mercer's story: Mercer knew that Bowman claimed that she had been raped by Kennedy Smith. Yet Mercer went through the house and grounds alone with Kennedy Smith looking for Bowman's shoes.

During pretrial preparation you constructed the following argument based on this inconsistency:

If: Bowman had told Mercer she had been raped by Smith. . . .

Then: We would *not* have expected Mercer to have gone through the house and grounds alone with Kennedy Smith looking for Bowman's shoes. . . .

Because:

---

18. This section focuses on inconsistencies with common experience and inconsistencies with established facts. For a discussion of how to impeach a witness with inconsistent statements see Sec. 3 d *infra*. When an inconsistency relates to statements made by two or more adverse witnesses, you may have to wait until closing

(1) Mercer would have wanted to get her friend away from the scene of the rape as soon as possible.

(2) Mercer would have wanted to get her friend medical attention as soon as possible.

(3) Mercer would have been afraid to be alone at night in the house and on the grounds with an alleged rapist.

Therefore Mercer's story is inconsistent with common experience.

During your cross examination of Mercer you want to ask safe, leading questions that communicate your argument that Mercer's story is inconsistent with common experience. Your cross may go as follows:

Q: Ms. Mercer, when Ms. Bowman called you she was distraught, she told you she'd been raped, and you immediately drove to the Kennedy estate to pick her up, is that right? [19]

Q: When you got there, Ms. Bowman was outside the house?

Q: You didn't immediately take your friend home, did you?

Q: And you didn't immediately take your friend to a hospital, did you?

Q: After you arrived at the estate, Ms. Bowman wanted to know where her shoes were, correct?

Q: So you tried to find them?

Q: You asked Mr. Smith if he knew where her shoes were, isn't that right?

Q: This is the man who you thought had just raped your best friend, correct?

Q: And you and Mr. Smith went into the house to look for her shoes, right?

Q: And it was dark in the house, wasn't it?

Q: You and he were alone walking through the dark house, looking for a pair of shoes, correct?

Q: You and this man you had been told was a rapist?

Q: And then you walked outside the house with him, correct?

Q: You walked down to the beach with him looking for the shoes, is that right?

Q: The two of you were alone on the beach, right?

Q: It was dark, wasn't it?

Q: Just you and the man you thought was a rapist? [20]

to develop your argument. See Sec. 7 e *infra*.

19. This question obviously violates the "one item question" rule of cross. But you are doing nothing more than repeating the adversary's version of events to set up the inconsistency. Thus, you may choose to lump the evidence into a single question to avoid emphasizing it.

20. This cross example was suggested by Roy Black's cross examination of Mercer in the actual trial.

This planned cross relies on safe, leading questions to elicit testimony supporting your argument that Mercer's story is inconsistent with common experience. As before, you emphasize certain portions of the argument with several questions (e.g., the "alone at night" aspect), and ask only one question to support other portions (e.g., for "didn't take her to the hospital").

(2) Arguments Based on Inconsistencies With Established Facts

A story may also be inconsistent with established facts (usually a document or a more believable witness). Here, your typical goal on cross is to commit a witness to the position that conflicts with the established fact or prior statement, so that you can later impeach the witness.

For example, assume that you are the prosecutor in a murder case. The defendant, John Menendez, admits shooting his parents, but claims that he did so in self defense. Your theory is that the self defense claim is a sham, and that the defendant had acquired the gun much earlier and was waiting for an opportunity to kill his parents, claim self defense and collect his inheritance.

In a pretrial statement to the police, Menendez stated that on October 2, a week before the killing, he bought the gun he used to kill his parents at a Big 6 Sporting Goods store that was near to his house. He said that he bought it to protect himself from his parents when they threatened his life on October 1. Les Ammo, the owner of Big 6 and your more believable witness, is prepared to testify for the prosecution that Big 6 stopped selling guns March 1, seven months before the defendant claims to have bought it.

Assume that on direct, Menendez testifies to purchasing the gun at Big 6 on October 2. In this situation, you may forego cross on this point entirely, and later call Ammo, the Big 6 owner, to contradict the defendant's testimony. However, a primary disadvantage of foregoing cross is that after Ammo testifies, the defendant may retake the stand and offer an explanation. Here, for instance, after Ammo testifies Menendez may offer the following explanation if you fail to commit him to his story:

Q: Mr. Menendez, do you wish to change your testimony as to where you bought the gun?

A: Yes, I guess I'm not really sure where I bought it. I really thought it was at Big 6, but apparently it wasn't. It must have been at SportShop or one of the other sporting goods stores near the house. I was so scared that I didn't pay that much attention to where I was buying the gun, I just knew that I might need it for protection.

This explanation largely undercuts the importance of the inconsistency. Hence, consider whether during cross you can safely commit the witness to the testimony creating the inconsistency with the more believable witness. Consider this series of questions:

1. Q: After your parents threatened you on October 1, you went out the next day and bought a gun, right?

2. Q: You bought it at the Big 6 sporting goods store?

3. Q: And you went to the Big 6 store because it was near your house, right?

4. Q: It was less than a mile from your house, correct?

5. Q: Other than the fact that the Big 6 store was close to your house, was there any reason you decided to buy the gun at Big 6?

6. Q: And when you bought the gun at Big 6, what did the clerk ask you for in the way of identification?

7. Q: Do you remember whether you dealt with a male or female sales clerk when you bought the gun?

This cross commits the defendant to the inconsistent testimony. There is little chance that a factfinder will believe a possible explanation like "I must have been confused when I said Big 6." Almost all the questions are safe, for they are based on the witness' prior statements. While you have included non-leading, open questions in the cross (Nos. 5, 6 and 7), such questions are safe here because any answer the witness gives further commits the witness to the testimony which Ammo, your more believable witness, will later contradict.[21]

Note that if Menendez had not testified on direct to the evidence which is inconsistent with Ammo's story, you may yourself elicit the evidence from Menendez for the purpose of later contradicting it with Ammo's testimony.[22] For example, based on Menendez's prior statement to the police, you may ask him, "You bought the gun at a Big 6 store, correct?" The rest of the cross may then proceed as above.

d. Using "Ultimate Conclusion" Questions

All the above cross examination examples have one thing in common: the conclusion you ultimately want the factfinder to draw is *not explicitly* stated in any of your questions. For example, the argument in Section 2 a above tries to convince the factfinder to accept the conclusion that Bollinger did not tell Evans about the leaky roof because she

---

21. This "firmly commit the witness" approach during cross carries some risk. The witness may become suspicious of your interest in the testimony creating the inconsistency with established facts and recant during the cross. For example, in response to question number 3 above the witness might respond: "Well I think it was Big 6 but I'm not sure. I didn't know where to buy a gun so I went to a sporting goods store near my house. I'm not sure which one. There were several near my house." You could still call your witness to testify that Big 6 did not sell guns when the defendant claimed to have bought one in that store, but the impact of the inconsistency may have been significantly reduced by the witness' recantation during cross.

22. You may not, however, impeach a witness on a "collateral matter." See, e.g., *United States v. Kozinski*, 16 F.3d 795 (7th Cir.1994).

thought the roof might have to be replaced. But this conclusion is not explicitly stated anywhere in the cross. Instead, the cross juxtaposes several items of evidence tending to prove this conclusion. Similarly, defense counsel's cross of Ms. Mercer in the Kennedy–Smith rape trial (Sec. 2 c) juxtaposes evidence suggesting an inconsistency but does not explicitly state what conclusion should be drawn from the inconsistency.

However, you can often use "ultimate conclusion questions" to help communicate any type of argument to a factfinder. As an example, again consider the cross examination of Bollinger based on the undisputed evidence that she knew that the roof was patched in January and leaked in February. Below is the same cross examination of Bollinger that was set forth in Sec. 2 a. Notice how inserting into the beginning of that cross one or two ultimate conclusion questions explicitly identifies the conclusion you want the factfinder to accept:

Ultimate Conclusion Question # 1: Ms. Bollinger, when you agreed to sell the house to Mr. Evans in June you knew very well that it needed a new roof, didn't you?

Ultimate Conclusion Question # 2: Well, isn't it a fact that because you didn't want to pay for a new roof before you sold the house, you didn't tell Mr. Evans about the problems you'd had with the roof?

1. Q: You had owned the house for about 15 years before you sold it to Mr. Evans, is that right?

2. Q: And during the 15 years you'd owned the house you never put a new roof on it, did you?

3. Q: So when the roof first leaked in January it was 15 years old?

4. Q: When your roof leaked in January, you had a roofer come out to look at it?

5. Q: Before the roofer came out to look at the roof in January, you were not positive that the leak in the roof could be fixed with a patch, isn't that right?

6. Q: Before the roofer came out, you thought your old roof might have to be replaced, isn't that correct?

7. Q: Now after the roof was patched, it leaked again in February, right?

8. Q: And that was just a month after you'd had the roof patched?

9. Q: And when the roof leaked only a month after being patched, you thought the patch on the roof had not completely corrected the problem, isn't that right?

10. Q: And you thought that if the patch hadn't completely corrected the problem, you might need a new roof, isn't that true?

11. Q: Mr. Evans told you that he wanted his inspector to inspect your house before he bought it, isn't that correct?

12. Q: You didn't want to pay to replace the roof of the house if it wasn't necessary, isn't that correct?

13. Q: Ms. Bollinger, when Mr. Evans said he wanted to have someone inspect the house, weren't you a little concerned that the inspector would recommend you pay for a new roof?

Bollinger will almost certainly refuse to agree with the assertions in your ultimate conclusion questions. But you expect her to refuse. The main point of these questions is to preview for the factfinder the argument you are trying to develop with the remaining questions.[23]

You can insert ultimate conclusion questions into any cross examination. For example, your cross based on Bollinger's failure to mention the problems with the roof in the documents she signed in connection with the sale of the house might begin with the following ultimate conclusion question:

"Ms. Bollinger, in the documents you signed in connection with the sale of your house you never mentioned the problems you'd had with the roof because you didn't want Mr. Evans to know the roof had leaked, isn't that true?"

Similarly, defense counsel's cross of Ms. Mercer might begin with the following questions:

"Ms. Mercer, isn't it true that on the night you picked Ms. Bowman up at the Kennedy estate she did *not* tell you that she had been raped?"

"Well, you went into the house with Mr. Smith because you did *not* think he was a rapist, isn't that right?"

While ultimate conclusion questions often make it easier for a factfinder to understand the argument you are trying to communicate during cross, they carry an increased risk of an explanation. The reason is that the argumentative tone of an ultimate conclusion question often provokes a witness into answering with an argument of her own. Many judges will permit a witness' argumentative response, out of a feeling that "you asked for it" by asking an argumentative question. Consider the following example:

Ultimate Conclusion Question # 1: Ms. Bollinger, when you agreed to sell the house to Mr. Evans in June you knew very well that it needed a new roof, didn't you?

---

23. The ultimate conclusions questions in the text precede the questions designed to communicate your argument. You could, however, place ultimate conclusion questions in the middle or at the end of the questions designed to communicate your argument. However, the witness is more likely to volunteer rebuttal when you place such questions in the middle or at the end of questions designed to communicate your argument.

A: No. That's not right.

Ultimate Conclusion Question # 2: Well, isn't it a fact that because you didn't want to pay for a new roof before you sold the house, you didn't tell Mr. Evans about the problems you'd had with the roof?

A: That's not true. I did tell him about the problems I'd had with the roof. I told him that when we negotiated the price of the house. And I didn't think. . . .

You: Your Honor, I move to strike everything after "that's not true" as non-responsive. I believe she's answered the question.

The Court: Counsel, you asked the argumentative question and I'm going to permit the witness to finish her answer. Ms. Bollinger, are you finished with your answer?

A: I was just going to say that I didn't think that the house needed a new roof. As I said, it had rained several times after February and the roof hadn't leaked at all. So why would I think the house needed a new roof. No one ever told me that, they said a patch would do the job. And I'm not a roofing expert, so how would I know that it needed a new roof? Besides when Mr. Evans said he wanted his inspector to look at the house I thought he'd look at the roof and see the patch, so I had no reason to try to hide anything from him.

Here, the ultimate conclusion questions provoke Bollinger into telling her own rebuttal story.[24] Had these questions not been asked, you could have communicated your argument without the factfinder hearing the counter argument during your cross. Indeed, but for the ultimate conclusion questions the counter argument might never be made, or would at least be delayed until redirect examination.[25]

Ultimately, whether to use an ultimate conclusion question is (like almost everything else) a matter of judgment. Typically, you will not use an ultimate conclusion question if you think that a factfinder will understand your argument without it. On the other hand, you may use an ultimate conclusion question if you think it is necessary to communicate your argument and an adverse witness is unlikely to argue back (or unlikely to argue back effectively) in response.[26]

---

24. Because judges often permit witnesses to argue in response to ultimate conclusion questions, you may get the best of both worlds if a judge sustains opposing counsel's "argumentative" objection. You get to ask the question and preview your argument, but the witness doesn't have a chance to argue in response. For this same reason, you may not want to object to an ultimate conclusion question asked of your witness.

25. This risk makes ultimate conclusion questions potentially the most unsafe question you can ask on cross examination. Most unsafe questions are risky because they may elicit a single item of unfavorable evidence undercutting your argument during the cross examination. Ultimate conclusion questions risk a witness inserting numerous unfavorable items of evidence and opinions into the cross.

26. Another potential risk of asking ultimate conclusion questions is that such questions preview an argument for a witness as well as for a factfinder. Consequently, a witness may "see where you are going" with your cross, and will almost certainly not provide helpful answers to your questions. Of course, to the extent that a cross relies on safe questions, you

3. RESPONDING TO UNANTICIPATED AND/OR UNDESIRED ANSWERS TO SAFE QUESTIONS

Fortunately for manufacturers of upset stomach remedies, your cross examinations will not always unfold exactly as you planned. Even if your questions are safe, witnesses may give answers that you did not anticipate and do not desire. For example, witnesses may offer explanations, give non-responsive or evasive answers, claim failure of recollection and change their stories. This section suggests techniques for responding to witnesses who give such answers.

a. Witness Gives Non–Responsive or Evasive Answer

You are entitled to insist in a professional manner on responsive answers to unambiguous questions. Moreover, a factfinder may discredit the testimony of a witness who is repeatedly evasive and non-responsive. The sections below illustrate techniques for insisting on an answer while emphasizing the evasiveness of the witness' original response.

(1) Repeat the Question

Assume that in support of one of your arguments you want to ask a witness whether he saw the bear go over the mountain. The question is safe because the witness so testified during his deposition. Nevertheless, when you ask the question the following ensues:

Q: On that Friday, you saw the bear go over the mountain, correct?

A: That Friday was a really busy day and I didn't have time to pay much attention to the bear.

Here, while the witness has not denied your assertion, the witness has not answered your question. One technique for dealing with such non-responsive and evasive answers is to simply "repeat the question." Thus, your follow-up question might be:

Q: But on that Friday, you did see the bear go over the mountain, correct? [27]

A slight variation is the "I Didn't Ask You X—I Asked You Y" technique, which tends to give greater emphasis to a witness' attempt to evade. To use this technique in the context of this same evasion, you might have used this follow-up question:

Q: Mr. Smith, I didn't ask you whether Friday was a busy day. What I asked you was, on that Friday, you saw the bear go over the mountain, correct?

may not care if the witness sees where you are going with the cross. With safe questions, the witness must still either give you the answer you expect, or be impeached or testify inconsistently with common experience.

27. As an alternative to personally repeating the question, you may ask the judge to have the court reporter reread your question.

(2) Repeat Your Question and Move to Strike the Non–Responsive Answer

Often you will combine a motion to strike a non-responsive answer with repetition of your question. For example:

Q: On that Friday, you saw the bear go over the mountain, correct?

A: That Friday was a really busy day and I didn't have time to pay much attention to the bear.

You: Your Honor I move to strike the witness' answer as non-responsive.

Court: Motion granted. [Judge instructs jury to disregard the stricken testimony]

Q: Mr. Smith, perhaps you didn't understand my question. Let me repeat it. On that Friday, you saw the bear go over the mountain, correct?

A: Yes, I did.

A successful motion to strike may prevent the factfinder from taking into account the stricken testimony in reaching a decision in the case. The motion to strike does, however, interrupt the flow of your cross, and may also call the factfinder's attention to the testimony they are instructed to disregard.

(3) Ask the Judge to Instruct the Witness to Answer

You may also ask the Judge to instruct a witness to answer your question. For example:

Q: On that Friday, you saw the bear go over the mountain, correct?

A: That Friday was a really busy day and I didn't have time to pay much attention to the bear.

You: Your Honor, will the Court please instruct the witness to answer the question.

Court: Mr. Smith, please answer counsel's question.

A: Yes I did.

In front of a jury, such an instruction from the judge may appear to align the judge with your client. In addition, a witness who has been instructed by the court may feel compelled to limit subsequent answers to "Yes" or "No." As a result, some judges will not instruct a witness to answer unless the witness has been repeatedly non-responsive.[28]

---

28. Some judges may allow you to personally instruct a witness to answer. However, unless a judge explicitly authorizes you to do so, make your requests through the judge.

Again, if you want the non-responsive answer stricken from the record, you must make a motion to strike it in conjunction with your request that the court instruct the witness to answer.

(4) Accept a Witness' Less Than Perfect Answer

You could cross examine some witnesses from now until Sunday and they will still equivocate. If you've established the point you set out to elicit, consider moving on to another topic. The repeated evasiveness is likely to have damaged the witness' credibility. Moreover, if you continue to insist on an unequivocal answer the factfinder may resent your effort to squeeze blood from a turnip.

For example, assume that you are cross examining Bollinger, who sold a house to Evans while allegedly failing to disclose that the house had a leaky roof. You are attempting to communicate the argument that Bollinger did not reveal the problems with the roof because she did not want to have to pay for a new roof. Your cross proceeds as follows:

1. Q: You had owned the house for about 15 years before you sold it to Mr. Evans, is that right?

2. A: I'm not exactly sure. It was about 15 years, I guess.

3. Q: And during the 15 years you'd owned the house you never put a new roof on it, did you?

4. A: No. I'd never had trouble with the roof, so I didn't need to replace it.

5. Q: So when the roof first leaked in January it was about 15 years old, isn't that correct?

6. A: I guess so.

7. Q: When your roof leaked in January, you had a roofer come out to look at it, correct?

8. A: Yes. I called someone and he came out right away.

Here, Bollinger's answers are less than perfect. She expands on some answers (e.g., No. 4), and qualifies others (e.g., Nos. 2 and 6). However, the deviations are minor, and any attempt on your part to attempt further control over the witness is likely to interrupt the flow of your cross and alienate judge and jury. Hence, you reasonably decide to accept the answers and move on.

b. Witness Offers an Explanation

A potentially more troublesome situation arises when a witness volunteers an explanation in response to a safe question. Typically, the witness initially provides your desired response. But recognizing the argument which the answer supports, the witness launches into an immediate explanation in an effort to undercut the answer's significance. The situation is one that can arise even though you prepared arguments diligently prior to trial and satisfied yourself that no "except whens" were evident.[29]

For example, assume that you represent the plaintiff, Ms. Jones, in an age discrimination/wrongful termination matter. You want to establish that her supervisor, Mr. Bishop, knew that Ms. Jones was the oldest employee in his department at the time she was fired. The question is safe because Bishop acknowledged this in a conversation with another employee. If Bishop volunteers an explanation, your options are the following.

(1) Repeat Your Question

If Bishop volunteers an explanation, you may use one of the techniques suggested above for non-responsive or evasive answers. For example, consider the following:

Q: You knew that Ms. Jones was the oldest employee in the shipping and receiving department, isn't that true?

A: Sure, but I didn't take her age into account when I decided to let her go.

Q: But you knew that Ms. Jones was the oldest employee in the shipping and receiving department, isn't that true?

A: Yes, I knew that.

When following this technique, you ignore the explanation and emphasize the evidence supporting your argument.

(2) Cut Off the Explanation by Interrupting a Witness' Answer

When you realize that a witness is about to launch into an explanation, another alternative is to stop the witness in mid-response. For example:

Q: You knew that Ms. Jones was the oldest employee in the shipping and receiving department, isn't that true?

A: I did, but that's not the reason . . .

Q: Excuse me, Mr. Bishop, you've answered my question. Now let me ask you. . . .

When you interrupt a witness as above, opposing counsel may object and argue that the witness should be permitted to finish his or her answer. Some judges will sustain such an objection, on the ground that counsel cannot force an incomplete answer on a witness. Yet other judges will support your interruption on the ground that a witness is not entitled to volunteer information, and leave it to opposing counsel to

---

29. Alternatively, you may have identified a likely explanation during pretrial preparation, but decided to go ahead with your argument anyway.

elicit the explanation on redirect.[30]

(3) Emphasize an Unbelievable Explanation

Often, a witness who recognizes the significance of your questions is so rattled that she or he offers an explanation which in the light of everyday experience makes no sense. In such situations, an effective response is simply to use leading questions to emphasize the explanation's implausibility.

For instance, assume that you are prosecuting Dunfor for stealing a car belonging to Edwards. Dunfor admits that he was driving the car belonging to Edwards, but testifies that he was walking down the street when an unidentified driver pulled over and asked Dunfor to wait with the car while the driver ran to pick up his child from a nearby day school.[31] When the driver did not return in 10 minutes, Dunfor says that he drove around trying to find her and was arrested. Your cross unfolds as follows:

Q: So your story is that a man you had never seen before asked you to wait with his car while he picked up his child from a day school?

A: That's right.

Q: After 10 minutes, he hadn't returned?

A: That's right.

Q: So you started to drive around to look for him?

A: Correct.

Q: You didn't walk over to the day school to look for him?

A: No, I thought that maybe he didn't remember where the car was.

Q: Oh, you drove around because you thought the driver might have forgotten where he left the car?

A: Yes.

Q: Yet it had been no more than about 10 minutes since he walked over to the school, correct?

A: That's right.

Q: And you thought that in that 10 minute period he had forgotten where his car was, right?

A: Sure, people forget stuff all the time.

Q: Including where they parked their car 10 minutes earlier, right?

---

30. Though opposing counsel may elicit an explanation on redirect, nevertheless it is frequently to your advantage to try to cut off an explanation. Frequently opposing counsel will not return to the explanation, fearing that doing so will require repetition of the harmful evidence the witness was seeking to explain away.

31. As preposterous as this story may sound, it is a common defense to car theft charges.

A: I suppose.

Here, with a few safe, leading questions you emphasize the implausibility of the defendant's explanation as to the reason he drove off in the car.

c. Witness Claims, "I Don't Remember"

Even if you ask safe questions based on a witness' prior statements, a potential obstacle arises when the witness claims a failure of recollection.[32] For example, assume that during her deposition a witness stated that, "it was raining heavily at the time of the accident." During cross, this dialogue ensues:

Q: It was raining heavily at the time of the accident, correct?

A: I don't remember.

How do you proceed? First, remember that a response of "I don't remember" enables you to refresh a witness' recollection. Thus, in the situation above you could show the witness her deposition testimony, ask her to read it to herself, and then ask her if it refreshes her recollection. If her recollection is refreshed, re-ask your question.[33]

What if the witness persists in claiming a failure of recollection? If the witness is a *party* the prior out of court statement is not hearsay; it is an admission.[34] Thus, you will probably be allowed to impeach the witness with the prior statement.[35]

If the witness is not a party, you may not be able to impeach the witness with the prior statement because it is often inadmissible hearsay. The reasoning is that it is not inconsistent for a witness to recall something at an earlier time and be unable to recall it at a later time. Therefore the prior statement does not qualify under the "prior inconsistent statement" exception to the hearsay rule.[36] However, the following steps may enable you to introduce the prior statement of a non-party witness.

Many evidence codifications deem a witness who has a failure of recollection to be "unavailable" with respect to that topic.[37] That enables you to read the deposition statement into the record under the hearsay exception for "former testimony."[38] Note that this exception commonly applies only to prior statements made under oath during a

---

32. If your safe question is based on common experience and a witness testifies "I don't recall" you will often accept the witness' answer and move on. For example, assume you ask the witness "Generally, you wanted to keep your important customers satisfied, correct?" and the witness answers "I don't recall." The witness' answer is inconsistent with common experience and you can move on to your next question.

33. If when you reask your question the witness testifies inconsistently with the pri-

or statement, you would then impeach the witness.

34. FRE 801 (d) (2).

35. For the techniques for impeaching a witness with a prior statement see Sec. d *infra*.

36. See e.g. *People v. Sam*, 71 Cal. 2nd. 194, 77 Cal.Rptr. 804, 454 P.2d 700 (1969).

37. See FRE 804(a)(3).

38. FRE 804(b)(1).

former trial or deposition. If the prior statement is a letter or informal statement, you will probably not be allowed to read it into evidence even if a witness is unavailable.

Second, evidence doctrine in some jurisdictions authorizes a judge to find that a claimed inability to remember is feigned, conveniently made up in an effort to prevent the disclosure of harmful evidence. If you can establish such a foundation, you can then read the prior statement (whether made in a deposition or informal statement) into the record under the "prior inconsistent statement" exception to the hearsay rule.[39]

d.   Witness Changes the Story—Impeach With a Prior Statement

Typically, many of the safe questions with which you communicate arguments on cross are derived from a witness' prior statements. And when a witness' response conflicts with a prior statement, you can impeach the witness by introducing the prior inconsistent statement into evidence. The procedures for impeaching a witness with a prior inconsistent statement vary slightly depending on the source of the prior statement.

(1) Impeaching With a Prior Deposition Statement

Assume that you represent the plaintiff, Ms. Pine, in a wrongful termination suit. During a pretrial deposition, Ms. Pine's ex-supervisor, Mr. Dent, testified that he thought your client "displayed good judgment when handling the Campbell account." You plan to elicit this favorable evidence during cross of Dent. Compare the following approaches to impeachment when the witness fails to provide your desired answer:

(a) Enhancing the Credibility of the Prior Statement

1. Q: Mr. Dent, you thought that Ms. Pine displayed good judgment when she handled the Campbell Account, correct?

2. A: I wouldn't say that.

3. Q: Well, you had your deposition taken in this case, did you not?

4. A: Yes, I did.

5. Q: And when you testified at your deposition you took an oath to tell the truth, correct?

6. A: Yes.

7. Q: Your Honor, I would like to read from Page 27, lines 14 through 17 of Mr. Dent's deposition.

39. See *United States v. Thompson*, 708 F.2d 1294 (8th Cir.1983): C. Mueller and L. Kirkpatrick, *Evidence* Sec. 6.55 (1995). Often, you will be able to convince a judge that a failure of recollection is feigned when common experience suggests that the witness should recall the information or when a witness' memory goes blank only as to harmful evidence.

Court: You may proceed.

8.   Q: (Reading from the deposition) Question: How would you characterize her work on the Campbell account? Answer: I thought she did a pretty good job on that one. There were some difficulties that came up and I thought she showed good judgment when she handled the Campbell account (You put down the deposition transcript). That was the testimony you gave at your deposition in this case, isn't that right Mr. Dent? [40]

9.   A: I guess so, I really don't remember.

10.   Q: Well, please look at the signature on the last page of your deposition transcript and tell us if it is your signature?

11.   A: Yes, it is.

12.   Q: And you read your deposition over before you signed it, didn't you?

13.   A: Yes.

14.   Q: And when you read it over you knew you that you could change anything that was wrong, correct?

15.   A: Yes.

16.   Q: But you didn't change your answer where you said Ms. Pine exercised good judgment on the Campbell account, did you?

17.   A: No.

18.   Q: When your deposition was taken you were told that if you were unsure of an answer you were not to guess, is that right?

19.   A: I remember that.

20.   Q: The oath you took at your deposition was the same as the oath you took in court today, wasn't it?

21.   A: Yes.

22.   Q: And you told the truth at your deposition, didn't you?

23.   A: Yes.

24.   Q: And your memory about the facts of this case was better when you had your deposition taken two years ago than it is today, isn't that right?

25.   A: Generally speaking, yes.

---

40. In lieu of reading the inconsistent deposition testimony into the record yourself, you might have the witness do so. The advantage of the latter procedure is that the witness is truly impeached out of the witness' own mouth; the disadvantage is that the witness may not read the contradictory material with as much gusto as you do.

26. Q: Now, Ms. Pine worked on the Campbell account dur-
         ing. . . .

(b) The "Bare Bones" Approach

1. Q: Mr. Dent, you thought that Ms. Pine displayed good judg-
        ment when she handled the Campbell Account, correct?
2. A: I wouldn't say that.
3. Q: You had your deposition taken in this case, did you not?
4. A: Yes, I did.
5. Q: And when you testified at your deposition you took an oath
        to tell the truth, correct?
6. A: Yes.
7. Q: Your Honor, I would like to read from Page 27, lines 14
        through 17 of Mr. Dent's deposition.

Court: You may proceed.

8. Q: (Reading from the deposition) Question: How would you
        characterize her work on the Campbell account? Answer:
        I thought she did a pretty good job on that one. There
        were some difficulties that came up and I thought she
        showed good judgment when she handled the Campbell
        account (You put down the deposition transcript).
9. Q: Now, Ms. Pine worked on the Campbell account dur-
        ing. . . .

*(c) Analysis of "Enhance Credibility" and "Bare Bones" Ap-
proaches*

In each example, you immediately impeach Dent with the inconsistent deposition testimony when he fails to provide your desired answer.
By juxtaposing the two inconsistent statements you make the impeachment apparent to the factfinder.

In the first example, you also ask a series of questions designed to
convince the factfinder that the favorable deposition testimony is more
likely to be accurate.[41] The approach is especially important when a
prior statement not only impeaches a witness but also provides affirmative support for one of your arguments. Moreover, all of your questions
are safe, either because they are based on the witness' deposition (e.g.,
No. 18) or because they are consistent with common experience (e.g., No.
24).[42]

41. Since judges understand the significance of deposition testimony, you may decide not to ask these follow up questions in
cases tried to a judge.

42. The series of questions set forth in
the text to enhance the credibility of the
prior statement is only illustrative. For
example, some attorneys ask questions Nos.

A potential disadvantage of the "enhance the credibility of the prior statement approach" is that it creates a substantial digression from the argument you are attempting to communicate. Moreover, if you impeach witnesses with depositions several times in the course of a trial, you are likely to bore the jury to death if you always follow this approach. Therefore, it sometimes makes sense to conduct a "bare bones" impeachment, which creates only a brief digression from an argument.

Though these examples may suggest that the two approaches are utterly distinct, they are but two ends of a continuum. As your judgment dictates, you may add a few questions to the bare bones approach to quickly suggest that the prior statement is more credible, or you may delete some questions from the "enhance the credibility of the prior statement approach" to keep the cross moving more quickly.

(d) The "Pin Down" Approach: Using Multiple Inconsistencies Between Direct Examination Testimony and a Deposition to Discredit a Witness

Sometimes, you begin cross knowing that on direct examination an adverse witness has contradicted a previous statement which supports one of your arguments. In such a situation, it may be useless to ask a question based on previous statement in the hope that the witness will switch back and testify consistently with the previous statement. Instead, you can move immediately into an impeachment mode and offer the previous statement to impeach the direct examination testimony.[43]

When you impeach direct examination testimony, the conflict between the direct testimony and the prior statement may not be apparent to the factfinder. After all, hours or even days may have intervened. To make the conflict apparent, you may "pin down" (have the witness repeat) the direct examination testimony before impeaching him. Admittedly, pinning down forces you to repeat a witness' unfavorable testimony. But particularly when you can bring out a number of conflicts, the cumulative effect of pinning down may discredit the witness' credibility.

For example, in the same wrongful termination case, assume that Mr. Dent testified on direct examination that Ms. Pine showed poor judgment on the Campbell account, undermined Dent's supervision by frequently contradicting him in the presence of other employees and that he had complaints about her work from the firm's accountants. This

10–26 before reading into the record the prior deposition testimony. This is a stylistic choice, but one that has the disadvantage of separating the two inconsistent statements.

43. You may nevertheless use the prior statement as affirmative support for an argument if the previous statement was given under oath (See Fed.R.Evid. 801(d)), or if your jurisdiction admits all inconsistent statements for the truth of their contents. See, e.g., Cal.Evid.Code 1235.

testimony conflicts with statements Dent made during his deposition.
You pin down his direct testimony before impeaching him:

Q: Mr. Dent, you testified on direct that Ms. Pine showed poor
    judgment on the Campbell account, correct?

A: That's right.

Q: You had your deposition taken in this case, did you not?

A: Yes, I did.

Q: And when you testified at your deposition you took an oath to
    tell the truth, correct?

A: Yes.

Q: Your Honor, I would like to read from Page 27, lines 14 through
    17 of Mr. Dent's deposition.

Court: You may proceed.

Q: (Reading from the deposition) Question—How would you char-
    acterize her work on the Campbell account? Answer—I
    thought she did a pretty good job on that one. There were
    some difficulties that came up and I thought she showed good
    judgment when she handled the Campbell account. (You put
    down the deposition transcript)

Q: You also stated during your direct examination that she fre-
    quently undermined your supervision by contradicting you in
    the presence of other employees?

A: Yes.

Q: Again reading from the deposition, Your Honor, this time at
    page 57, lines 9–12. Question—How did you and Ms. Pine get
    along in the office? Answer—I'd say we had a pretty good
    business relationship. She'd occasionally voice a different point
    of view from mine, but that was never a problem.

Q: Now, you also testified on direct that you had complaints about
    Ms. Pine's work from the firm's accountants?

A: That's my best recollection, yes.

Q: Once more reading from the witness' deposition, Your Honor, at
    page 112, lines 19–24. Question—Did you ever receive any
    complaints about Ms. Pines' work from other employees of the
    firm? Answer—I remember a complaint or two from a sales-
    man, something about her not getting orders filled as quickly as
    they wanted. But that's all.

Here, the "pin down" approach emphasizes the inconsistency between Dent's direct examination testimony and statements in his deposition. The cumulative effect may cause the factfinder to conclude that
Dent is unreliable.

(e) Other Techniques for Enhancing Your Impeachment Skills

As the sample dialogues demonstrate, when you impeach with a deposition you generally do not have to show the witness the deposition or mark it as an exhibit. With the court's permission, simply read the question and the inconsistent answer from the deposition into the record. Of course you must identify the page and line number you are reading from so that opposing counsel and the court may determine if the testimony you wish to read in is actually inconsistent with the witness' in-court testimony.[44] And you must read the entire question and answer from the deposition verbatim, unless the judge explicitly permits you to do otherwise.

(2) Impeaching With a Document Prepared or Signed by the Witness[45]

When a witness' testimony conflicts with a statement the witness has previously made in a document, the impeachment techniques are largely the same as they are with a deposition. The principal difference is that unless a document has already been admitted into evidence, you have to incorporate foundational questions about the document into your impeachment questioning.[46] For example, assume that in the wrongful termination case, Dent prepared an Employee Evaluation form in which he stated that Ms. Pine "displayed good judgment when handling the Campbell account." You plan to elicit this information during cross of Dent, and impeach him if he testifies inconsistently. As before, you may follow either an "enhance credibility" or "bare bones" approach:

(a) Enhancing the Credibility of the Prior Statement

Q: Mr. Dent, you thought that Ms. Pine displayed good judgment when she handled the Campbell Account, correct?

A: I wouldn't say that.

Q: May I approach the witness, Your Honor? Mr. Dent, I am showing you a document marked Exhibit 25 for identification. Do you recognize it?

A: Yes.

Q: Exhibit 25 is an employee evaluation of Ms. Pine that you prepared?

44. If the deposition testimony is not inconsistent you usually will not be allowed to read it into the record at that time. If the witness is not a party, the out of court statement in the deposition is often inadmissible hearsay unless it is inconsistent with the in court testimony. And even if the deposition testimony is admissible, if it is not inconsistent with the in court testimony the court may prohibit you from reading it into the record at a point where doing so would create a false appearance of impeachment.

45. You cannot impeach a witness with a document prepared or signed by someone else. See discussion *infra* Sec. 6(e).

46. For a discussion of the questions necessary to lay the foundation for the introduction of documents and other tangible exhibits, see Chapter 16.

A: Yes.

Q: That's your signature at the bottom of it, correct?

A: Yes.[47]

You: Your Honor, I ask that Exhibit 25 be received into evidence.

Court: It will be received.[48]

Q: Mr. Dent, you prepared Exhibit 25 about a month after Ms. Pine had finished working on the Campbell account, correct?

A: Yes.

Q: And you knew that Exhibit 25 would go into Ms. Pine's personnel file, correct?

A: Yes.

Q: And you knew that if Exhibit 25 was in Ms. Pine's personnel file it might be relied on by other people at the company evaluating Ms. Pine, isn't that right?

A: That's possible.

You: Your Honor, I ask permission to read the first two sentences of the third paragraph of Exhibit 25 to the jury.

Court: You may proceed.

You (Reading from the Exhibit): "I thought she did a pretty good job on the Campbell account. There were some difficulties that came up and I thought she showed good judgment when she handled the account." [49]

Q: You wrote that in Exhibit 25 about a month after you observed Ms. Pine's work on the Campbell account, isn't that true?

A: Yes.[50]

Q: Now, Ms. Pine worked on the Campbell account during. . . .

(b) The "Bare Bones" Approach

Q: Mr. Dent, you thought that Ms. Pine displayed good judgment when she handled the Campbell Account, correct?

47. If the witness refuses to admit that she prepared the document, you must later call a third party to testify that the witness did prepare the document, and then read in the impeaching statement.

48. Many judges will not insist that you offer a document containing an inconsistent statement into evidence. Once you lay the same foundation needed to admit the document into evidence, they will allow you to read the impeaching statement into the record.

49. As with a deposition, you may ask the witness to read the portion of the document containing inconsistent testimony.

50. When impeaching with a statement in a document, you may have more difficulty enhancing its credibility than when you impeach with a statement in a deposition. Unlike with a deposition, you have no "standard" list of safe questions that you can incorporate into your cross. Nevertheless, you can often rely on common experience to suggest safe questions enhancing the credibility of the prior statement (e.g., "And you knew that Exhibit 25 would go into Ms. Pine's personnel file, correct?").

A: I wouldn't say that.

Q: Your Honor, may I approach the witness? Mr. Dent, I am showing you a document marked Exhibit 25 for identification. Do you recognize it?

A: Yes.

Q: Exhibit 25 is an employee evaluation of Ms. Pine that you prepared?

A: Yes.

Q: That's your signature at the bottom of the evaluation, correct?

A: Yes.

You: Your Honor, I ask that Exhibit 25 be received in evidence.

Court: It will be received.

You: Your Honor, I ask permission to read the first two sentences of the third paragraph of Exhibit 25 to the jury.

Court: You may proceed.

You (Reading from the Exhibit): "I thought she did a pretty good job on the Campbell account. There were some difficulties that came up and I thought she showed good judgment when she handled the account." [51]

Q: Now, Ms. Pine worked on the Campbell account during....

(c) The "Pin Down" Approach

When a witness' direct examination testimony conflicts with a statement in a document, you may emphasize the inconsistency by having the witness repeat the testimony and then using the document to impeach:

Q: Mr. Dent, you testified on direct that you thought Ms. Pine displayed poor judgment on the Campbell account, correct?

A: That's right.

Q: Isn't it true that you thought Ms. Pine displayed good judgment when she handled the Campbell Account?

A: No. That's not true.

[Complete the impeachment using either the "bare bones" or "enhance the credibility of the prior statement" approach.]

(3) Avoid Triumphant But Argumentative Follow–Up Questions

In the warm afterglow of successfully impeaching a witness with a prior statement, you may be tempted to follow up with an argumentative

---

51. Again, while some attorneys would ask the witness to read the portion of the document containing the inconsistent testimony, there are disadvantages to following this approach. See footnote 40, *supra*.

question such as, "When were you lying—when you testified under oath at your deposition or when you said on direct that Ms. Pine frequently contradicted you in the presence of other employees?" Resist the temptation: Not only is such a question objectionable, it may provoke an explanation that undermines the inconsistency.

(4) Impeaching With a Statement Made by the Witness to a Third Party

You can also impeach a witness with a prior inconsistent statement made to another person. But unlike when the prior statement is part of the witness' deposition or a document prepared by the witness, you cannot immediately "prove up" the inconsistency if the witness denies making the prior statement. Instead, you must call the other person as a witness when it is your turn to present evidence.[52]

For example, assume that Ms. Brown is Dent's supervisor. According to Brown, Dent said that Ms. Pine displayed good judgment when she handled the Campbell account. If on cross Dent refuses to admit that Pine displayed good judgment on the Campbell account, you cannot immediately impeach him. Instead, after the cross you will have to call Brown to testify to the prior inconsistent statement by Dent. For example, the cross of Dent might go as follows:

Q: Mr. Dent, you thought that Ms. Pine displayed good judgment when she handled the Campbell Account, correct?

A: I wouldn't say that.

Q: Well, Barbara Brown was your supervisor when Ms. Pine worked for Dorox Inc., correct?

A: Yes.

Q: And you told Ms. Brown that Ms. Pine displayed good judgment when Ms. Pine handled the Campbell Account, didn't you?

A: No. I don't remember saying that to Ms. Brown.[53]

(5) Impeachment By Omission

A final situation in which you can impeach based on a change in a witness' story arises when a witness provides information during cross that the witness should have but did not mention prior to trial. The witness' omission of the information in a statement made prior to trial often creates an inconsistency with common experience that you can illustrate during cross.

For example, in Ms. Pine's wrongful termination case, assume that Dent explains for the first time during cross examination that one reason

---

52. If the court regards the inconsistency as pertaining to a "collateral matter," the court may not permit you to prove up the inconsistency with "extrinsic evidence" (testimony of another witness).

53. Federal Rule of Evidence 613(b) states that you must either give the witness an opportunity to explain the inconsistent statement on cross examination, or not excuse the witness from giving further testimony.

he decided to discharge Pine is because she left work early without authorization on several occasions during the last two months of her employment. However, the Employee Evaluation form Dent prepared for Pine covering the last three months of her employment makes no mention of her leaving work early. Dent's change of story supports an argument that his testimony is inconsistent with common experience. That argument would go as follows:

If: Pine had left work early without authorization....

Then: We would expect Dent to have mentioned that in Pine's employee evaluation....

Because:

(1) An employee leaving work early without authorization may cause problems for the employer.

(2) Leaving work early without authorization is a significant breach of the employee's obligation to the employer.

(3) Dent would want to make the employee evaluation as complete and accurate as possible.

Therefore Dent's testimony that Pine left work early without authorization is inconsistent with common experience.

During Dent's cross, you might ask the following questions to communicate this argument to the factfinder:

Q: Mr. Dent, you testified on direct that Ms. Pine left work early without authorization on several occasions during the last two months of her employment, correct?

A: That's correct.

Q: When an employee you are supervising leaves work early without your permission, that may cause problems for you, isn't that right?

A: It can, yes.

Q: Mr. Dent, wouldn't you agree that an employee leaving work early without authorization is a serious breach of the employee's obligation to his or her employer?

A: Yes.

Q: You prepare employee evaluations for the people you supervise at work, right?

A: Yes.

Q: And if you know that an employee has committed a serious breach of their obligation to your employer you generally note that in the employee evaluation, correct?

A: Generally.

Q: And if you know that an employee has committed a serious breach of their obligation to your employer on several occasions

you'd be especially likely to note that in the employee evaluation, correct?

A: Yes. I suppose so.

Q: You want the evaluations you prepare to be accurate, don't you?

A: Yes.

Q: And you anticipate that your supervisors might rely on your
evaluations when making decisions about whether to promote
or discharge an employee, isn't that right?

A: Yes.

Q: Your Honor, may I approach the witness? Mr. Dent, I am
showing you Exhibit 25, which has previously been admitted
into evidence. Exhibit 25 is the employee evaluation you prepared for Ms. Pine?

A: Yes.

Q: Your evaluation covers the last three months of her employment, correct?

A: Yes.

Q: Your evaluation covers the period when you say that on several
occasions Ms. Pine left work early without authorization, correct?

A: Yes.

Q: Mr. Dent, in your evaluation of Ms. Pine you didn't indicate
that she had left work early without authorization on several
occasions, did you?

A: No.

Q: In fact, your evaluation says absolutely nothing about Ms. Pine
leaving work without authorization, isn't that true?

A: Yes.

Q: And your evaluation says absolutely nothing about Ms. Pine
leaving work early, isn't that true?

A: Yes.

4. UNSAFE QUESTIONS

Ideally you want to ask only safe questions during cross examination. The following subsections discuss situations in which you might
decide to ask unsafe questions. That is, you might decide to ask
questions which may elicit undesirable answers that you cannot impeach. But be aware at the outset that it is when they leave safe
harbors for open seas that ships have been lost. If the invitation to ask
unsafe questions goads you into rehashing and thus reemphasizing
everything opposing witnesses say on direct, or blindly disregarding
safety concerns, your cross examinations are likely to resemble the
voyage of the Titanic.

a. Information a Factfinder Will Assume Exists

Sometimes, an unsafe question may be low risk in the sense that a favorable answer will provide helpful evidence, yet an unfavorable answer will not significantly damage your case. Usually, the reason that an unfavorable answer will not do significant damage is that in the absence of the answer the factfinder will assume that the unfavorable evidence is true. In such situations you may decide to ask the unsafe question.

For example, assume that you represent a criminal defendant whose defense is mistaken identity. At trial, you notice that an eyewitness who claims to have identified your client from a distance of 50 feet is wearing glasses. You do not know whether the witness needs glasses to see accurately at that distance, or whether the witness was wearing glasses at the time of the incident. Nevertheless, you may ask unsafe questions such as, "Why do you need to wear glasses?" and "Were you wearing your glasses at the time you saw someone holding the gun?" If the witness admits that she wasn't wearing glasses at the time of the incident you have probably helped your case. On the other hand, unfavorable answers would probably not damage your case significantly. The factfinder would probably have assumed that the witness was wearing glasses at the time of the incident had you not asked the questions.

b. Asking Unsafe Questions to Bolster Existing Arguments

A common situation in which you have to decide whether to ask unsafe questions arises when you consider strengthening an existing argument. For instance, an argument may have some force, but you realize that an additional "especially when" or two would be a dandy way of making the argument more persuasive. If you have to rely on unsafe questions to elicit the "especially whens," you run a risk that unfavorable answers will undermine your argument.

For example, assume that you represent Della Rocha, a plaintiff who is suing a police officer for assault and battery. The officer, Laura Petrich, denies attacking Rocha; Petrich claims that she only defended herself when Rocha attacked her when Petrich went to Rocha's house to execute a search warrant. An argument on which you rely is that Petrich had a motive to attack Rocha because six months previously, Rocha had filed a complaint against Petrich with the Police Department for stopping Rocha's car without legal cause. Thus, your argument is as follows:

Evidence: Six months before the incident, Rocha filed a citizen's complaint against Petrich claiming that Petrich had stopped Rocha's car without proper cause.

Generalization # 1: "Police officers who have been subjected to a citizen's complaint sometimes are angry with the citizen."

Especially When

- The officer was disciplined by the department as a result of the complaint.

- The officer had to hire a lawyer to represent her in the disciplinary proceedings.

- The filing of the complaint delayed the promotion that the officer hoped to get.

Generalization # 2: "Police officers who are angry with a citizen sometimes will strike that citizen if they later come in contact with that citizen."

Assume that the only safe questions you can ask pertain to Rocha's filing of the complaint and Petrich's subsequent discipline. Thus if you hope to strengthen the argument with the other "especially whens," you will have to use unsafe questions. And if Petrich denies that she had to hire a lawyer or had a promotion delayed, you have undermined your argument that Rocha's filing of the complaint gave Petrich a motive to attack.

One technique that may enhance your chances of eliciting favorable answers to unsafe questions in these circumstances is to ask the unsafe questions before advancing the rest of your argument. That way, the witness may not realize the import of the questions and therefore be less inclined to fudge an answer. For example, before asking Officer Petrich about Rocha's complaint and Petrich's subsequent discipline, you might inquire about whether she had been scheduled for a promotion. The officer may be more inclined to provide a favorable answer than if questions about Rocha's complaint and the ensuing discipline have put her on her guard as to your argument.

Ultimately, you'll have to rely on your judgment to decide when to ask unsafe questions to try to bolster an existing argument. If an argument is fairly strong without the evidence that unsafe questions might produce, you should probably not ask them. If an argument is weak without the evidence that unsafe questions might produce and you lack strong arguments that rely on safe questions, you will be more likely to ask unsafe questions. And sometimes you may decide to try to strengthen an argument that you had initially regarded as secondary, but which takes on new importance when an argument you had regarded as stronger before trial has evaporated.

5.   THE "NO QUESTIONS" CROSS

"No questions" is often the most overlooked yet most useful of an attorney's cross examination strategies. Whenever you cross examine, you risk eliciting additional harmful evidence. At the very least, you will probably allow a witness to repeat some harmful evidence already given on direct, and allow opposing counsel an opportunity to elicit additional damaging information on redirect. Consequently, you may want to forego cross examination in the following circumstances:

- A witness has not provided damaging testimony on direct. Although almost all witnesses will provide testimony favoring your adversary during direct, if the testimony is not particularly probative on a crucial proposition, you have little to gain and potentially much to lose when you cross examine.

- You can safely elicit evidence supporting your arguments through the cross examination of other adverse witnesses.

- A witness has provided evidence in support of a factual proposition you are prepared to concede. (This rationale applies primarily to defense counsel, who may focus on specific propositions. A plaintiff who concedes a defense position with regard to a factual proposition loses the legal claim to which that proposition pertains.)

- A dispute centers around the interpretation of a normative standard rather than around disputed historical events. For example, assume that your primary argument is that your allegedly negligent client acted reasonably in driving 60 m.p.h. in order to rush his sick child to the hospital. You should probably not cross examine a witness who testifies to how your client drove. If you unsuccessfully attack the witness' credibility, the factfinder may reject your argument that "what's really in dispute is the proper interpretation of reasonableness," and decide against you because it believes your adversary's version of what happened.

Foregoing cross is, of course, a matter for your best professional judgment. Recognize, however, that whenever you cross examine, you implicitly suggest that the adverse witness' testimony was important, and that you will develop favorable information. If you fail to make any headway, you may damage your case in the mind of a factfinder even if the witness doesn't disclose any new and damaging information.

6. "FISHING"

"Fishing" refers to a type of cross examination in which you ask numerous unsafe questions in the hope of obtaining evidence to support arguments you have *not* constructed prior to trial. This type of cross is rare. But sometimes a witness will provide extremely damaging testimony on direct and you have no prepared arguments to undermine the witness' testimony. Your options may be lose the case or fish.

Here are some suggestions to improve your chances of a successful fishing voyage:

a. Ask Open Questions

When fishing, you often have to reverse the normal cross examination practice of asking leading questions. One reason for this is that many judges consider it improper to suggest through a question that a fact is true when you have no good-faith basis to believe the fact is true.[54] For example, assume that you are defense counsel in a criminal case and

---

54. See 6 J. Wigmore *Evidence* Sec. 1808 (Chadbourn Rev. 1976).

you are cross examining an eyewitness who has identified your client as the culprit. The witness claims to have seen your client after walking out of an office building. You should not ask, "You were in the building to have your vision checked, correct?" unless you can point to information giving you a good-faith reason to believe that your suggestion is true. To fish for helpful information, you have to use an open question such as, "What were you doing in the building?"

Open questions are also helpful when fishing because they encourage adverse witnesses to testify in their own words. Though contrary to the Received Wisdom of cross examination, this may be your only hope of developing evidence to support an argument. Under the "give a person enough rope and he'll hang himself" rationale, an adverse witness just might disclose favorable evidence that would not otherwise have come out.

For instance, assume that you represent a defendant in a negligence action. The plaintiff has produced a witness who insists that your client ran a red light and was steering her car with her toes. Your client insists that neither claim is accurate. You have decided that not to cross examine this witness would be tantamount to conceding liability, and that you need to fish if you are to have any chance of developing favorable evidence. Consider such questions as:

- "Tell us what you were doing in the four hours preceding the accident."

- "Please describe what the plaintiff did following the collision."

- "Tell us what contacts you've had with the plaintiff from the date of the accident until today."

Responding to such open questions, a witness may reveal evidence that supports your client's version of events. Or, you might uncover evidence from which you can argue that the witness' story is in some way inconsistent. While your chances of doing so may not be high, you may reasonably decide to take this approach if the alternative is almost certain defeat.

b. Focus Your Questions on Evidence That Would Normally Exist If a Witness' Testimony Were True

Rarely will a witness admit that something she said on direct examination was incorrect. Therefore, if you are to develop favorable evidence when fishing, your questions typically have to focus on evidence that would be consistent with the witness' testimony. Use your knowledge of how the world operates to identify evidence that would be consistent with a witness' assertion. If you can show that evidence that would normally exist if what the witness says is true does not in fact exist, you have a basis for arguing that the witness' testimony is incorrect.

A silly example will demonstrate the technique. An adverse witness testifies, "I am the defending Olympic high jump champion." You want to cast doubt on this testimony, but have no safe bases for doing so. So ask yourself, "If what the witness says is true, what else is very likely to be true?" Based on everyday experience, you expect an Olympic high jump champion to know the height of the winning jump, the names and countries of origins of, and heights cleared by the second and third place finishers, to have participated in prior meets, to be able to spell at least eight steroid-related chemicals, etc. Such information can be put to the witness on cross examination:

- "What was the height of your winning jump?"
- "Please tell us the nationalities of the second and third place finishers." [55]

c. Probe for Details

As the name implies, the "probe for details" cross examination technique typically consists of detailed probing of events to which a witness has already testified on direct examination. You have two chances of casting doubt on that testimony. The witness may remember either so few details or so many details that either way, the factfinder disbelieves his testimony.

For example, assume that you are cross examining a waiter who claims to have overheard your client enter into an agreement during a lunch meeting that your client insists never took place. Consider this type of cross:

Q: Who arrived first at the restaurant?

A: Your client, Ms. Robinson.

Q: How was she dressed, if you recall?

A: I remember she was wearing a blue suit with some sort of gold pin.

Q: And how long after that did Mr. Hoffman arrive?

A: Just about five minutes later.

Q: And you're sure of that?

A: Pretty sure.

Q: You were busy serving other customers in the restaurant?

A: I had some other customers, yes.

Q: Now once they were seated, what's the first thing you heard either of them say?

A: Ms. Robinson asked what the specials were for that day....

Even without seeing the rest of the examination, you can see the beginnings of an argument that the witness' story is inconsistent with everyday experience; that it is highly unlikely that someone other than The Amazing Kreskin would remember such details.

---

55. Remember that when you have no reasonable basis to believe a fact is true, you can not suggest it is true through your questions, see Sec. 6 a *supra*.

The converse might also occur. The waiter might have professed inability to recall anything other than, "I heard Ms. Robinson say that she would pay $3 million for the plastics factory." In this situation, you argue that the witness' memory is so sparse that he is unworthy of belief.

d. Rely on Your Judgment

Even though fishing necessarily implies a lack of safe questions, you may yet have some basis for deciding what areas to inquire into. Has your adversary avoided certain topics during pretrial negotiations and conferences? During direct examination, did a witness seem to lack confidence with respect to certain topics? Do you have some information, even though not the sort you can offer into evidence, that suggests you might get a favorable answer? Asking yourself these questions may improve your chance of a successful fishing trip.

7. IMPORTANT EVIDENCE RULES GOVERNING CROSS EXAMINATION

a. Scope of Cross

The traditional "American rule" is that cross examination is limited to the scope of direct examination. In general, this means that you can ask questions pertaining to (a) the subject matter of direct; and (b) a witness' credibility. The policy behind this rule is that each side to a trial has the right to limit the scope of its presentation. Therefore, if you wish to go outside the scope of your adversary's presentation, you should call the witness when it is next your turn to present evidence.[56]

The application of this rule is committed to judges' "sound discretion," and they vary greatly in how strictly they apply it. Some judges tend to ignore it completely, reasoning that avoiding the delay and inconvenience of forcing a witness to return on a separate day for additional testimony is a stronger policy than enforcing a technical rule of trial procedure. Other judges prefer to narrowly define the scope of direct. Thus, if you anticipate an objection in a close case, be prepared to argue why it makes sense to take all the witness' testimony at once, and how the scope of direct is broad enough to encompass the questions you wish to ask.

b. Character Evidence

A full analysis of the character evidence rules as they relate to cross examination is beyond the scope of this text. In general, the Federal Rules of Evidence permit you to impeach a witness with a conviction of a felony, with a misdemeanor conviction for a crime involving dishonesty, and, subject to judicial discretion, with evidence of specific acts of dishonesty.[57]

---

56. In most jurisdictions, you could probably call the witness as a "hostile witness" and ask leading questions. See FRE 611(c).

57. Fed.R.Evid. 608, 609.

As when you are fishing, you can not suggest the existence of damaging character evidence unless you have a good faith believe that the evidence is true.[58] The reason for this is that a juror may assume that no matter what the witness' answer, counsel would not have been permitted to ask the question unless it were true. For instance, examine this possible cross examination of a bystander in a traffic accident case:

Q: Mr. Johnson, how far away from the traffic signals were you?

A: About 15 yards.

Q: Mr. Johnson, were you under the influence of cocaine at the time of the accident?

Opp. Counsel: Object, Your Honor. There's absolutely no evidence that Mr. Johnson was under the influence of any substance whatsoever.

Cross Examiner: If that's the case, Your Honor, he can say so.

Judge: So you have no basis for asking the question?

Cross Examiner: Well, no.

Judge: The objection is sustained, and I'll see both counsel in chambers.[59]

You don't really want to know what might go on in chambers, particularly if this is not the first such incident. A mistrial, sanctions, contempt of court, and a report to the Bar Association for disciplinary proceedings are all possible. When in doubt about whether you have sufficient information to establish a good faith belief, consider seeking an advance ruling from the judge.

c. Don't Argue With a Witness or Answer a Witness' Questions

Particularly when you believe that an adverse witness is being purposely evasive, you may tend to argue or answer a witness' questions. Though the emotional impulse is understandable, as a professional you are expected to resist them. Better that you keep your professional cool and seek the judge's help when necessary.

Examine this exchange:

Q: What time did you arrive there?

A: I'd say about 3 o'clock.

Q: You're not sure of much, including the time, are you?

---

58. See Sec. 6 a *supra*.

59. Compare this example with the one described in Sec. 6 a, *supra*. When fishing, in general you have to ask a non-leading question if you lack a good faith basis to believe that it is true. But if the subject matter is socially embarrassing, you cannot even ask a non-leading question.

The last question is improperly argumentative. Though phrased as a question, it's really a comment on the evidence which belongs in final summation.

And this one:

Q: You immediately blew down the house made of straw, right?

A: What would you have done?

Q: Well, I would have gotten an environmental permit, as you should have done.

Again, a witness has baited a questioner into an improper response. Your role during cross is to ask questions, not give testimony. After the witness' evasive response, the cross examiner might properly have done one of the following:

1. "What I would have done is not the issue, and I am not under oath. You did immediately blow down the house made of straw, correct?"

2. "I didn't ask you what I would have done, I asked you if it isn't a fact that you immediately blew down the house made of straw."

3. "Your Honor, I move to strike the witness' remark. Will Your Honor please instruct the witness to answer the question?"

4. "Please just answer my question. You immediately blew down the house made of straw, correct?"

d. Elicit Evidence From a Prior Statement Without Referring to It

As this chapter has emphasized, safe cross examination questions frequently emanate from a witness' prior statements. In such a situation, you should not refer to the prior statement unless the witness contradicts it. Only then will you refer to the prior statement, in order to impeach the witness.

For example, assume that Jack and Jill have brought suit against a landowner for personal injuries based on the landowner's negligent maintenance of a well. On direct examination, Jack's friend Hansel testified that he saw Jack and his sister Jill go up a hill, fetch a pail of water and slip on loose bricks near the base of the well. During cross examination of Hansel, you want to elicit the following evidence based on testimony Hansel gave during his deposition: he had seen Jack and Jill go to the well many times before. You want to elicit this information to support your argument that Jack and Jill were themselves negligent. On direct, Hansel was not asked and he said nothing about whether he had ever seen Jack and Jill at the well before.

In this situation, compare the following two questions:

Improper Question: Q: Hansel, you testified during your deposition that Jack and Jill had gone to the well many times before, correct?

Proper Question: Q: Hansel, you had seen Jack and Jill go to the well many times before, correct?

This first question is improper because whether Hansel made this statement during his deposition is *irrelevant*, and the deposition testimony is *hearsay*. The second question properly elicits the evidence without referring to its source. If Hansel says "No" in response to the second question, you can then read his inconsistent deposition testimony into the record to impeach him.

e. *You Cannot Impeach One Witness With the Prior Inconsistent Statement of a Different Witness*

Only a prior statement of the witness you are cross examining is admissible to impeach that witness. You cannot impeach one witness with the prior statement of another.

For instance, assume that you represent the defendant in a personal injury action. Chuck, a plaintiff's witness, signed a statement indicating that it was raining heavily at the time of the accident. Linda, a second plaintiff's witness, then testifies that it was not raining when the accident occurred. In this situation, you cannot impeach Linda with Chuck's prior inconsistent statement. Consider this dialogue:

You: You say it was dry when the accident occurred?

Linda: That's right.

You: Your Honor I would like to read in the first sentence of Exhibit 32 [the statement signed by Chuck], previously admitted into evidence.

Your Adversary: I object your Honor. This is improper impeachment.

Court: Objection sustained.

The objection and the ruling are proper. You may argue whatever inferences you think should be drawn from the conflict between Chuck and Linda, but you cannot impeach one witness with the contradictory statement of another.[60]

f. *Distinguish Impeachment From Refreshing Recollection*

Impeachment with prior statements and refreshing recollection are two different techniques. Evidence rules authorize impeachment with a prior statement when it conflicts with a witness' in-court testimony, and

---

60. Some judges may permit you to ask Linda the following questions: "Did you hear Chuck testify on direct examination that it was raining heavily at the time of the accident? Isn't it true that it had stopped raining when the accident occurred?" These questions may be permitted because they simply juxtapose a conflict between two of the plaintiff's witnesses. The improper questions in the text, on the other hand, may mislead the factfinder into thinking that Linda has made two inconsistent statements. Even if you are permitted to juxtapose an inconsistency between two of your adversary's witnesses you should not follow up with questions such as, "Then how can you explain the fact that Chuck says that it was raining heavily?" Not only is this question objectionable as argumentative and calling for speculation, it is tactically unwise: it openly invites the witness to explain away the inconsistency.

refreshing recollection when a witness is unable to recall an item of evidence. Thus, it is improper (yet far too common) for a cross examiner to attempt to refresh recollection though a situation requires impeachment. Consider this example:

Assume that you represent the defendant in a personal injury action. You are cross examining Linda, and based on a statement in her deposition want to elicit testimony that it was raining heavily when an accident occurred. The following dialogue takes place:

> You: Now, it was raining heavily when the accident occurred, correct?

> Linda: No, I'd describe it as more of a steady drizzle.

> You: Well, let me show you your deposition testimony and see if it refreshes your recollection.

Your last question is improper, because no foundation exists for refreshing Linda's recollection. Linda has not claimed inability to recall the weather conditions. When a witness' testimony is at variance with the witness' prior statement, what you may do is impeach the witness, not refresh her recollection.[61]

8. MISCELLANEOUS STRATEGIC ISSUES

a. *Prepare Your Witness for Cross Examination*

Unnerved by the dramatic depictions of cross examination in movies and on television, many witnesses are genuinely fearful of it. Therefore, when you prepare a witness for direct examination, save time to review your adversary's expected cross. Following the lead of many attorneys, you may want to bring in a colleague for a practice cross, so as not to breach a sense of trust between you and a witness. Also, assure the witness that you will protect the witness against sharp tactics by opposing counsel. For example, tell a witness that you will step in if opposing counsel asks an improper question, misquotes the witness, does not allow the witness to finish an answer, or begins arguing with the witness.[62]

b. *Order of Cross Examination Topics*

As you know, the typical format of a direct examination is chronological. But in cross examination, you generally aim to establish support for discrete arguments rather than elicit a story. Thus, when you seek to elicit evidence supporting more than one argument, it is often more effective to elicit the evidence pertaining to one argument before you

---

61. Of course, if in response to your question Linda had said that she could not remember whether it was raining heavily, it would be perfectly proper for you to attempt to refresh her recollection.

62. If a witness is not your client, what you say to her when preparing for cross is not privileged. Consequently, when pre-paring witness you will typically emphasize that you want them to answer opposing counsel's questions truthfully and responsively. Then, if opposing counsel suggests on cross that you improperly prepared a witness, you can have the witness testify to your instructions.

move on to the evidence supporting a different argument, regardless of the overall chronology of events. For example, assume that you plan to ask an adverse witness one set of questions to elicit evidence of bias, and another set supporting your argument that your client mentioned a problem with the roof to the purchaser of her house. The temporal relationship of the evidence for the two arguments probably will not matter. A factfinder's assessment of the arguments is unlikely to be affected by the order of the arguments.[63]

Instead of chronology, such considerations as these normally influence the order of topics during cross examination:

- Of the arguments you plan to develop, which is the "strongest," in the sense that it is either most crucial to a favorable outcome or supported entirely by safe questions? Since a factfinder may be most attentive at the outset of cross, you may want to begin with your "strongest" argument.

- Consider eliciting evidence to support your affirmative arguments before attacking a witness' credibility with inconsistencies in the witness' story.

- Consider starting your cross on whatever topic direct examination concludes. This topic may be freshest in a factfinder's mind.

- A traditional ordering tactic described in the trial advocacy literature is "hop, skip and jump." This refers not to questions asked by an Olympian during a track meet, but to flitting randomly back and forth with questions to different parts of a witness' story. The idea is to coax inconsistent replies from a witness who can tell a straight story only in chronological order. This technique is useful, if at all, only when you are fishing and you are hoping to catch the witness testifying inconsistently with his direct examination. This technique reduces the witness' opportunity to simply retell his story.

c. *Mid-Course Maneuvering*

Because the questions you ask on cross examination typically flow from your arguments, this Chapter has emphasized that you can plan many of your cross questions prior to trial. But pretrial preparation, no matter how thorough, cannot completely eliminate the unpredictable, dynamic nature of trial. Adverse witnesses sometimes provide evidence that you didn't expect, and when they do trials come closest to the hoary maximum that to be a good trial lawyer you have to be able to think on your feet.

One possibility is that the unexpected evidence will constitute additional support for one of your arguments. If so, you can safely ask the

---

63. On the other hand, ordinarily you can foster factfinder understanding of a discrete argument by eliciting the evidence supporting that argument in chronological order. For instance, you might elicit the evidence supporting an argument that your client told the purchaser of her house about a problem with the roof in chronological order.

witness to repeat the testimony on cross. If the witness changes her or his story, you can impeach the witness with the inconsistent direct examination testimony.

A second possibility is that the unexpected evidence undermines one of your arguments. If you hope to respond to the evidence, you'll have to do some quick thinking. Is the unexpected testimony inconsistent with anything the witness has previously said, with an established fact, or with everyday experience? If so, you may safely try to show that the unexpected testimony is not accurate. But if no safe questions challenging the accuracy of the unexpected testimony come to mind, you'll have to consider how to proceed. For example, if the unexpected evidence explains away an inconsistency and thus vitiates an argument you planned to develop, you may decide to abandon that argument.

A third possibility is that the unexpected evidence serves as the basis for an entirely new argument, perhaps one that will supplant an argument you had intended to make. Unlike some lawyers in movies, you will probably not have the good fortune of having a new argument handed to you on a golden platter at the last minute by an adverse eyewitness bumping into counsel table and the hatrack on the way to the witness box. But if you learn about highly probative evidence for the first time in the middle of trial, do not hesitate to treat it just like any other undisputed highly probative evidence. Try to enhance its probative value with "especially whens," and seek to elicit those "especially whens" both on cross of the same witness and the examinations of other witnesses.

Chapter 14

CLOSING ARGUMENT

Closing argument is something of an enigma. Typically blending a highly partisan interpretation of unique events with an appeal to neutral concepts of liberty and justice, closing argument conveys an image of powerful oratory whose flourishes captivate a rapt factfinder. Its potential power is partly a product of the past, for many of history's most charismatic public speakers have been lawyers who have bestowed their most dramatic words on courtrooms. Though the bombast of earlier times is not common today, closing argument may retain a hold on your imagination as your primary chance to win over a skeptical factfinder.

Contrasting with this powerful image is an attitude exemplified by the judicial response which frequently greets attorneys who object to an adversary's remark during final argument: "Overruled; it's only argument." The judicial response suggests an attitude that closing argument is relatively unimportant, a crass attempt to divert attention from evidentiary shortcomings. The attitude is supported by empirical evidence suggesting that jurors often do not change their tentative verdict preferences at the close of the evidence as a result of closing arguments.[1]

At the end of the day, it matters little which of these perspectives is more likely to be accurate. For example, whatever your success in communicating your arguments throughout a trial, an effective summation may reach factfinders who are on the fence. Too, an effective closing may help those jurors already inclined in your client's favor to win converts or resist counter arguments during jury deliberations. And surely some factfinders do change their minds based on closing arguments. Convincing one factfinder to change his or her mind may be the difference between winning and losing a trial. Thus, whatever a factfinder's state of mind, you want your last chance to speak to be effective and persuasive.

This chapter describes and illustrates a variety of effective closing argument techniques, including using analogies, preemptive arguments and inoculation. The chapter also explains the most important legal rules governing closing argument. But the chapter's emphasis is on techniques for making arguments explicit. One reason for this emphasis is, as you recall, that many different inferences or conclusions can be drawn from circumstantial evidence. Explicit arguments explain to a factfinder what inferences you want them to draw an why, and are thus often more persuasive than implicit arguments. Moreover, you will probably find explicit arguments much more difficult to make than implicit ones. Explicit arguments are difficult to articulate because most of us are socialized to be implicit. In everyday conversation, implicit arguments are the rule because we rely on verbal and non-verbal feedback from our audience to determine when we have "made our case." But rarely in everyday conversation do you confront an audience that must sit in stony silence as you speak, and then listen to your adversary who is trying to convince them that everything you say is hogwash. Thus, you may have to break your socialized shackles to become the explicit orator your parents always hoped for.

You should not infer, however, from the chapter's emphasis of explicitness that an explicit argument is always more effective than a more implicit one. Implicit arguments have their advantages, and the chapter endeavors to point them out.

1. INTRODUCTION TO A CLOSING ARGUMENT

Just as opening statements typically have Introductions, so too do closing arguments. You have considerable flexibility when deciding

---

1. V. Hans & K. Swigert, Jurors' Views of Civil Lawyers: Implications for Courtroom Communication, 68 Ind. L.J. 1297, 1314–15 (1993).

what to say in an Introduction. Some counsel like to begin by thanking the jurors for paying close attention to the evidence, while others like to point out any failure by their adversary to produce the evidence promised in the adversary's opening statement.

However you begin, an Introduction will often briefly identify the legal elements the law requires you to prove and the factual propositions you contend you have proven to satisfy each element. You then indicate which propositions you will concentrate on in your closing. After your Introduction, a factfinder should understand why a favorable resolution of the issues you've outlined compels a verdict for your client.

For example, a plaintiff's Introduction in a fraud case may go as follows:

"If you'll look at the overhead, you'll see that I've put up the instruction that the judge will give you shortly which defines what the law requires us to prove in order to show fraud.[2] As I'll discuss, the evidence we've introduced clearly establishes everything the law requires us to prove. We've proven that on the afternoon of February 2, defendant Bank told Ms. Palmer that it would provide construction financing for her miniature golf course. This satisfies the first requirement, that there be a representation (pointing to overhead of jury instruction). Next, we've shown that Bank knew that the statement was false. . . .

"If you find that we have met each of these requirements, under the law Ms. Palmer is entitled to a verdict and damages in the amount of $68,000. Now, let's look at the evidence that establishes that we've satisfied each of these legal requirements.

"First, let's look at the evidence that the Bank told Ms. Palmer that it would provide construction financing for her miniature golf course."

In many cases, during an Introduction it will not be necessary for you to review each of the legal requirements you have to meet. It may be clear from the evidence that only a single issue or two is in serious dispute, and if so your Introduction may focus on that issue.[3] For instance, assume that in the case of Palmer v. Bank, the only real dispute between the parties is whether Palmer reasonably relied on Bank's offer of construction financing. In this situation, the heart of your Introduction may go as follows:

"As you've listened to all the evidence, you know that there's only one issue that you have to consider to decide whether Bank committed fraud, and that is whether Ms. Palmer reasonably relied on Bank's offer of construction financing. Bank does not dispute that

2. In lieu of an overhead, you might write out the elements on a blackboard or an easel. Of course, the simplest but perhaps least memorable option is to state them orally.

3. Though your Introduction and ensuing argument may focus on one or two propositions, as the plaintiff or prosecutor you will at some point want to establish that you have proved all of the required propositions, crucial or not.

the offer was made, nor does it dispute that it failed to provide the financing. I will now discuss why the evidence clearly shows that Ms. Palmer did reasonably rely on Bank's offer, and that she's entitled to recover damages in the sum of $68,000."

Often criminal cases involve only one or two seriously disputed issues, and those issues are often obvious to a factfinder. For example, in a typical armed robbery case, often the only issue in serious dispute is the identity of the robber. In such a case, the prosecution's Introduction will briefly review the elements of the crime and indicate that only identity is in dispute.

Typically, defendants do not challenge every element of a plaintiff's claim.[4] Therefore, a defendant's Introduction will usually more closely resemble the second example than the first. For example, assume that Methusela Enterprises has been sued by a former employee, Leon Ponce, for age discrimination. Methusela admits discharging Ponce, but contends that the discharge was based on Ponce's poor work performance and was not age-related. Defense counsel's Introduction may focus on the single element Methusela disputes:

"The judge will instruct you that if you find that Methusela would have discharged Mr. Ponce even if he had been under 40 years of age, you must return a defense verdict. Now let's look at the evidence proving that Mr. Ponce would have been terminated no matter what his age."[5]

2. ORDER OF ARGUMENTS

Once past your Introduction, you launch into the arguments themselves. No standard pattern exists for the order of arguments you discuss during closing. For example, it is impossible to set forth rules such as, "Make arguments based on undisputed evidence before arguments based on disputed evidence or inconsistencies in adverse witnesses' stories."

However, you can consider the following factors when deciding on the order of arguments. Especially when you have the burden of proof, you will usually want to begin with your strongest affirmative arguments.[6] You are the party who has to move a factfinder off dead center,

---

4. A criminal defendant whose only defense is the prosecution's failure to prove its case beyond a reasonable doubt will of course not set forth a defense factual proposition in an Introduction. Instead, defense counsel will typically begin by focusing on the jury instruction defining the burden of proof and asserting that the prosecution has failed to meet it.

5. You may also emphasize in your Introduction what is *not* an issue that the factfinder should focus on. For example, in a criminal case the prosecution may emphasize that the issue is *not* whether the police did a flawless job when collecting blood samples from the scene of the crime, but whether the defendant committed the brutal murders of two innocent people. Including such a statement in your Introduction may undercut arguments made by the defense during trial and help to focus the factfinder's attention on the issues you see as most important.

6. Since a factfinder's attention will often be sharpest at the beginning of closing, it makes sense to start with your strongest arguments. R. Lawson, *Order of Presenta-*

so you should emphasize your affirmative case by presenting it first. You would then turn to the weaknesses in your opponent's case.

A second factor to consider is what issues a factfinder probably sees as most important. Based on what happened at trial, you may conclude that a factfinder is most likely to be concerned about the credibility of a particular witness or a particular evidentiary dispute. If so, you may want to begin closing with arguments responding to those issues. After all, you encourage an audience to listen by beginning with the issues the audience thinks are most salient.[7]

3. MAKING ARGUMENTS EXPLICIT

During a single summation, you typically make several of the arguments discussed throughout this book. That is, you will make:

- Arguments based on undisputed evidence;
- Arguments based on disputed evidence;
- Arguments attacking the credibility of the adversary's witnesses' stories; and
- Arguments about a normative standard.

The following subsections explore techniques for making these arguments explicit. Understand at the outset that "explicitness" is a matter of degree; few arguments are either fully explicit or fully implicit. In general, however, an explicit argument is one that identifies the important evidence supporting your desired inferences, points out and illustrates the principal generalizations underlying the argument, and explains why the factfinder should reach your desired conclusion. As you can see, the arguments you've learned how to prepare prior to trial put you well on your way towards delivering an explicit argument in closing.

a. *Explicit Arguments Based on Undisputed Evidence*

During pre-trial preparation of an argument based on undisputed evidence, you link highly probative evidence to a factual proposition, formulate the generalization(s) underlying the linkage, and strengthen the argument with "especially whens."[8] Typically, summation is your only chance to communicate an argument explicitly, because witnesses cannot ordinarily testify to generalizations and "especially whens" are usually scattered through the testimony of different witnesses.

To understand how to communicate an argument explicitly, assume again that you represent the plaintiff in *Prager v. Dolinko*. As you may recall from Chapter 4, Pauline Prager was allegedly struck and killed by a truck driven by the defendant Dolinko. Prager's husband is seeking to

---

tion as a Factor in Jury Persuasion, 56 Ky. L.J. 523, 529–30 (1968).

7. Indeed, in a court trial you may ask the judge at the beginning of closing if there is an issue the court would like you to address. And if the judge tells you, for example, that she is not sure you have proven that the defendant was speeding, you would usually address that factual proposition first in closing.

8. If you did not identify generalizations and "especially whens" prior to trial, you will need to do so prior to summation to make an explicit argument.

recover damages in a wrongful death action.   One crucial factual proposition you are trying to prove is that Dolinko was momentarily inattentive to the road just before he struck Prager.   You prepared and offered evidence supporting the following argument:

Undisputed Item of Evidence: Just before the accident, Dolinko got a phone call informing him of a problem with one of his remodeling jobs.

Generalization 1: "Building contractors who receive a call on their car phone informing them of a problem with one of their remodeling jobs are sometimes thinking about the problem as they drive."

Especially when:

1. The problem has to be dealt with before the job can continue.

2. The problem is a large one.

3. The contractor receiving the call is the owner of the company.

4. The contractor receiving the call is in the vicinity of the job site.

5. The contractor receiving the call changes his route to go to the job site.

Generalization 2: "Building contractors who are thinking about a problem with one of their remodeling jobs as they drive are sometimes inattentive to the road."

Therefore. . . .

Factual Proposition: Dolinko was momentarily inattentive to the road just before he struck Prager.

An explicit version of this argument may go as follows:

1   "Ladies and Gentlemen, as I mentioned just a moment ago, one
2   of the issues you must decide is whether the defendant was
3   inattentive to the road just before he struck and killed Ms.
4   Prager.   You will recall that the defendant admitted during
5   cross examination that just moments before the accident, he got
6   a phone call while driving in his truck informing him of a
7   problem with one of his remodeling jobs.   And building contrac-
8   tors, like the defendant, who receive a call on their car phone
9   informing them of a problem with one of their remodeling
10 projects often think about that problem as they drive.   Especial-
11 ly when they hear about the problem in the vicinity of the job
12 site, and the problem they hear about is a large one.   And what
13 sort of problem had the defendant been told about?   It wasn't
14 just a minor problem.   Remember the defendant's testimony?
15 He said that this was a large problem.   And he's especially
16 likely to have been thinking about the problem as he drove
17 because it was a large problem that required his immediate
18 attention.   We know the problem required his immediate atten-
19 tion because, as the defendant told you, the problem had to be
20 dealt with before the job could continue.   And since the defen-
21 dant was the owner of this construction company, if the job

22   couldn't continue immediately he might have lost money. So
23   the defendant had lots of reasons to be thinking about the
24   problem as he drove. And as a result he was at least momen-
25   tarily inattentive to the road when he struck Ms. Prager just
26   moments after receiving the phone call."

Here, you identify an undisputed item of evidence (lines 4–7), a generalization linking the evidence to your desired conclusion (lines 7–11), and the evidence supporting your "especially whens" (lines 11–24). In addition, you clearly assert your desired conclusion (lines 24–26). To make the above argument more explicit and enhance its persuasiveness, you can "validate" your generalization(s) and "especially whens" (i.e. establish their accuracy) by pointing out that they are consistent with the factfinder's own personal experiences. For example, a more explicit version of the above argument might go as follows:

"Ladies and Gentlemen, as I mentioned just a moment ago, one of the issues you must decide is whether the defendant was inattentive to the road just before he struck and killed Ms. Prager. You will recall that the defendant admitted during cross examination that just moments before the accident, he got a phone call while driving in his truck informing him of a problem with one of his remodeling jobs. And building contractors, like the defendant, who receive a call on their car phone informing them of a problem with one of their remodeling projects often think about that problem as they drive. Especially when it is a large problem. And remember the defendant admitted on cross examination that this was a large problem he was told about. *Now, I know none of you are building contractors, but you've probably all been listening to the car radio when you've heard some distressing news. When you did, wasn't your instinctive reaction to think about the bad news and about how it might affect you? Such a reaction is quite common, its something we all do.* And the evidence shows that that's just what the defendant did.

"What other evidence indicates that the defendant was thinking about this problem just before the accident? We know that when he got the call, he was near the remodeling job that had the problem. *So when he gets the call isn't it natural for him to be thinking: 'That job's near here. I could swing by and fix the problem right now.'* And that's just what he did. He changed direction to go to the remodeling job because he was thinking about the problem just before the accident.

"There's other evidence that tells us the defendant was probably thinking about this problem immediately before the accident occurred. Remember the defendant admitted on cross examination that the remodeling job couldn't continue until this problem was fixed. *And we all know that time is money.* He's not just an employee who gets paid by the hour, he's the owner of the company. So if the defendant can't fix this job he's going to lose money and he knows it. *What do people often do when they have a problem that involves losing money. Don't they do what you would do, think about how to solve the problem so that they can limit their losses?*

"Thus, after the defendant gets this call he has every reason in the world to be thinking about how to solve the problem and what he's going to do to rearrange his schedule if the problem can't be solved and work on the remodeling job is stopped or delayed. *How do you know that? Because your common sense—what you know about how people behave—tells you that's what most likely happened.* And as the court will instruct you, you are the ones who have to use your common sense, look at the evidence and decide what really happened.

"If the defendant was thinking about this problem while he was driving isn't it also likely that he was momentarily inattentive to the road? *How many of you have caught yourself thinking about a business or personal problem and consequently not paying strict attention to what your doing or what someone is saying to you? How many times have we heard someone say: 'I'm sorry. I didn't hear what you said. I was thinking about something else.' In fact, while driving haven't you or someone you know had the experience of missing a turn or almost getting in an accident because your mind was on something other than the road?* That's what happened here. The defendant was inattentive to the road for just a moment and struck Ms. Prager." [9]

Here, you validate the generalizations and "especially whens" by referring to the factfinder's own personal experiences.[10] The validation technique tacitly says to the factfinder: "If you look at the personal experiences I've touched on in my argument, you'll see that the defendant's actions in this case were similar to how you and others behave in similar circumstances."[11] Establishing similarity is persuasive because people typically decide what they believe "really happened" by making similarity assessments.[12]

b. *Explicit Arguments Based on Disputed Evidence*

Arguments that your version of disputed evidence is accurate are drawn from the Credibility Checklist.[13] An explicit credibility argument sets forth the disputed evidence, communicates the Checklist arguments,

---

9. The language of these arguments is illustrative only. What you say will vary from case to case, depending on such factors as type of case and your argument style.

10. When making explicit arguments you need not validate every generalization and "especially when." So doing may detract from your argument's persuasiveness by making it seem stilted or too long.

11. Analogous personal experiences may be either actual or vicarious. If you refer to an experience the factfinder has had

("you've heard distressing news over the radio"), that's an actual analogous experience. If the experience is one that the factfinder has read or heard about ("we've all had friends who have heard about distressing news while driving"), that is a vicarious experience.

12. Albert J. Moore, Trial by Schema: Cognitive Filters in the Courtroom, 37 UCLA L.REV. 273 (1989).

13. See Chapter 5, Sec. 1.

and tells a factfinder both why your version of a dispute is accurate and an adversary's is not.[14]

(1) Explicitly Supporting Your Version of Disputed Evidence

Assume that you continue to represent the plaintiff in *Prager*. Recall that Ms. White testified that she saw Ms. Prager in the crosswalk moments before the accident occurred. But White's testimony is disputed; defendant Dolinko claims that Prager ran out from between two parked cars approximately 50 feet north of the crosswalk. Assume that you have identified the following Checklist arguments to support White's version of the dispute: [15]

Credibility Checklist

1. *Physical Ability* : White was close enough to observe Prager in the crosswalk, the lighting was good at the time and her view was unobstructed.

2. *Reason or Motive to Engage in Conduct*: White had a reason to observe Prager because Prager was wearing clothing White thought she might want to buy for herself.

3. *Internal Consistency*: White's testimony about returning to the scene after the accident is consistent with her having seen Prager in the crosswalk. White returned to the scene to identify herself as a witness.

4. *Neutrality*: White has no financial interest in the litigation. She has no motive to lie about what she saw.

5. *Reason to Recall*: White remembers seeing Prager in the crosswalk because the accident occurred seconds later.[16]

As you argue the significance of each item on the Checklist, you can validate your argument with analogous personal experiences. For example, to explicitly communicate an argument based on White's "physical ability," you might say something like the following:

"Recall that the testimony of Cynthia White and Steve Dolinko differed on one important point. Ms. White said she saw Ms. Prager in the crosswalk just moments before she was struck and killed by the defendant's truck. Mr. Dolinko testified that Ms. Prager ran out from between two parked cars about 50 feet north of the crosswalk just before he struck her. If you look at the evidence

14. If the disputed item of evidence is circumstantial evidence, you may also have to make a second argument explaining why the evidence supports your desired inference, as in the previous subsection illustrating an argument based on undisputed evidence.

15. If you did not prepare the Credibility Checklist prior to trial because you did not think the evidence would be disputed,

you would have to prepare it prior to delivering your closing.

16. Based on the trial testimony, you may sometimes identify additional arguments which were not included in your pretrial Credibility Checklist. If so, you would add those arguments to the Checklist prior to closing.

you'll see that Cynthia White is correct and that Ms. Prager was in the crosswalk when she was killed.

"First of all, let's look at where Ms. White was when she saw Ms. Prager in the crosswalk. She was the first car in line at the light because she had arrived at the intersection just as the light turned red for traffic going in her direction. She was stopped in the lane closest to the curb, parked right here where she placed a 'W' on the diagram. Ms. White also told us that there were no cars immediately to her left, so she had a clear view of the crosswalk. And she saw Ms. Prager step off the curb right here, where she placed a 'P' and start to walk across the crosswalk. And she did what we all do from time to time when we're stopped at a light that has just turned red. She looked to her left and noticed someone directly in her line of sight: a woman in the crosswalk. So Ms. White had a clear, unobstructed view of Ms. Prager in the crosswalk. And remember that this accident didn't take place at 9 o'clock at night or even at dusk; it happened at 3 o'clock in the afternoon. All this indicates that Ms. White is correct when she says she saw Ms. Prager in the crosswalk seconds before the accident.

"There is additional evidence that Ms. White saw Ms. Prager in the crosswalk. We know that Ms. White had a reason to be looking at Ms. Prager moments before her death...."

Here, you do more than assert a conclusion that White was close enough to observe Prager and had an unobstructed view. Instead, you explicitly review the individual items of evidence supporting your desired conclusion, and refer to the factfinder's analogous personal experience ("And she did what we all do ... looked to her left....") [17] You would complete the argument by discussing the other evidence in a similar fashion.[18]

---

17. Note that we have not suggested that you articulate generalizations and "especially whens" connecting a specific item of evidence to the conclusion that White had the physical ability to see Prager in the crosswalk. You could do so, however. For example, in *Prager* you might construct the following: Item of Evidence: White was parked only a street width away from Prager. Generalization: Drivers who are parked only a street width away from a pedestrian usually are able to see whether that pedestrian is in a crosswalk. Especially When: (1) Nothing obstructs the driver's view. (2) It is 3:00 P.M. Therefore, White had the physical ability to see Prager in the crosswalk. You could, of course, articulate similar generalizations and "especially whens" for any category on the Credibility Checklist. You will have to use your judgment to determine if articulating generalizations and "especially whens" in this fashion will help you to clearly explain to the factfinder how your evidence proves that your witness is accurate.

18. Of course, you must exercise some judgment about whether to mention an argument from the Credibility Checklist at all during your closing. In pretrial preparation, you identified all the *potential* arguments you might make to resolve an evidentiary dispute. Before closing you must reassess the arguments on your Checklist and decide if they are strong enough to warrant mention during closing. Consider, for example, the "Internal Consistency" argument. You may conclude that this is a weak argument (after all if she had seen someone hit in a crosswalk why didn't she stop immediately and identify herself as a witness) and not mention it at all in support of your witness' version of this evidentiary dispute. See R. Klonoff & P. Colby, *Sponsorship Strategy: Evidentiary Tactics for Winning Jury Trials* 95–105 (1990).

(2) Explicitly Attacking the Adversary's Version of Disputed Evidence

In addition to supporting your version of disputed evidence, you can explicitly attack the adversary's version in much the same way. For example, in *Prager*, Dolinko contradicts White; he testified that Prager ran out from between two parked cars north of the crosswalk. To explicitly attack Dolinko's testimony, refer to the arguments drawn from the Credibility Checklist and consider validating each argument by referring to a factfinder's analogous personal experience.

For example, assume that one of your arguments attacking Dolinko is that he lacks neutrality: He says Prager ran from between two parked cars because he does not want to feel responsible for her death.[19] You might deliver this argument as follows:

> "... And if Ms. White is correct, then the defendant must be wrong when he says that Ms. Prager ran from between two parked cars just before he struck her. That doesn't mean that he lied to you.[20] What he told you is the way he wishes it had happened, because he doesn't want to feel responsible for Ms. Prager's death. Like any of us, he'll try to remember things in a way that makes a tragic accident not our fault. The defendant may have seen two cars parked 50 feet north of the crosswalk and subconsciously convinced himself after the accident that Ms. Prager ran out from between them. But you have to base the verdict on what really happened, not on what the defendant wishes had happened."

You'll have to exercise judgment when, as often occurs, you dispute the accuracy of two or more things an adverse witness says and the same Checklist argument applies to both. For instance, assume that in addition to disputing Dolinko's version of where Prager was, you also dispute his testimony as to how fast he was going. The "lack of neutrality" argument applies to both. Do you attack each item of evidence separately, repeating the lack of neutrality argument? Do you make the full-fledged argument the first time, and offer a briefer version the second? Or do you group the items together and make just one argument? You'll have to exercise judgment based on such factors as the complexity of a case, how much time you can allot to a witness, and the centrality of the disputes to the outcome.

Similarly, you will have to exercise judgment when it comes to the order of arguments. For example, the discussion above assumes that you first offer all the arguments supporting White's version of a dispute,

---

19. Another "lack of neutrality" argument you might make involves Dolinko's financial interest in the outcome.

20. Sometimes, you may choose to argue explicitly that an adverse witness is lying. But a factfinder may have difficulty accepting an argument that a witness has lied. By arguing only that a witness is mistaken, you satisfy such factfinders at no cost: factfinders who believe that an adverse witness is lying will be favorably disposed to you no matter what your argument.

and then attack Dolinko's version. But you might choose to juxtapose the conflicts. That is, you might argue that White had the physical ability to see Prager in the crosswalk and that Dolinko did not. Then you might argue that White is neutral and Dolinko is not, and so on. Such decisions are dictated not by rules, but by your best professional judgment.

c. *Explicitly Attacking Inconsistencies in Adverse Stories*

An argument that inconsistencies in an adverse witness' story render it unbelievable consists of the inconsistencies and your desired inference.[21] When the inconsistencies are apparent, you can deliver an explicit argument simply by recounting them and stating your desired conclusion. For example, assume that you have offered evidence of the following internal inconsistencies in the testimony of "Shaw:"

- Shaw testified at trial that he did not attend a January 1 business meeting. However, on cross you read into the record a portion of Shaw's deposition testimony, in which Shaw stated that a plaintiff's fraudulent statement was made during a business meeting on January 1.

- Shaw testified on direct that he never told anyone that his employer needed to buy a new computer system. However, on cross Shaw admitted that he told Ms. Brown that his employer needed a new computer system to help him keep track of inventory.

Since the inconsistencies are plainly apparent, you will not need to convince the jury that Shaw's story is in fact internally inconsistent. Thus, your explicit argument would simply point out the inconsistencies and identify your desired inference:

"Ladies and Gentlemen, Mr. Shaw's testimony just doesn't make sense. He testifies here under oath that he didn't attend a business meeting on Jan. 1. Yet if you'll remember Mr. Shaw's deposition testimony that I read to you during his cross examination, Mr. Shaw testified under oath that he was present at the January 1st meeting between the plaintiff and my client. Both of Mr. Shaw's statements can't be correct. Either he was at the meeting or he wasn't. And I'd also like to call your attention to Mr. Shaw's conflicting statements about whether his company needed a new computer system. On direct examination he told you that he never told anyone that his employer needed to buy a new computer system. But on cross examination Mr. Shaw again changed his story. He admitted that he told Ms. Brown that his employer needed a new computer system to help him keep track of inventory. His story is too filled with inconsistencies to be believable; you should disregard it entirely."

Even when, as above, inconsistencies in a story are readily apparent, to make your argument explicit you may have to do more than simply

---

21. See Chapter 8.

point out the inconsistencies. For example, a factfinder may be unwilling to conclude from a seemingly minor inconsistency or two that a witness' entire story is unreliable. Therefore, you might have to amplify an argument by telling the factfinder why the inconsistencies are significant. For example, to persuade a factfinder of the importance of Shaw's inconsistency concerning whether he told Brown of his employer's need for a new computer system, you might say something like the following:

> "On direct examination Shaw told you that he never told anyone that his employer needed to buy a new computer system. But on cross examination, Mr. Shaw again changed his story. He admitted that he told Ms. Brown that his employer needed a new computer system to help him keep track of inventory. This is not merely a slip of the tongue, or a minor inconsistency. It is critically significant, as Mr. Shaw is in charge of computer operations and this whole case is about a contract for the sale of computer equipment. Together with the other inconsistency, Mr. Shaw's testimony is unreliable; you should disregard it entirely."

A second situation in which you have to do more than simply point out apparent internal conflicts arises when you attack a story as inconsistent with common experience. In such situations, you often have to explain to the factfinder the basis of your contention that the story is inconsistent. For an example of such an argument, assume again that you represented the defense in the well-publicized rape trial of William Kennedy Smith. Smith was a member of one of America's most powerful families. While in a bar, he met a young woman by the name of Patricia Bowman. As you recall, Bowman claimed that Smith raped her after she gave him a ride home from the bar to the lavish Kennedy Palm Beach estate. Smith's defense was consent. During the trial, Ann Mercer, a prosecution witness who was a close friend of Bowman's, testified that she arrived at the Kennedy estate shortly after the rape to pick up Bowman, who was distraught. Mercer testified that Bowman told her, "Smith raped me."

As the defense attorney, you attack Mercer's story as inconsistent with common experience. Mercer had given a statement to the police stating that after Bowman told her that Smith had raped her, Mercer went through Kennedy's house and down to the beach with Smith looking for Bowman's shoes. During pretrial preparation you constructed the following argument based on this inconsistency with common experience:

If: Bowman had told Mercer she had been raped by Smith. . . .

Then: We would *not* have expected Mercer to have gone through the house and to the beach with Smith looking for Bowman's shoes. . . .

Because:

(1) Mercer would have wanted to get her friend away from the scene of the rape as soon as possible.

(2) Mercer would have wanted to get her friend medical attention as soon as possible.

(3) Mercer would have been afraid to be alone at night in the house and on the beach with an alleged rapist.

(4) Mercer could have returned to pick up the shoes the following day.

Therefore Mercer's story is inconsistent with common experience.[22]

Your explicit argument attacking Mercer's story as inconsistent with common experience can recount the evidence creating the inconsistency, convey through generalizations and "especially whens" that the story is inconsistent, validate the argument with the factfinder's analogous personal experience, and state the inference you want the factfinder to draw from the inconsistency. The argument might go as follows:

"Ms. Mercer's testimony about what happened that night just doesn't make sense. Supposedly, as soon as Ms. Mercer arrives at the Kennedy estate, Ms. Bowman tells her that Mr. Smith had raped her. But Ms. Mercer admits that after supposedly hearing this, she went into the house with Mr. Smith searching for Ms. Bowman's shoes. And when they couldn't find the shoes in the house, she and Mr. Smith went through a dark house and grounds, down to the beach, looking for them.

"It just doesn't make sense that Ms. Mercer would have searched all through a dark house and grounds for Ms. Bowman's shoes if Ms. Bowman really had told Mercer she had been raped. We all know that rape is a traumatic experience. Wouldn't a woman whose best friend had suffered such a traumatic experience want to get their friend away from the place where it happened as soon as possible? Especially if the friend is distraught, as Ms. Bowman says she was? Common sense will tell you that people don't usually leave friends alone at the scene of a rape while they go off in the dark to look for a pair of shoes with the alleged rapist.

"Moreover, if Mercer had been told that a rape had occurred, wouldn't she have been concerned about getting her friend medical attention as soon as she could? If you had a friend who had been assaulted and was distraught, wouldn't your first thought be to get her checked out by a physician and away from the scene of the assault as quickly as possible? Would you bother to look for a pair of shoes in the dark that could be picked up the next day?

"Also, if Ms. Mercer really had been told by her friend that Mr. Smith was a rapist, a violent criminal, surely she would not have walked alone with him all around the estate in the middle of the night. People do not knowingly go off alone in the middle of the night with violent criminals, especially when they think the violent criminal has just committed a rape.

---

22. Many of the points in the argument developed in the text were suggested by the cross examination of Ms. Mercer by Roy Black, counsel for Kennedy Smith.

"So what can you conclude from the fact that Ms. Mercer went with Mr. Smith to look for a pair of shoes? Just this: Ms. Bowman did not in fact tell Ms. Bowman that Mr. Smith was a rapist. Change this one fact, and everything makes sense. If Ann Mercer was coming to pick up her good friend after Ms. Bowman and Mr. Smith had consensual intercourse, just as Mr. Smith testified, then it is perfectly reasonable for Ms. Mercer to have gone off with Mr. Smith to hunt for Ms. Bowman's shoes. After all, there is no reason for a woman to fear a man who has done nothing to harm her friend. Thus, the only sensible conclusion is that Ms. Bowman did not tell Ms. Mercer that Mr. Smith was a rapist. What is true is exactly what Mr. Smith told you: he and Ms. Bowman had consensual intercourse."[23]

d. *Explicit Arguments About Normative Standards*

As explained in Chapter 6, many elements of claims and defenses require factfinders to determine more than the credibility of witnesses or what happened in the past. Some elements also require factfinders to evaluate the propriety of a party's conduct according to community norms. Elements which require this additional determination contain normative standards.

An explicit normative argument explains why your normative factual propositions are accurate, and then points out how these propositions do (or do not) satisfy the normative standard. To illustrate this two step process, assume that you represent the defendant in an automobile accident case, *Porter v. Deng*. Porter contends that Deng negligently weaved in and out of traffic, causing Porter's injuries. Deng was driving her daughter to the hospital at the time of the accident. She admits that she was weaving in and out of traffic, but denies that she was negligent.

Here, you will have to argue that under the circumstances, it was reasonable for your client to have weaved in and out of traffic. Assume that during pretrial preparation, you identified the following normative factual propositions to support your claim that your client's conduct was reasonable:

(1) Deng thought her daughter might die from a snake bite if she didn't get to the hospital quickly.

(2) Because she was told that an ambulance was not available, Deng had to drive her daughter to the hospital in order to get her daughter there quickly.

(3) Given an unanticipated traffic jam on route to the hospital, Deng had no alternative other than to weave in and out of traffic to get her daughter to the hospital.

---

23. Although you have included generalizations, "especially whens" and analogous personal experiences to support some of your reasons that Mercer's behavior was implausible, you have not done so for each. You could do so, however, and the more of those you include the more explicit your argument would become.

(4) Deng tried to minimize the risk of injury to others by driving within the speed limit.

At trial, you introduced evidence tending to establish each of these propositions. Your explicit argument that these normative factual propositions are true and that your client's conduct was reasonable might go as follows:

"Ms. Deng has told you forthrightly that she was changing lanes just before her car struck the plaintiff's car. But given the emergency facing her, it was reasonable for Ms. Deng to drive as she did.

"At the time of the accident Ms. Deng was taking her 3 year old daughter to the hospital. As she told you, she was afraid her daughter might die if she didn't get to the hospital right away. And the evidence shows that Ms. Deng is telling you the truth.

"Ms. Deng told you that she saw her daughter bitten by a rattlesnake, and the hospital report confirms that child was suffering the effects of rattlesnake poison. Immediately after Ms. Deng saw her daughter bitten she called the hospital to ask what she should do. No one disputes that Ms. Deng made this call. And when she talked to the people at the hospital they told her that her daughter might die if she didn't get to the hospital right away. We know that's what the hospital told Ms. Deng because we heard the recording of Ms. Deng's call to 911 at 3:16 P.M. On that recording Ms. Deng said, 'My daughter has just been bitten by a rattlesnake and if I don't get her to the hospital right away she may die.' She must have been told this by someone at the hospital. People listen carefully when they call a hospital for emergency instructions, especially when they personally lack medical training and the patient is their young child. So the evidence of the 911 call clearly shows that Ms. Deng had been told and believed that her daughter might die if she did not get to the hospital immediately. Ms. Deng weaved in and out of traffic because she was trying to save her child's life.

"And there is other evidence indicating that Ms. Deng's conduct was reasonable under the circumstances. Ms. Deng really had no alternative but to drive her daughter to the hospital. It is undisputed that the dispatcher at 911 told Ms. Deng that no emergency vehicle could reach her daughter for at least 30 minutes. You've heard the 911 recording; it leaves no doubt on that point. Likewise, it is undisputed that the hospital is only a 10 minute drive from Ms. Deng's house in normal driving circumstances. Officer Pace confirmed this fact for you during his direct examination and plaintiff has never argued otherwise. In a medical emergency, people don't wait 30 minutes for an ambulance when they can drive to the hospital in 10. Would you wait if it were your child? No. The risks are too great. It would be unreasonable to expect Ms. Deng to wait for 30 minutes.

"While driving to the hospital, Ms. Deng was caught in an unanticipated traffic jam. So Ms. Deng could either sit and wait in traffic and put her daughter's life at risk, or try to work her way through the traffic. She kept the risks to a minimum by not even exceeding the speed limit, and all the evidence shows that she drove at a safe rate of speed. Again, Ms. Deng behaved reasonably.

"In thinking about whether Ms. Deng's conduct was reasonable ask yourself whether, if it had been your child, you would have weaved in and out of traffic to get your child to the hospital on time. Wouldn't anyone? Don't we want people to get to hospitals in emergencies, especially when they keep the risks to a minimum? You shouldn't decide she was unreasonable if any of us would do the same thing. The law shouldn't prohibit what all of us would do.

"The judge will instruct you that negligence is a failure to exercise reasonable care under the circumstances. It's up to you to decide if Ms. Deng behavior was reasonable, and I think the evidence clearly demonstrates that it was. Ms. Deng was not negligent, and you should return a verdict for the defense."

Here, you argue that your normative factual propositions are accurate. For example, you assert that Deng thought her daughter might die from a snake bite if she didn't get to the hospital quickly, and support the assertion with a generalization ("People listen carefully when they call a hospital for emergency instructions, especially when they personally lack medical training and the patient is their young child."). You also validate a generalization with an analogous personal experience ("In a medical emergency, people don't wait 30 minutes for an ambulance when they can drive to the hospital in 10. Would you wait if it were your child? No.") Lastly, you argue that your normative propositions prove that Ms. Deng acted reasonably. You point out that waiting for an ambulance and remaining in a traffic jam were not reasonable alternatives.[24] And again, you refer to the factfinder's analogous personal experience. ("[A]sk yourself whether, if it had been your child, you would have weaved in and out of traffic to get your child to the hospital on time.")

e. Conclusion

This is a good time to remind you that you can vary the explicitness of an argument on a sliding scale. For example, in the *Deng* argument in the previous subsection, you explicitly explained to the factfinder why the 911 call proved that Ms. Deng thought that her child might die. But you could have made the argument more implicit by neither reminding the factfinder of what Ms. Deng said in the 911 call nor identifying the connecting generalization. You might have said only, "Think back to the evidence of the 911 call. Doesn't that show that she really believed

---

24. Remember, one way to support a normative argument is to convince a fact-finder that, under the circumstances, a client lacked less restrictive alternatives. See Chapter 6, Sec. 2 (c).

that her child's life was in danger?" You thereby allow the factfinder to reason through this part of the argument on its own. Although an explicit argument tends to be more persuasive than an implicit one, some factfinders respond better to the latter than the former.[25] Moreover, explicit arguments are lengthier and you will probably be unable to hold a factfinder's attention if you make every argument as explicit as possible.

4. ADDITIONAL ARGUMENT TECHNIQUES

Explicitness is but one characteristic of effective arguments. The subsections below examine other persuasive techniques.

a. Use the Question Form of Argumentation

Substituting questions for assertions adds variety (and therefore interest) to a summation and softens the explicitness of an argument. Don't you sometimes find questions to be a welcome change of pace?

The general rule of thumb is that you can convert any assertion to a question. For example:

- *Assertion* (from *Deng* argument above): "You shouldn't decide she was unreasonable if any of us would do the same thing." *Question*: "Should you pronounce her unreasonable if any of us would do the same thing?"

- *Assertion*: (attacking the credibility of an eyewitness to an early-morning convenience store holdup): "Mr. Tilvon admitted that he went to the store at 3 A.M. because he had a headache. When someone is awakened at 3 A.M. by a headache that causes him to get out of bed and go to a store for aspirin, that person is probably woozy and has difficulty seeing straight and concentrating." *Question*: "Didn't Mr. Tilvon admit that he went to the store at 3 A.M. because he had a headache? And if someone is awakened at 3 A.M. and goes to a store for aspirin, what is that person's physical condition? Is he likely to be woozy? Have difficulty seeing straight and concentrating?"

As you can see, the content of these pairs of examples is virtually identical. By incorporating questions into your argument, you give a factfinder a bit more room to think for him or her self.

b. Make Preemptive Strikes (Anticipate an Adversary's Response to Your Arguments)

Confrontational beasts that they are, adversaries will typically try to undermine your arguments. If you argue first, you can preempt an adversary's likely response to your argument by raising and then refut-

---

25. See J. Freedman, J. Carlsmith & D. Sears, *Social Psychology* 289–91 (2d ed. 1974)(suggesting that explicit form of argument may be more effective when the issues are complex and the audience is less intelli-gent). See also W. McGuire, *Attitudes and Attitude Change* in Vol. II, The Handbook of Social Psychology 270–271 3rd ed. 1985 (discussing the effects of implicit vs. explicit arguments).

ing the adversary's response. Knocking down potential responses is a way of shoring up your own affirmative arguments. Also, if the adversary does make the response you've preempted, there's a good chance that a factfinder will be thinking of your response as it listens to the adversary's argument.

The preemption technique is not unique to litigation. Indeed, you probably have practiced it frequently. For example, perhaps you said something like this during your teen-age years:

> "Mom, I ought to be allowed to have the car tonight, because I haven't used it in three weeks. I know you've said I don't have enough experience to drive at night, but I'll be with Hilary, who's a really experienced driver."

Here, you make an affirmative argument (you should have the car because you haven't had it in three weeks), preempt your Mother's likely response (you don't have enough experience to drive at night) and then counter her response (you'll be with a really experienced driver). So doing may take the wind out of Mother's sails.

Consider an example of the preemption technique in the context of a closing argument. Assume that you are again the defense attorney in the Kennedy Smith rape case, discussed above. During cross examination of Ann Mercer (the alleged victim's friend), you emphasized the implausibility of her going through a darkened house and out onto the beach with someone who she supposedly thought had just committed a violent crime. On redirect, the prosecution emphasized how distraught Mercer became on hearing what had happened to her close friend. Based on this redirect, you expect the prosecution to respond to your closing by arguing that distress and anxiety led the friend to behave in a dangerous and foolish manner. After making your argument that Mercer's testimony is inconsistent with common experience, you might then raise and refute the adversary's likely response as follows:

> "The State may claim that the reason Ms. Mercer acted this way is that hearing what happened to her friend so distressed her that she behaved in a foolish and dangerous manner. But ask yourself if this really explains what happened. Ms. Mercer didn't wander around the estate with Mr. Smith in a daze. They had a conversation, she asked him questions, he responded. They talked about knick-knacks in the house. This is not the behavior of someone who was distraught and irrational. No, the only explanation for the friend's behavior that night is that Patricia Bowman had said nothing to her about a rape."

Here, you discuss the prosecution's likely response, immediately counter it, and conclude by reiterating your desired conclusion.

The extent to which you preempt must be left to your judgment. Overuse often makes your closing too long, and detracts from your affirmative arguments by spending too much time discussing the adversary's case. But if you are virtually certain that the adversary will eventually make the responsive argument, and you have a strong response to it, consider preemption.

c. *Respond to an Adversary's Affirmative Arguments*

When you deliver your own affirmative arguments and preempt an adversary's likely responses, you are telling a factfinder why you deserve a verdict. But factfinders typically want to hear not only why you should win, but also what's wrong with your adversary's arguments. That's why you prepare responses to an adversary's arguments prior to trial. Assuming that you've offered evidence to support these responses (e.g., "except whens" that undermine the force of an adversary's undisputed evidence), you will usually want to put forth those responses during summation.

As suggested above, normally you deliver your affirmative arguments before responding to an adversary's.[26] And you need feel no compunction to respond to every argument an adversary makes. Doing so will probably detract from the force of your own arguments, and may give a factfinder the impression that if you have to devote so much attention to it, the adversary's case must be a strong one. Many times, therefore, you may choose to select one or two of the adversary's arguments (ones to which you have strong responses), and ignore the rest.

Responding to an adversary's arguments may be difficult if you argue first and will not have a chance to make a response. You are put in the uncomfortable position of having to predict and assert the arguments an adversary is going to make. In such a situation, you should generally identify and respond only to an argument you are almost certain that the adversary will make.

For example, assume that you represent the plaintiff in a wrongful termination matter. You will argue first, and will not have an opportunity to respond to the defendant's argument.[27] Based on the adversary's presentation of evidence, you are certain that the adversary will argue that your client's occasional tardiness constituted "just cause" for the dismissal. Thus, you may begin your response as follows:

> "Now, defendant Chronos will undoubtedly argue that Mr. Shpate's occasional tardiness gave it just cause to fire him. But if you examine the evidence, you'll see that there's no substance to this claim. First, ..."

If you were uncertain as to whether Chronos would make an argument based on evidence of tardiness, you would be hesitant to make this argument.

The general rule that you respond only to arguments that an adversary is almost certain to make is subject to an important qualifica-

---

26. See Sec. 2, *supra*.

27. Forbidding plaintiff a responsive argument is generally within a trial judge's discretion.

tion. Regardless of what your adversary says, factfinders may come up with arguments of their own. And you should consider responding to such arguments, just as you might if an adversary was making them. For instance, return to Mr. Shpate's wrongful termination case against Chronos. Evidence of Mr. Shpate's occasional tardiness emerged during the trial. However, Chronos did not stress the evidence, and you think it unlikely that Chronos will argue that the tardiness constitutes just cause for the dismissal. Nevertheless, you are concerned that the factfinder may consider the tardiness just cause. If so, you might respond to the argument:

> "You've heard some evidence that Mr. Shpate was occasionally tardy, and you may be wondering whether the tardiness gave Chronos just cause to fire him. If you examine the evidence, you'll see that there's no substance to this claim. First,...."

The tactic of referring to an argument that an adversary will not make is particularly important when you are responding to silent arguments. As you know, silent arguments often grow out of negative racial, ethnic and economic stereotypes.[28] An adversary can not explicitly put forth a silent argument because such an argument is legally improper (e.g., "You shouldn't believe Ms. Fenton because she speaks with a heavy accent;" or, "You shouldn't find for the plaintiff because she is rich enough already."). However, factfinders may be influenced by such considerations, and summation is a chance for you to point out their impropriety.

For example, assume that a particular case pits your nervous, uncomfortable-looking day laborer against an adversary's polished, sophisticated corporate executive. Even if your adversary does not explicitly argue that these factors make the executive more credible, you think the factfinder may well be influenced by this distinction. An argument undermining this silent argument may go as follows:

> "This case boils down to who you believe, Mr. Herr or Ms. Shearer. Now, defense counsel might argue that you ought to believe Ms. Shearer. And it's true that she has more education, is more sophisticated and is used to speaking in front of people in important meetings. So she isn't nervous like most people would be, and like Mr. Herr no doubt was. But those factors should play no part whatsoever as you think about the case. Under our system of justice, everyone deserves to be evaluated on their own merits, and whether someone has years of education and years of experience sitting in the witness chair does not automatically make them more credible. They can't necessarily see or hear better than anyone else coming into court and seeking justice."

Defense counsel would not have been permitted to make the argument you have put into its mouth, at least not in the blatant way you suggest. But a factfinder may be influenced by such factors. Respond-

---

28. See Chapter 9.

ing to the silent argument not only gives you a chance to persuade the factfinder to ignore such factors, but also allows you to make your adversary bear the onus of a seemingly unfair argument.

d. Inoculate Against Persuasive Aspects of an Adversary's Arguments

To inoculate is to begin an argument by acknowledging the validity of a widely-accepted generalization supporting an adversary's position.[29] When an adversary's argument rests on such a generalization, you can try to inoculate the factfinder against accepting the argument by acknowledging the legitimacy of the generalization but then pointing out why it is inapplicable to the particular dispute. Research suggests that inoculation makes it easier for the factfinder to accept an argument that is an exception to the generalization on which beliefs are founded.[30]

For example, assume that you represent a defendant accused of robbery. At trial, a police officer testified that your client confessed to the crime. Your client testified that he never confessed. During closing, the prosecution argues that the officer is unbiased and his testimony establishes your client's guilt. You have concluded that you must argue that the officer is lying when he says that your client confessed. Before developing the evidence that indicates the officer is lying you want to inoculate because you believe the factfinder will be extremely reluctant to accept your argument that the police officer knowingly lied. Your argument might begin as follows:

"I know that you've heard the prosecutor argue that Officer Carlson is an honest, unbiased witness, and that he says my client confessed to the robbery. And you're probably thinking that police officers are usually honest, and that they wouldn't lie just to get a conviction. And you're absolutely right. Most police officers are honest, unbiased witnesses and we can generally rely on their testimony. Indeed, our system of justice works because that's the way most police officers behave. But you have to do more than just decide how police officers usually behave. You can't just say 'Well, I think that police officers are usually truthful, so the police officer must have been telling the truth here.' You have to go beyond that. You have to examine the evidence and decide what happened *in this particular case*. So let's look at the evidence *that in this particular case* Officer Carlson did not testify truthfully...."

Here, you inoculate in an effort to overcome the widely held belief that we need to and generally can rely on the honesty of police officers.[31] You expressly acknowledge and validate the generalizations underlying

---

29. See generally, W.J. McGuire, *Inducing Resistance to Persuasion: Some Contemporary Approaches, in Advances in Experimental Social Psychology,* 191–229 (L. Berkowitz ed., 1964).

30. See W.J. McGuire & D. Papageorgis, *The Relative Efficacy of Various Types of Prior Belief–Defense in Producing Immunity Against Persuasion,* 62 J. Abnormal & Soc. Psychol. 327 (1961).

31. Obviously, this belief may be held more strongly in some communities than in others.

these beliefs, but remind the factfinder that those beliefs do not necessarily dictate the outcome of this case.[32]

e. Use Analogies

Analogies are a widely used and often effective argument technique.[33] Analogies can be powerful because they respond to the basic human reasoning process of treating like situations alike. When you demonstrate to a factfinder that some aspect of a case has an analogue in a familiar, every-day social setting, the factfinder is likely to think about the case in the same way as it does the familiar analogue.[34] And you can use analogies to illustrate and add vividness to any portion of a summation.

For example, you might use an analogy to explain the meaning of a normative standard. Assume that you represent the plaintiff in a personal injury action. Your client took the prescription drug "pantol" to relieve severe arthritis pain, and allegedly as a result suffered kidney damage and had to have a kidney removed. The drug's warning label stated in part, "Take two tablets every four hours. DO NOT EXCEED 6 TABLETS IN ANY 24 HOUR PERIOD." Your client took 8 tablets per day for 3 weeks. You contend that the drug's manufacturer breached its duty to provide a "reasonable" warning label because the warning did not specifically warn of the potential (and known) severe consequences of exceeding the recommended dose. A portion of your argument that the warning was defective might go as follows:

> "We submit that the warning was defective not because of what it said, but because of what it failed to say. It said absolutely nothing about the dire consequences that might result from taking more than 6 pantol tablets per day. And that's not a fair or reasonable warning. Think about your own experience. Most all of us take, or know someone who takes, vitamins of one sort or another. Suppose you buy a bottle of vitamins and the label says 'TAKE ONE TABLET PER DAY.' If you forget to take the vitamins for a few days, maybe you'll take two a day for a while to catch up. The label

---

32. You can also use inoculation to respond to arguments a factfinder may make. Assume, for example, that you want to argue that a police officer reasonably believed he was in danger when he shot a suspect after making a traffic stop. One reason the officer has given for feeling in danger is the traffic stop occurred in a "high crime" neighborhood. A factfinder who lives in such a neighborhood (or who has a friend or relative who does) may think that any argument relying on this information suggests that the police are free to shoot motorists they stop in such an area. You can inoculate by acknowledging the factfinder's legitimate concern and then explaining why your argument does not rely on this position.

33. For an earlier illustration of the analogy technique, see Sec. 3 (a) *supra* (validating generalizations through analogous personal experience).

34. Obviously, an analogy will not be persuasive if a factfinder is unconvinced of the parallels between a case and your analogous illustration. For example, assume that you're arguing that a driver involved in an automobile accident was driving carefully because he had a flower arrangement in the back seat. You analogize to the care drivers take when they have a baby on board. If the factfinder is unwilling to see a parallel between flowers and infants, your analogy will fail.

said not to, but you wouldn't expect that you were putting yourself at risk for kidney damage or some other drastic consequence. If taking more than one vitamin per day was going to put you at such great risk, you'd expect the manufacturer to tell you that on the label. And if they didn't tell you, you'd say it wasn't reasonable or fair. The same is true here. The warning wasn't reasonable because it said nothing about the horrible consequences of taking 8 tablets instead of 6.''

Here, since the factfinder is probably unfamiliar with "pantol," you analogize to the more familiar setting of vitamins. Based on the fairness principle of treating like cases alike, you argue that just as a failure to warn would be unreasonable in the familiar vitamin context, so too is it with pantol. The analogy will be successful if the factfinder believes that the analogous case is like the one the factfinder must decide.[35]

Similarly, you can use analogies to illustrate the meaning of legal concepts and terms used in jury instructions. Consider the following examples:

Example: "The Judge will instruct you that we have to prove our case by a preponderance of the evidence. What does this mean? Well, assume that you have a balance scale and you place all our evidence on one side of the scale and all of the defendant's on the other side. If our side of the scale is heavier even by the weight of a single feather, then we have proved our case by a preponderance of the evidence."

Example: "The Judge will instruct you that you can use your common sense to draw inferences from circumstantial evidence. What does that mean? Well, suppose you saw someone walk into the courtroom wearing a wet raincoat. Your common sense would tell you that it was raining outside. Maybe you haven't looked outside and no one has told you that it's raining, but common sense leads you to draw an inference that it is raining. And it is perfectly proper for you to draw inferences from the testimony of witnesses in this case."

In both of these examples, the analogies may help the factfinder understand the meaning of abstract legal principles.

If you examine the analogies set forth above, you'll note that they refer to concrete situations: taking vitamins, looking at a balance scale, drawing inferences from a wet raincoat. That concreteness tends to make the analogies more vivid and memorable, and hence more persuasive. But you can also use abstract analogies distilled from the experi-

---

35. Unless an analogy is within a factfinder's experience, it is unlikely to be persuasive. For example, analogizing some aspect of a trial to "that feeling you get when you pole vault over 20 feet" is unlikely to be persuasive, as few people have accomplished that feat. Similarly, analogizing to "the anger you feel when a caterer over- cooks the filet mignon" is likely to be demeaning to a juror who has to struggle to feed her family. And an analogy to a little-known Biblical incident may have little impact on a factfinder with no religious background. Just as with all arguments, an analogy that impresses you is of little use if it is outside a factfinder's experience.

ences of a collective community. Such analogies are usually thought of as aphorisms, maxims, adages or proverbs. Though often less vivid, these abstract analogies may be convincing because a factfinder is likely to be quite familiar and comfortable with them.

For example, return to pantol warning label case. An abstract analogy you might use would go as follows:

"It is conceded that the warning label said nothing about the risk of severe kidney damage. To see why the label was inadequate and unreasonable, think about the familiar saying that an ounce of prevention is worth a pound of cure. This saying reflects the wisdom that it's better to try to prevent injuries than to cure them after the fact. If the defendant had used an ounce of prevention and taken the small step of indicating on the label that taking more than the required dosage might have caused my client to lose his kidney, would we be here today? The defendants' warning is inadequate and unreasonable because it didn't bother to use that ounce of prevention."

This analogy does not direct the factfinder to any concrete personal experience. Instead, you attempt to show that the defendant's conduct is inappropriate because it is inconsistent with the collective experience underlying the "ounce of prevention" adage.

f. Discuss the Burden of Proof

Some reference to the burden of proof is standard in closing argument. You might refer in a separate portion of closing argument (often near the beginning and/or the end) to the applicable burden and argue either that you have, or that your adversary has not, satisfied that burden. Perhaps more effectively, you may integrate references to the burden of proof into your arguments. Consider how as defense counsel you might have integrate a discussion of the burden of proof into your argument about the inferential significance of Ann Mercer's testimony in *Kennedy Smith*:

"The testimony of Ann Mercer strongly supports Mr. Smith's testimony that he and Ms. Bowman had consensual intercourse. If Ms. Mercer really believed that Mr. Smith was a rapist, a violent criminal, surely she would not have walked alone with him all around the estate in the middle of the night. Remember, the State has to convince you of Mr. Smith's guilt beyond a reasonable doubt. That means you must think about whether Ann Mercer's implausible testimony about walking around a dark house with someone she supposedly believed was a rapist, along with other evidence, leaves you convinced that the only reasonably possible conclusion is that Mr. Smith committed a violent act of rape. But far from demonstrating guilt beyond a reasonable doubt, Ms. Mercer's implausible testimony is strong evidence of Mr. Smith's innocence."

By directly juxtaposing the prosecution's heavy burden with a specific defense argument, you may enhance an argument's persuasiveness.

Many jurors automatically think of the criminal standard of "beyond a reasonable doubt" when they hear the words "burden of proof." After all, jurors with previous jury service are more likely to have served on criminal than on civil juries. And, people with no previous jury service have usually been exposed to numerous legal dramas on television and in films, most of which focus on criminal cases. Hence, when you represent a civil plaintiff, you should take particular care to emphasize the difference between civil burdens such as "preponderance of the evidence" and "clear and convincing evidence," and the criminal burden.

g. Discuss Other Important Jury Instructions

Many jury instructions are written in abstract legal terms that are difficult to understand.[36] And even when instructions are written in layperson's language, a judge typically reads dozens of instructions to the jury with the same emotive force as a teenager reading a list of the night's homework assignments to a parent. Thus, jurors are hard pressed to remember their contents.[37] Therefore, you want to review the language and meaning of important instructions during summation.[38]

For example, jurors are typically given an instruction defining circumstantial evidence. But if your case rests heavily on inferences drawn from circumstantial evidence, you shouldn't trust the jurors' understanding to the jury instruction. Explain its terms, and perhaps illustrate the instruction with an analogy:

> "Her Honor will instruct you shortly that circumstantial evidence is simply evidence from which an inference can be drawn. You've probably heard this term a lot, but you may not be certain what it means. An inference is simply a conclusion you reach based on evidence. These conclusions are perfectly proper; you draw these kinds of conclusions every day. For instance, if you're stopped at a red light and the driver behind you honks as soon as the light turns green, you may infer that the driver is in a hurry. This is exactly the kind of common sense reasoning that you should use in this case to conclude that Jones was the robber...."

You will have to confine such explanations to the most important instructions. And if you try cases often enough, you can develop "stock" explanations for instructions such as the ones dealing with the burden of proof and circumstantial evidence, since they are given in every case.

36. The California civil jury instructions for "burden of proof," for example, read as follows:

"The plaintiff has the burden of proving by a preponderance of the evidence all of the facts necessary to establish: _____. The defendant has the burden of proving by a preponderance of the evidence all of the facts necessary to establish: _____." BAJI 2.60 (7th ed. 1986).

37. Some judges allow jurors to take the instructions with them when they deliberate. However, most judges do not because of the supposed danger that jurors will focus on one or two instructions and overlook others that may modify them.

38. You will know the exact language of the instructions because the judge will have decided on the instructions she will give prior to counsel's closing.

h. Summations in Judge–Tried Cases

To what extent should you modify what you say during closing argument in judge-tried cases? Obviously, you might adjust the order in which you address the issues if a judge indicates a particular issue is critical to her decision. However, you generally need not modify the substance of your arguments. After all, these arguments pertain to unique historical events. While a judge may have more legal sophistication than the average juror, a judge is not necessarily gifted with greater insight into historical interpretation. Thus, explicitness, inoculation, analogies and the other techniques discussed above are usually as appropriate in bench as in jury trials.

However, some of the subjects you might cover in jury trials are largely unnecessary in bench trials. For example, you would not explain the meaning of "preponderance of the evidence" or other common legal concepts to a judge.[39]

i. Tell the Factfinder What Your Client Wants

An effective closing argument typically discloses your desired verdict to the factfinder. If you represent a criminal defendant, for example, you might say something like, "The evidence requires a verdict of not guilty." Or, if you do not want to goad the jury into an all-or-nothing decision, you might argue that, "The evidence requires a verdict of not guilty on the charge of assault with a deadly weapon. Even if you look only at the prosecution's evidence, and totally ignore that of the defendant, at the most you could convict her of simple assault."

Similarly, if you represent a civil plaintiff, you might argue that "the evidence demonstrates that Ajax Co.'s promise to produce a limited edition series of Great Law Professors trading cards was false, and that it knew the statement to be false. Thus, you should find that Ajax Co. committed fraud, and assess damages as follows...."

You might sometimes be reluctant to disclose a bottom line for fear of aiming too low and not getting as good a result as a factfinder might be willing to give. However, the risk of this occurring is less than the risk that your failure to indicate a bottom line will leave the factfinder confused about what action you want it to take on your client's behalf. Besides, through adept wording you can perhaps have your cake and eat it too: "You should award damages of *at least*...."

j. Use Effective Oral Speaking Skills

(1) Talk, Don't Read

Close your eyes (figuratively will do) and think of a model advocate giving an effective closing argument. Probably your advocate is looking

---

39. Unless you are prepared to cope with a nasty scowl and a well-hurled evi- dence code.

directly at the factfinder, not reading. Nevertheless, you may tell yourself that it makes sense to prepare by writing out your argument ahead of time. After all, during closing you have as much control over the information you present as you ever will have inside a courtroom. There's no witness to muck things up, and opposing counsel probably won't object. Then, you may take your speech with you to court, so you can "refer" to it if absolutely necessary. Resist the temptation! You will quickly have your head buried in your papers, and your argument will sound something like stale toast when it breaks. Yes, prepare an outline. Go ahead and write down testimony or legal principles whose exact text is so important that you want to read it correctly. But otherwise, leave your speech at home and just talk to the factfinder.

(2) Use Exhibits and Other Visual Aids

Using exhibits and other visual aids makes your arguments easier to understand and remember, and provides a bit of a change of pace. With the court's permission, you may hand out ("publish") copies of exhibits admitted at trial so the jurors can follow along with your argument. In addition, you can use visual aids ranging from specific language from an important jury instruction hand written on large paper and placed on an easel, to computer graphics or simulations shown on a large screen television.[40] You cannot, however, use visual aids which refer to inadmissible evidence or impermissible inferences. You should usually obtain approval to use visual aids from the judge prior to the commencement of closing.

5. RULES OF CLOSING ARGUMENT

Though closing argument is the most freeform phase of trial, you are not free to say anything you please. This section considers the rules you are most likely to encounter.

a. Arguing Inferences (OK) vs. Arguing "Facts Outside the Record" (Not OK)

Perhaps the most sensible and widely agreed-upon rule of closing argument is that you must "confine your argument to the record." This means that you cannot refer to evidence that was (a) never offered; (b) offered but not admitted; (c) admitted conditionally and later stricken; or (d) admitted for a limited purpose (e.g., for "state of mind"), and you refer to it for a different purpose.

However, the application of the "confine argument to the record" rule is not always obvious, because another rule states that you may "argue reasonable inferences from evidence in the record."[41] This latter

---

40. See T. Brown, *Animations Add a New Dimension*, Nat'l L.J., May 27, 1991, at 19; R. Parloff, *Now Showing in a Courtroom Near You*, Am. Law., May 1990, at 4.

41. What constitutes a "reasonable" inference from evidence in the record may vary from judge to judge. As is the case whenever a "reasonableness" standard

rule is no minor exception; without it, you would be unable to draw inferences to connect evidence to factual propositions or to draw conclusions about credibility. And as is obvious from the earlier discussion of explicit arguments, you may refer to the generalizations upon which you ask a trier to make inferences, even though those generalizations are not a proper subject of testimony. Unfortunately, sometimes it's difficult to distinguish between a proper inference and an improper reference to a fact not in evidence.

For example, assume that a case involves a young child injured by a dog bite. There's no evidence of the precise events leading up to the bite. An attorney argues, "The dog must have been provoked into biting the child." Is this an improper assertion of a fact not in the record, or a legitimate inference to ask the factfinder to draw? Typically, close rulings are committed to a trial judge's discretion, and objections are often met with the rejoinder, "It's only argument." Thus, often your only counter to an argument which you consider improper is to emphasize during your own argument that the adversary has given a misleading argument. On the other hand, if your objection is sustained, in a jury trial you may ask the judge to admonish the jury to disregard counsel's remark. If the misstatement is serious enough, or opposing counsel has repeatedly misstated the record, you may ask for a mistrial and sanctions.

b. Puffing

"Puffing" refers to the exaggerated claims that sellers sometimes make in an effort to induce customers to do business. Puffing is generally acceptable, because consumers are unlikely to be misled by a claim like, "Eating in our restaurant is like stepping into Paradise." Also, in a market economy, some excess of zeal is predictable and tolerable. Thus, a diner could not sue the restaurant for breach of warranty, claiming that "I ate there and it was nothing like Paradise. It wasn't even like McDonalds."

For the same reasons, you may puff somewhat during closing argument. For example, you might argue that "liability could not be clearer," even though your adversary has in fact raised a serious defense. Or, you might argue that "Ms. Anthrope testified in a way that was totally believable," even though your adversary might point out a number of weaknesses in her demeanor.

But again, limits exist. You cannot puff if the effect is to ask a factfinder to substitute emotion for reason. For example, as a prosecutor, you probably could not ask a jury to "lock up this filthy wild beast." Similarly, at some point "puffing" becomes "evidence outside the record." For instance, your reference to your client as "a driver with an impeccable record" may refer to improper character evidence, and therefore constitute argument outside the record.

comes into play, reasonable people can disagree about its application.

c. Stating Your Personal Opinion

You may not directly ask the factfinder to evaluate your or opposing counsel's personal credibility along with the evidence.[42] Thus, statements such as the following are typically improper:

- "Never in all my years of practice have I represented someone with as much integrity in business as Lem Bezzle."

- "I do not take cases unless I think they are completely meritorious."

- "Opposing counsel is the kind of person who will stop at nothing to take your mind off the evidence."

Each statement injects counsel's personal background and integrity directly into the case, and that you cannot do.

Since all of closing argument is in a sense the "opinion of counsel," you are allowed to give your opinion about the *probative worth or credibility of evidence*. As a general guideline, if you can substitute the phrase "I submit that the evidence shows" for "I think," your argument is proper. For example, examine the following argument:

> "Jack would have you believe that he went up the hill to fetch a pail of water. However, as Jill testified, and as you might expect, the well was located at the bottom of the hill. I think Jill's evidence demonstrates that Jack went up there for another purpose entirely. I think that purpose will become clear if you look at Hansel's testimony...." [43]

In this excerpt, you do not place your personal credibility in issue. You confine your statement of belief to conclusions to be drawn from the evidence. Hence, your argument is proper.

d. Asking the Factfinder to "Send a Message" With Its Verdict

Factfinders are supposed to resolve questions of guilt or innocence, or liability and damages. Factfinders should render the verdict on these issues without regard to the message that their verdict might send to the public at large. Therefore, it is improper for you to argue about the "message" that a particular verdict should or might send to third parties or the community at large.[44] For example, in a prosecution for the illegal sale of drugs, it would be improper for the prosecutor to argue as follows: "And it's time we sent a message to all the drug dealers out there that we won't tolerate this sort of criminal conduct in our community." The factfinder's job is to render a verdict based on the evidence, not to render a verdict which the factfinder thinks will have the "right" effect on third parties.

---

42. Of course, you cannot help but do so in an indirect way constantly, whether through the clothes you wear or your manner of speech. This is a form of non-testimonial silent argument; see Chapter 9.

43. The argument excerpt is from Paul Bergman, *Trial Advocacy in a Nutshell* 231 (1989).

44. See D. McCormick, "The Permissibility of Consequentialist Closing Arguments," 38 Trial Lawyer's Guide 399 (1995).

Chapter 15

EXPERT TESTIMONY

Joe Pesci as Vincent Gambini thanks expert witness Marisa Tomei as Mona Lisa Vito as Fred Gwynne looks on in disbelief. Still photograph from "My Cousin Vinny". © 1992. Twentieth Century Fox Film Corporation. All rights reserved.

Expert testimony is a frequent feature of modern trials. Though many decry the trend,[1] expert testimony appears to be a growth industry. Among the factors responsible for this growth are:

- Statutes such as the Federal Rules of Evidence have tended to eliminate common law restrictions on the use of expert testimony.[2]

- Appellate opinions have likewise tended to expand the scope of

---

1. See, e.g., P. Huber, *Junk Science* (1991).

2. For example, experts may deliver opinions about "ultimate issues" (See FRE 704) and may support their opinions with hearsay and other kinds of inadmissible evidence (FRE 703).

permissible expert testimony.[3]

- Fields of expertise have both mushroomed and narrowed. Experts can now tell us "more and more about less and less." The combination of diverse subjects and experts' depth of expertise about those subjects increases the likelihood that expert testimony will be relevant to a particular dispute.

- Substantive legal rules often demand expert testimony.[4]

- Seeking to impress jaded jurors who live in the Information and Video Ages, attorneys routinely try to add impact to their arguments with expert testimony.[5]

As a result, if you plan to spend much time in the courtroom, you will routinely encounter expert testimony. Thus, you have to understand how to integrate expert testimony into arguments and to examine expert witnesses. This chapter explores these topics.[6]

SECTION A. CONSTRUCTING ARGUMENTS TO SUPPORT EXPERT OPINIONS

1. THE ROLE OF EXPERT TESTIMONY AT TRIAL

The primary function of experts is to deliver opinions about topics that are beyond a factfinder's everyday experience. Such opinions grow out of an expert's specialized "knowledge, skill, experience, training or education."[7] Experts' opinions are of two general types:

- Factual Assertions.

- Normative Conclusions.

The sections below examine the argument construction process for each of these types of opinion.

2. CONSTRUCTING ARGUMENTS FOR FACTUAL ASSERTION OPINIONS

An expert opinion constituting a factual assertion typically describes either past or future events or conditions. For instance, in a products liability case involving the cause of the sudden movement of a parked car, an expert may testify, "In my opinion, the sensor in the car's

---

3. For instance, in *Daubert v. Merrell Dow Pharmaceuticals*, ___ U.S. ___, 113 S.Ct. 2786, 125 L.Ed.2d 469 (1993), the U.S. Supreme Court voided the rule that in order to qualify for admission into evidence, scientific evidence had to be generally accepted within a relevant scientific community. Similarly, courts often permit experts to testify on the factors affecting perception and memory, a subject matter once left entirely to the domain of lay reasoning.

4. For example, it would be a rare malpractice case in which a plaintiff would not

have to call an expert to provide an opinion that the defendant doctor's actions did not comport with the relevant standard of care.

5. Publications aimed at practicing attorneys typically feature page upon page of expert witness advertisements.

6. The discussion assumes that you have admissible expert testimony, and that you have retained an expert who is prepared to testify to favorable evidence in the form of an opinion or otherwise.

7. FRE 702.

transmission failed and caused the car to slip out of park and roll forward." Similarly, an expert may deliver an opinion that the blood type on a victim's shirt is the same blood type as the defendant's, that a plaintiff's depression was caused by the stress of his job, and that a defendant's car was travelling 50 miles per hour when it struck the plaintiff's car. All of these opinions are factual assertions describing past events or conditions.

Experts may also make factual assertions about future events or conditions. For example, an expert may testify that a plaintiff will suffer back pain for the rest of her life, or that a plaintiff's lifetime earnings had she not been injured would have amounted to a million dollars.

To construct an argument supporting a factual assertion opinion, with your expert's assistance take the following steps:

- Identify the evidence supporting the factual assertion.[8]

- Develop one or more arguments by linking the evidence to the factual assertion with generalization(s).

- Validate the generalization(s) through the use of the expert's specialized knowledge.

- Identify other evidence ("especially whens") strengthening the argument through the use of the expert's specialized knowledge.

- Consider the adversary's likely responses to your argument.

As you can see, the argument-construction process for experts' factual assertions is similar to the process by which you construct arguments for factual propositions. The primary difference is that you cannot rely on a factfinder's everyday experience to validate (confirm) the generalization(s) on which arguments rests. Therefore, you have to identify the specialized knowledge or training which validates a generalization.

To construct persuasive arguments, you generally need to develop a symbiotic relationship with an expert. You will typically need an expert's help to identify evidence supporting the factual assertions and validating the underlying generalizations and "especially whens," and the expert may need your help to organize the evidence into a persuasive legal argument.

a. *Identify the Evidence Supporting Factual Assertions*

Let's examine the argument construction process in a case in which you represent the Department of Children's Services ("DCS") in a child neglect proceeding. The DCS contends that Rob and Laura are unfit parents of their two year old son, Ritchie, in that one of them intentionally broke his leg, and seeks to remove Ritchie from his parents' home.

---

8. If of a type reasonably relied on by experts in the particular field, the facts or data underlying an expert's opinion needn't be independently admissible in evidence. See FRE 703.

Rob and Laura claim that whatever injuries Ritchie suffered were a result of an accidental fall. In this case, you might phrase one factual proposition as follows:

"On February 2nd, either Rob or Laura intentionally broke Ritchie's leg."

Your expert is Dr. Carole Eule, who after examining Ritchie's x-rays and other medical records is prepared to testify to an opinion (factual assertion) that Ritchie's leg was intentionally broken. Since Ritchie's parents dispute this opinion, when preparing for trial you have to construct an argument that her opinion is correct. Assume that Dr. Eule has the necessary "knowledge, skill, experience, training, or education"[9] to provide an expert opinion as to whether Ritchie's injury resulted from child abuse. Your first step is to ask Dr. Eule for the evidence indicating that Ritchie's leg was intentionally broken.[10]

Assume that in response, Dr. Eule identifies the following evidence:

1. X-rays taken on February 2nd reveal a spiral fracture in Ritchie's leg.

2. Ritchie's parents told the DCS investigator that his injury resulted from a fall on the kitchen floor. Dr. Eule thinks it highly unlikely that a fall to the floor could have caused the spiral fracture.

3. The February 2nd x-rays revealed a separate fracture in Ritchie's other leg that occurred several months earlier.

At trial, you have to introduce the evidence underlying an expert's opinion. Sometimes, an expert can testify to the underlying evidence from personal knowledge. For example, Dr. Eule may be able to testify that the x-ray taken on February 2nd revealed a spiral fracture in Ritchie's leg. If the expert lacks personal knowledge of the underlying evidence, you must elicit it from other witnesses. For example, the DCS investigator would probably have to testify to the parent's account of how Ritchie was supposedly injured.

b. Link the Most Probative Evidence to the Assertion

With this list of evidence in hand, ask the expert for the strongest (most probative) evidence indicating that her opinion is correct. You ask an expert for the strongest evidence because not all the evidence will be strong enough to justify construction of a separate argument linking evidence to a factual assertion.[11]

In response to your inquiry, Dr. Eule may say, "I suppose the strongest evidence that these injuries were inflicted intentionally is the

---

9. See FRE 702.

10. Even experienced experts may have trouble isolating all the evidence supporting an opinion. Experts do not necessarily spend their waking hours marshalling discrete items of evidence around specific assertions. Thus, producing a useful list of evidence will often require a collaborative effort between you and an expert.

11. Ultimately, how many arguments you construct supporting a particular opinion must rest on your judgment.

spiral fracture." You then construct an embryonic argument by connecting the evidence to the conclusion via a single generalization:

"People who suffer spiral fractures to their legs have often been intentionally injured." [12]

Examine this generalization. Most factfinders lack the common experience to know if it is accurate.[13] Therefore, you will typically ask your expert to validate the generalization by explaining "the facts or data"[14] underlying its accuracy.

c. *Validate the Generalization in Your Argument*

Validating a generalization simply means having your expert identify the "scientific, technical or other specialized knowledge"[15] upon which a generalization is based. Such knowledge supplies the substitute for common experience which allows a factfinder to understand and accept your generalization.

For example, return to Ritchie's case. To validate the generalization in section "b" above, you would ask Dr. Eule to explain the scientific basis for her conclusion that a spiral fracture is indicative of intentional injury. Your conversation with Dr. Eule might go as follows:

Q: Dr. Eule, what exactly is a spiral fracture?

A: It's a fracture that has a coiled pattern rather than going in a straight line across the bone.

Q: And how do you know that a spiral fracture is caused intentionally rather than accidentally?

A: For a spiral fracture to occur, you usually have to twist the leg sharply, and with a great deal of force. That sort of twisting force isn't generated in a fall. You usually have to violently twist someone's leg with your hand to generate that sort of force.

Q: I'd like the jury to understand how you know that this sort of force is necessary to create a spiral fracture. Can you explain this in a little more detail?

A: Sure. The bone that was broken is the femur, the strongest bone in the body. It's just about impossible for a spiral fracture to occur with a femur unless one portion of the leg is held virtually immobile while another portion is subjected to violent twisting. According to a couple of recent studies....

---

12. You and your expert may decide that intermediate generalizations will make your argument more persuasive. See Chapter 3 Sec. 3.

13. Even if your factfinder did know that this generalization is valid, you would still need expert testimony because the generalization is not a matter of common knowledge.

14. See FRE 703.

15. See FRE 702.

This dialogue validates Dr. Eule's generalization by explaining the specialized knowledge on which it is based.[16] This information will become part of the evidence you elicit during an expert's direct examination. The information helps persuade a factfinder to accept your argument.

The information you elicit to validate a generalization will of course vary greatly depending on the field of expertise. But you need to validate a generalization even when an expert's opinion rests in part on the output of a machine. For instance, assume that you're trying to prove that the voice on a recorded telephone bomb threat is that of the defendant. An expert in sound spectrography (voice analysis) has opined that the voice on the recording is the defendant's.[17] That opinion is based in part on evidence that according to graphs produced by a machine known as a sound spectrograph, vowel sounds produced by the voice on the recording are nearly identical to vowel sounds produced by the defendant. The generalization linking this evidence to the expert's conclusion is something like, "Voice samples that produce very similar vowel sound graphs often come from the same person." To validate this generalization, you would explore with the expert the science of sound spectrography and the scientific basis for this generalization, as well as the basis upon which the expert acquired this knowledge.

d. Strengthen Your Argument With "Especially Whens"

Ordinarily, you complete an argument by identifying "especially whens" strengthening a generalization.[18] You follow the same procedure with an expert. The only difference is that your lack of specialized knowledge means that you will typically have to rely on the expert to identify the "especially whens." For instance, in the DCS proceeding on behalf of Ritchie, you might ask Dr. Eule: "Is there anything in this case that makes it especially likely that the spiral fracture was caused intentionally?" Dr. Eule might reply, "Well, Ritchie was only two years old when this injury occurred. The bones of a two year old are extremely soft and supple, so for a spiral fracture to occur in a child that young some forceful twisting must take place."

Based on this response, you have identified the "especially when" that Ritchie was only two at the time of the injury. Of course, just as most factfinders lack the common experience to know if a generalization is valid, so too do they lack the common experience necessary to assess the significance of an "especially when." Therefore, you will typically validate your "especially whens" by asking your expert to explain the scientific knowledge supporting their significance. For instance, you

---

16. Obviously, you might have obtained much of this information when you first decided to retain Dr. Eule as an expert. Nevertheless, a conversation such as the one in the text is common during pretrial preparation, because at that earlier time you might not have known the specific generalizations upon which your expert was going to rely.

17. One of a number of cases admitting sound spectrography evidence is *United States v. Smith*, 869 F.2d 348 (7th Cir. 1989).

18. See Chapter 3, Sec. 2.

would ask Dr. Eule to explain that the softness and suppleness of a two year old's bones indicate abuse. This information will also support your argument by becoming part of the evidence you elicit during an expert's direct examination.

e. Counter an Adversary's Likely Responses

As with any other argument, you need to consider an adversary's likely responses to an argument that your expert's opinion is correct, and counter them if necessary. The following subsections examine this aspect of preparation.

(1) Adversary's Response No. 1—Disputing the Accuracy of the Evidence Supporting Your Expert's Opinion

An adversary may attack an expert's opinion by disputing the accuracy of the evidence on which it is based. Such an attack raises the familiar issue of disputed evidence. And sometimes you may be able to prepare your response to an adversary's argument without the assistance of your expert. For instance, assume that Dr. Eule had based her opinion in part on Ritchie having said to a social worker, "I got hurt because my daddy got mad at me." If your adversary is likely to dispute Ritchie's making this remark, you wouldn't need Dr. Eule's help to prepare your response. You would use the Credibility Checklist[19] to help you prepare an argument that Ritchie's father did make the remark.

Other times, however, you will need your expert's help when an adversary disputes the accuracy of evidence relied on by your expert. For example, assume Ritchie's parent's expert claims that Ritchie's fracture is not a spiral fracture. You lack the specialized knowledge to identify arguments that the fracture is spiral, and the Credibility Checklist will be of little use since it applies to lay witnesses' assertions. To resolve this type of dispute, you will have to ask your expert to help you prepare arguments resolving the dispute in your favor.

The subjects you inquire into when you need an expert's help to resolve evidentiary disputes necessarily vary depending on the field of expertise. In general, you will ask your expert to identify the evidence supporting her version of the dispute. Your specific questions will often focus on such subjects as:

- The reliability of any tests performed by your expert.

- Whether your expert followed proper procedures in carrying out the tests.

- Whether your expert considered alternate hypotheses.

- Whether your expert considered the opinions of other experts as set forth in treatises or articles.[20]

---

19. See Chapter 5 Sec. 1.

20. You may be able to bolster your expert's opinion with statements in reliable publications. See FRE 803 (18).

(2) Adversary's Response No. 2—Using "Except Whens" to Weaken Your Generalization(s)[21]

As arguments supporting the accuracy of experts' opinions rely on generalizations, an adversary may attack your arguments by establishing exceptions to your generalization(s). To identify such attacks, ask your expert about potential exceptions to the generalizations on which your arguments rely.

For example, in Ritchie's child abuse case, you would ask Dr. Eule a question such as, "Doctor, you've said that children who suffer spiral fractures to their legs have often been intentionally injured. Are there any exceptions to this? Can a spiral fracture be due to other causes?"

If an expert identifies exceptions, check your file to determine whether your adversary has evidentiary support for any of the potential "except whens." Thus, if Dr. Eule states that a spiral fracture might result from an accidental fall if the child's foot is held in a fixed position while the child's body twists, you would want to know whether your adversary could muster evidentiary support for this "except when".

To counter an adversary's reliance on "except whens," you may argue that your generalizations and "especially whens" are more persuasive than your opponent's "except whens." For example, you might argue that while it is possible for a freak accidental fall to cause a spiral fracture, it is far more likely that Ritchie's spiral fracture was the result of an intentional injury. In addition, you may dispute the accuracy of an adversary's "except when." For example, if Ritchie's parents claim that he broke his leg in a fall from a chair, you may offer evidence that no such fall took place.[22]

(3) Adversary's Response No. 3—Challenging the Validity of Your Expert's Generalization(s)

An adversary may also respond to an argument by challenging the validity of the generalization underlying your expert's opinion. For example, again in the Ritchie child abuse case, the parents' expert may contend that spiral fractures to legs are commonly caused by accidental falls and therefore are not indicative of intentional injury.

To ferret out such a response by an adversary, ask your expert if other authorities in the field dispute the validity of the expert's generalization. If so, together with your expert you will need to develop arguments attacking the position of the conflicting authorities.[23]

---

21. For a discussion of the "except when" process, see Chapter 4 Sec. 2.

22. The Credibility Checklist in Chapter 5 can often help you construct arguments attacking an adversary's "except whens."

23. If a case merits the additional expense, you might consider engaging an additional expert to support the validate of your generalization.

(4) Adversary's Response No. 4—Your Expert Is Biased

A frequently-made argument is that an expert's testimony is a product of bias. An expert is subject to the same claims of bias as any lay witness. For example, a party may claim that an expert's testimony is a product of a desire for financial gain, personal friendship with a party or even with counsel, or to avoid the embarrassment of recanting an earlier position. For instance, Ritchie's parents may claim that Dr. Eule is biased because she filed the child abuse complaint with the DCS and is unwilling to embarrass herself by abandoning this position despite evidence to the contrary. Dr. Eule's testimony that she took into account the contrary evidence even before filing the complaint would counter this argument.

In addition to the bias claims to which all witnesses are subject, experts are potentially subject to a variety of unique bias arguments. Among these are the following:

- The amount of an expert's fees.

- Inconsistent positions taken by the same expert in other cases or writings. For example, has Dr. Eule previously testified or written that spiral fractures commonly result from accidental falls?

- An expert's previous employment by the same counsel or law firm.

- An expert's previous testimony on behalf of the same interest group, such as medical malpractice plaintiffs or products liability defendants.[24]

(5) Adversary's Response No. 5–Your Expert's Qualifications Are Lacking

Finally, an adversary may attack the credibility of an expert's opinion by trying to undermine the expert's qualifications.[25] For example, Ritchie's parents may contend that as Dr. Eule is only a general practitioner and not a Board-certified pediatrician, her opinion about the cause of a spiral fracture should not be believed. In another case, a party may argue that an appraiser's opinion as to the market value of an industrial park in County X should not be believed because all of the appraiser's professional experience has been in County Y.

To ferret out such a response, explore any weaknesses in an expert's background that occur to you, and ask your expert about any challenges that she anticipates. You should rely on your expert to develop responses. For example, ask your expert appraiser, "How is it that your experience in County Y allows you to arrive at an opinion about property

---

24. In an effort to attract business, many experts advertise that they've represented both sides.

25. This argument constitutes an attack on an expert's credibility, not on the admis-sibility of an expert's testimony. Thus, your adversary may make such an attack even after a judge rules that an expert has sufficient qualifications to give an expert opinion.

in County X?" [26]

3. CONSTRUCTING ARGUMENTS FOR NORMATIVE CONCLUSIONS

The second type of expert opinions constitute normative conclusions. As you know,[27] some legal elements require factfinders not only to determine what happened, but also to evaluate the propriety of a party's conduct according to community norms. Elements which require this latter determination contain a "normative" standard. An expert's opinion may assert that the normative standard has or has not been satisfied. Typical opinions constituting normative conclusions are, "the doctor was negligent in neglecting to take x-rays prior to the surgery," and "the police used reasonable force when making the arrest."

Fortunately, the process of constructing arguments supporting experts' normative conclusions is very similar to that for expert's factual assertions. The main difference is that you need to develop normative factual propositions supporting your expert's normative conclusion. To illustrate the argument construction process for normative conclusions, consider an example in which you represent a plaintiff in a legal malpractice case.[28] You want to prove that the plaintiff's former attorney, Brad Olsen, negligently represented the plaintiff in a previous automobile accident case. Your expert witness, Francis Anderson, has given an opinion that Olsen was negligent.

Your first step is to identify the historical factual propositions supporting Anderson's opinion. To do so, you would simply ask Anderson a question such as "What are all the things that Olson did (or failed to do) that constitute malpractice?" Assume that in response Anderson identifies the following historical propositions:

a. Olsen failed to advise the plaintiff of the meaning of the term "course and scope of employment" as used in a set of interrogatories served on the plaintiff on February 2nd.

b. Olsen neglected to interview an eyewitness to the accident.

c. Olsen failed to object to inadmissible evidence at the trial.

If your opponent disputes any of the expert's historical factual propositions, you would have to construct arguments supporting the accuracy of your propositions in the same way that you construct arguments for any other factual assertion.[29]

Assuming the accuracy of your historical factual propositions, you would then develop normative propositions to establish either a breach of or compliance with the normative standard. Thus, in the example

---

26. The process of constructing arguments to support your expert's opinion is presented as a linear one. In practice of course, you may deviate from this sequence as circumstances dictate.

27. See Chapter 6.

28. The example in the text is based on a case in which one of the authors served as an expert witness.

29. Since the arguments are historical in nature you may not need your expert's assistance when preparing such arguments.

above, for each historical factual proposition you would ask Anderson a series of questions such as:

- Why was it malpractice for Olsen to fail to mention the meaning of "course and scope?"

- Why was it unreasonable for Olsen to fail to mention "course and scope?"

- What were the risks resulting from Olsen's failure to mention "course and scope?"

- Were there alternative courses of action Olsen might have taken to avoid any risks associated with the failure to mention "course and scope?"

- Did Olsen's failure to mention "course and scope" violate an industry standard? [30]

The expert's answers would provide your normative propositions. For example, Anderson might identify the following normative propositions in response to the questions above:

- In response to the interrogatories the client erroneously admitted that an employee was in the course and scope of employment.

- As a result of the erroneous admission, the client had to pay a damage award of $300,000.

- A competent lawyer would have recognized the danger and consequences of the client not understanding the meaning of "course and scope," and would have explained the phrase before the interrogatories were answered.

You would then ask Anderson to identify the evidence proving your normative propositions. After Anderson identifies that evidence, you would construct arguments to prove your normative propositions just as you did when proving an expert's factual assertion in Section 2 above. That is, you would connect the most probative item of evidence to the normative proposition with a generalization; validate the generalization with the expert's specialized knowledge; strengthen the argument with "especially whens" and validate the "especially whens." Finally, you and the expert would consider the adversary's potential responses to the arguments tending to prove your normative propositions, and your counter arguments. As was true for an expert's factual assertion, an adversary may attack an argument supporting a normative factual proposition by disputing the accuracy of the evidence tending to prove the proposition, by challenging the validity of your generalization(s), by offering "except whens," by claiming that your expert is biased or by attacking your expert's qualifications. And you would counter the adversary's response just as you did in Section 2 above.

---

30. The questions in the text are those that you ask yourself when attempting to identify normative factual propositions in cases not involving expert opinions. See Chapter 6. The questions obviously overlap somewhat, but you want to be thorough when identifying normative propositions.

4. EXPERTS' OPINIONS—DIRECT v. CIRCUMSTANTIAL EVIDENCE

Like any other evidence, an expert's opinion will constitute either direct or circumstantial evidence. When an opinion is direct evidence, persuading a factfinder that the opinion is accurate establishes a legal element. For instance, in the legal malpractice case described in Section 3 above, Anderson's opinion that Olsen committed malpractice is direct evidence. The factfinder's acceptance of this opinion satisfies the element of negligence.[31]

When an opinion is circumstantial evidence, even if you persuade a factfinder that the opinion is true you have to construct an additional argument linking the opinion to a factual proposition. For example, assume that you contend that a defendant, Jeeves, physically assaulted your client, Wooster. One item of evidence is a taped message allegedly left by Jeeves on Wooster's telephone answering machine, threatening Wooster with bodily harm. Jeeves denies making the threatening phone call. To prove that Jeeves made the call, you call an expert in sound spectrography. The expert testifies to an opinion that the voice on the tape is that of Jeeves. This opinion is circumstantial evidence. Even if the factfinder accepts it, the factfinder will still have to draw an inference to link the opinion ("Jeeves made a threatening phone call to Wooster") to your desired conclusion ("Jeeves physically assaulted Wooster"). You would make an argument in support of that inference the same as for any other item of highly probative circumstantial evidence.[32]

5. "NON–OPINION" EXPERT TESTIMONY

In some situations, experts are allowed to provide a factfinder with specialized knowledge but are not allowed to deliver an opinion about the facts of a specific case.[33] Typically, the reason for the no-opinion rule is that an expert's field of expertise has not progressed to the point that an expert can opine about specific circumstances with sufficient scientific accuracy.[34]

Consider the following examples:

    a. A "rape syndrome expert" may be allowed to testify to the common behavior of rape victims following an attack, but typically cannot state an opinion as to whether a particular victim was raped.[35]

    b. An eyewitness identification expert may be allowed to testify as to the general circumstances affecting people's perceptions and

---

31. Normative expert opinions almost always constitute direct evidence. Expert's factual assertions may constitute either direct or circumstantial evidence.

32. See Chapter 3.

33. See 31A Am. Jur. 2d "Expert and Opinion Evidence" Sec. 51, at 58 (1994).

34. See C. Mueller and L. Kirkpatrick, *Evidence* Sec. 7.7 (1995).

35. See, e.g., *State v. Allewalt*, 308 Md. 89, 517 A.2d 741 (Md.1986). See also 1 John Myers, *Evidence in Child Abuse and Neglect Cases*, Sec. 4:34 at 291 (2d ed. 1992).

memories, but may be unable to state an opinion as to the accuracy of a particular identification.[36]

    c. An expert on "child abuse accommodation syndrome" may be allowed to describe the symptoms commonly exhibited by victims of child abuse, but may not be allowed to opine as to whether a specific child was a child abuse victim.[37]

    In situations such as these, the reason you call an expert is to validate the generalizations you will rely on when making an argument. For example, in a criminal case, you may argue that an eyewitness' identification of your client is mistaken, in part because the eyewitness was under a great amount of stress when he observed the crime. The generalization you are relying on is that, "People who observe a crime while under stress often misperceive the identity of the perpetrator." The expert's role would be to provide specialized knowledge validating this generalization.[38]

6. CONSTRUCTING ARGUMENTS CHALLENGING YOUR ADVERSARY'S EXPERT'S OPINION

    To this point, you have learned to construct arguments supporting your expert's opinion. Of course, in many cases your adversary will offer conflicting expert testimony. And, to the extent that time and a client's financial resources permit, you should construct arguments attacking an adversary expert's opinion. To do so, follow the same steps you would to construct arguments support your own expert's opinion, this time developing your own responses to those arguments. Your responses will be one or more of those discussed in Section 2 (e) above.

SECTION B. ELICITING EXPERT TESTIMONY

1. IN GENERAL

    Constructing arguments according to the principles described in Part One prepares you to conduct the direct or cross examination of expert witnesses. Those examinations tend to be very different from those of lay witnesses, and not just because experts often get to use pointers and display exhibits with funny-sounding names. Among the differences that make parents proud to brag that "my child is an expert witness" are these:

Direct Examination

    • To qualify a witness as an expert, you generally have to elicit extensive foundational testimony about a witness' education,

---

36. See e.g. *State v. Chapple,* 135 Ariz. 281, 660 P.2d 1208 (Ariz.1983); 31A Am. Jur. 2d *Expert and Opinion Evidence,* Sec. 370 at 371 (1994).

37. See, e.g., *State v. JQ,* 130 N.J. 554, 617 A.2d 1196 (N.J. 1993); 1 John Myers, *Evidence in Child Abuse and Neglect Cases,* Sec. 4:33 at 289 (2d ed. 1992).

38. In this situation, the factfinder's everyday experience would be sufficient to allow it to accept this generalization even without the expert's testimony. However, such testimony is sometimes allowable for the reason that it would "assist" the factfinder to decide the case. See FRE 702.

training, knowledge and experience.[39]

- Experts are not required to testify from personal knowledge. They may testify in response to hypothetical questions, or based on information supplied to them prior to trial.

- Because experts typically do not recount a series of events, expert testimony often does not emerge chronologically.

- Experts are often allowed to deliver narrative responses, reflecting judges' trust in them to keep to the point and not throw in inadmissible evidence.

- Experts may discuss otherwise inadmissible information, as long as they used it to arrive at an opinion and the information is of a type that other experts in the same field reasonably rely on to form opinions.[40]

- Experts may discuss the generalizations linking evidence to their conclusions, as a lay factfinder presumably lacks the specialized knowledge to be aware of them.

Cross Examination

- To explore an expert's possible bias, you may ask about the expert's compensation and previous services as an expert.

- You may offer the conflicting opinions of authors of authoritative treatises.[41]

The remainder of the chapter examines these unique aspects of expert witness testimony.

2. QUALIFYING A WITNESS AS AN EXPERT

The examination of an expert typically begins with foundational testimony demonstrating a witness' specialized "knowledge, skill, experience, training or education." [42] Thus, you routinely begin an expert's direct examination with such foundational evidence. And you may be able to emphasize background evidence that pertains directly to an argument by eliciting it twice, once when qualifying a witness as an expert and a second time when validating a generalization underlying the expert's opinion.

The content of foundational testimony necessarily varies according to a witness' field of expertise. In general, however, you will elicit evidence of the following types:

- Formal education: Undergraduate and graduate degrees, postgraduate specialty education. This background is important for the wide range of experts who have advanced professional degrees and training. For example, you may elicit evidence that a tax

---

39. See FRE 702

40. See FRE 703.

41. See FRE 803 (18).

42. See FRE 702.

attorney expert witness has completed a month-long certificate course on "Tax Planning for Retirement Funds."

- Professional experience: The duration and content of an expert's relevant work experiences, and any licenses an expert has. For example, if a trauma expert is to testify to your client's injuries following an automobile accident, you may elicit testimony that the expert has seven years of emergency room experience, and has seen patients with injuries similar to your client's at least 100 times. Or, if your expert is to testify to the value of Beatles collectibles, you may elicit testimony that the expert has dealt exclusively with such collectibles for over five years, attends at least half a dozen Beatles conventions a year where such items are bought and sold and is a licensed appraiser.

- Professional organizations to which an expert belongs. This evidence can be especially impressive if membership depends on fulfilling rigorous conditions rather than payment of a membership fee, and if your witness is an officer of the organization.

- Relevant educational courses that an expert has taught, whether at the undergraduate, graduate or post-graduate level. Such evidence suggests that other experts respect your expert.

- Articles or books written by an expert, unless it is this one.

- The number of times a person has previously qualified as an expert.

Before you begin to elicit such information, your adversary may graciously offer to stipulate that your witness is qualified as an expert. Be wary of accepting such an offer if your expert's background is particularly impressive and relevant to an argument. For while the primary goal of the foundational testimony is to qualify a witness as an expert, an important secondary goal is to add to the expert's credibility by impressing a factfinder with the expert's credentials. Thus, you may politely decline the offer to stipulate, if necessary assuring a judge with an anxious eye on the calendar that you'll "focus on those parts of the background which demonstrate how qualified Ms. Expert is to render an opinion in this case."

By way of example, assume that your client has filed a legal malpractice suit against an estate planner for failing to advise your client's father that he needed to change his will in order to disinherit a child born after the will was signed. Your expert, Arlene Wilkoff, will opine that the failure to do so violated professional standards and was therefore malpractice. Your foundational questioning of Ms. Wilkoff may proceed as follows:

1. Q: Ms. Wilkoff, what is your name and current occupation?
2. A: Arlene Wilkoff. I'm a lawyer who specializes in estate planning here in town, and I also teach part-time.
3. Q: You have a license to practice law?

4.   A: Yes.

5.   Q: Please describe your formal education.

6.   A: I graduated with a Bachelor of Sciences degree from Yale 15 years ago, then went to law school at the University of Chicago, where I graduated three years later. I then completed the University of Miami's year-long course in the Planning and Taxation of Estates.

7.   Q: Can you briefly describe your practice experience?

8.   A: Surely. For the first five years after completing the Estate Planning course I was an associate with the law firm of Hoffman & Lurie, where I worked exclusively on estate planning matters. I then took a three year leave of absence to work for the Enforcement Division of the State Bar, prosecuting lawyers for disciplinary rules violations. I handled primarily matters dealing with estate planning practitioners. Following that, I returned as a partner to Hoffman & Lurie, where I've been ever since.

9.   Q: Apart from your work at the State Bar, have you had any experience with professional standards for estate planning lawyers?

10.   A: Yes indeed. I teach a Continuing Education course for estate planners twice a year, and I've written a number of articles in the local county bar journal.

11.   Q: Are you affiliated with any professional organizations?

12.   A: Yes, I just wound up two years as the Chair of our State Bar's Task Force on Probate Code Reform. I'm also the Treasurer of our local bar's section on estate planning.

13.   Q: Have you ever previously qualified as an expert in a case involving alleged malpractice by an estate planning practitioner?

14.   A: Yes, I've actually testified in three matters, two on behalf of the person making the claim of malpractice and once on behalf of the attorney. I was retained in a few other matters, but they settled prior to trial.

15.   Q: Thank you, Ms. Wilkoff. Now, turning your attention to the matter at hand....

Here, you elicit testimony establishing a witness' expertise in the professional standards for estate planning lawyers. You focus on her formal education (No. 6), her professional experience, including relevant teaching and writing (Nos. 8 and 10), her service with relevant organizations (No. 12) and her past experience as an expert witness (No. 14). Whether in an actual case you would make a more in-depth probe of an expert's qualifications would depend in part on the closeness of a fit between the qualifications and the information on which the expert bases her opinion, and in part on the extent of a factfinder's familiarity with the expert's subject matter.

In accord with the practice of many judges, you do not make a formal motion for a ruling that Wilkoff is qualified to render an expert opinion. Rather, you move directly into the subject matter of her testimony (No. 15). However, always ask the court clerk about the procedures a judge follows. Some judges will want you to request a ruling that a witness is qualified as an expert, in order to clarify the record and to give opposing counsel a chance to contest an expert's qualifications through argument or voir dire questioning. In any event, in a jury trial you may want to request a ruling that your witness is qualified as an expert, for the jurors may take the ruling as an indication that the judge approves of an expert's testimony.

3. ELICITING AN EXPERT'S OPINION

The substance of an expert's testimony usually includes at least these three portions:

a. What an expert did to arrive at an opinion;

b. The opinion;

c. The facts or data supporting the opinion.

But unlike lay witnesses, whose testimony typically emerges in chronological order, no standard format for an expert's testimony exists. Among the reasons are these:

- Some attorneys prefer to begin by eliciting an expert's opinion, and then trace the process by which the expert arrived at it. Other attorneys prefer to build towards an opinion before eliciting it.

- You are not required to disclose the "facts or data" on which an expert basis an opinion.[43] In practice, however, most attorneys do so.

- Some attorneys are fond of presenting an expert with the data on which she is to base an opinion in the form of a hypothetical question. Other attorneys eschew hypotheticals in favor of presenting the necessary data to an expert before the hearing.[44]

- An expert may have to explain a field of expertise even before beginning to describe what the expert did to arrive at an opinion. For example, the testimony of an expert in sound spectrography will mean little to most factfinders in the absence of testimony explaining the science and mechanical technology underlying the production of sound spectrographs.

Rather than trying to fit the testimony of all experts into a single mode, be flexible and consider an expert's suggestions. Many experts have had loads of experience describing their field of interest not only in court, but in more natural social settings like dinner parties. As a

---

43. See FRE 705.

44. FRE 703, which states that an expert may testify on the basis of "facts or data ... made known to the expert at or before the hearing," authorizes either procedure.

result, an expert may have good insight into how to explain an opinion in a convincing manner to a non-expert.

For one example of how you might elicit an expert's opinion, assume that you have called Dr. Peter Laddy to provide an expert opinion that the voice on a tape recorded bomb threat is that of the defendant. After he qualifies as an expert, you might elicit his testimony as follows:

1. Q: Dr. Laddy, you're here as an expert in the field of sound spectrography. Can you briefly tell the jurors what this is.

2. A: Surely. Sound spectrography is the science of analyzing the vocal qualities of speech with the help of a machine known as a sound spectrometer. The machine produces printouts known as sound spectrograms. Those printouts allow one to study speech patterns visually.

3. Q: I've heard the term voiceprints. Are these what you've referred to as sound spectrograms?

4. A: Voiceprints is not a term I would use; I think it's misleading. It makes one think of fingerprints, which to my understanding are rather fixed on each individual. Speech sounds are different. Nobody would pronounce the word "movie," for example, the same way every time, so the sound spectrogram would be a little different each time.

5. Q: How do sound spectrograms help you to identify a speaker's identity?

6. A: It's based on the principle that the variation in speech sounds made by one person is less than the variation in speech sounds made by different people. With a sound spectrograph machine, we can separate a sound according to its pitch and duration, and by comparing a series of printouts identify whether a speech sample was made by the same or by different speakers.

7. Q: You used the term "pitch." Can you please explain what you mean by that?

8. A: Yes . . . .

[Dr. Laddy continues to explain sound spectrography.]

15. Q: Now, Dr. Laddy, as an expert in sound spectrography, can you tell the jury if you've been able to arrive at an opinion as to whether the voices on Tapes A and B, as they've been labeled, are the voices of the same individual.

16. A: Yes, I have.

17. Q: And what is that opinion?

18. A: In my opinion, the voices on both tapes are the voice of the same individual.

19. Q: Can you please describe how you went about arriving at that opinion?

20. A: All right. I was given two tapes, A and B, and asked to compare them with the aid of a sound spectrometer.

21. Q: Let me interrupt you there. Were you involved in any way in the making of these two tapes?

22. A: Not at all. I was just sent them and asked to render an opinion as to whether they were made by the same person, if I could.

23. Q: OK, please continue.

24. A: The first thing I did was to encode the tapes through a sound spectrometer into my computer. I then listened to the tapes numerous times in various ways.

25. Q: What do you mean, in various ways?

26. A: Once the statements have been computerized, I can play each one all the way through or I can put pieces of them next to each other for immediate comparison.

27. Q: About how many times would you say that you listened to the tapes?

28. A: In one way or another, well over 50 times, I should think.

29. Q: What else did you do?

30. A: I also prepared sound spectrograms for 12 words or phrases that were common to both tapes, and analyzed those spectrograms.

31. Q: Why did you do that?

32. A: Well, an identification made on the basis of as many as 12 points of comparison is extremely likely to be accurate.

33. Q: Can you explain how you went about making these spectrograms?

[Dr. Laddy continues to explain how he went about arriving at his opinion.]

53. Q: Dr. Laddy, you've told us how you went about doing the analysis to arrive at an opinion that the voices on both tapes are the voice of the same person. I'd now like to ask you about the bases for that opinion. Is your opinion based on listening to the tapes or on comparing the sound spectrograms?

54. A: Oh, both. I always listen to voice samples numerous times as well as compare spectrograms from the samples before I'm able to arrive at an opinion.

55. Q: All right, let's first talk about the sound spectrograms themselves. Do you have those with you?

56. A: Yes. What I did was to prepare a series of overheads, each one containing a phrase or word from Tape A and the corresponding phrase or word from Tape B that I used as the basis of my comparison.

57. Q: We've got an overhead projector here. Can you please place one of the transparencies on it.

58. A: OK.

59. Q: For the record, Dr. Laddy has placed a transparency labeled "Keller–1" on the overhead projector. Dr. Laddy, what does this transparency represent?

60. A: The case name is Keller, and I gave each transparency a number from 1 to 12. Number one contains the phrase, "in one hour," from both tapes. The top printout is from Tape A, the bottom one is from Tape B.

61. Q: Can you please tell us how these printouts support your opinion that both were made by the same person.

62. A: Surely. First note that the duration of the "ow" sound in the word "hour" on each printout is nearly identical, and that the speaker gives a slight pronunciation of the "h" sound.

63. Q: Is there anything especially significant about these similarities?

64. A: Well, they are particularly indicative here, because in each case the word "hour" was preceded by the same words, "in one...."

Whatever the precise subject matter of an expert's testimony, it should reflect the arguments you constructed prior to trial. Here, the expert's opinion consists of a factual assertion: both tapes were made by the same individual. You first identify and begin to validate the generalizations underlying the expert's opinion (No. 6). This is a good idea, given a factfinder's likely unfamiliarity with sound spectrography. After eliciting the opinion (No. 18), you then set about asking the witness to describe the process by which he arrived at it (Nos. 19–33). Based on an argument you constructed before trial, you elicit the important evidence supporting the expert's opinion (No. 62), as well as an "especially when" (No. 64).

In further questioning, you and an expert might anticipate an adversary's likely response and counter it. For instance, if you are aware that Keller intends to attack Dr. Laddy's opinion on the basis of excessive background noise on one of the tapes, you might question Dr. Laddy on the extent of background noise and whether it affected his ability to arrive at an opinion.[45]

---

45. Alternatively, you might delay countering this response until Keller's counsel explores the subject with Dr. Laddy on cross examination. Then, if Keller's counsel does not cross examine on this point, but instead calls a second expert to testify

As you can see, it is very difficult to conduct the examination of a Dr. Laddy or any other expert unless you are familiar with an expert's field of expertise.[46] Your task is to help an expert convince a lay factfinder that an opinion is accurate, and to do that you must be sufficiently well versed to carry on meaningful direct and cross examinations.[47] But familiarity can be a double-edged sword. Through your questions, you try to translate an expert's knowledge into evidence that a lay factfinder can understand. Yet, the more knowledgeable you are, the more the danger that you will overlook the difficulty in understanding that a factfinder may have when hearing the information for the first time.

For example, many experts, be they scientists, lawyers, economists or others, are prone to use jargon. As a result, you and an expert may proceed blithely on with testimony as a factfinder struggles in your wake. To prevent this from happening, always keep in mind your own frustration and even anger when a teacher or other lecturer assumed knowledge that you didn't have. Make sure that an expert explicitly sets forth the generalizations underlying an opinion, and validates them with personal background qualifications, the results of empirical testing, and other such bases. Be alert for jargon, remembering that even a simple term may have technical meanings within a given field of expertise. For example, in No. 6 above Dr. Laddy uses the term "pitch." This is an everyday word, but one that may have special meaning to a linguist. Thus, No. 7 asks Dr. Laddy to explain the meaning of this term.

4. HYPOTHETICAL QUESTIONS

Hypothetical questions set forth factual information, and ask an expert to deliver an opinion on the assumption that the information is accurate.[48] Once, hypothetical questions were the exclusive method of eliciting experts' opinions not based on the expert's first hand knowledge.[49] They are now rarely necessary, as modern evidence rules permit you to furnish an expert with information prior to trial.[50]

For a brief example of a hypothetical question, assume that you represent a civil plaintiff who is suing two police officers for using excessive force to effect an arrest of the plaintiff. Your expert, Chris

---

that excessive background noise prevents an accurate determination, you would recall Dr. Laddy and elicit the countering testimony.

46. Some commentators would put an even greater burden on you, suggesting that you must possess even greater expertise than your expert. This is an unattainable goal unless you continuously specialize in a single type of case, and even then you would be asking your first clients to subsidize much of your education. Besides, even among the medical malpractice lawyers we know who are quite expert about medicine,

there are none we would allow to operate on us.

47. If you have need of expertise in a field with which you are unfamiliar, your expert can probably supply you with the articles or books that will get you "up to speed."

48. The factual matter in a hypothetical question must be based on evidence in the record.

49. 2 J. Wigmore *Evidence* Sec. 672 (Chadbourne rev. 1994).

50. FRE 703.

Littleton, is a former commander of the police force. Based on information furnished by you to her, Littleton is prepared to opine that the officers used excessive force.[51] During trial, you might elicit this opinion in response to a hypothetical question such as the following:[52]

> "Ms. Littleton, I'll ask you to assume the accuracy of the following information. Assume that two police officers stop a car for failing to have an illuminated rear license plate. Assume further that the driver of the car pulls over immediately and.... Based on all this information, do you have an opinion as to whether the officers used excessive force in making the arrest?"

As you can see, in addition to serving as the basis of an expert's opinion, a hypothetical question allows you to recapitulate favorable evidence during questioning. However, frequently opposing counsel will object to such questions on the grounds that you have not introduced evidence to establish all the facts assumed in the hypothetical.[53] Moreover, hypotheticals are often complex and therefore difficult for factfinders to understand. Such questions also invite an adversary to point out on cross examination that if the true facts are other than as stated in the hypothetical, the expert's opinion might be diametrically different. Therefore, be wary of using hypothetical questions.[54]

5. CROSS EXAMINING AN EXPERT

Perhaps the most difficult of all cross examination tasks is cross examining an expert witness. One of two outcomes often results. When the cross examiner is insufficiently knowledgeable about the expert's field of expertise, the expert gets to repeat all the conclusions she already gave on direct examination—except this time with a sneer. Or, if the cross examiner is thoroughly knowledgeable about the expert's field of expertise, the cross turns into a complex battle of wits that leaves a baffled factfinder shaking its head.

The best way to steer between the horns of this dilemma is to rely on the arguments you constructed prior to trial and to ask safe, leading questions. Before trial, you generally have a chance to consult with your own expert in the process of planning for cross. Even if you cannot afford an expert of your own, you may be able to consult with one or at least look at books or articles analyzing an adverse expert's field of expertise. Such sources will often enable you to write down a series of

---

51. As you probably realize, this opinion constitutes a normative conclusion. See Part 1 above.

52. Since Littleton has no personal knowledge of the underlying events, you would of course have to prove them through the testimony of other witnesses.

53. For a hypothetical question to be proper, all of the facts assumed in the question must be testified to by a witness, either before or after such a question is posed to

an expert. See e.g., *Iconco v. Jensen Construction Co.*, 622 F.2d 1291 (8th Cir.1980).

54. Hypothetical questions are generally not practical when an expert's opinion rests on tests the expert has to conduct prior to trial. For instance, in the example in Section 9 above, Dr. Laddy based his testimony on tests of two tape recordings that he conducted before he testified. You would therefore be unable to put a hypothetical question to Dr. Laddy.

questions probing potential weaknesses' in an adverse expert's opinion, and during cross you diverge from this list at your peril.

Part One of this chapter described five methods by which an adversary might attack your argument supporting an expert's opinion. Obviously, these are the same bases you might use to develop arguments attacking an adverse expert's opinion. The following subsections explore techniques for conducting cross examination based on such arguments.

a. Disputing the Accuracy of Evidence on Which an Expert Relies

One method of cross examining an expert involves challenging the accuracy of evidence on which an expert relies in arriving at an opinion. How you cross depends on whether disputed evidence is furnished to an expert by another source, or whether the evidence is within an expert's personal knowledge. Briefly examine each of these common situations.

In one type of situation, disputed evidence on which an expert relies is furnished to the expert by another source. In such situations, you typically cannot challenge the accuracy of the evidence during cross of the expert. What you often can do is illustrate on cross that the expert is relying on evidence that you dispute, and that if the factfinder resolves the dispute in your favor, the expert's opinion is of no value.[55]

For example, assume that an adverse expert has testified to an opinion that a fire was of incendiary origin (intentionally set). He stated that his opinion was based in part on information furnished by Colonel Mustard as to where and when flames from the fire were first seen. You dispute Colonel Mustard's information, and will offer evidence that flames were first seen at a different time and place.[56] You cannot dispute the accuracy of Colonel Mustard's testimony while cross examining the expert. But you can demonstrate that the opinion is no better than the information on which it is based. Your cross may go as follows:

Q: Mr. Expert, your conclusion is that the fire was intentionally set, correct?

A: That's correct.

Q: In arriving at this opinion, you relied heavily on information given you by Colonel Mustard, didn't you?[57]

A: I took his statement into account, yes.

Q: Well, he told you that he saw the first flames from the fire in the Conservatory around 7:30 P.M., right?

---

55. As with other disputed evidence, you would use the Credibility Checklist to prepare an argument that your version is accurate. See Chapter 5, Sec. 1.

56. You can do this both by cross examining Colonel Mustard and by offering testimony of your own witnesses.

57. Remember, experts may consider inadmissible information (in this case, hearsay) to arrive at an opinion. FRE 703.

A: Yes.

Q: But if it should turn out that the first flames from the fire were seen by another witness in the Library around 7:00, your conclusion as to whether the fire was intentionally set might be different, mightn't it?

A: If that were true, I'd certainly have to re-assess the situation.

Q: And you personally have no knowledge as to where or at what time the flames from the fire were first seen, do you?

A: No.

Q: If Colonel Mustard was wrong, your conclusion might well be wrong?

A: That's true.

This cross supplies the basis for an eventual argument that since the expert's opinion relies on inaccurate evidence, the factfinder should pay no heed to the expert's opinion.

By contrast, you can dispute the accuracy of disputed evidence on cross examination when evidence supporting an expert's opinion is within the expert's personal knowledge. Sometimes, the disputed evidence does not rest on specialized knowledge. In such situations, you cross examine an expert as you would any other witness, using arguments suggested by the Credibility Checklist. For example, in the arson hypothetical, assume that the disputed evidence is what Colonel Mustard actually said to the expert. The expert claims that Mustard told him that the flames were first seen in the Conservatory around 7:30; your contention is that Mustard said that the flames were first seen in the Library around 7:00. You would simply develop arguments that your version is correct using the categories set forth in the Credibility Checklist.[58]

Other times, however, the disputed evidence on which an expert relies is based on specialized knowledge. For instance, an adverse medical expert may state that an x-ray depicts a spiral fracture; your medical expert says that it shows only a simple fracture. In such instances, you will have to work with your expert to identify evidence supporting your version of the dispute.

b. *Attack the Generalization Underlying an Expert's Opinion*

Attacking a generalization underlying an expert's opinion typically involves casting doubt on a generalization on which an expert claims specialized knowledge. To conduct such an attack, you personally have to become knowledgeable about the expert's field of expertise. Unless you bring the specialized knowledge to a case, you will have to develop

---

58. For example, you might explore the expert's opportunity to hear and recall   what Mustard said.

your knowledge either by studying the relevant body of specialized knowledge yourself or by consulting your own expert.

For example, a medical expert may opine that, "Spiral fractures in the legs of two year old children are almost always the result of intentional injuries." Or, an expert in speech analysis may opine that, "The variation in speech sound from one person to another is greater than the variability in speech sounds made by the same person."

In each instance, to attack the generalization is to attack the expert's knowledge in his field of expertise. In the first, you would try to show that research has not proven a necessary link between spiral fractures and intentional injuries; they often result from non-intentional injuries. In the second, you would try to show that research suggests that the variation in speech sounds made by one person is apt to be as large as the variation in speech sounds made by different speakers. And to carry out these cross examinations, you would have to be familiar with research into the causes of spiral fractures and into speech analysis.

Identifying the generalization on which an adverse expert's opinion rests is obviously the first step in conducting this type of cross examination. Then, and often together with your own expert, you develop arguments attacking a generalization. The cross you produce may go something like this:

Q: Dr. Laddy, your opinion is that interspeaker variability is greater than intraspeaker variability, correct?

A: Yes.

Q: You're suggesting in other words that there is a greater variation in speech patterns when two different people speak the same word than when one person says the same word at two different times?

A: That's basically right.

Q: And your opinion that interspeaker variability is greater than intraspeaker variability is crucial to the conclusion that you've arrived at in this case, correct?

A: I'd have to agree with that.

Q: But not all voice analysts share this opinion, do they?

A: Most of them do, certainly the ones whose opinions I value.

Q: Well, about two decades ago you testified as an expert in the case of *State v. Shapiro*, didn't you?

A: I recall that case, yes.

Q: And didn't you at that time testify that the science of voice identification did *not* permit one to conclude that interspeaker variability was greater than intraspeaker variability?

A: I may have done, but I've since changed my views as research by myself and others has continued.

Q: Dr. Laddy, are you familiar with a treatise by Dr. Ian Maddenson called *Voice Identification Analysis in a Nutshell*?

A: I am.

Q: You regard that as a generally authoritative work, correct?

A: Yes, that's generally true of all nutshell books.

Q: Handing you Ex. 4, this is a copy of that book, isn't it?

A: Yes.

Q: And reading from page 136, Dr. Maddenson writes, and I quote, "To date, a conclusion that interspeaker variability is greater than intraspeaker variability is still uncertain."[59] That is Dr. Maddenson's statement, correct?

A: That's his opinion, yes. I disagree.

Here, you attack the generalization underlying an adverse expert's opinion in two ways. You offer evidence of the same expert's previously conflicting opinion, and of a different expert's contradictory opinion. You hope that the cross (together with additional evidence you might offer, including perhaps testimony of your own expert) will persuade the factfinder that the generalization is inaccurate.

c. Attack the Applicability of the Generalization to a Particular Case by Eliciting Evidence of "Except Whens"

Offering evidence of "except whens" that arguably render a generalization inapplicable to a particular case is an oft-used method of attacking an adverse expert's opinion. To succeed, you need only show that evidence exists in a particular case negating a generalization which might be true in other cases. Again, carrying out this type of cross requires that you be familiar with the adverse expert's field of expertise.

For an example of this type of cross, assume that you are cross examining the voice identification expert, Dr. Laddy, in a case in which your client, a ship captain, is prosecuted for drunkenly causing a cargo ship to run aground. Dr. Laddy's opinion, based on a comparison of recorded messages made by the captain before and around the time that the ship ran aground, is that the captain was under the influence of alcohol when the ship ran aground. That comparison showed that the captain's voice around the time of the accident was deeper and huskier, and the captain spoke much more slowly, than when the captain spoke many hours before the accident. Thus, the generalization underlying Dr. Laddy's opinion is that, "People whose voices are deeper and huskier than their normal speaking voices and who speak more slowly are frequently under the influence of alcohol."

Assume for the moment that you accept this generalization. However, with the help of your own expert, you have constructed an argument that "except whens" render the generalization inapplicable to this particular case. That is, people who speak more slowly and whose

59. This type of cross is authorized by FRE 803 (18).

voices are lower and huskier than usual often are under the influence of alcohol—except when:

- they speak when they have just been awakened;

- they speak under conditions of great stress; and

- the duration of the abnormal speech sample is only five seconds.

A cross examination based on this argument might go something like this:

Q: Dr. Laddy, your opinion is that the variation in the captain's speech was due to the effect of alcohol, correct?

A: That's right.

Q: But the speech effects that you noted are consistent with other causes too, aren't they?

A: It's possible.

Q: For example, even if someone has had no alcohol, if the person speaks after just being awakened, the person's voice may be deeper and huskier than normal, correct?

A: That's true.

Q: And even if someone has had no alcohol, if the person has just been awakened the person may speak more slowly than normal, right?

A: Yes.

Q: Stress too can affect a person's manner of speech, correct?

A: That's true.

Q: A person who speaks under the influence of stress may have a voice that is huskier and deeper than normal, regardless of whether the person has had any alcohol, right?

A: Well, this is not a consistent finding.

Q: But Dr. Allenson's study, to which you referred earlier, did find that people who are under stress have a voice that is huskier and deeper than normal, didn't it?

A: Yes, in a number of the subjects who participated in that study.

Q: Finally, you would agree that the more of a speech sample you have to analyze, the more sure you can be of your conclusion, wouldn't you?

A: A number of factors can affect my ability to arrive at an opinion, and the quantity of the sample certainly is an important one.

Q: The speech sample on which you base your conclusion that the captain was under the influence of alcohol was barely five seconds long, right?

A: Yes, I believe so.

Q: And that's the bare minimum you would accept as the basis for a conclusion, isn't it?

A: That's true.

Q: You would be more confident of your conclusion if you had a longer sample to analyze?

A: That's correct.

Here, you suggest the existence of additional factors that might negate the generalization on which the expert relies. Of course, you would have to establish by other evidence that, at the time the tape was made, your client had just been awakened and was under stress. The cross furnishes the factfinder with a basis for concluding that these other causes, and not alcohol, account for the change in the captain's pattern of speaking.

A common "except when" with which you may attack an adverse expert's generalization is to show that the expert did not perform a test that might have been or often is performed. Your argument then takes the form, "Generalization A is correct, except when it has not been validated by Test C." For example, assume that an adverse blood analysis expert concludes that "The victim's blood was HIV positive." The expert arrived at this conclusion based on the results of a test known as the ELISA test, but did not verify those results by conducting the more accurate Western Blot test. On cross, you might elicit evidence explaining the importance of the Western Blot test and showing the expert's failure to conduct it.

d. Attack an Expert's Qualifications

Part of validating an expert's generalization is demonstrating that an expert is sufficiently qualified to formulate it. On cross, then, you may undermine a generalization by attacking an adverse expert's qualifications. Note that you may properly conduct this type of cross even after a judge rules that the witness is qualified as an expert. Your cross examination questions go to the weight of the expert's opinion, not to its admissibility.

A few brief examples should suffice to illustrate this type of cross:

• An appraiser testifies to the market value of an industrial park in County Y. You ask, "Ms. Appraiser, isn't it true that prior to making this appraisal, all of your experience had been in County Z?"

• A pediatrician testifies that your clients had allowed their infant child to become malnourished. You ask, "Dr. Casey, in your seven years of practice, you've only seen the cases of two children who have been severely underweight, correct?" "And any pediatrician can join the Royal Academy of Pediatricians just by paying an annual fee, correct?"

- A lawyer testifies that another lawyer committed malpractice by failing to inform a client of the likely consequences of including a claim for punitive damages in a complaint. You ask, "Mr. Hegland, you've never been a practicing attorney, have you?" "You've spent your entire career teaching law, isn't that right?"

In each example, your questions suggest that the adverse expert is insufficiently qualified to arrive at a believable opinion. While the qualifications were not so lacking that judges would not permit the experts to testify, you will argue that they are so minimal (especially as compared to your superbly-qualified expert) that the opinions are not believable.

In one important respect, this type of cross is less risky than the ones above. Since you do not probe an opinion itself, but only an expert's qualifications for arriving at it, you do not give an adverse expert an opportunity to repeat the damaging direct examination testimony during your cross.

e. *Offer Evidence That the Adverse Expert Is Biased*

Finally, experts are as subject to bias arguments as lay witnesses. But whereas the bias charges against lay witnesses usually grow out of claims of personal friendship, those against experts typically arise out of their professional affairs. Questions pertaining to experts' compensation and partisanship to a particular point of view are most common. For example:

- "Dr. Emdy, you have been paid a total of $7000 to testify in this case, right?"

- "Dr. Emdy, this is the fifth case in the last two years in which Anna Turney (opposing counsel) has hired you as an expert, correct?"

- "And in every case in which you have been hired by Ms. Turney, you have concluded that a doctor committed malpractice, right?"

Again, this type of cross examination is relatively low risk, because you do not give an expert an opportunity to repeat damaging direct examination testimony.

Chapter 16

EXHIBITS

Trials set factfinders awash in a sea of oral communication. Everyone talks at them—witnesses, lawyers and judges to jurors. Given the short life span of the spoken word and its tendency to numb listeners when used to excess, it's easy to understand why lawyers are so fond of offering tangible objects—"exhibits"—into evidence.

Rarely are exhibits mandatory. Subject to the Original Writing Rule,[1] you can almost always prove or disprove claims strictly through

1. FRE 1000.

oral testimony. But tangible objects further your persuasive goal by adding visual interest to a presentation and making oral testimony more memorable and easier to understand. Also, they often have a long shelf life. Especially since factfinders can often review exhibits while deliberating, exhibits may trigger recollection of oral evidence that may otherwise have been forgotten. Finally, exhibits typically enhance credibility; witnesses who nervously answer questions often gain assurance when holding tangible objects.

This chapter summarizes the process of offering exhibits into evidence, and describes and illustrates the foundational requirements for many common types of exhibits.

1. LAYING THE FOUNDATION FOR AN EXHIBIT

In order to lay a foundation for the admission of any exhibit into evidence you will generally follow a four step process:

- mark the exhibit and show it to opposing counsel;
- authenticate the exhibit;
- establish that the exhibit is relevant;
- establish that the exhibit is admissible.

Once you have completed these steps you have "laid the foundation" for the exhibit, and you can move it into evidence and publish it to the factfinder.[2] As part of your pretrial preparation, you will typically identify the evidence and arguments you will use to authenticate your exhibits, and establish the relevance and admissibility of each exhibit you plan to admit at trial.

a. *"Mark" an Exhibit and Show It to Opposing Counsel*

Marking an exhibit consists of tagging it with a number or letter that distinguishes it from all other exhibits. By tradition, plaintiffs' exhibits are assigned numbers while defense exhibits are assigned letters, though many judges now prefer to mark all exhibits sequentially by number or letter regardless of which party offers them.

Often you mark all exhibits for purposes of identification at a pretrial conference. If you need to introduce an exhibit which has not been previously marked, either you or the court clerk will mark it before you first refer to it during trial. Before you examine a witness about an exhibit you should show the exhibit to opposing counsel and state on the record that you have done so. This permits opposing counsel to make timely objections to any questions you have relating to the exhibit.

For example, the marking process for a photograph may go as follows:

---

2. You can, of course, dispense with the need to lay a foundation through a "stipulation" to an exhibit's admissibility. When the ultimate admissibility of an exhibit is not in doubt, attorneys commonly offer to stipulate to its admissibility. Thus, you will resort to the following four step procedure only if you can't arrive at a stipulation with opposing counsel.

"Your Honor, I have here a photograph which I have previously shown to defense counsel. I ask that it be marked as Plaintiff's 3 for identification. May I show it to the witness?"

Then, either you or the court clerk can ink in a small "3" on the back or front of the photograph. Finally, either you or the bailiff will hand Exhibit 3 to the witness.

Once an exhibit is marked, refer to it by its exhibit number. Especially when a number of exhibits have been offered, you muddle up the record if you ask a witness to "look at that piece of paper there and tell us if you recognize what it shows." Leave no doubt as to what you're referring to: "Please look at the photograph, Exhibit 3, and tell us if you recognize what it shows."

b. *Authenticate an Exhibit* [3]

Authenticating an exhibit typically involves eliciting testimony tending to prove that the exhibit is what you contend it is. For example, assume that you are trying to authenticate a photograph of your client's living room as it looked just after it was damaged in a rainstorm. Your client is testifying on direct and the examination proceeds as follows:

Q: The bailiff has handed you Exhibit 3. Do you recognize Exhibit 3?

A: Yes.

Q: Can you please tell us what this is?

A: Yes, it's a photograph of the living room of my house showing what it looked like after the rainstorm on December 8th.

This testimony authenticates the photograph by providing evidence that the photo is what you contend it is.

Often, as above, you can quickly authenticate an exhibit by showing it to the witness, asking her if she recognizes it, and then asking her what it is. However, if it is not obvious to the court that the witness has personal knowledge that allows her to identify an exhibit, you may have to elicit testimony establishing that the witness has such personal knowledge. For example, assume you represent the plaintiff Sendor Inc. in a breach of contract action against Reliable Widget Co. You want to introduce what you contend is a copy of a letter sent by Bonnie Davis, the former president of Sendor, to Reliable. Davis died prior to trial. To authenticate the letter, you call Davis' secretary Wally Woods on direct. After marking the letter as Exhibit 22 and showing it to opposing counsel, your examination proceeds as follows:

---

3. Some courts will try to resolve all issues relating to authentication prior to trial. The trial judge, for example, will often ask the parties if they will contest the authenticity of any of the adversary's exhibits. If not, both sides will be required to stipulate to the genuineness of the exhibits. Such a stipulation will relieve you of the obligation to authenticate the exhibit at trial. The opposing party may still object to the exhibit on the grounds that it is irrelevant or for some other reason inadmissible.

Q: Mr. Woods, directing your attention to Exhibit 22, which you have before you, do you recognize that document?

A: Yes.

Q: And what is Exhibit 22?

Opposing Counsel: Objection, lack of foundation and lack of personal knowledge.

Court: Sustained.

Q: Mr. Woods, you testified that you were Ms. Davis' secretary for 5 years, during that time did you type any letters for Mr. Davis to sign?

A: Yes. Hundreds of times.

Q: And when you typed a letter for Ms. Davis' signature, did you put your initials anywhere on the letter?

A: Yes, I always typed my initials on the bottom left side of the last page of the letter.

Q: Mr. Woods, do you see your initials anywhere on Exhibit 22?

A: Yes, they are on the bottom left side of the last page.

Q: Mr. Woods, during the time you were Ms. Davis' secretary did you ever observe Ms. Davis sign any letters?

A: Yes. Hundreds of times.

Q: Do you recognize the signature on Exhibit 22?

A: Yes, it's Ms. Davis' signature.

Q: Do you know what Ms. Davis typically did with a business letter after she signed it?

A: She put it in her out box.

Q: And what, if anything, would you do with the letter after Ms. Davis placed it in the out box?

A: I'd pick it up, make copies for our files, put it in an envelope addressed to the addressee on the letter and put the envelope in the company's box for outgoing mail.

Q: You previously testified that you recognized Exhibit 22, could you now tell us what it is?

A: It's a copy of a letter from our files that Ms. Davis sent to Reliable Widget Co.

In this example, you contend that the exhibit is a copy of a letter written by Davis and sent to Reliable. But because Woods is not the author of the letter, it is not obvious that Woods has personal knowledge of what the exhibit is. To authenticate the exhibit, you first have to introduce evidence establishing his personal knowledge of the exhibit. You will often be required to follow this procedure when authenticating exhibits.[4]

Note that the evidence you elicit to authenticate an exhibit may not remove all doubt about whether the exhibit is what you contend it is. Woods may be wrong about the signature being Davis', or Woods may have failed to mail the letter after receiving it from Davis. But as long as you introduce enough evidence to allow a factfinder to conclude that the exhibit is what you contend it is, you have authenticated it.[5]

c. Establish an Exhibit's Relevance

After authenticating an exhibit you must next establish its relevance. Once authenticated, some exhibits are obviously relevant because they consist of the very objects involved in an underlying dispute, such as a murder weapon or an allegedly-breached royalty agreement. Other exhibits are obviously relevant because their logical connection to an issue in dispute is readily apparent. For example, in an assault case a photograph showing what the plaintiff looked like after the fight is obviously relevant to show the injuries inflicted on the plaintiff.

With other exhibits, however, you will have to introduce additional testimony or make an offer of proof to the judge to establish their relevance. For example, assume that on cross examination of the plaintiff Casey you want to introduce a letter written by Casey. The letter is relevant because one of the statements in the letter is inconsistent with statements made earlier by Casey to Orin, a witness you will call to testify in your case. You can authenticate the letter through Casey, but the judge will not know why it is relevant until you elicit additional testimony from Casey establishing that he made a prior inconsistent statement to Orin. And if on cross Casey refuses to admit making the prior inconsistent statement to Orin, then you will have to make an offer of proof to establish that the letter is relevant. In your offer of proof you must explain why the exhibit is relevant. In this example, in your offer of proof you would explain to the judge that you will call Orin as a witness, and that Orin will testify that Casey made a statement inconsistent with what he wrote in the letter.[6]

d. Establish an Exhibit's Admissibility

Not all relevant exhibits are admissible in evidence. All of the evidence rules which exclude relevant oral testimony apply to exhibits. Thus, you may authenticate and establish the relevance of a letter, but it may still be excluded because it is hearsay or inadmissible character evidence. Consequently, you will often need to introduce additional

---

4. For example, you typically must do so when establishing the chain of custody for fungible exhibits. See Sec. 4 (b) *infra*.

5. See FRE 104 (b).

6. If the judge accepts your offer of proof, she will admit the letter on cross conditioned on Orin's testifying to the prior inconsistent statement. If Orin should la-

ter fail to testify to the inconsistent statement the letter will be stricken from the record. Alternatively, notwithstanding your offer of proof, the judge, exercising her discretion, may decide not to admit the letter until Orin testifies to the prior inconsistent statement.

testimony or make an argument to the judge to establish that a relevant and authenticated exhibit is admissible. For example, you may authenticate and establish the relevance of a letter sent by Company X to your client, but you may not be permitted to introduce it into evidence until you have introduced testimony satisfying the business records exception to the hearsay rule. And you may authenticate a gruesome photograph of the deceased victim of an auto accident, but you may not be able to admit the photograph until you convince the court that its probative value outweighs its prejudicial effect.

e. A "Mini–Trial" on the Adequacy of a Foundation

You can establish the foundation (i.e. authentication, relevance and admissibility) for many exhibits with a handful of questions to a single witness. For other exhibits, a mini-trial may take place when a dispute arises over the adequacy of the foundation. In a mini-trial, which may be held either in or outside the presence of the jury,[7] you and your opponent elicit evidence pertaining to the sufficiency of the foundation. Typically, evidence rules do not apply during a mini-trial.[8] A mini-trial can be quite extensive, with both parties calling witnesses and making arguments. At its conclusion, the judge decides whether the proponent of the exhibit has laid a sufficient foundation and the trial then proceeds with or without the exhibit.

2. MOVING EXHIBITS INTO EVIDENCE

Once you have laid the foundation for your exhibits, remember to move them into evidence. You will typically move each exhibit into evidence as soon as you believe that you have laid the necessary foundation. Then, if the court sustains an adversary's objection to your foundation, you will often be able to elicit additional foundational testimony from your witnesses.[9]

The process for admitting exhibits into evidence often goes something like this:

You: Your Honor, I ask that Exhibit 3 be received in evidence.

Judge: Any objection?

Opp.: None, Your Honor.

Judge: All right, Exhibit 3 is received in evidence.

Once a judge receives an exhibit into evidence, it is the property of the court until formally released. Don't accidentally put admitted exhibits into your briefcase at the end of the day, lest you join the exhibit in a locked overnight courthouse stay.

---

7. See FRE 103.

8. FRE 104.

9. Some attorneys, fearing that they might forget to move one or two of numerous exhibits into evidence, prefer to move all of their exhibits into evidence just before they "rest." However, if the court sustains an objection to one or more exhibits at this time, the witnesses who might provide additional foundational testimony may be unavailable.

3. "PUBLISHING" EXHIBITS

An exhibit typically goes from lawyer to judge, sometimes via the bailiff, then judge to witness. When the witness is finished testifying about the exhibit, it goes to the clerk's desk until shown to another witness. Jurors are frozen out of this neat little process. They may not actually see or know the contents of an exhibit until an attorney displays it during final argument or they take it with them into the jury deliberation room.

When a witness' testimony makes the contents of an exhibit obvious, the delay in jurors' examining an exhibit may be fine with you. But an exhibit often has a power to convey information that oral testimony cannot match. For example, a witness cannot verbally describe everything depicted in a photograph. Similarly, jurors' seeing a party's signature on a piece of paper may have greater persuasive impact than the oral counterpart, "This is her signature at the bottom." And you may want the contents of an important document read to the juror early in your case, rather than waiting until closing argument. In such situations, you may ask the judge for permission to communicate the contents of an exhibit to the jurors as soon as it's been admitted in evidence. The formal, little-used name for this request is "publishing an exhibit."

A judge will not necessarily be sympathetic to your request to publish an exhibit because publishing takes time. You may do two things to overcome such judicial reticence: be prepared to justify your request and, whenever possible, publish the exhibit without causing undue delay.

By way of example, assume that you are the prosecutor in a child sexual assault case. You have offered into evidence a photograph of the room where many assaultive acts allegedly took place. Your request to have the jurors examine the photograph immediately may go as follows:

You: Your Honor, I request permission to publish Exhibit 4, the photograph, by showing it to the jurors at this time.

Judge: Counsel, they can look at it while they deliberate.

You: If I may be heard, Your Honor? Jimmy will shortly be testifying as to certain actions the defendant engaged in before each act of assault. The jurors will be much better able to understand Jimmy's testimony if they first look at the photograph. I might add, Your Honor, that my office has prepared a copy of the photograph for each juror, so we will not be wasting the court's time.

Judge: Very well, counsel. We'll take a moment for the jurors to examine Exhibit 4.[10]

---

10. When you distribute copies of an exhibit to the jurors, you will typically want to collect the copies from the jurors before the testimony resumes. If you do not, the factfinder may be looking at the exhibit rather than listening to your witness' testimony.

You can publish an exhibit to the factfinder in many ways. For example, the photograph in the sexual assault case could be published to the jurors by placing an enlargement of the photo on an easel that Jimmy could refer to during his direct testimony. And you might publish only selected sections of a multipage exhibit. To do so, you might display one important portion of the document on an overhead projector or computer while the witness explains the importance of that portion. Then move on to the next important section of the document and repeat the process. The techniques you use to publish exhibits to a factfinder are limited only by your imagination, a client's pocketbook and the court's discretion.[11]

4. ESTABLISHING THE FOUNDATION FOR COMMON TRIAL EXHIBITS

The general foundational requirements for every exhibit are the same: authentication, relevance and admissibility. The subsections below examine methods of satisfying these requirements for the types of exhibits routinely used at trial.

a. *Illustrative Exhibits*

Illustrative exhibits help a factfinder understand oral testimony.[12] For example, a diagram or model of the human heart is an illustrative exhibit which helps a factfinder better understand the oral testimony about the process of open heart surgery. Most illustrative exhibits are prepared by or at the request of counsel in anticipation of trial. As a result, such exhibits are generally relevant only if they help a factfinder understand oral testimony. Any device which helps a factfinder understand oral testimony is a potential illustrative exhibit.

(1) *"Look–Alike" Exhibits*

If your client has been unable to gain possession of "the real thing," you may be able to illustrate testimony by offering a "look-alike" exhibit. For instance, assume that Harold, your client in a personal injury action, claims that while in a shopping mall, the defendant Doris negligently tossed a boomerang which struck him in the head and caused serious injuries. After your client was taken to the hospital, a mall security officer picked up the boomerang and subsequently lost it. At trial you want to offer a similar boomerang to the one that struck your client. Assume that on direct Harold has already described being hit by a boomerang thrown by Doris. To offer a look-alike boomerang into evidence, you might elicit the following testimony:

Q: Could you please describe the boomerang for us?

---

11. If you wish to use a new or unconventional method of publication, you may make a motion in limine prior to trial to obtain prior approval from the court. See Chapter 17 for a discussion of motions in limine.

12. Illustrative exhibits are sometimes referred to as "demonstrative" exhibits.

A: Well, it was about a foot from tip to tip and about three inches wide, with an angle in the middle that gave it a half-moon shape.

Q: Did you pick up the boomerang?

A: Yes, but about a minute later one of the security guards asked for it. I gave it to her, and that's the last I saw of it.

Q: I want to show you what has been previously marked Plaintiff's 2. Is Exhibit 2 similar to the boomerang with which you were hit.

A: Yes, I'd say almost identical. The one I was hit with was a lighter color, but other than that they're about the same.

Q: That includes the length, width and weight?

A: Yes.

Q: Your Honor, I offer Exhibit 2 into evidence.

In this example, you authenticate the exhibit by having your client testify that it is similar to the boomerang that struck him. The exhibit is relevant because it will help the factfinder understand Harold's testimony about the pain he experienced when he was hit. It may also help the factfinder understand the medical testimony about his injuries. The exhibit is admissible if the look-alike is so substantially similar that it is not misleading. If, for example, the look-alike were heavier or larger than the original, it might well tend to mislead the factfinder more than it would help them. But as the testimony establishes the near-identity of the look-alike exhibit and the real object, there is no danger of misleading the factfinder and you have laid an adequate foundation for admission of the exhibit.

(2) Diagrams

In part because of their low cost, diagrams are among the most popular illustrative exhibits. Diagrams are useful for illustrating a witness' testimony about how events unfolded in relatively large spaces, such as the movement of cars through an intersection. Typically, you and a witness can draw a skeleton diagram on a large sheet of white paper in your office, prior to testimony. In the courtroom, mount the skeleton diagram on a blackboard or similar object.

Some attorneys try to use a diagram to get "two for the price of one." In other words, they take a witness through a story twice, once orally and once with the use of the diagram. However, some judges will not permit this, and will force you to ask a witness to mark a diagram as a story unfolds in the first place.

As an illustration of how to lay the foundation for a diagram and incorporate a diagram into testimony, assume that you represent the plaintiff in *Prager v. Dolinko*, a personal injury case in which a pedestrian was allegedly struck in a crosswalk. The foundational testimony may go something like this:

Q: Now, Ms. Prager, turning to the events of Dec. 18 at about 3 P.M., where were you?

A: I was on the northeast corner of Elm and Main, just about to cross the street.

Q: Your Honor, the bailiff has placed a diagram previously marked as Exhibit 1 on the easel. May I ask the witness to step down from the witness chair so that she may refer to that diagram?

The Court: You may.

Q: All right, Ms. Prager, please step over to the diagram and tell me if you recognize what it depicts.

A: Yes, it shows the intersection of Main and Elm Streets. Elm runs east-west, and Main runs north-south.

Q: How do you know this?

A: Well, I'm familiar with the area and I drew it up in your office last night.

Q: What are the other markings you've put on the diagram?

A: There's a solid line down the middle of each street because they're each two way streets, and then there's a broken line on either side of the solid lines because they each have two lanes of traffic in each direction. I also marked in a left turn lane for eastbound cars on Elm to turn north onto Main, and I put in the crosswalks on all sides of the intersection.

Q: I notice a "P" and the northeast corner of the intersection. What does the "P" stand for?

A: That's where I was standing just before I started to cross the street.

Counsel: Your Honor, I move Exhibit 1 into evidence, for illustrative purposes only.

Judge: Hearing no objection, it will be received.

Here you have authenticated the diagram by having Prager testify that it depicts an intersection with which she is familiar and by asking Prager to identify the skeletal markings already on the diagram. Again the exhibit is relevant because it helps the factfinder understand subsequent oral testimony. And the exhibit is admissible, even if not drawn exactly to scale, so long as it will not tend to mislead or confuse the factfinder. As you take Prager through the rest of her testimony, have her illustrate the major movements of people and objects as follows:

Q: All right, Ms. Prager, where was the defendant's car when you first noticed it?

A: He was on Elm Street, headed towards Main.

Q: Please draw a small box on the diagram to indicate the approximate location of the defendant's car when you first noticed it.

A: OK.

Q: To make it clear for the record, put a D–1 inside the box you've drawn and an arrow on the front of the box to indicate the car's direction.

A: There ... like that?

Q: Thank you.   Now, after you noticed the defendant's car at location D–1, what happened?

A: Well, I had the green light so I stepped off the curb into the crosswalk.   Then I heard the loud noise of an engine and I looked to my left and saw Mr. Dolinko's truck heading right for me.

Q: Where were you in the crosswalk when this happened?

A: I was about halfway across the intersection.

Q: Please mark "P–2" on the diagram to indicate about where you were when you saw the defendant's truck heading right for you.

In this example, the witness marks the diagram as she tells her story.   The marking process enables the witness to add persuasiveness to her testimony by illustrating it graphically for the factfinder.   Moreover, the details will enable a reader of the written transcript (such as an appellate court judge) to understand what the markings mean.   Be careful not to overdo it, however, lest you drown witness, factfinders and transcript readers in an incomprehensible mass of lines, squares and arrows.

(3) Photographs

You typically arouse a factfinder's interest and add impact to a story when you illustrate testimony with photographs.   Everyone knows the aphorism that "a picture is worth a thousand words."   In trial it may be more like "a thousand and eighty words," because before you introduce a photograph into evidence you have to lay a foundation.

You typically authenticate a photograph through the testimony of a witness who has personal knowledge of whatever the photograph depicts.   Authentication often requires no more than having the witness testify that a photograph is an accurate representation of whatever it depicts.   Because you authenticate the exhibit with such testimony rather than through technical details of photographic technique, it does not matter whether the authenticating witness took the photograph, knows when the photograph was taken or knows what type of film or camera was used to take it.   Once you have authenticated a relevant photograph, it is generally admissible unless its probative value is outweighed by its tendency to mislead, confuse or appeal to the emotions of the factfinder.

For example, assume that you are involved in a personal injury action.   You want to offer into evidence a photograph depicting the appearance of your client's car after the accident, to illustrate your client's testimony about where and how his car was struck and to help the factfinder understand why your client sustained such serious injuries. After marking the exhibit, showing it to opposing counsel and handing it to the client, you may proceed as follows:

Q: Please look at Exhibit C and tell us if you recognize what it shows.

A: I sure do. That's my car after the accident.

Q: Is Exhibit C, the photograph, a fair and accurate representation of your car's appearance immediately after the accident?

A: Yes, it is.

Q: Your Honor, at this time I ask that Exhibit C be received in evidence.

This foundational testimony establishes the photograph's admissibility even if it was taken months after the accident. The witness' testimony, based on personal knowledge, that the photo accurately depicts the condition of the car immediately after the accident authenticates the exhibit, and it is relevant to prove damages.

(4) Other Illustrative Exhibits

A chart or graph depicting your client's profits and losses, a blowup of a document with key phrases pulled out and highlighted, a "Day in the Life Video," showing the effect of the plaintiff's personal injuries on her daily life, an expert's videotape reenactment of the breakdown of an allegedly defective product, a computer-generated re-creation of the last moments of a stricken private jet or the manufacturing and testing process a product underwent before being put on the market; are all illustrative exhibits. To lay a proper foundation, you must be able to authenticate the exhibit by having a witness explain what it is and convince the court the exhibit will aid the factfinder in understanding other testimony. And with all illustrative exhibits the danger always exists that a court will exclude it as confusing or misleading, or deem its unduly prejudicial impact to outweigh its probative value. For example, perhaps a "Day in the Life" video exaggerates the extent to which injuries have altered a plaintiff's lifestyle, or a computerized re-enactment is based only on partial data. You should be able to anticipate and avoid most admissibility problems with illustrative exhibits since they are almost always created by you or at your direction in preparation for trial.

b. "Chain of Custody" Exhibits

Usually, accounting for an exhibit's whereabouts prior to trial is not necessary for admissibility. But when an exhibit is "fungible" [13] or susceptible to tampering and has passed through a number of hands for purposes of pretrial analysis, you may have to elicit testimony account-

---

13. An exhibit is fungible when it has no readily apparent distinguishing characteristics. For example, a plastic baggie of white powder, a blood smear, or a common safety pin are all fungible. You can not readily distinguish one bag of white powder from another, or one safety pin from another.

ing for an exhibit's whereabouts between the time events took place and trial. Accounting for an exhibit's whereabouts prior to trial is typically done by establishing a chain of custody.

To elicit a chain of custody, ordinarily you need not account for an exhibit at every relevant moment of its existence, nor need you demonstrate that it could not possibly have been tampered with. As long as the chain of custody is sufficient for a judge to conclude that an exhibit is genuine and that its condition is not so materially altered as to be misleading, the exhibit is likely to be admissible.

For a typical example of when you may need to establish a chain of custody, assume that you represent Eileen Johnson, a civil plaintiff who claims that Ron Houston, the defendant, negligently caused personal injuries by driving under the influence of cocaine. After the accident the plaintiff saw a baggie of a white powdery substance she thought might be an illegal drug on the passenger seat of the defendant's car, and took it for use as possible evidence. At your direction, prior to trial the contents of the baggie were tested by a local laboratory and determined to be cocaine. Now at trial you want to offer the baggie of cocaine into evidence. To lay the foundation, you will have to elicit a chain of custody proving that the baggie given to the laboratory was the one taken from the defendant's car, that the contents were unchanged, and that the exhibit in court consists of that same baggie and contents. After your client describes the accident and its immediate aftermath, the foundational testimony may go as follows:

Q: Ms. Johnson, I hand you Exhibit 1, a clear plastic baggie and its contents. Do you recognize it?

A: Yes, this is the baggie that was on the driver's seat in Mr. Houston's car.

Q: And how do you know that?

A: When I got home I put this little sticker on it and marked it with the date and my initials.

Q: After you took it home, what did you do with it?

A: I have a small room that I use as an office with a file cabinet in it, so I put it in the top drawer of the cabinet.

Q: Does anyone besides yourself have access to the file cabinet?

A: Well, I don't usually keep it locked. But the kids can't even reach the top drawer, so the only other person would be my husband Rich.

Q: As you look at Exhibit 1, does it appear to be in any way different from when you saw it in the defendant's car?

A: No.

Q: Has the baggie remained in your file cabinet the entire time before trial?

A: No. You called and said that you had arranged to have it tested at Speidel Laboratory, so I brought it over to them that same day.

Q: And what day was that?

A: December 18th of last year, I believe.

Q: And how do you know that?

A: I marked the date down on the sticker I had placed on the baggie when I first took it home.

Q: Did you ever see the baggie again?

A: Yes, a couple of days later I got a call from Speidel saying they were done with the test and that I could come down and pick it up, so I did.

Q: That was on December 20?

A: Yes.

Q: Did you look at it?

A: Yes, quickly.

Q: Did it appear to be the same baggie and contents you had given Speidel two days earlier?

A: Yes.

Q: And then what did you do with it?

A: I put it back in the file cabinet, and that's where it stayed until today.

To this point, you've built only part of the chain. You have shown that this baggie is the one taken from the defendant's car. To establish the relevance of the baggie you also next need to show that it contains cocaine. To do that, you will need a witness from Speidel Laboratories to that testify that the powdery substance in the baggie was tested and found to be cocaine. Depending on witness availability and the discretion of your trial judge, you may interrupt Johnson's testimony to have a witness from Speidel establish that the exhibit is relevant, or make an offer of proof that the witness from Speidel will so testify when later called to the stand, and ask the judge to admit the exhibit conditionally during Johnson's testimony.[14] In either event, the link in the chain establishing relevance will go something like this:

Q: Please state your name for the record.

A: Richard Speidel.

Q: Mr. Speidel, what is your occupation?

A: I'm a state-licensed forensic chemist.

---

14. Under FRE 104, the judge has dis-   cretion to make either ruling.

(Remainder of foundation showing witness' qualifications to render an expert opinion that the powdery substance in Exhibit 1 is cocaine omitted.)

Q: Mr. Speidel, I hand you Exhibit 1 and ask if you have ever seen it before?

A: Yes, on Dec. 18 of last year. Ms. Johnson personally brought it into the lab.

Q: And how do you know that?

A: I placed this lab sticker on it immediately and filled in my initials, the date and the name of Eileen Johnson as the person who asked that the contents be tested.

Q: Can you briefly describe the testing procedure?

A: Certainly. After Ms. Johnson left, I took from the baggie a small amount of the powder and placed it in a vial labeled to identify it as coming from her baggie. I then placed the baggie itself in a locked storage facility in the lab. It remained there until I called Ms. Johnson to pick it up. She picked it up two days later. I again put my initials on the lab sticker and wrote in the date of Dec. 20 to indicate when it was returned to her.

Q: Before you returned the baggie to Ms. Johnson, did you test the contents of the vial?

A: I did; it was cocaine.

Q: Could you describe the tests you conducted that led you to conclude the substance was cocaine?

A: Yes. (Remaining details pertaining to the expert's findings omitted.)

Q: Your Honor, at this time I ask that Exhibit 1 be received in evidence.

The Judge: Any objection from opposing counsel? All right, Exhibit 1 in evidence.

c. Signed or Handwritten Documents

Our judicial system accepts little at face value. The fact that a handwritten letter is signed by "Jenni Johnson" is not itself sufficient evidence that Jenni Johnson wrote the letter.[15] For authentication, you have to elicit testimony establishing that signature was made by the person who you claim authored the letter. There are a variety of statutory options for doing so.[16]

For instance, assume that you have brought suit against Johnson for failing to make payments to your client pursuant to the terms of a written personal guarantee. The printed personal guarantee is signed "Jenni Johnson," but absent a stipulation you will have to authenticate

---

15. For some modern exceptions to this principle, see FRE 902.

16. See FRE 901.

the exhibit by establishing that the defendant is the person who signed the guarantee. The foundational testimony may go like this:

Q: Handing you Plaintiff's 2, can you tell me if you recognize what this is?

A: Yes, that's the personal guarantee that Jenni Johnson signed.

Q: And how do you know this?

A: Well, this is my signature here in the lower right hand corner, and Ms. Johnson's right above it.

Q: And how do you know this is Ms. Johnson's signature?

A: I was sitting next to her at the desk and I watched her sign it.

Although this testimony authenticates the exhibit, some attorneys prefer to foreclose factfinder suspicions about authenticity by demonstrating that the exhibit has been well cared for since it came into existence. The additional testimony may go as follows:

Q: What happened to the document after you both signed it?

A: Well, we made a copy, which Ms. Johnson took. I kept the original, made a few copies, and put the original and copies in a file cabinet in my office.

Q: Did you ever remove the original from your file cabinet?

A: Not until I brought it with me to my deposition. Since then you attorneys have had it.

When you offer documentary exhibits, you must of course also comply with the Original Writing, nee Best Evidence, Rule.[17] This means that if your offered document is not an original, and you have a legitimate reason for not being able to produce it, you may offer (a) a duplicate copy; (b) a written copy which does not qualify as a "duplicate;" or (c) oral testimony reciting the contents of the absent original.

d. Unsigned Documents—Faxes, Form Letters, Brochures, Etc.

Under the Federal Rules of Evidence and most state codifications, many business documents are "self-authenticating."[18] For example, you needn't elicit testimony that a can of peas bearing the label "Jolly Green Giant" actually was packed by the Green Giant Company, nor need you elicit testimony that a recall notice bearing the heading "Chrysler Motors" actually was issued by that company.

What if you want to authenticate an unsigned, unheaded fax transmission or similar document? Often, such documents will have distinctive characteristics linking it to its claimed author. For example, a fax transmission may indicate the telephone number from which it was sent, thus establishing its place of origin. Or, it may recite matters peculiar to a particular transaction, thus demonstrating that it shares a common

17. See FRE 1001.   **18.** See FRE 902 (7).

origin with other documents of known authenticity. Such evidence is typically sufficient to authenticate these exhibits.

e. Business Records

When the exhibit you are offering is a written document, almost always your goal is to offer the words of the document into evidence rather than the pieces of paper on which the words are written. Hence you usually need to qualify the words under an exception to the hearsay rule. And one of the most used exceptions is to show that a document is a business record.

To comply with the business record exception to the hearsay rule, you have to establishing that exhibit is trustworthy because it was prepared according to regular practice in the normal course of a business and that it was prepared around the time of the event to which it pertains.[19]

To comply with the business records exception, you often call as a witness the person who prepared a business record. In many large businesses, however, numerous people may contribute to a single record. For example, a salesperson may prepare a invoice for Customer A, another employee may enter the information from the invoice the company's computer records, and a third employee may prepare a printout of all transactions with Customer A during the period relevant to a lawsuit. You may then want to establish that the printout qualifies as a business record for purposes of the hearsay rule. In such a situation, the foundational testimony may emerge through the testimony of a "custodian of records" whose primary business function is to maintain the business' records. For example, assume that you represent JCN Inc., a manufacturer of computers. JCN claims that one its customers, a multi-state computer retailer named Hard Ware, owes a large sum of money on shipments extending back over a two year period. You seek to offer into evidence a computer-generated printout showing all transactions between JCN and Hard Ware during this period. The witness is Brad Apple, whose testimony is as follows:

Q: Mr. Apple, how are you employed?

A: I'm a records keeper with JCN, in the sales department.

Q: And what does that job entail?

A: I maintain sales records for wholesale sales to JCN customers in the southeast region of the country.

Q: Is Hard Ware one of the customers whose account you maintain?

A: Yes, it is.

Q: Mr. Apple, with the court's permission I'm showing you what has been marked Plaintiff's Exhibit 2. Do you recognize what this is?

---

19. See FRE 803 (6).

A: Sure, this is a Master Account which is a record of all computer shipments from JCN to Hard Ware during the last two years, the invoice amount for those shipments, and payments received from Hard Ware. The top page shows the current balance due from Hard Ware.

Q: Can you tell us how a record like this is prepared?

A: Well, the actual sales are recorded by salespeople in the various states. They fax orders to the sales department in company headquarters. When it gets here, a copy goes to the shipping department and another copy goes to bookkeeping. Bookkeeping prepares an invoice and sends it to the customer and a copy to me, and when the products are shipped the shipping department sends me a confirmation. I enter the data in a Master Account for the customer. When payment is received from the customer, I also receive written confirmation from bookkeeping and I enter that information into the Master Account.

Q: Do you keep the written confirmations you receive from bookkeeping and shipping?

A: No.

Q: For how many customers do you maintain Master Accounts?

A: Well of course it varies from month to month, but at any one time about 150.

Q: And do you follow the procedure you've just described for each of these accounts?

A: That's correct.

Q: And was that the procedure you followed in preparing Exhibit 1?

A: Yes.

Q: Now, you told us that this document covers the last two years. How far back does the Hard Ware Master Account extend?

A: At least 10 years, if I remember correctly.

Q: Is Exhibit 1 a complete printout of JCN records for the last two years pertaining to Hard Ware?

A: It is.

Q: Your Honor, at this time I offer plaintiff's exhibit 3 into evidence.

Judge: Hearing no objection, it will be received.

The records of entities such as hospitals are routinely qualified as business records at trial. And to save such entities the trouble and expense of constantly sending their custodians of records to court, over half the states have adopted a shortcut procedure known as the Uniform Photographic Copies of Business and Public Records as Evidence Act. The Act provides for admissibility of otherwise admissible records without a further foundation when, in response to a subpoena duces tecum, an entity mails a record to the court accompanied by a custodian's affidavit as to how such records are prepared and kept.

f. Public Records

Modern evidence rules have lessened the foundational requirements for the admission of government reports and records. The records, reports and compilations of public offices and agencies, including factual findings resulting from investigations made by public offices and agencies, are admissible as an exception to the hearsay rule unless the party opposing their admission can show that they are untrustworthy.[20]

Moreover, you may authenticate an exhibit as a public record by offering evidence (typically in the form of a seal or attestation from a public employee) either that it was recorded in a public office or, if it is not the type of document that gets recorded, that it emanates from the office where such records are kept.[21]

Not even the Original Document Rule poses an obstacle. You may offer a copy of a public record into evidence if the copy is accompanied by a public employee's attestation that it is a correct copy. And if you cannot with reasonable diligence secure a copy, oral testimony of a record's contents is admissible.[22]

5. ODDS AND ENDS

a. General Procedures

When introducing exhibits you should typically conform to the following procedures. Before showing an exhibit to a witness, you should ask the judge's permission to approach the witness, at least until the judge indicates that you need not do so, and indicate on the record that you have shown the exhibit to opposing counsel.[23] Also, when you show an exhibit to a witness, always refer to the exhibit number or letter. That keeps the record clear as to which exhibit testimony refers. Finally, when you are laying foundation you should refer to an exhibit *only* by number or letter. Thus, you should not do the following: "Q: Mr. Jones, I'm showing you what has been marked as exhibit 3, a letter which you sent to the defendant confirming that deliver of the computers was to be completed before January 23rd, do you recognize exhibit 3?" In the guise of a question the attorney is improperly testifying as to what the exhibit is. Your opponent may object on this ground and ask the court to admonish you not to testify. Avoid this problem by referring to an exhibit only by number or letter until it has been admitted into evidence.

b. Partially Admissible Exhibits

Some exhibits contain both admissible and inadmissible information. For example, a letter may contain admissible information as well as inadmissible character evidence or speculation. As the proponent of

---

20. See FRE 803 (8).

21. FRE 901 (b)(7).

22. FRE 1005.

23. In many courtrooms, the bailiff takes exhibits back and forth.

such an exhibit you are responsible for redacting (or "whiting out") the inadmissible portions before it can be received in evidence. When you are concerned that one of your exhibits may be only partially admissible, you may want to make a motion in limine to have the court make a decision on which parts of the exhibit must be redacted. Such a motion will allow you to smoothly admit the exhibit at trial.

c. Laying Foundation on Cross Examination

Although most of your exhibits will be introduced through your witnesses on direct, you will often lay foundation for exhibits on cross examination. The foundational requirements are the same.

d. Prepare Written Stipulations

Attorneys commonly stipulate to the admissibility of many exhibits. When you do so, be careful to write out the terms of a stipulation and have it signed both by you and your adversary. For if in reliance upon an oral stipulation you fail to have a foundational witness available, and your adversary suddenly reneges in the middle of trial you may have no way to get an exhibit into evidence.

For example, assume that you represent a tenant in an eviction suit brought by a landlord, and that you want to offer into evidence the report of a termite inspection company. In reliance on opposing counsel's oral offer to stipulate, you offer the report into evidence. Opposing counsel objects, denying that he agreed to stipulate. Or opposing counsel claims that you misunderstood the terms of the stipulation: he says that he agreed to stipulate that he would not make a hearsay objection, but that he did not stipulate to the authenticity of the report. Protect your client against such sharp practices by securing written stipulations.

e. Commercially Prepared Exhibits

If a client can pay the freight, you can offer illustrative exhibits prepared by a vast array of commercial enterprises.[24] Unless you personally are aware of the range of commercially prepared exhibits, approach commercial exhibit preparers as you would other experts. That is, describe a case to them and let them help you select the most effective illustrative exhibit.

Commercially prepared exhibits are illustrative and consequently the danger always exists that a court will exclude it as misleading, or deem its unduly prejudicial impact to outweigh its probative value. You may spend lots of a client's money only to have a judge exclude an exhibit from evidence. Thus, no matter how high tech an exhibit (or maybe the more high tech an exhibit), you have to exercise professional judgment about admissibility. Solicit a commercial preparer's suggestions, but do not forget that you are the one who will have to convince a judge of an exhibit's admissibility.

---

24. Many of these enterprises advertise in magazines distributed to members of the trial bar.

Chapter 17

OBJECTIONS

Gene Hackman as Jedediah Ward and Colin Friels as Michael Grazier subtly argue an objection as Mary Elizabeth Mastrantonio as Maggie Ward looks on. Still photograph from "Class Action." © 1991 Twentieth Century Fox Film Corporation. All rights reserved.

Trials, like any other contest intended to produce a fair outcome, are played by predetermined rules. These governing rules are primarily rules of evidence.[1] Many rules have been codified by the Federal Rules of Evidence and similar enactments. Others are unwritten; they are embedded in the legal culture's trial processes and enforced through a judge's power to "exercise reasonable control over the mode and order of

---

1. Not all governing rules fall within the intellectual domain of "evidence." For example, you would probably think of the rule that a defendant in a criminal case has a privilege to remain silent as a constitutional principle rather than a rule of evidence.

interrogating witnesses."[2]

To a large extent, both the written and unwritten evidence rules are self-executing; testimony generally conforms to legal requirements. Thus, just as prehistoric creatures are visible primarily through their fossilized remains and football rules are visible primarily through the way players run, catch, and tackle, evidence rules are visible primarily through the manner of testimony.

During trial, the accepted method of explicitly invoking a rule is by objecting; no dropping of yellow flags allowed. An objection is the culmination of three events, all of which typically take place in the same amount of time it takes a cabby stopped behind you to honk when a traffic light turns green. You have to (a) recognize a proper ground of objection; (b) decide that the benefits of objecting outweigh the potential disadvantages; and (c) state your objection properly and in a timely manner.

Successfully accomplishing all these tasks during the maelstrom of trial can be a formidable task. But do not overemphasize the importance of objections to the outcome of most trials. Dramatic portrayals notwithstanding, some trials sail through from beginning to end with few objections. Moreover, it is unlikely that you will sit idly by as crucial evidence of doubtful propriety sails past. Almost always, you are aware of such evidence prior to trial. If you do not object before trial, you will almost certainly be prepared to do so when your adversary offers the evidence.

1. PRETRIAL OBJECTIONS

As suggested above, you may seek a ruling on the admissibility of evidence before trial, typically through a "Motion In Limine."[3] A Motion in Limine is essentially an objection made prior to the start of trial. If a judge grants your motion, your adversary cannot refer to the stricken evidence during trial. Thus, such motions are particularly important in jury trials. If you wait to object until your adversary offers crucial evidence, the jury may hear and be influenced by the evidence even if it is stricken and the judge instructs the jurors to "forget what you've just heard."

If time permits, you may serve a written notice of a Motion in Limine on your adversary. Your notice should identify the evidence you seek to exclude and the legal arguments (often in the form of a "Memorandum of Points and Authorities") supporting its exclusion. But if you find out about inadmissible evidence on the eve of trial, you may often make a Motion in Limine orally. To do so, inform the court clerk prior to the call of the case that you want to be heard before trial on the motion.

---

2. FRE 611.

3. You may also use a motion in limine to seek a pretrial ruling that evidence is *admissible*. For convenience, we refer only to the use of pretrial motions to object to admissibility.

As you would expect, judges have a good deal of discretion when it comes to ruling on Motions in Limine, especially those made orally on the eve of trial. But even if you have filed a written notice, a judge may prefer to postpone a ruling until your adversary offers the evidence. Delay serves two purposes for a judge. The adversary may decide not to offer the evidence, obviating the need for a ruling. And if the adversary does offer the evidence, the delay allows the judge to gauge the relevance and potential prejudice of the disputed evidence in the light of all the other evidence.

Your argument in support of a Motion in Limine should stress not only the inadmissibility and unfair prejudice of the evidence, but also your need for an immediate ruling. For example, assume that you represent the defendant in a criminal case. You might argue that you would cross examine one way if the defendant testifies, and another if the defendant does not, and that whether the defendant testifies depends on the judge's ruling about the admissibility of a prior conviction. If your argument does not produce an immediate pretrial ruling, it may at least produce one before you cross examine.

2. DECIDING WHETHER TO OBJECT

Before you can object, your obvious first task is to recognize that a ground for objection exists. This requires that you be familiar with evidence rules. However, assuming that you recognize a ground for objection, your second task is to balance the benefits against the disadvantages of making it. The poetic question you must subconsciously ask yourself is, "If my objection is sustained, what have I gained?"

Generally, the gain you derive from objecting is the exclusion of evidence. Therefore, the more important evidence is to an adversary's argument, the more likely you are to raise an impropriety. However, sometimes you might object to evidence of little significance. For example, you might object to try to establish firm "ground rules" for your trial. Assume that you let three or four "improper opinions" pass without objection because they are insignificant. Your inaction may encourage your adversary to try to elicit potentially improper opinions about important evidence. And when you then object, the judge may overrule the objection because "we've been allowing this form of testimony all along." Thus, objecting to evidence whatever its significance communicates your knowledge of evidence rules and your intention to conduct the trial "by the book." [4]

Balanced against these potential gains is the disadvantage that instead of excluding evidence, you may goad an adversary into eliciting more effective testimony. For example, assume that an important issue is the identity of the person asleep in a bed, and the following testimony occurs:

---

4. It is improper to make groundless objections to intimidate witnesses and opposing counsel, or to interrupt the flow of adverse counsel's impressive evidence or argument.

Q: The next thing you noticed was that Goldilocks was asleep in your bed?

You: Objection, leading.

Judge: Sustained.

Q: What happened next?

A: I looked towards my bed, and saw somebody lying in it. So I went right over to get a closer look, and saw that it was her, Goldilocks.

Q: Are you sure about that?

A: Oh, yes. I stood right next to her for a good 5–10 seconds. I have no doubt whatsoever it was her.

In this example, your "leading" objection excludes nothing. Instead, it results in the introduction of evidence in a way that strengthens the witness' identification. Thus, if your objection goes only to the "form" of a question or answer, and counsel is almost certain to elicit the evidence properly, you may well decide not to object.

Unfortunately, it is nearly impossible to weigh these factors in the abstract. For example, if your adversary and judge are both experienced professionals, you may see no need to object to insignificant evidence merely to set "ground rules." On the other hand, if you find that a nervous adversary is unable to rephrase objectionable questions, you may become more aggressive in your objections. Thus, whether you object routinely or pick your evidentiary fights carefully rests on your judgment in an individual case.

3. MAKING OBJECTIONS PROPERLY

Just as some people look at dust on a mantel as an indication of the overall cleanliness of a house, some judges and jurors gauge the persuasiveness of your case in part by the professionalism with which you object. Ironically, then, while the evidence to which you object may be insignificant, how you make and respond to objections may influence a factfinder's evaluation of evidence. Hence, this section examines essential objections techniques.

• Object as soon as you become aware of an objectionable question, answer or comment:

Q: What happened next?

A: The wolf ran over to a nearby house, this one built of sticks. Then I heard the person standing next to me say that. . . .

You: Excuse me. Objection to what the witness heard the person say. Hearsay.

Here, you object at your first opportunity, before the witness can blurt out the inadmissible hearsay. By prefacing the objection with "excuse me," you stop the witness from talking and prevent the awkwardness that can result when you try to talk over a witness.

• If you are unable to object before inadmissible evidence is referred to, make a motion to strike the evidence at the same time that you object or immediately after the judge sustains your objection. Otherwise, the factfinder may properly consider the evidence despite your successful objection. In addition, you might ask the judge to instruct the jury to disregard the stricken evidence:

Q: What happened next?

A: The idiot finally ran out the back of the house. Then....

You: Object and move to strike the characterization as an improper and inflammatory opinion.

Judge: Objection sustained; the remark is stricken.

You: I also ask that Your Honor instruct the jurors to disregard that remark.

Judge: Yes, the jurors are instructed that the witness' remark was improper, and they are to disregard it.

• Stand when objecting as a sign of respect to the court.[5] Also, standing may silence an adverse witness who has launched into an inadmissible tirade, giving you a chance to object before the witness can spew additional inadmissible information.

• Object as concisely as possible. "Objection" followed by the ground(s) will do it: "Objection, hearsay;" "I object—improper opinion, irrelevant and unduly prejudicial under Rule 403." Do not try a judge's patience with "speaking objections:"

Q: What then happened?

A: After running out of the little pig's house, he went into the woods. Now, the woods are rather thick at this point, so I lost sight of him for a couple of moments. But then I saw him again, running with a basket towards Grandma's House.

You: Your Honor, what does any of this have to do with this case? This is a case about....

Judge: Counsel, if you have an objection to make, please make it.

You: Excuse me, Your Honor. I object and move to strike, irrelevant.

Judge: Sustained. The witness's reference to a different wolf tale is stricken.

Here, your first objection is an improper "speaking objection." Instead of stating a precise ground of objection, you launch into an argument about the vileness of the answer.

• After making a concise objection, support it with argument only if the judge asks you to do so:

Q: And what was the wolf doing?

---

5. You can begin stating your objection as you rise.

A: He was huffing and puffing, and I'd say that he was trying to blow the house down.

You: Objection, improper opinion.

Judge: Counsel, what is the basis of that objection?

You: Your Honor, the witness can testify to what he observed, but he's speculating about what the wolf's intent was.

Judge: I agree, objection sustained.

● If you fail to state a ground for an objection, or if you state the wrong ground, a judge has the power to overrule your objection even though a proper ground for objection exists. Many judges do not exercise this power if it is clear that a proper ground for objection in fact exists. Or, they may ask you to amend your objection to state the proper ground:

You: Objection, hearsay.

Judge: Counsel, I don't think it's hearsay. But if you were to object that it is irrelevant, I would sustain your objection.

You: Objection, irrelevant.

Judge: Yes, well done. Sustained.[6]

● When you object, use a professional tone of voice; do not whine. When objecting, some attorneys adopt a vocal tone and a physical bearing suggesting that their entire life has been wasted fending off improper evidentiary thrusts by the adversary. Maintain your dignity, even if opposing counsel (either through ineptitude or craft) repeatedly errs.

If the judge sustains your objection, sit down. An obsequious "thank you" is improper, as it implies that the judge was doing you a favor instead of enforcing a legal rule. High-fiving a spectator in the front row is even worse.

● If the judge overrules your objection, you might ask the judge to reconsider. Judges often rule immediately on objections, and may be open to argument demonstrating that their immediate ruling was mistaken. The key is to seek the judge's permission before making your argument:

Q: And what was the wolf doing?

A: He was huffing and puffing and trying to blow the house down.

You: Objection, improper opinion; speculation.

Judge: Overruled.

You: Your Honor, the witness testified to the wolf's subjective . . . .

Judge: Counsel, did you hear my ruling?

---

6. If the judge then overrules the "irrel-
evant" objection, your problems go beyond   this evidentiary issue.

You: I apologize, Your Honor. Might I be heard further on that ruling?

Judge: Go ahead.

You: My objection goes only to the last part of the witness' answer, which consists of speculation as to the wolf's subjective state of mind.

Judge: All right. The objection as to what the wolf was trying to do is sustained; that portion of the answer is stricken.

4. RESPONDING TO AN ADVERSARY'S OBJECTION

Your immediate reaction to an adversary's objection may be that the objection is proper. For example, at the same moment that your adversary objects to a question as "vague and unintelligible," you may notice a look of bewilderment on your witness' face. Or, when you seek to elicit a hearsay statement as an "excited utterance," a "lack of foundation" objection may remind you that you neglected to establish how much time elapsed between the event and the hearsay statement.

In such circumstances, one option you have is to wait for the judge to sustain the objection and then to ask another question. A second is to ask the judge's permission to withdraw the question.[7] The advantage of the second option is that it may stamp you as knowledgeable about evidence, and thus give added force to your later evidentiary arguments. However, withdrawal of a question waives any right to claim on appeal that the question was proper, so withdraw only when you genuinely concede the error.

Respond to an objection only with the judge's permission. The judge may be prepared to overrule the objection immediately. Even if that is not the case, the judge may not want to hear argument:

You: Mr. Wolf, did you huff and puff on the houses of the three little Puerco children in order to harm them?

Opp: Objection, leading.

You: I don't think it's leading. I'm simply asking the witness....

Judge: Counsel, please do not argue an objection without permission. The objection is sustained. Ask another question.

You: Mr. Wolf, why did you huff and puff on the houses?

Opp: Objection, calls for a conclusion.

You: Your Honor, the witness is entitled....

Judge: I'll instruct you just one more time to refrain from arguing without permission. However, I will overrule the objection.

You: Mr. Wolf, do you remember the question?

7. Many judges will not insist that you ask permission; you may simply state that you "withdraw the question."

A: Yes. I huffed and puffed because. . . .

Make an "offer of proof" when a judge erroneously sustains an adversary's objection. An offer of proof is simply a statement of the evidence you expect to elicit, and a concise argument as to its admissibility. In the same example as the previous section, assume that the testimony goes as follows:

You: Mr. Wolf, why did you huff and puff on the houses?

A: I huffed and puffed because of what their grandmother had told me.

You: What did their grandmother tell you?

Opp: Objection to what he was told, hearsay.

Judge: Sustained.

You: Might I make an offer of proof, Your Honor?

Judge: Briefly. Counsel will approach the bench.[8]

You: The witness will testify that he had been told that they were lazy, so he blew on the houses just to teach them a lesson about the need for hard work. So we're not offering the grandmother's statement to Mr. Wolf for its truth, but only to show the reason he huffed and puffed. It goes to his state of mind.

Judge: I'll allow the testimony for state of mind. The objection is overruled.

Offers of proof are important because they are often your only way to explain to a judge why her ruling was erroneous.[9]

5. TRANSCRIPT FOR ANALYSIS

Below is a hypothetical transcript. In order to give you practice analyzing the form and content of objections, the transcript necessarily conflicts with the earlier assertion that many trials sail through with few objections. As you read through it, consider the propriety of the objections, and compare your thinking with the analysis that follows.

For the purpose of this exercise, focus only on objections that you *might* make. Remember that in an actual case, you might forgo making even the valid objections.

---

8. In a jury trial, make offers of proof at the bench lest the jury hear evidence that a judge ultimately decides is improper. Furthermore, when a judge's ruling depends on specific details in a witness' story, your offer of proof might consist of having the witness testify in a foundational direct and cross examination. Again, a jury would be excused during the foundational testimony. Then, if the judge decides to allow the testimony, the witness would testify again in front of the jury.

9. An offer of proof is also your avenue for convincing the appellate court that not only was the trial judge's ruling in error, but also that the error prevented the jury from hearing testimony that might have affected the outcome. Consequently, you will want to be sure that the court reporter includes your offer of proof made at side bar in the record.

Namb v. Pambee

This is a suit for malicious prosecution; you represent the plaintiff Namb. Namb and Pambee own competing shopping centers that occupy the same city block. About a year before you filed the present suit, Namb had erected a fence on his side of the property line separating the two shopping centers. The fence made it impossible for people who wished to go to Pambee's center to drive there through Namb's center.

In an earlier lawsuit, Pambee sued Namb, seeking an order that Namb take down the fence. Pambee claimed that the City had designated both shopping centers a single regional center. Summary judgment in favor of Namb was granted. You then filed the present suit seeking damages for malicious prosecution, claiming that Pambee had no reasonable basis for filing the earlier lawsuit.

The witness whose testimony follows is Hy Watermark, a defense witness called by Pambee. Watermark is the assistant manager of the shopping center owned by Pambee, and Pambee has called him to establish that Watermark's investigation demonstrated that Pambee had a reasonable basis to claim that the shopping centers constituted a single regional center.

Q: Mr. Watermark, how are you employed?

A: I am the assistant manager of the Waikoloa Shores Shopping Center in downtown Akron.

Q: Are you married?

A: Yes I am. I've got two children, ages 8 and 3.

Q: What are your general duties as assistant manager?

You: Objection to the testimony that the witness has three children, that's irrelevant.

1. Judge: Overruled.

   You: I also object to the witness describing his job duties, as improper character evidence.

2. Judge: I'll allow it.

   A: My main duties involve negotiating leases with tenants and supervising security and maintenance operations within the center.

   Q: Do you find your job challenging?

   You: Objection, that's improper.

3. Judge: Sustained.

   Q: I want to direct your attention to a conversation you had with Ms. Pambee about the status of your shopping center on the afternoon of September 22, three years ago. Do you recall that conversation?

4. You: Objection. This is direct examination, but counsel is putting words into the witness' mouth instead of letting the witness tell what happened in his own words.

5.　Judge:　The objection is overruled.

　A:　Yes, I do.　Ms. Pambee called me into her office and asked me if I was aware that the night before, a fence had been erected between our shopping center and the one to the east of us.

6.　You:　Objection to everything after "Yes, I do" as beyond the scope of the question; move to strike.

　Judge:　Sustained.

　Q:　What did Ms. Pambee tell you in this conversation of Sept. 22?

　A:　She told me that Namb had erected a fence across his property the night before, and that unless we could somehow force him to take it down our shopping center would lose a lot of business.

7.　You:　Would you make a hearsay objection to this testimony concerning what Ms. Pambee said?

　Q:　What else did she say?

　A:　Just that we were going to meet with her lawyer later that afternoon.　She also said that she wasn't surprised by what Namb did, that he was doing it to retaliate against her for refusing to sell her shopping center to him.

8.　You:　Is the witness speculating, Your Honor?

　Judge:　I'll strike the last sentence as improper speculation.

9.　You:　I appreciate that, Your Honor.　I'd ask that you instruct the jury to disregard the remark.

　Judge:　Yes, the jury is instructed to disregard the remark.

　Q:　Well, why do you think that Mr. Namb erected the fence?

10.　You:　Counsel, the judge just sustained my objection to that same information.　It's highly improper for you to ask the witness about it again.

　Q:　I'll move on.　Mr. Watermark, when was it recognized by Ms. Pambee that the city had designated the entire area a single regional center?

11.　You:　What if any objection is available?

　A:　I'm not sure, but this is the idea that I looked into.

　Q:　What did you do?

　A:　The first thing I did was phone the city clerk's office at City Hall.　I asked if they kept minutes of City Council meetings, and if I could look through them.　Whoever I talked to said they did keep minutes, and that they were available for inspection any business day.

12.　You:　Would a hearsay objection to what the person in the City Clerk's office said be proper?

13.　You:　Assuming that a hearsay objection would have been proper, could the judge properly rule that you had waived the objection by failing to make it before the witness testified to what the person said?

Q: Then what happened?

A: The very next morning, I went down to the city clerk's office to look through minutes of City Council meetings.

Q: And you were looking for a decision of the City Council that its approval for Mr. Namb to build his center was based on the idea that both centers together constituted a single regional center?

14. You: Objection, leading. Counsel is doing the testifying and telling the witness what to say, and I object to it.

Judge: Sustained.

Q: Let me just ask you what if anything you found concerning a regional shopping center.

A: The minutes that I found made it reasonable to think that the City Council considered both centers to be a single regional center.

15. You: On what basis might you object?

Q: Did anyone else accompany you?

A: No, but the next day I asked my assistant, Helene Pear, to look through additional minutes. She did, and after talking to her I realized that on two other occasions, the council had talked about the two centers as a single regional center.

You: Objection, hearsay.

Judge: Overruled.

16. You: But Your Honor, when this witness testifies to what he realized after talking to Ms. Pear, he is really testifying that, "This is what Ms. Pear told me." Since her statement is offered to prove that the city council had talked about the two centers as a regional center, what he learned from Ms. Pear is hearsay.

Judge: You heard my ruling.

Q: Nothing further at this time.

Judge: Cross examine?

You: Just briefly. Mr. Watermark, didn't Ms. Pambee tell you that unless you testified that you had checked through city hall records, she would fire you?

Opp.:   I must object; that's highly argumentative.

17. You: I'll withdraw the question.

You: Now Mr. Watermark, you went to the city clerk's office to examine minutes of city council meetings?

Opp.:   Objection, asked and answered on direct.

18. You: Your Honor, I clearly have a right on cross examination to go into matters that were covered on direct.

Judge: Objection overruled.

A: Yes, I did.

You: And according to people in the city clerk's office, you were there for less than half an hour, right?

Opp.:   Objection, improper cross examination.

19.   You: You did spend less than 30 minutes in the city clerk's office looking at minutes, correct?

A: Yes.

You: Nothing further.

Analysis of Numbered Portions of Transcript

No. 1: The objection is untimely. You waited until after an unrelated question was asked to make the objection.

No. 2: Improper objection. The evidence goes to the witness' general background, and also shows that the witness is a person to whom Pambee properly turned for help in investigating a possible lawsuit against Namb.

No. 3: The objection does not state a proper ground for objection, as the term "improper" does not specify a particular evidentiary defect. A proper ground would be "irrelevant." But where, as here, the question is obviously improper, a judge may well do what this judge did: sustain the objection anyway.

No. 4: The objection is an improper "speaking" version of "leading."

No. 5: Correct ruling. The question is not leading; it properly calls the witness' attention to the subject matter of his testimony.

No. 6: A classic example of a useless objection. Technically you may be correct; the question called for a simple "yes" or "no" answer. But what the witness is saying is admissible, so the objection only serves to let counsel repeat the testimony.

No. 7: No. What Ms. Pambee said is not offered for its truth, but as part of the basis on which the earlier lawsuit was filed.

No. 8: You identified a correct ground of objection. But you stated the objection in a mousy manner. Phrase objections as declarations that make a judge feel that you have confidence in your objection: "Object and move to strike the last sentence, speculation."

No. 9: "I appreciate that" is an improper remark suggesting that the judge is doing you a favor rather than making a legal ruling. Your request for the instruction to the jury is proper.

No. 10: You cannot speak directly to opposing counsel on the record. Make your objection to the judge: "I object. Counsel seeks the same information that Your Honor has just ruled inadmissible."

No. 11: Your best choices would be, "Assumes facts not in evidence" and "Calls for a legal conclusion." The question assumes that the city had designated the centers as a single regional center, and that Ms. Pambee recognized this fact.

No. 12: No, again the statement is not offered for its truth, but to show a reasonable basis for filing the earlier lawsuit.

No. 13: No; had it been proper, your objection would have been timely. You could not tell from the question that the witness' answer might include hearsay testimony.

No 14: The first sentence is a properly phrased objection. The second sentence adds nothing but improper verbiage.

No. 15: Two good bases of objection are that the answer constitutes an improper conclusion and violates the Best Evidence (Original Writing) Rule.

No. 16: Your argument is a correct statement of evidence law. But you should not argue after the judge has ruled until you get the judge's permission to do so.

No. 17: Your question is proper to show bias on the witness' part. You should not have withdrawn it; do not be cowed just because an adversary makes an emphatic objection.

No. 18: As a matter of evidence law, you are absolutely correct. But you should not argue the objection without leave of court.

No. 19: Your opponent's objection was correct: you cannot cross examine a witness with the hearsay statements of other people. However, before asking another question, you should either wait for the judge to rule or withdraw your initial question.

6. TROUBLESHOOTING

a. "Continuing" Objections

Normally, you want to make as few objections as possible. Yet, you may want to object to an entire series of questions because you think they all share a common impropriety. For example, perhaps an adverse witness is to be asked a series of questions about "the events of May 23," or about "all conversations with Aunt Mary." Your position is that the events of May 23 or the conversations with Aunt Mary are irrelevant. How can you preserve your objections for appeal without risking antagonizing the factfinder with constant objections?

A good solution to this dilemma is the "continuing objection." A continuing objection is a single objection that relates to all testimony on a particular topic. Once a judge grants you permission to make a continuing objection, you need not object each time the topic arises to preserve your position for appeal. Remember to get a clear indication on the record that you have a continuing objection:

Opp: Next, turning to the events of May 23, what is the first thing you can recall?

You: Objection, irrelevant; also object pursuant to Rule 403.

Judge: Both objections are overruled.

You: Your Honor, may I be heard? Our position is that any testimony concerning the events of May 23 is irrelevant and improper under Rule 403. May I have a continuing objection to all testimony, whether from this witness or any other witness, to the events of May 23?

Judge: That request will be granted. I will note for the record your continuing objection to testimony concerning the events of May 23.

b. "I Know It's Wrong, But I Can't Put My Finger on It"

You have undoubtedly had the experience of having someone's name on the tip of your tongue, but been unable to think of it immediately. A similar experience may occur in the courtroom: your adversary asks a question which you are certain is improper and warrants objection, but you are unable to come up with proper ground.

Just like a trust does not fail for want of a trustee, a valid objection should not fail for lack of the proper label. If you are uncertain of the magic legal ground, object. Often, a judge will say "Sustained" as soon as you begin to rise and begin to mouth the word "objection," sparing you from having to specify a precise ground. If the judge does not rescue you, a moment or two of "filler" may be all you need for the proper ground to come to mind:

Opp: Which chair did Goldilocks first sit in?

You: Objection, Your Honor. It's improper, lack of foundation; no personal knowledge.

As in this example, "lack of foundation" is often your best "filler." Since all evidence is subject to one sort of foundation or another, no other objection applies to as many potential evidentiary sins.

c. "How Do I Object If I Don't Know What the Witness Is Going to Say?"

As a general rule, it is in your interest to keep harmful information from the jury altogether rather than to strike damaging testimony already given. But if you are uncertain of what an adverse witness will say, you cannot readily object before the jury hears what the witness has to say.

One solution is to request that the adversary make an offer of proof. The offer is typically made at the bench, out of hearing of the witness and jurors. If the offer reveals objectionable evidence, you make your objection at the bench. If the objection is sustained, the jurors do not hear what the witness' testimony would have been:

Q: You had seen Goldilocks about three weeks prior to this incident, correct?

A: Yes.

Q: And what did you see on that occasion?

You: Your Honor, may we approach the bench? I'm not sure what counsel is after here, so I'd ask that counsel make an offer of proof.

Judge: All right, both counsel will come over to the sidebar with the court reporter. (All parties at the bench) Mr. Even (opponent), what is it the witness will say?

Opp: Your Honor, she'll testify that on the earlier occasion she saw the defendant enter the bears' home and eat their lunches, which consisted of cold pasta salads. This testimony goes to Goldilocks' intent in the case at hand.

Judge: Your response, counsel?

You: In that case, I object. It would be character evidence.

Judge: All right, I'll sustain that objection. Mr. Even, do you have any other questions for the witness, or should she be excused?

d. *"When Objecting Just Isn't Enough"*

Normally, objections are sufficient to give all sides a fair trial. Not all rulings are accurate, and jurors must sometimes be asked to perform the difficult feat of forgetting what they've heard. But neither trial nor any other human system is perfect.

But on occasion, you cannot achieve fairness through a judge's sustaining of your objections. For example, perhaps an adverse witness repeatedly peppers testimony with improper vituperatives which are likely to color jurors' attitudes no matter how many instructions to the contrary are given. Or, an adversary may continuously bombard your direct examination with objections, almost all of which are groundless. The flip side of this is an adversary who persists in getting improper evidence before the factfinder by referring to it in questions.

When such situations arise, an objection and a striking of improper matter may be insufficient to balance the books. While you might hope to avoid these situations, here are additional remedies you might seek:

● Ask the judge to instruct a runaway witness to listen carefully to the questions, and confine answers strictly to the questions. In very serious cases of abuse, ask the judge to strike the witness' testimony in its entirety.

● Ask the judge to instruct obstreperous counsel that continued ground-less objections and improper questioning will be dealt with by sanctions. In very serious cases of abuse, you might ask for a mistrial and costs. In many jurisdictions, judges also have the power to report counsel who conduct themselves improperly to the state's licensing authority for possible discipline.

7. CHECKLIST OF COMMON OBJECTIONS

a. *Objections to the Form of Questions*

(1) *"Vague, Unintelligible or Ambiguous" (FRE 611)*

Problem: You cannot anticipate a witness' answer, and therefore do not know whether to object.

Examples:

- "Is there anything about any of these incidents that perhaps you noticed at the time but which on later reflection has perhaps changed in your own mind based on what they did afterwards?"

- "What happened next?" (asked when the testimony the witness has previously given has not referred to any particular point in time)

(2) *"Compound" (FRE 611)*

Problem: You do not know whether the witness will answer one or both parts, and thus cannot anticipate the scope of the answer.

Example: "What time did he arrive and what did he do when he got there?"

(3) *"Calls For a Narrative Response" (FRE 611)*

Problem: The broad scope of the question allows witnesses (especially inexperienced ones) to refer to improper evidence before you can anticipate and therefore object to it.

Example: "Please describe the events that culminated in the signing of the contract."

Note: Even when a question does not "call for a narrative response," a witness may give one. You may interrupt the answer to object that "the witness is narrating."

(4) *"Asked and Answered" (FRE 611)*

Problem: Counsel wastes the court's time and unfairly tries to emphasize testimony by rehashing it.

Example: Counsel asks a witness to "tell us what you saw from your window one more time."

Note: Judges often permit you to ask specific questions more than once. This is especially true when you seek to clarify the record or end testimony on a crucial point.

(5) "Misquotes a Witness or Mischaracterizes Testimony" (FRE 611)

Problem: Counsel distorts prior testimony in a way that does not allow the witness to correct the distortion. (You may make this objection whether your adversary is questioning the witness whose testimony is misquoted, or a different witness.)

Example: Your adversary is cross-examining an eyewitness to Goldilocks' burglary of the bears' home:

Q: Your testimony is that you saw Goldilocks for a couple of seconds from a distance of about 15 feet, correct?

A: Yes.

Q: Now, after you got this pretty good look, what did you do?

You: Objection; counsel has misquoted the witness. He did not say he got a "pretty good look."

(6) "Leading" (FRE 611)

Problem: The question tells a cooperative witness counsel's desired answer. Counsel, not the witness, determines the content and the wording of the evidence.

Example: "Neither of the other bowls of porridge had been touched?"

(7) "Argumentative" (FRE 611)

Problem: A witness is unable to fairly answer a question because the question refers to counsel's argument rather than to the evidence on which the argument rests.

Examples:

- "How can you expect anyone to believe that you were able to see her well enough to identify her?"

- "If you called the Building and Safety Department the next day, you couldn't have thought that the roach problem had been taken care of."

(8) "Assumes Facts Not in Evidence" (FRE 611)

Problem: Counsel inserts evidence into the record by making an assertion without asking a witness to respond to it.

Example: "Doctor, spiral fractures are readily seen on X-rays. Please explain why you didn't notice this one."

b. *Objections to the Content of Testimony*

(1) "Speculation or Improper Opinion" (FRE 701); "Lack of Personal Knowledge" (FRE 602)

Problem: Testimony concerning hypothetical situations or to matters beyond the witness' powers of observation or scope of expertise is unreliable and invades the function of the factfinder.

Examples:

- "Why did the chicken cross the road?" (The witness cannot know another's state of mind.)

- "If you had seen the defendant, what would you have done?"

Practice Note: As the multiple heading suggests, you can typically use any of these objections and cover much the same evidentiary ground.

(2) *"Hearsay" (FRE 801)*

Problem: In the interest of common decency, you are spared another explanation of hearsay dangers. As you should know from your Evidence course, hearsay is an out of court statement offered to prove the truth of the matter asserted.

(3) *"Irrelevant" (FRE 402)*

Problem: Irrelevant evidence wastes court time and may lead a factfinder to rely on information that has no logical connection to factual propositions.

Example: Seeking to disprove Citron's testimony that he was able to identify a person he had seen from a distance of 20 feet at night, Collins is asked, "Could you identify somebody at a distance of 20 feet at night?" (Collins' ability to observe is not logically connected to Citron's ability.)

(4) *"Probative Value Substantially Outweighed By Unfair Prejudice" (FRE 403)*

Problem: Factfinder may give evidence far more weight than it logically deserves, often because the emotional impact of the evidence will override the factfinder's rational faculties. Or, the evidence may be excluded because it will consume an undue amount of court time.

Examples:

- In a personal injury case, the plaintiff offers her actual severed leg into evidence.[10]

- Rhoda recounts the details of an oral agreement that she and Bernie allegedly entered into on June 3. On cross examination,

---

10. The late and much-remembered expert on trial advocacy, Irving Younger, used to say that evidence was inadmissible if it "would make the average juror throw up."

Rhoda is asked to recount all other conversations she had on June 3.

Practice Note: Whenever you object that evidence is "irrelevant," you should almost always also object "under Rule 403." If you object only that evidence is irrelevant and the evidence does have minimal probative value, a judge may properly overrule the objection.

(5) "Lack of Foundation" (See FRE 104)

Problem: Evidence which fails to meet foundational requirements is unreliable.[11]

Examples:

- A proponent of a business record fails to show that it was prepared "in the ordinary course of business."

- A witness is asked to give an opinion that Franklin was under the influence of alcohol, but only saw Franklin for a brief moment.

(6) "Cumulative" (FRE 611)

Problem: Cumulative evidence wastes court time and gives undue emphasis to testimony.

Example: A tenant suing a landlord for breach of the warranty of habitability seeks to call 12 different visitors to testify to the leaking ceilings and roaches in the tenant's apartment.

Practice Note: If you are the would-be proponent of cumulative testimony, instead of trying to call multiple witnesses ask your adversary to stipulate "that if witnesses 3 through 12 were called, they would testify as follows. . . ." The stipulation only records what the witnesses would have said had they testified; it allows the adversary to contest that testimony.

(7) "Character Evidence" (FRE 404)

Problem: See the description under FRE 403, as the rule against character evidence is a specific instance of evidence made inadmissible by that section.

Example: To prove that Eileen was speeding, the adversary seeks to prove that she often drives over the speed limit.

---

11. For an extensive discussion of foundational requirements for exhibits, see Chapter 16.

Chapter 18

SELECTING A JURY

Henry Fonda, Ed Begley, Jack Klugman, Edward Binns and Lee J. Cobb are
among the jurors deciding the fate of a murder defendant. "Twelve Angry
Men," © 1957 Orion-Nova Twelve Angry Men. All rights reserved.

The jury trial is one of the hallmarks of the Anglo–American legal
system.[1] Once you (or your adversary) opt for a jury trial, you've got a
ticket to participate in the fascinating and uniquely American process of
selecting a fair and impartial jury. This chapter describes that process,
explains how the arguments you've prepared prior to trial influence your

---

1. Research has shown that 98% of the world's civil jury trials take place in the United States. H. Zeisel, "The American Jury," in *The American Jury System: Final* *Report of the 1977 Chief Justice Earl Warren Conference on Advocacy in the United States* (1977).

jury selection strategy and examines factors you generally consider when deciding whether to excuse a juror.

1. OVERVIEW OF THE JURY SELECTION PROCESS

You are probably familiar with the general process of jury selection. Citizens are called to serve as jurors, for a term of typically between one to two weeks. When a jury trial is about to begin, a clerk in a jury assembly area draws the names of potential jurors at random and makes them leave the jigsaw puzzles they were trying to assemble and sends them to the appropriate courtroom. From this group, the courtroom clerk conducts a similar random draw and a potential venire is seated in the jury box.[2] The potential jurors are then questioned.

The process by which potential jurors answer questions on the way to becoming actual jurors is known as "voir dire."[3] Literally translated, the term means "to speak the truth." During voir dire, potential jurors respond to questions about their personal backgrounds and their attitudes towards issues that will arise as evidence unfolds. Traditionally, lawyers themselves did much of the questioning. However, never ones to recoil at the thought of gaining an advantage, many litigators have treated voir dire as an opportunity to persuade jurors of the righteousness of their cause. On occasion, voir dire has taken even longer than the trial. As a result, many judges now conduct voir dire themselves, and require counsel to submit in writing any questions they would like the judge to put to the jury panel.

After both sides (or the judge) have questioned the initial venire, attorneys can excuse unacceptable jurors by exercising "challenges." Challenges come in two convenient sizes—challenges for cause and peremptory challenges. A challenge for cause asks a judge to disqualify a potential juror on the ground that the juror is legally disqualified from serving. The usual reason for a disqualification is that a potential juror is not fair and impartial. However, other infirmities, usually defined by statute, may give rise to a challenge for cause, such as a potential juror's lacking the mental capacity to understand testimony. You may exercise an unlimited number of challenges for cause, though it's up to the trial judge to decide whether such a challenge has merit. Peremptory challenges allow you to remove potential jurors you think *might* be biased or predisposed against your client, even though you cannot establish bias to the judge's satisfaction. Although the basis upon which lawyers can exercise peremptories has been shrinking,[4] peremptories allow lawyers to excuse potential jurors without needing a judge's consent. However, statutes in all jurisdictions strictly limit the number of peremptories a

---

2. The number of jurors on a panel typically varies between six and twelve according to jurisdiction.

3. Don't worry if your pronunciation of the term is different from someone else's. Like recipes for 1000 Island dressing, no two pronunciations are the same.

4. Counsel can no longer excuse jurors on the basis of race, *Batson v. Kentucky*, 476 U.S. 79, 106 S.Ct. 1712, 90 L.Ed.2d 69 (1986), or gender, *J.E.B. v. Alabama Ex Rel. T.B.*, ___ U.S. ___, 114 S.Ct. 1419, 128 L.Ed.2d 89 (1994).

lawyer can exercise, lest a zealous obstructionist send a county full of potential jurors packing. Typical is the federal law, which in civil cases allows a party only three peremptories.[5]

As the judge excuses potential jurors in response to counsel's challenges, others take their place and respond to questions. When the parties complete the challenge process, alternate jurors may be selected in the same way if the judge and the attorneys think it necessary. Eventually, the court clerk swears in the jurors and the trial itself commences.

2. THE SCOPE OF VOIR DIRE QUESTIONING

The scope of questioning permitted on voir dire varies. Some jurisdictions permit you only to seek information supporting a challenge for cause, while others also permit questions seeking information that might assist you in exercising peremptory challenges.[6] Whether a question seeks information supporting a challenge for cause is often a matter about which otherwise reasonable judges tend to differ. As a result, each judge's interpretation of permissible scope of voir dire will vary. Consequently, you will have to examine the law in your jurisdiction and the practice in your judge's court to determine the latitude you will have when questioning prospective jurors.

3. DRAWING INFERENCES FROM CIRCUMSTANTIAL EVIDENCE DURING VOIR DIRE

Your goal during jury voir dire is to identify jurors who are likely to be biased or predisposed for or against your client. When attempting to identify such jurors, you will inevitably have to draw your conclusions from circumstantial evidence because direct evidence of bias is rarely available. Jurors who want to remain on a jury will never admit to a bias against any party. Consequently, you must typically infer a juror's potential bias from the information that emerges during voir dire. This information is really circumstantial evidence tending to prove the conclusion of potential bias.

As you well know, circumstantial evidence can support contradictory inferences. Thus, jury selection is necessarily something of a guessing game. For example, assume that your opponent will call a university professor as an expert witness; your expert is someone who "works in the field." A potential juror tells you she has worked in the administration office of a local university for 20 years. She contends, of course, that she will be unbiased when assessing the credibility of all the witnesses. But reasonable generalizations can connect this circumstantial evidence to at least two competing inferences:

---

5. 28 U.S.C. sec. 1870.

6. In California, for example, in a criminal case you may be restricted to questions directed to a challenge for cause, while in a civil case you may also ask questions enabling you to intelligently exercise your peremptory challenges. See Calif. Code of Civil Proc. Sec. 222.5 and 223.

● People who have worked in university administration for 20 years sometimes think that university professors are unbiased, objective, thorough and intelligent. Get her off the jury.

● People who have worked in university administration for 20 years sometimes think that university professors are close-minded, arrogant and know nothing about the problems of the real world. Keep her on the jury.

You can't be certain which generalization is more consistent with this juror's experiences while working at the university. You might, of course, expand your data base through additional questions seeking "especially whens" or "except whens" for the competing generalizations. For example, you might postulate that the juror will have a favorable attitude towards university professors, especially when she has worked for the same professor for several years. You would then inquire about the juror's university work experience.

In the limited time available for voir dire, a judge is likely to prevent you from making a detailed inquiry into "especially" or "except" whens. Moreover, a juror who wants to keep her seat on the panel may try to conceal her real attitude towards university professors. In the end, your conclusions about jurors' potential bias will almost always be uncertain inferences drawn from circumstantial evidence.

4. IDENTIFYING JURORS' PREDISPOSITIONS

The main legal justification for juror voir dire is to permit counsel to select a fair and impartial jury. Under the adversary system, you will attempt to identify and remove jurors who may be biased or predisposed against your client and identify and retain those jurors who are predisposed in favor of your client. Your adversary will do the same for her client. The result is theoretically an impartial factfinder.

The subsections below examine the general topics you will commonly consider or inquire about when seeking to uncover jurors' predispositions. Remember, however, that within each of these categories judges have tremendous discretion to limit the scope of voir dire questioning.

a. *Identification With or Hostility Against a Party or Witness*

One source of jurors' predispositions emanates from personal feelings of identity or hostility. Jurors often identify with and therefore tend to believe parties or witnesses with whom they share personal attributes.[7] For example, if a juror and a party have similar ages, race, gender, ethnicity, socio-economic class, or work background, the juror may well closely identify with and be predisposed towards that party.[8]

---

7. Research confirms that people tend to like witnesses with whom they share similar characteristics, backgrounds or attitudes, and therefore to believe them. See G. Lindzey & E. Aronson (eds.), II *The* *Handbook of Social Psychology* 266–267 (3d ed. 1985).

8. As discussed above, you will recognize here the influence of generalizations in the voir dire process. To say that a juror

The contrary is also quite possible: a resident of a wealthy white suburb may not identify with a minority group member living in the inner-city. Similarly, a day laborer may be hostile towards a corporate president and a corporate president may harbor resentment towards a personal injury lawyer.

Often, gauging a juror's personal feelings is not as simple as observing obvious physical or socio-economic similarities and differences. For example, assume that your client and a juror are both young mothers. Do not be too quick to assume, "That's one for me." Voir dire probing of the juror's family background and close friendships may reveal circumstantial evidence of a different predisposition. For instance, further inquiry into the young mother's background may reveal that one of her best friends is a police officer. If your adversary will rely heavily on the testimony of a police officer, the juror's sympathies may not lie with you.

A juror's work experiences frequently furnish the circumstantial evidence from which you infer personal identification or hostility. For example, assume that your client is the president of a large corporation, and a juror states that she works as a computer programmer. Again, do not automatically assume that the juror will identify with your client as "one businessperson to another." Instead, you will want to probe the juror's personal and employment background. Your voir dire questioning may go as follows:

Q: Ms. Megabyte, I believe you told the judge that you worked as a computer programmer at Pear Electronics. Please tell me a little bit about your work history.

A: I graduated with a degree in computer engineering about five years ago and went to work for a small company called JCN Inc. I left a couple of years later and went to Macrohard Drive for another couple of years. I've been at Pear for about six months now.

Q: I'm sure that three changes in five years has required a lot of adjustments on your part. Can you briefly describe how those changes came about?

A: In both instances, the companies I worked for were taken over by larger companies. There was a reduction in staff after the takeovers, and as I was always one of the newer employees I was let go.

This juror may harbor hostility toward your client because she sees him as the symbol of the corporate culture that "threw her out of" two

will favor a party with whom she shares a common attribute is to accept a broad generalization, or a "stereotype." That is, to say that a juror who is a senior citizen is likely to favor the older of two parties is to rely on a stereotype. As with any general-ization or stereotype, exceptions exist. Thus, in some instances people may be predisposed *against* those with similar attributes or backgrounds. See G. Lindzey & E. Aronson (eds.), II *The Handbook of Social Psychology* 266 (3d ed. 1985).

jobs.[9]

b. Acceptance or Rejection of Your Important Generalizations

Recall that arguments typically rely on circumstantial evidence, and the persuasiveness of these arguments typically depends on the jury's acceptance of underlying generalization(s). Jurors tend to accept generalizations which are consistent with their actual or vicarious personal experience.[10] Consequently, a juror whose personal experience is consistent with the generalizations underlying your most important arguments may be predisposed toward your case. Conversely, a juror whose personal experience is inconsistent with the generalizations underlying your most important arguments may be predisposed against your client. For example, assume that you represent the plaintiff in an auto accident case. Your most important argument will be that the accident happened because the defendant was momentarily inattentive to the road when he was distracted by his two children arguing in the back seat. The generalization underlying your argument is something like: "People whose children are arguing in the back seat of a car are sometimes momentarily inattentive to the road." A juror whose personal experience is consistent with this generalization is likely to be receptive to your argument.

But, as always, contradictory generalizations are available. For instance, a juror may be hostile toward your argument if her personal experience is consistent with the following generalization: "People whose children are arguing in the back seat of a car sometimes are worried about their children's safety and are particularly attentive to the road."

During voir dire you would like to find out which jurors have had actual or vicarious personal experiences consistent with the generalization you would like them to accept. Thus, you might inquire about any auto accidents (or near accidents) they or their friends and family have been involved in and what they perceived were the causes of those accidents.[11]

Of course, many jurors will not have had actual or vicarious personal experiences that directly validate your generalization(s). For instance, in the above example, some jurors may not have been personally involved in or heard about an auto accident or near accident being

---

9. The topics you will ask about to identify feelings of personal identification or hostility will obviously depend on the nature of your case and the breadth of questioning permitted by the judge. Typical topics that you might want to inquire into include: Knowledge of parties, witnesses or the facts of a case; educational and employment history; and involvement of a juror or family members or close friends in similar lawsuits or transactions.

10. See discussion in Chapter 14, Sec. 3.

11. And if they do have experiences consistent with your generalizations, the juror will often be stricken by your opponent. For example, a juror who says that his father twice rear ended another car when distracted by his children may be seen as very favorable to your case and thus stricken by your adversary.

caused by a parent being distracted by a child. Ideally, you would like to determine if such a juror has had consistent analogous personal experience. For example, you would like to ask if such a juror has been distracted by children's arguments when watching television, trying to talk on the telephone, or when assembling a Christmas present. Such analogous personal experiences (either actual or vicarious) might tend to make the jurors more receptive to your argument.[12] Again, the extent to which you will be able to ask questions about such analogous experiences during voir dire depends upon the scope of questioning permitted by the judge.[13]

In addition to identifying jurors with consistent personal experiences, you would also want to identify jurors with inconsistent personal experiences. For example, in the auto accident case, assume that a juror is a father of a two and a four year old. Your voir dire might include the following:

Q: Do you ever drive with both of your children in the car?

A: Yes, quite often.

Q: I'm sure that if your kids are anything like mine they bicker on occasion when you're driving?

A: Sometimes, sure.

Q: Could you tell me how, if at all, this affects your ability to concentrate on your driving?

A: Not much. When I'm driving with my kids in the car I think I'm especially cautious. I just don't want to take any chances on getting in an accident when they're in the car. If they're arguing in the back seat, I may say something, but I basically just ignore it.

This father might be predisposed to reject your argument that your adversary was negligent because he was distracted by his children.[14]

---

12. If you have prepared a draft of your closing argument prior to trial, you may have already identified the analogous personal experiences you will rely on in closing. See Chapter 14, Sec. 3. During voir dire you want to select jurors for whom the analogous personal experiences you will discuss in closing ring true.

13. Thus, in the example in the text, if you try to ask a juror about whether his children ever distracted him while he was on the telephone or while he attempted to assemble a Christmas present, many judges would prohibit the question. To the court, such a question probably does not appear to relate to a challenge for cause or to the intelligent exercise of a peremptory challenge.

14. Of course, this father may think that many people are distracted by their children, and he is an exception to the general rule. You will have difficulty determining when such is the case. You typically can not ask a juror to express an opinion about the validity of a generalization. You probably could not, for example, ask the father. "Mr. Jones, regardless of how you behave, do you think that when people have their children in the car they are often to be distracted from their driving?" Most judges would rule such a question improper because it asks a juror to "prejudge" the evidence by agreeing that your generalization is valid. A "prejudge the evidence" question is generally objectionable because it asks the juror what inference he will probably draw from the evidence. And the inferences to be drawn from the evidence is a subject for closing argument, when all the testimony bearing on that question has been introduced.

You will also want to identify the jurors whose personal experiences make them predisposed to accept your adversary's strongest arguments. For example, assume that you represent the plaintiff in a sexual harassment case. Your client claims that her boss asked her out on dates, made inappropriate sexual remarks to her and physically touched her in a sexual way when they were alone. Your client found the situation intolerable and felt forced to quit. Her boss denies all. Your client admits that she never mentioned her boss' inappropriate behavior to anyone before she talked to a lawyer because she was embarrassed and humiliated. You know that your adversary will argue that her failure to mention the boss' alleged behavior to anyone is strong evidence that no inappropriate behavior occurred.

What generalization(s) underlie your adversary's argument and what questions might you ask to identify jurors with personal experiences consistent or inconsistent with such generalization(s)? What inferences would you like the jurors to draw from your client's failure to mention the inappropriate behavior? What generalizations underlie your inferences and what questions would you ask to identify jurors with personal experiences consistent or inconsistent with your generalizations? The answers to such questions would guide your beliefs about what types of jurors will best be able to give your client a fair trial.

c. *Favorable or Unfavorable Socio–Political Attitudes*

Apart from their identification with an opposing party or witness, and apart from whether their life experiences are consistent or inconsistent with generalizations relating to the accuracy of historical facts, jurors' socio-political attitudes toward legal claims or defenses may cause them to be biased. For example, a juror may think that possession of marijuana is common and its use relatively harmless, and be biased against the prosecution in such cases. Some jurors may think the "entrapment" defense reflects a left wing overreaction to appropriately aggressive police investigatory techniques. Other jurors may harbor negative opinions on important legal concepts or doctrines, such as a criminal defendant's right not to testify and entitlement to a presumption of innocence, the prosecution's heavy burden to prove guilt beyond a reasonable doubt and a civil plaintiff's lighter burden to prove a case only by a preponderance of evidence. For example, assume that you are plaintiff's counsel in a civil suit against two police officers for allegedly using "excessive" force during an otherwise admittedly legitimate arrest. You are concerned that the some jurors may not be receptive to this type of suit because they think it unfairly hamstrings police and rewards criminals. In this case, an inquiry along the following lines might be appropriate:

Q: Mr. Sklansky, my client in this case admits that he was disturbing the peace on the night he was arrested. This suit involves his claim that arresting officers used excessive force when they arrested him. Do you have any feelings about whether suits like this one are legitimate?

A: I suppose that depends on the facts of the case.

Q: That's fair and I'm not asking you to come to any conclusions about the facts of this case. I just want to know what you think about the right of a person who is arrested to complain if the officers used excessive force?

A: I think the police have a very difficult job and I don't like to second guess everything they do. But they shouldn't use any more force than they have to when they make an arrest.

Q: You say that the police have a difficult job. Would you be worried about whether this kind of case will make police officers reluctant to arrest someone for fear that they'll later get sued?

A: I suppose there is a risk of that, but if the evidence shows excessive force I won't have any trouble holding the officers responsible.

Q: The judge will instruct you that in reaching your verdict, you shouldn't take into account the effect it may have on police officers' future conduct in other situations.[15] Will you be able to follow such an instruction?

A: Well. . . .

Mr. Sklansky's answers thus far do not display overt bias against lawsuits for excessive force. Hence, a challenge for cause is at best premature. And you may be uncertain about whether to exercise a peremptory challenge, as the attitudes he's expressed so far are likely to be shared by many people in the community. By asking additional open questions that encourage Mr. Sklansky to talk in his own words, you hope to obtain circumstantial evidence of whether he harbors unfavorable socio-political attitudes towards excessive force lawsuits.

5. INOCULATING JURORS

Regardless of how successful you have been in removing biased jurors, your case will sometimes have significant weaknesses that your adversary is certain to raise and that may adversely influence jurors who are neutral or even predisposed in your client's favor. Jury selection is an opportunity to inoculate the jury against such weaknesses. You do so by disclosing the weakness and seeking the jurors' commitment not to decide the case solely on the basis of that weakness. Inoculation tends to remove the shock value from an adversary's mid-trial disclosure of the weakness, and reduces the likelihood that the jury will be unduly influenced by it.

For example, assume that Sue Gillig, one of your witnesses, has previously been convicted of felony embezzlement. During jury selection you might inoculate the jury as follows:

Q: One of our witnesses will be Sue Gillig. You'll hear testimony that a few years ago, Ms. Gillig was convicted of embezzlement.

---

15.   See Chapter 14, Sec. 5 (d).

Will any of you automatically assume before you even hear her testimony that nothing she says is true because she's previously been convicted of a crime?

A: (No response.)

Q: If you're selected to serve on the jury, you all agree that it's wrong to prejudge any witness' testimony, and that you'll keep an open mind until you've heard all the evidence?

A: (No response.)

Q: Mr. Charles, you wouldn't just automatically assume that Ms. Gillig's testimony must be inaccurate just because she's been convicted of embezzlement, right?

A: No, I'll listen to what she has to say just like I will with any other witness.

Q: Would anyone else's answer be different than Mr. Charles's?

A: (No response)

Here, you inoculate the jurors by securing their pledge not to prejudge the evidence. Of course you have no guarantee that the inoculation will "take." There's little you can do if a juror decides not to believe Gillig largely because of the prior conviction. But by surfacing the issue and obtaining the jurors' commitment to keep an open mind, you hope to prevent them from being unduly influenced by the conviction.[16]

Often, you will employ the inoculation technique to undercut an opponent's silent arguments.[17] For example, assume that the president of the local university will testify as a witness for your adversary. You are concerned that the jurors will credit whatever the president says just because of her high status. To inoculate against this improper reasoning you might question the jurors as follows:

Q: The plaintiff will call Funda Raysa as a witness. Ms. Raysa is the president of our local university. Without even listening to the evidence, do any of you believe that Ms. Raysa's testimony must be accurate solely because she is a university president?

A: (No response.)

Q: If you're selected to serve on the jury, you all agree that it's wrong to prejudge any witness' testimony, and that you'll keep an open mind until you've heard all the evidence?

A: (No response.)

---

16. Inoculation obviously carries a risk: you call attention to weaknesses in your case even before opening statement. Consequently, you will seldom try to inoculate against more than one or two weaknesses.

17. For a discussion of silent arguments, see Chapter 9.

Q: Mr. Lowwa, you wouldn't just automatically assume that Ms. Raysa's testimony must be accurate just because of who she is, right?

A: No, I'll treat her just like any other witness.

Q: Would anyone else's answer be different than Mr. Lowwa's?

A: (No response)

Consider a second example of inoculating against an adversary's silent argument. Assume that a witness who will testify on your behalf speaks with a heavy foreign accent. Your concern is that the jurors may subconsciously discount his testimony because they'll have difficulty understanding him. Again, you may try to inoculate:

Q: One of the witnesses we will call is Mr. Higgins, who speaks with a pronounced Cockney accent that you may have some difficulty understanding. Is there anyone who would be inclined to discount Mr. Higgins' testimony simply because he's a bit difficult to understand?

A: (No response)

Q: Miss Epburn, if you have to expend a little extra effort to understand what Mr. Higgins says, you won't hold that against him, correct?

A: No, I wouldn't hold his accent against him.

You can even inoculate against an opponent's non-testimonial silent arguments. For example, you may be prosecuting Bryant, who is charged with committing a violent assault. In court, Bryant appears dressed in preppie attire. To counter the defense's silent argument that Bryant doesn't look like someone who would have committed a violent act, you may ask a question such as the following: "The defendant is charged with a violent attack on Felix Katz. In court, you see that the defendant is dressed like a college student. You understand that how he dresses in court is irrelevant, and if you're selected to be on the jury you won't be influenced by how he's dressed, right?"

Inoculation questions are generally proper as going to a challenge for cause. A juror who states that he's prejudged a witness' credibility or that he'll be influenced by a witness' accent or manner of dress is not fair and impartial, and should be excused for cause. Admittedly, you probably do not expect a juror to answer in a way that will support a challenge for cause. But as inoculation commits jurors to listen to all the evidence before making up their minds and seeks to minimize the influence of improper and unstated arguments, such questions further the purpose of jury voir dire.

6. THE RULE AGAINST ASKING JURORS TO PREJUDGE EVIDENCE

A well-settled and nearly universal rule is that you cannot ask jurors to "prejudge the case." What this means is that you cannot commit jurors to the inference they would draw if the evidence is as you describe it. The tactic is improper because it asks a juror to commit to a position based on less than all the evidence.

For example, consider this question that a plaintiff might ask in a case in which the claim is that the defendant drove while under the influence of alcohol:

"If we establish by a preponderance of the evidence that the defendant drank three martinis an hour or so before driving, will you conclude that she was driving under the influence of alcohol?"

Most judges would deem this question an objectionable request to ask the juror to prejudge the case, as it asks a juror to draw an inference before hearing all of the evidence.

Lawyers often try to evade the spirit of the "can't prejudge" rule while obeying its letter. For instance, contrast the question above with the following one:

"If we establish by a preponderance of the evidence that the defendant drank three martinis an hour or so before driving, will you be willing to consider that as evidence that the defendant may have been driving under the influence of alcohol?"

Technically, this question does not ask a juror to prejudge the case. Rather, the question only seeks a juror's willingness to consider relevant evidence. A juror who stated that he would not consider this legitimate argument would be subject to a challenge for cause. However, since it is so unlikely that a juror would reject such obviously relevant evidence, it may be apparent to a judge that counsel's real purpose is to preview an argument that counsel hopes the juror will ultimately find persuasive. If so, the judge may deem the question an improper attempt to convince the juror to prejudge the case.

By contrast, "inoculation" questions typically avoid the rule against prejudging the case. The reason is that they seek a jurors' commitment only to follow a proper decision-making process, and do not have the effect of previewing an argument. For example, assume that in the same case, defense counsel asks a slight variation on the question above:

"You will hear evidence that my client drank three martinis an hour or so before driving. Would you conclude solely from that evidence that he was driving under the influence of alcohol?"

Here, defense counsel's question seeks to inoculate the jury against an obvious weakness in the defense case. Since the question seeks the juror's commitment to a proper decision-making process and does not preview a defense argument, the question probably does not violate the rule against asking jurors to prejudge evidence.

7. BUILDING RAPPORT DURING VOIR DIRE

You will want to establish rapport with the jurors as you question them. One reason for this is instrumental: when you treat jurors with respect and show consideration for their feelings they are more likely to accept your arguments. Moreover, jurors deserve respect for setting aside their normal activities to serve on a jury. This section examines several rapport building techniques.

a. Explain the Reason for Your Inquiry

Answering voir dire questions would not be most people's first activity of choice. Few people would say, "I think I'd like to go down to the courthouse and have lawyers probe my feelings and attitudes about all sorts of private matters in front of a bunch of people I hardly know." Since jurors often resent voir dire questioning, you can enhance rapport by empathizing with their possible discomfort and explaining the purpose of particularly personal or embarrassing inquiries.

For example, assume that you represent a woman who is relying on "battered wife syndrome" evidence as a defense to a murder charge. On voir dire, you will have to explore jurors' experiences with and attitudes towards physically abusive men. Many jurors are likely to be embarrassed and reticent to talk about such matters. To encourage full disclosure and build rapport, you might do the following:

- Preface your overall questioning by empathizing with their discomfort:

"Ladies and gentlemen, as you know, this case involves a woman whose defense rests on her claim that she was subjected to years of physical abuse by her husband. Both counsel therefore are obligated to ask you about your experiences with and attitudes about spousal abuse. It's certainly not my purpose or wish to embarrass any of you, and if anything I ask becomes too personal please let me know and we'll see what we can do to solve the problem. For example, both counsel and the judge have discussed the possibility of examining you individually in the judge's chambers." [18]

- Preface specific questions that are likely to be embarrassing with an explanation as to why you are seeking the particular information:

"Ms. Hurley, there will be evidence that alcohol was often involved when abuse occurred. Therefore, while I don't want to pry unnecessarily into your personal affairs, I'll need to ask you some questions about your experiences and attitudes relating to alcohol."

b. Use a Conversational Manner

Voir dire is most effective when you treat it as a series of conversations between you and the panel members. Jurors don't want to feel like they are being cross examined and you can build rapport by talking to them as you would a friend or acquaintance. For example, don't use legalese or ten dollar words that many lay people will not understand.

18. Whenever you think a juror is embarrassed to discuss a particular subject, you can ask the judge to allow you and opposing counsel to question the potential juror in the privacy of the judge's chambers.

Refer to the jurors as "Ms. Jones" or "Mr. Smith," rather than as "Juror No. 3." [19] If you ask a question that appears to confuse a juror, take the blame on yourself and rephrase it. For example, you might say something like, "I guess my question wasn't very clear. What I meant to ask was...." And though a courtroom is a formal and serious setting, you can even respond to humorous situations when a juror does something like making a lighthearted remark.

8. QUESTIONING TECHNIQUES

During voir dire you will obviously use a combination of open and closed or leading questions.

Open questions have several advantages. They are efficient because they allow jurors to narrate in their own words. They tend to make the jurors feel an active part of the voir dire process. Jurors can often reveal personal or potentially embarrassing information in the most favorable light if they are allowed to narrate about their experiences or attitudes, rather than being "cross examined" with a series of questions calling only for an unequivocal "yes" or "no." Finally, you may obtain unexpected circumstantial evidence of a favorable or unfavorable disposition toward your case from a jurors relatively unconstrained response to open questions. For all these reasons, questions such as "Tell me about your experiences with....," "What are your attitudes toward....," "How do you feel about ...," will be quite common on voir dire.

Closed and leading questions also have advantages. They permit you to focus on specific information a juror may have omitted in response to an open question. And they are particularly useful when you want to ask questions to inoculate the jurors,[20] or, as you will see in the next section, when you want to challenge a juror for cause.

9. LAYING A FOUNDATION FOR CHALLENGES FOR CAUSE

If you think that a juror's background or responses to voir dire questioning demonstrate bias against your client, you can remove that juror with a peremptory challenge (assuming you have a peremptory left). But if you can convince a judge to excuse that juror for cause, you can save a precious peremptory.[21]

In typical cases, successful challenges for cause are relatively rare. As long as a juror claims to have an open mind and agrees to base a decision strictly on the evidence, many judges are reluctant to excuse a juror for cause. As a result, you may have to lay a foundation through

19. Most attorneys prepare a simple chart consisting of boxes for each juror position, with room to write down the name and information about the juror occupying that position. The chart enables you to refer to potential jurors by name and provides a ready reference to the information upon which you might want to base a challenge.

20. See, for example, the questions used in Section 5 *supra*.

21. Unfortunately, you can not carry over peremptories from one case to another. Thus, the following argument will fall on deaf ears: "Your Honor, I have three peremptories left over from my last trial and I'd like to use them now."

your questions to convince a judge that a juror is biased. For example, assume that you represent the defendant in an auto accident case. Your client, Norm Malone, admits he had a "couple of beers" prior to the accident, but contends it had no effect on his driving. You know that plaintiff will claim that your client was driving under the influence of alcohol. A portion of your voir dire of juror Shelley Claven might go as follows:

1. Q: Ms. Claven, as you know my client admits that he had a very small amount of alcohol to drink shortly before the accident. You wouldn't conclude that just because he had had some alcohol, no matter how small an amount, that he was at fault in this case, would you?

2. A: No, of course not.

3. Q: Please tell me what your attitudes are toward people who drink alcohol?

4. A: Well, I myself don't use alcohol and I don't permit people to drink it in my house, but I know lots of people like to drink.

5. Q: And how do you feel about these people who like to drink?

6. A: To tell you the truth, I'm not really comfortable around people when they are drinking. I've never used alcohol and I don't see the need for it.

7. Q: Ms. Claven, I can understand why you'd feel that way. But if I understand you correctly, you think that society would be better off if people didn't drink at all, don't you?

8. A: I suppose I do.

9. Q: And you would think it was wrong if a member of your family had any amount of alcohol before they drove a car, correct?

10. A: That's right. I don't want anyone in my family to have anything to drink, especially if they will be driving a car.

11. Q: And now that you know my client had some amount to drink you think that he wasn't behaving appropriately, isn't that right?

12. A: I guess that's right.

13. Q: It's fair to say, Ms. Claven, that Mr. Malone has a strike against him in your mind because he admits he had some amount of alcohol?

14. A: Well, let's just say I don't approve of that sort of thing.

15. Q: Your Honor, I challenge Ms. Claven for cause.

16. Judge: Ms. Mason, do you wish to question this juror before I rule on opposing counsel's challenge?

17. Mason: Thank you, Your Honor. Ms. Claven, you haven't made up your mind about this case already have you?

18.   A: No, I haven't even heard any of the testimony.

19.   Mason: And you will listen to the testimony for both sides before you reach a decision, won't you?

20.   A: Of course.

21.   Mason: Can you put aside your personal feelings about alcohol use and be fair to both sides?

22.   A: Absolutely.

23.   Mason: Your Honor, this juror has been candid about her feelings toward alcohol use, but she can be fair and impartial to both sides. The challenge for cause is not appropriate.

24.   Judge: Counsel for defense, would you care to respond before I rule.

25.   You: Your Honor, Ms. Claven never drinks, she does not associate with people who drink, and she thinks that nobody should drink. She is entitled to that belief, but I don't think that someone who has those beliefs can give my client a fair trial. There will be some evidence that Mr. Malone consumed a small amount of alcohol, and from what she said, it's clear that she'd be biased against him.

26.   Judge: Well, based on what I've heard....

In this example, you attempt to inoculate the juror (No. 1), and then ask open questions to learn about her attitudes toward alcohol (Nos. 3 and 5). When you have decided that you do not want her on the jury, you switch to closed and leading questions to try to lay a foundation for bias. It is uncertain how a judge would rule in this situation. But even if you lose the challenge for cause, you will still be able to remove Ms. Claven with a peremptory challenge.[22]

10.   JURY SELECTION AIDS

Drawing inferences about jurors' predispositions is a risky business. Among other things, the uncertainty of jury selection has produced a long, colorful and even embarrassing literature about the perceived stereotypical qualities of various racial, ethnic and social groups.[23] However, there are at least two alternatives to relying strictly on the information you obtain through voir dire, on the one hand, and outdated aphorisms passed down from one generation of lawyers to the next, on the other.

One such alternative is "shadow juries." As you know, a shadow jury is a group of people convened shortly before trial to evaluate both sides' arguments.[24] If you convene a shadow jury, you may present

---

22. If you have used all your peremptory challenges, you will be more reluctant to challenge a juror for cause. If you lose the challenge, the juror may well hold it against you or your client.

23. See e.g. F. Bailey and H. Rothblatt, *Fundamentals of Criminal Advocacy*, Secs. 336–337 (1974).

24. See Chapter 10.

evidence in summary form and inform the jurors of the relevant legal principles. The shadow jury then deliberates a produces a "verdict." You may even videotape the deliberations.

By convening a shadow jury, you may gain insight into the reactions of people of different backgrounds and experiences to both parties' arguments. Among other things, you can use the information to help you identify the predispositions of actual jurors with similar backgrounds and experiences.

A second type of jury selection aid consists of empirical research by social science "experts." For a fee (usually a handsome one), jury research firms will conduct public opinion research in the geographical area from which the jurors will be drawn, directed at both parties' arguments.[25] The firms typically provide profiles of how people with different backgrounds and experiences react to those arguments. You can in turn use that information to determine which jurors to challenge.

11. JUDGE OR JURY?

Many cases are tried to judges sitting without juries.[26] Sometimes the reason is that rules make certain issues triable only to a judge.[27] Most often, however, cases are tried to judges rather than juries because the parties prefer judge trials. This section reviews some of the important considerations affecting the determination of whether to seek a judge or jury trial.

Despite the centrality of a jury in the collective American legal conscience, in most jurisdictions a judge trial is the "default" selection. This means that you will have a judge trial unless you request a jury trial. And you typically have to observe strict guidelines to avoid waiving your right to a jury trial. For example, in a federal civil action you must serve a request for a jury trial on your adversary no later than 10 days after service of the last pleading.[28] Even if your request is timely, you may forfeit a jury trial if you fail to deposit fees in advance of trial. For instance, one state prone to earthquakes requires that a party requesting a jury trial deposit the one day fee for 20 jurors (a total of $100 at this state's current paltry rate of payment of jurors) at least 25 days prior to the date set for trial.[29]

The choice between a judge and jury trial has been the subject of much lawyer lore. For example, plaintiffs' attorneys in civil cases and defense attorneys in criminal cases traditionally choose juries. Civil plaintiffs tend to think of jurors as more forgiving of case weaknesses

25. Most notably, a jury research firm was employed by the defense in the highly publicized 1991 rape trial of William Kennedy Smith. Following the acquittal of Kennedy Smith, the defense described how extensive social science research underlay its selection of the jurors.

26. During the decade 1979–89, 55.5% of all federal court trials were judge trials. See Clermont & Eisenberg, "Trial by Jury or Judge: Transcending Empiricism," 77 Cornell L. Rev. 1124, 1127 (1992).

27. For instance, juries are usually not allowed in bankruptcy cases nor in child custody disputes in most state courts.

28. FRCP 38 (b).

29. Cal. Code of Civil Proc. sec. 631.

and more willing to award large damages. Criminal defense attorneys often hope to avoid a conviction by finding at least one juror who holds out for a "not guilty." Empiricists have analyzed some of this traditional wisdom, with inconclusive results.[30]

In any individual case, the choice between a judge and jury should at least take account of which factfinder you think will be more likely to accept your arguments.[31] For example, in a wrongful termination case your strongest argument may be that your client should not have been discharged because her errors were caused by the inadequate training provided by the employer. You may conclude that a judge will be reluctant to accept this argument because the judge fears that every employee who feels they have received inadequate training from an employer may sue and "overwhelm" the courts with wrongful termination trials. A jury may be less likely to be influenced by such extra-merits considerations. By contrast, perhaps you represent the defendant employer, and your primary argument is that employee's suit is barred by the Statute of Limitations. Trying to sustain this more "technical" defense, you might opt for a judge trial.[32]

You may consider a number of other factors when choosing between a judge and jury trial. Two are time and money. As compared to judge-tried cases, jury trials are typically longer and more formal—and therefore more expensive. Moreover, judges tend to have a "track record" that you can investigate, often making the result of a judge-tried case more predictable than jury trial. Also, if in your opinion the judge assigned to preside over your trial is unacceptable, some states allow you a limited right to disqualify the judge even in the absence of a showing of prejudice.[33] By contrast, you almost always have the right to excuse some jurors who are unacceptable to you, although all jurisdictions strictly limit the number of jurors you are allowed to excuse.[34] Hence, in a jury trial you may have to accept a juror or two who you may have wanted to excuse.

30. See, e.g., Clermont & Eisenberg, "Trial by Jury or Judge: Transcending Empiricism," 77 Cornell L. Rev. 1124 (1992); Saks, "Do We Really Know Anything About the Behavior of the Tort Litigation System—And Why Not?" 140 U. Pa. L. Rev. 1147 (1992).

31. An oft-repeated bit of lawyer folk wisdom is to "select a judge when the law is on your side and a jury when the facts are on your side." Evaluating your decision in the context of the arguments you want a trier to accept is a more case-specific version of this traditional wisdom.

32. In many cases, of course, you may not have settled on your arguments before the time you have to submit your request for a jury trial. In such a situation, you may preserve your options by at least submitting the jury request. Then, if you ultimately decide on a judge trial, you usually can drop the request without penalty.

33. See, e.g., Cal. Code of Civ. Proc. sec. 170.6.; James, Hazard & Leubsdorf, *Civil Procedure* sec. 7.4 (4th ed. 1992). Cf. 28 U.S.C. sec. 144. Despite the broadly permissive wording of the federal statute, federal caselaw makes it very difficult to remove the federal judge to whom a case has been assigned. Cases permit disqualification only when the litigant seeking to disqualify a federal judge establishes actual prejudice. See *Toth v. Trans World Airlines*, 862 F.2d 1381 (9th Cir.1988); James, Hazard & Leubsdorf, *supra*.

34. For example, parties in federal civil jury trials are allowed only three peremptory challenges. 28 U.S.C. sec. 1870.

How thoroughly you can evaluate the background and proclivities of the judge assigned to preside over a trial depends in part on whether a jurisdiction uses a system of "all purpose judges" or "specialized judges." In an all purpose judge system (used in all federal court jurisdictions and many state court jurisdictions), a single judge presides over all hearings, settlement discussions and the trial in a case from the moment it is filed until its conclusion.

By contrast, in a specialized judge system you encounter different judges as a case wends its way from initial filing to trial. For example, one judge may hear motions relating to pleadings and discovery, another may conduct settlement conferences, and yet another may preside over the trial. The specialized judge system is used in conjunction with a "master calendar" system, which funnels all cases to a single judge on the day the cases are set for trial, who then parcels them out to different courtrooms for trial. This may prevent you from learning the identity of the judge who will preside over your case until the day it is assigned for trial.

You can conduct a more efficient investigation into the background of a judge in an all purpose judge system than in a specialized judge system. In the former, you almost always know the identity of the judge who will ultimately preside over a trial at the inception of a case. Hence, you can focus your factual investigation on that one judge.

But in a specialized judge system, the point at which a case is assigned to a judge for trial is often too late for you either to investigate the judge or (if you have neglected to do so in advance) to request a jury trial. Hence, you may have to investigate the backgrounds of the various judges who may be assigned to preside over your trial, and evaluate the wisdom of requesting a jury trial according to your evaluation of the judges as a group.

Whether your investigation focuses on one or on a number of judges, here are some of the sources of information you may look to when deciding whether to request a jury trial:

- Sit in a courtroom and watch a judge in action, at least during pretrial hearings but preferably during a trial.

- Consult attorneys who have appeared before a judge.

- If you are a member of a local lawyers' group (e. g., plaintiff's personal injury lawyers), you may have access to the files which that group may maintain on various local judges.

- If you have access to a legal newspaper, check to see whether it publishes "judicial profiles" providing evaluations of local judges.

- If your client is in a position to do so, ask the client to check out how a judge has reacted to similarly situated litigants. For example, a tenant may be able to check with a tenants' rights organization, a banker with others in the banking industry.

Once you and a client have gathered information from sources such as the above, review it jointly before the deadline for making a jury request. Just as when you select jurors, you'll have to draw inferences about whether a judge will personally identify with or feel hostility against a party or witness, whether the judge's background and experiences will lead to acceptance or rejection of your important generalizations, and the judge's socio-political attitudes. The decision is an important one, and once you have discussed the advantages and disadvantages of each option the final decision as to judge or jury should be the client's whenever practicable.

Index

References are to Pages

---

†